EYEWITNESS TRAVEL

JERUSALEM,
ISRAEL, PETRA & SINAI

EYEWITNESS TRAVEL

JERUSALEM,
ISRAEL, PETRA & SINAI

Penguin Random House

Project Editors Nick Inman, Ferdie McDonald
Art Editors Jo Doran, Paul Jackson
Commissioning Editor Giovanni Francesio
at Fabio Ratti Editoria S.r.l.

Editors Elizabeth Atherton, Cathy Day, Simon Hall,
Freddy Hamilton, Andrew Humphreys
Designers Chris Lee Jones, Anthony Limerick,
Sue Metcalfe-Megginson, Rebecca Milner, Johnny Pau
Picture Research Monica Allende, Katherine Mesquita
Map Coordinator Dave Pugh
DTP Designer Maite Lantaron
Researcher Karen Ben-Zoor

Main Contributors
Fabrizio Ardito, Cristina Gambaro, Massimo Acanfora Torrefranca

Photography
Eddie Gerald, Hanan Isachar, Richard Nowitz,
Magnus Rew, Visions of the Land

Illustrators
Isidoro Gonzáles-Adalid Cabezas (Acanto Arquitectura y
Urbanismo S.L.), Stephen Conlin, Gary Cross, Chris Forsey,
Andrew MacDonald, Maltings Partnership, Jill Munford,
Chris Orr & Associates, Pat Thorne, John Woodcock

Printed and bound in China

First published in the UK in 2000
by Dorling Kindersley Limited, 80 Strand, London WC2R 0RL

16 17 18 19 10 9 8 7 6 5 4 3 2 1

Reprinted with revisions 2002, 2007, 2010, 2012, 2014, 2016

Copyright 2000, 2016 © Dorling Kindersley Limited, London

A Penguin Random House Company

A CIP catalogue record is available from the British Library.

ISBN 978-0-2412-0968-4

Floors are referred to throughout in accordance with European usage;
ie the "first floor" is the floor above ground level.

Note The term "Holy Land" has been used to describe
the areas covered by this guide.

MIX
Paper from
responsible sources
FSC
www.fsc.org   FSC™ C018179

Front cover main image: The historic centre of Jerusalem

◀ The lavishly decorated interior of the Dome of the Rock in Jerusalem

Mount of Olives, Jerusalem

Contents

Old Jaffa's attractive waterfront

Bedouin camel,
Western Jordan

Middle Eastern handicrafts

Pomegranates

The remote St Catherine's Monastery in Sinai

HOW TO USE THIS GUIDE

This guide helps you to get the most from your visit to Jerusalem and the Holy Land, by providing detailed practical information. *Introducing Jerusalem, Israel, Petra & Sinai* maps the region and sets it in its historical and cultural context. The Jerusalem section and the four regional chapters describe important sights, using maps, photographs and illustrations. Features cover topics from food to wildlife. Recommended hotels and restaurants are listed in *Travellers' Needs*, while the *Survival Guide* has tips on travel, money and other practical matters.

Jerusalem Area by Area

The city is divided into five areas, each with its own chapter. A last chapter, *Further Afield*, covers peripheral sights. All sights are numbered and plotted on the chapter's area map. The detailed descriptions of the sights are easy to locate, as they follow the numerical order on the map.

A locator map shows where you are in relation to other areas of the city centre.

Each area of Jerusalem has its own colour-coded thumb tab, as shown inside the front cover.

Sights at a Glance lists the chapter's sights by category, such as Holy Places, Historic Districts, Museums and Archaeological Sites.

1 Area Map
For easy reference, sights are numbered and located on a map. The central sights are also marked on the *Street Finder maps* on pages 160–63.

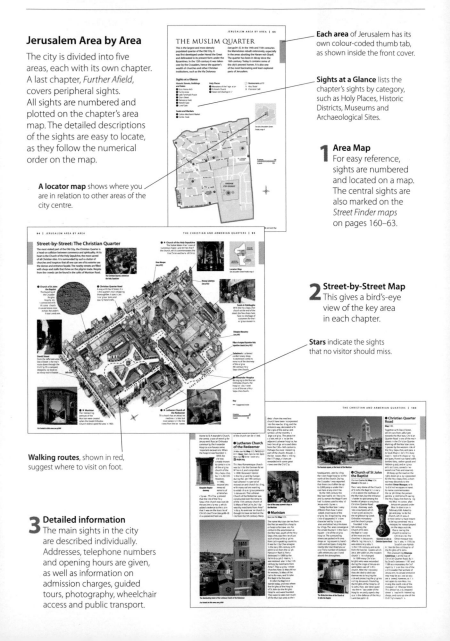

Walking routes, shown in red, suggest where to visit on foot.

2 Street-by-Street Map
This gives a bird's-eye view of the key area in each chapter.

Stars indicate the sights that no visitor should miss.

3 Detailed information
The main sights in the city are described individually. Addresses, telephone numbers and opening hours are given, as well as information on admission charges, guided tours, photography, wheelchair access and public transport.

Israel, Petra & Sinai Region by Region

Apart from Jerusalem, the Holy Land has been divided into four other regions, each of which has a separate chapter. The most interesting cities, towns, historical and religious sites and other places of interest are located on a *Regional Map*.

1 Introduction
The landscape, history and character of each region is outlined here, showing how the area has developed over the centuries and what it has to offer the visitor today.

2 Regional Map
This shows the road network and gives an illustrated overview of the whole region. Interesting places to visit are numbered and there are also useful tips on getting to and around the region by car and public transport.

Each region of the Holy Land can be quickly identified by its colour-coded thumb tabs (see inside front cover).

3 Detailed information
All the important towns and other places to visit are described individually. They are listed in order, following the numbering on the *Regional Map*. Within each town or city, there is detailed information on important buildings and other sights.

For all major sights, a Visitors' Checklist provides the practical information you will need to plan your visit.

4 The Top Sights
These are given two or more full pages. Historic buildings are dissected to reveal their interiors. Other interesting sights and areas are mapped or shown in bird's-eye view, with the most important features described.

INTRODUCING JERUSALEM, ISRAEL, PETRA & SINAI

DISCOVERING THE HOLY LAND

The following tours have been designed to take in as many of the region's highlights as possible, while keeping travel times manageable. First come ideas for making the most of a week in Jerusalem, then follows a one-week tour of northern Israel, taking in all the must-visit sites along the Coast and Galilee. Next, a five-day round-trip covers the Dead Sea and the Negev Desert. There is also a six-day tour covering western Jordan, with two days in the magnificent city of Petra, as well as an itinerary maximizing three days by the Red Sea in Sinai, Egypt. Travellers with time can combine all five itineraries to a make a superb one-month tour of the whole region. Pick, combine and follow your favourite tours, or simply dip in and out and be inspired.

Masada, overlooking the Dead Sea
Famous for the siege in the Jewish-Roman war, the fortress at Masada offers some ethereal views of the Judaean Desert.

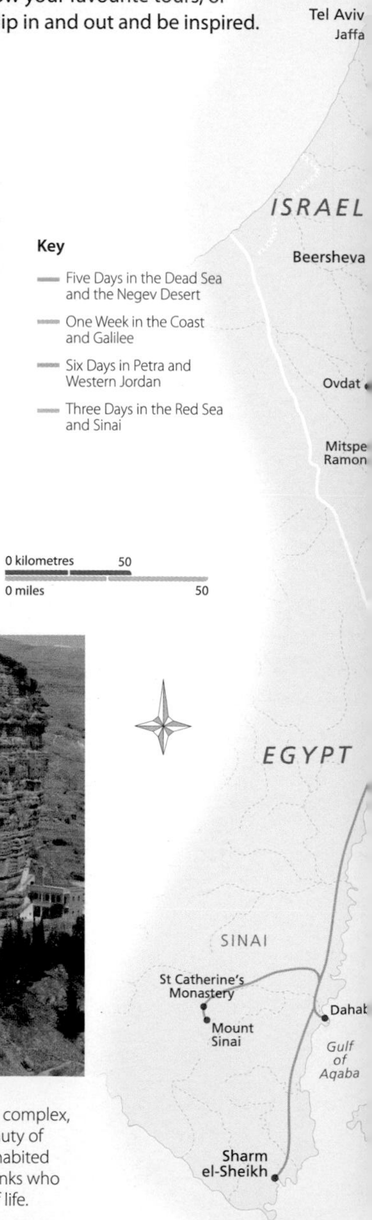

Key

— Five Days in the Dead Sea and the Negev Desert

— One Week in the Coast and Galilee

— Six Days in Petra and Western Jordan

— Three Days in the Red Sea and Sinai

Map labels: Tel Aviv, Jaffa, ISRAEL, Beersheva, Ovdat, Mitspe Ramon, EGYPT, SINAI, St Catherine's Monastery, Mount Sinai, Dahab, Gulf of Aqaba, Sharm el-Sheikh

0 kilometres 50
0 miles 50

Five Days in the Dead Sea and the Negev

- Escape the crowds at **St George's Monastery** and see remarkable views of the Judaean Hills across the gorge.

- Smear yourself with mineral-rich black mud, before soaking in the salty waters of the **Dead Sea**.

- Scale the heights of the historic **Masada** and admire the superb views from Herod's clifftop palaces.

- Splash around in the Red Sea at **Eilat** and enjoy the nightlife along the attractive seafront boulevard.

- Go hiking and biking through the staggering vastness of the **Ramon crater** in the Negev Desert.

- Explore the ruins at **Ovdat** and **Beersheva**.

St George's Monastery
The spectacular cliff-hanging complex, located amid the rugged beauty of the Judaean Desert, is still inhabited by a few Greek Orthodox monks who maintain their ancient way of life.

◄ The monastery at Petra *(see p234)* as depicted in a 19th-century engraving by David Roberts

One Week in the Coast and Galilee

- Have fun on the beach, relax in fashionable café-bars and sample eclectic Israeli cuisine in white-washed **Tel Aviv**.

- Appreciate the emerald slopes of the Baha'i Gardens from **Haifa's** gorgeously restored German Colony.

- Contrast **Akko's** mosques with the Jewish tombs in **Safed**.

- Walk in Jesus Christ's footsteps through the green hills around **Nazareth**, and see the sites of his ministry on the northern edge of the **Sea of Galilee**.

- Relish the fresh fish and famous Galilean cuisine at one of the many unique restaurants in the region.

- Marvel at remarkable **Beth Shean**, a ruined city that flourished for millennia and is now known for Israel's best-preserved Roman theatre.

The Monastery at Petra
One of the most striking monuments in Petra is the Monastery, which boasts a massive façade carved into the sandstone hill. It was most likely a temple for the Nabataeans.

Three Days in the Red Sea and Sinai

- Snorkel or dive down and be stunned by Sinai's luminous, colourful underwater world.

- Make the climb up **Mount Sinai** in the footsteps of Moses, either on foot or by camel, as the sun rises.

- Visit one of the world's oldest monasteries – the walled fortress of **St Catherine's**, which preserves a priceless collection of icons.

- Enjoy the ambience of an Egyptian-style coffee shop and let your hair down in the clubs of **Sharm el-Sheikh**.

- Relax on cushions at **Dahab's** mellow restaurants on the beach promenade, after diving or trekking

Six Days in Petra and Western Jordan

- Be awed by the extensive ruins at **Jerash**, one of the best-preserved Roman cities in the Middle East.

- Soak up the buzz of lively **Amman**, which has a great restaurant scene alongside Roman-era attractions.

- Admire the Byzantine-age map at **Madaba**, a town with a wealth of mosaics.

- Chill out in a premier spa-resort idyllically located on the **Dead Sea**, while trying out its reputed healing properties.

- Gaze up at the pink perfection of the hidden city of **Petra**, where one day is simply not enough.

- Sprawl by a campfire under the stars in **Wadi Rum**.

- Wind down on **Aqaba's** long stretch of beach, to indulge in water sports and savour fresh fish for lunch

One Week in Jerusalem

The Old City is crammed with many fascinating sites and it is possible to see a great deal in a short span of time, as it is a small area.

- **Arriving** Arrive at Ben Gurion Airport. A private taxi or shared *sherut* takes 45 minutes to the city.
- **Transport** The alleys of the Old City can be negotiated only on foot. For outlying sights, take a taxi or use the Light Rail and bus services.
- **Booking ahead** Western Wall Tunnel tour and the Night Spectacular.

Day 1
Morning Start early at the **Western Wall** (*p89*), then ascend the **Haram esh-Sharif** (*pp72–7*) to see the **Dome of the Rock** (*pp76–7*). Exit via the Bab el-Asbat and walk along **Via Dolorosa** (*pp34–5*), which traces the last footsteps of Christ. Stop at the **Monastery of the Flagellation** and **Ecce Homo Arch** (*p68*) and eat a houmous lunch.

Afternoon The Via Dolorosa culminates with the **Church of the Holy Sepulchre** (*pp96–9*), the most sacred site in Christendom. Next, absorb Jerusalem's history in the museum at the **Citadel** (*pp106–9*), before exiting via Jaffa Gate to the shops on Mamilla Avenue. Mamilla Hotel's rooftop bar has great views of the Old City; nearby **Nakhalat Shiva** (*p127*) has many options for dinner.

Day 2
Morning Head to the exceptional **Israel Museum** (*pp136–41*). Three hours is the minimum needed here, and when fatigue sets in, make use of the cafés for lunch. The biggest draws are the Shrine of the Book and the re-created synagogue interiors – but make time for the Fine Arts Wing, where new exhibits seamlessly showcase ancient pieces alongside contemporary work.

Afternoon Visit the **Jewish Quarter** (*pp80–91*) to see the **Cardo** (*p84*) and the **Sephardic Synagogues** (*p86*), or just watch life on **Hurva Square** (*pp84–5*). In the early evening, opt for the **Western Wall Tunnel tour** (*p89*), then savour an Israeli-fusion meal in the **Cinematheque** (*p154*) or the **First Station** complex (*p152*), where you can also take a stroll along converted train tracks.

Day 3
Morning Explore East Jerusalem – **Solomon's Quarries** (*p130*), **Garden Tomb** (*p130*) and **Palestinian Pottery** (*p150*) – before relaxing in the garden of the **American Colony Hotel** (*p131*).

Afternoon Call in at the **Rockefeller Museum** (*p131*), then tread Crusader-era steps down to the **Tomb of the Virgin** (*p118*). From the sublime **Basilica of the Agony** (*p118*), ascend the **Mount of Olives** (*pp114–15*). The **Dominus Flevit Sanctuary** (*p117*) is just one beautiful church along the route. Then it's a short ride for Palestinian food and Taybeeh beer just north of **Damascus Gate** (*pp70–71*).

Day 4
Morning Begin at **Yad Vashem** (*p142*), the museum of the Holocaust. Take the trail through the pine forest (or a bus) to delightful **Ein Kerem** (*pp142–3*), where cafés nestle alongside quaint galleries.

Afternoon Walk the **Old City walls** (*pp146–7*) in the late afternoon light, from Jaffa Gate to Lions' Gate. Pop into atmospheric **St Anne's Church** (*p71*), before enjoying a drink and the superb views at the Austrian Hospice. In the evening, watch the **Night Spectacular** (*p107*) at the Citadel.

Day 5
Morning Stroll the flower-filled lanes of **Yemin Moshe** (*pp124–5*), see the inspiring architecture of the **YMCA** and **King David Hotel** (*p126*), then cross the New City to **Mahane Yehuda** market (*p135*). Enjoy fantastic eateries, bars and shops among the hollering vegetable vendors.

Afternoon Return to the Old City to wander **Muristan** (*pp102–3*) and do souvenir shopping on **Christian Quarter Road** (*p103*) or in the **souks** (*p70*). Continue on to the **City of David** (*p119*) for an exciting walk in thigh-deep water through Hezekiah's Tunnel. In the evening, try the trendy **Russian Compound** (*p128*) for a meal.

Day 6
Morning Visit the magical **Monastery of the Cross** (*p134*) for its wonderful Georgian frescoes. Then choose between two museums nearby: the **Bible Lands Museum** (*pp134–5*), displaying archaeological treasures, or the **LA Mayer Museum of Islamic Art** (*p134*) which also exhibits a collection of antique watches and clocks.

Afternoon Explore **Mount Zion** (*p120*) to see the glittering interior of the **Church of the Dormition** (*p120*) and **King David's Tomb** (*p121*). If the time is right (3pm), pop into **St James's Cathedral** (*p110*) to hear the clergy's hypnotic singing; otherwise, head straight to the

The interior of the Catholikon, at the centre of the Church of the Holy Sepulchre

For practical information on travelling around the Holy Land, see pp302–9

Boats docked at the picturesque port of Tel Aviv

Jerusalem Archaeological Park (pp90–91), which has an intriguing subterranean visitors' centre.

Day 7

Morning Make an early start to **Bethlehem** (pp196–9), either by taxi or bus 21 from Damascus Gate. Beneath the atmospheric grotto of the **Church of the Nativity** (pp198–9), a silver star marks Jesus's birthplace. The souks and **Baituna Al-Talhami** (p197), a Palestinian house-cum-museum, are also worth a visit.

Afternoon Take a taxi to the **Herodion** (p196), topped with the ruins and riddled with tunnels dug nearly 2,000 years ago. Return to Jerusalem for an early dinner in the **German Colony**, then take in a film, concert or theatre show.

One Week in the Coast and Galilee

- **Airport** Arrive and depart from Ben Gurion Airport. Collect a hire car from the airport, or take a taxi or train to Tel Aviv, then arrange car rental there.
- **Transport** Requires a hire car.

Day 1: Tel Aviv

Survey the city's Bauhaus architecture on **Rothschild Avenue**, arty **Bialik Street** (p176) and fashionable **Dizengoff Street** (p174). The buzzing **Carmel Market** (p176) leads south to the run-down yet chic **Neve Tzedek** (p177), where you can eat at the beautifully restored **HaTachana** (p177). Stroll down the promenade

to **Jaffa** (pp178–9). Here, explore the quirky flea market and Artists' Quarter, and feast on contemporary Israeli cuisine.

Day 2: Tel Aviv

Spend the morning at **Beit Hatfutsot** (p172), Museum of the Jewish People, then laze or surf the afternoon away at one of the beaches. Alternatively, culture buffs could view the masterpieces at the **Museum of Art** (p174). Come sunset, head to the **Old Port** (p173) for dinner. You could also take in some culture – the Bat Sheva dance company is world-renowned.

Day 3: Caesarea and Haifa

Set off for Herod's port of **Caesarea** (p180), which has a splendid seaside setting. Then go north to multicultural **Haifa** (p181). Look in at the **Carmelite Monastery** and **Elijah's Cave**, or one of the many museums. Dinner on the Germany Colony's picturesque avenue, with views of the **Baha'i Gardens** (p181), is a must.

Day 4: Akko and Nazareth

Be at the **Baha'i Shrine and Gardens** (p181) when it opens at 9am, then take the short drive to **Akko** (pp182–3) to explore the subterranean Crusader City. Move on to historic **Nazareth** (pp184–5) and squeeze in a visit to the **Basilica of the Annunciation** (p185, closes 9pm), before sampling the rich food culture of this Arab town.

Day 5: Nazareth to the Sea of Galilee

Devote a couple of hours to exploring Nazareth's old centre,

a jumble of churches and little shops. Next, see the fascinating Mona Lisa mosaic and ruins at **Tsipori** (p185). If so inclined, see the basilica on **Mount Tabor** (p185), which boasts extraordinary views; otherwise head straight down to **Tiberias** (p188) on the **Sea of Galilee** (pp186–7), with its vibrant Roman history, strong Jewish flavour, striking basalt-stone buildings, beaches and hot springs.

Day 6: Sea of Galilee and around

In the morning, visit the sites of Christ's ministry, commemorated in the pretty churches at **Tabgha** and the remains of **Capernaum** (p188). Then twist uphill, past the **Church of the Beatitudes** (p188), to Kabbalist **Safed** (p185) for a complete contrast – explore old synagogues, the Artists' Quarter and the rabbis' tombs. Spend the night in Safed, or return to Tiberias.

A 6th-century mosaic in the synagogue at Beth Alpha

Day 7: Sea of Galilee and around

Wind upwards to the Crusaders' bastion of **Belvoir Castle** (p188), for astounding views across the Jordan Valley. Spend a couple of hours wandering the splendid Roman-Byzantine ruins at **Beth Shean** (p189) and drop in to admire the vivid 6th-century mosaic floor at **Beth Alpha** (p189). Pick a spot for lunch in the Lower Galilee. Explore the site of **Megiddo** (p184), before making your way back to Tel Aviv.

The Ramon Crater as viewed from the observation deck of the Mitspe Ramon Visitors' Centre

Five Days in the Dead Sea and the Negev

- **Airport** Arrive and depart from Ben Gurion Airport. Collect a hire car from the airport, or take a private taxi or shared *sherut* to Jerusalem and arrange car rental there.
- **Transport** Requires a hire car.
- **Booking ahead** Book at least 2 weeks in advance for snorkelling or diving with dolphins in Eilat.

Day 1: Jerusalem to Ein Gedi
Detour off the Jerusalem– Dead Sea road to picturesque **St George's Monastery** *(p194)*. Those with a historical bent should then stop at **Qumran** *(p200)*, where the Dead Sea Scrolls *(pp140–41)* were discovered. Floating in the **Dead Sea** *(p201)* is an absolute must – a good spot is the **Ein Gedi** beach *(p201)*. In the afternoon, hike in the **Ein Gedi Nature Reserve** *(p200)* or just relax in thermo-mineral waters at the lowest point on earth.

Day 2: Masada and Ein Bokek
Energetic folk should do **Masada** *(pp204–5)* at dawn, walking up the Snake Path to see the sunrise over the Dead Sea; otherwise, the cable car starts at 8am. Allow at least three hours to explore the fortress itself. Have another dip in the Dead Sea at the free beach in **Ein Bokek** *(p201)*, before travelling down to the

scenic **Eilat** *(p209)* in time for a delectable fresh-fish dinner.

Day 3: Eilat
Eilat, by the Red Sea, is the best place in Israel for diving and water sports. You can swim with dolphins at **Dolphin Reef**, or just enjoy the beach, good food and a dash of nightlife.

To extend your trip...
Cross the border into Jordan or Egypt, to visit Petra or laze by the beach in Sinai for a couple of nights.

Day 4: Makhtesh Ramon
Start early to drive through the heart of the Negev to breathtaking **Makhtesh Ramon** *(p208)*. It is excellent for hiking and mountain-biking, or you can take jeep tours through the wildly beautiful landscape. The town of **Mitspe Ramon** – perched on the crater's edge – has a frontier feel, yet it has amazing accommodation, plus interesting shopping and eating spots in the Spice Route Quarter.

Day 5: Ovdat and Beersheva
Travel on to Jerusalem, stopping to visit either the Nabataean and Roman-Byzantine remains at **Ovdat** *(p206)* or make a circular walk through the gorge **Ein Ovdat** *(p206)*, where there are ice-cold pools. Have lunch and a leg-stretch in **Beersheva** *(p207)*, which has some attractive Ottoman-era architecture and a fun Bedouin market, before continuing on to Jerusalem.

Six Days in Petra and Western Jordan

- **Airport** Arrive and depart from Queen Alia International Airport, Amman.
- **Transport** By taxi, or hire a car in Amman and drop it off in Aqaba.
- **Booking ahead** Internal flight from Aqaba to Amman.

Day 1: Amman
In the morning visit the Roman ruins of **Jerash** *(pp214–15)*, an hour north of Amman. This expansive site has a splendid colonnaded Cardo and an oval-shaped plaza. In the afternoon, head up to Amman's **Citadel** *(p216)* for fantastic city views and the on-site **Archaeological Museum** *(p217)*. Make an exploration of the **Downtown** area *(p216)* and its lively markets in the evening, before feasting on a Middle Eastern meal.

Day 2: Madaba to the Dead Sea
Go to **Madaba** *(pp220–21)* to view the extraordinary map – a 6th-century mosaic of the Holy Land depicting Jerusalem, the Jordan River and many other places covered in this guide. It's a short drive to **Mount Nebo** *(p219)*, where tradition holds Moses died after seeing the Promised Land. Spend the afternoon soaking in the salty waters of the **Dead Sea** *(p201)*, relishing the facilities of a top-class resort.

The ancient Roman ruins of the Cardo in Jerash

Coral Bay Resort by the beach in Aqaba

Day 3: Kerak to Petra
Visit the magnificent Crusader fortress of **Kerak** *(p219)* before moving on to **Petra** *(pp224–35)* – the highlight of any trip to Jordan and one of the world's great archaeological wonders. After an early lunch in Wadi Musa village, walk the narrow **Siq** *(pp226–7)* to be awestruck by the glowing-pink **Treasury** *(p228)* at the gorge's end. You'll pass by the rock-hewn **Theatre** and have time to explore the **City of Petra** *(pp232–3)*, as well as the museums, before dusk.

Day 4: Petra
Attempt to get up at dawn – it's worth it, to have the Siq to yourself and see the sun rise over the Treasury. Take in Petra's outlying sites, starting with the impressive façade of the **Royal Tombs** *(pp230–31)* and the **Tomb of Sextius Florentinius** *(p233)*, then climb to the spectacular **Monastery** *(p234)*. After lunch and a rest, energetic visitors should go to the **High Place of Sacrifice** *(p234)*; it's a stunning walk with tombs and monuments along the path. Alternatively, return through the Siq and take a taxi to secretive **Little Petra** *(p235)*: no less impressive but much less visited. After a long day, treat yourself to dinner at the Movenpick Resort.

Day 5: Wadi Rum
From Petra, make the journey to ethereal **Wadi Rum** *(pp236–8)*, a rose-sanded swathe of desert interspersed with wind-hollowed canyons and peaks. There are many rewarding hikes, or you can take a jeep or camel safari with local Bedouin, then spend a surreal night camping by the fire under star-filled skies.

Day 6: Aqaba
Take a one-hour journey to **Aqaba** *(p239)* on the Red Sea. There are archaeological sites in town, otherwise the stretch of sand south of the port is perfect for some pure beach-time or water sports action. From Aqaba, a flight back to Amman takes 45 minutes.

Three Days in the Red Sea and Sinai

- **Airport** Arrive and depart overland via Eilat in Israel; or take a flight to Sharm el-Sheikh Airport, 17 km (11 miles) north of town.
- **Transport** By taxi or bus.

Day 1: Dahab
Cross the **Taba** *(p246)* border and head south along the coast to **Dahab** *(pp246–7)*. A swathe of cute cafés lines the shore; just spend the afternoon swimming and relaxing, or experienced divers could check out the marine life at the famed Blue Hole. Dahab is also a great place to try kite-surfing or trekking.

Day 2: Mount Sinai to Sharm el-Sheikh
Make a pre-dawn start to St Catherine's (hire a taxi or join a tour) and ascend mystical **Mount Sinai** *(p253)*, holy to Muslims, Christians and Jews alike. Then enter **St Catherine's Monastery** *(pp250–52)* to see priceless icons and the radiant early-Byzantine Mosaic of the Transfiguration. Have lunch in El-Milga village, before journeying to **Sharm el-Sheikh** *(p247)* for a swim and a lively night out in the town's busy markets, pubs and coffee shops.

> **To extend your trip…**
> From St Catherine's, go on a camel safari in the desert plateaus or trek through the mountains and gardens with local Bedouin guides.

Day 3: Sharm el-Sheikh
Spend the day immersed in the warm waters of the Red Sea – diving, snorkelling, glass-bottomed boat trips and other water sports are all easily arranged. It's just over three hours by car back to the border at Eilat *(open 24 hours)*. Note that it's possible to connect Sinai and Jordan by ferry between Nuweiba and Aqaba (daily; visas can be arranged on board the vessel to/from Jordan, or on exiting the vessel in Sinai).

St Catherine's Monastery, at the foot of Mount Sinai

Putting the Holy Land on the Map

The crossroads of three continents – Africa to the
south, Asia to the east and Europe to the west – the
Holy Land encompasses the whole of Israel and the
Palestinian Autonomous Territories, and parts of Jordan
and Egypt. Its boundaries could be said to stretch from the
Mediterranean in the west, inland to the Jordanian deserts,
and from Galilee in the north to the southern tip of the Sinai
peninsula. At the core of the Holy Land is Jerusalem, an
ancient walled city which stands on the Judaean Hills, just
to the west of the Dead Sea, the lowest point on earth.

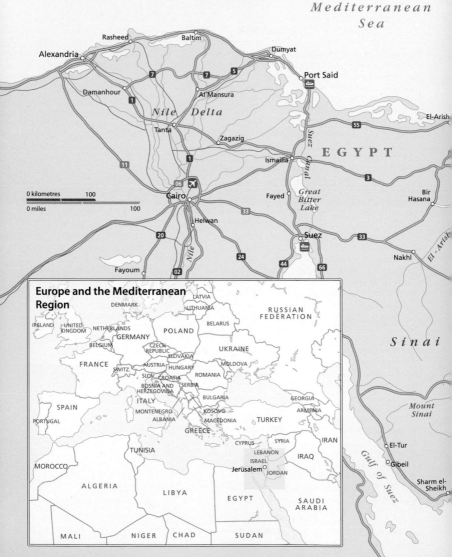

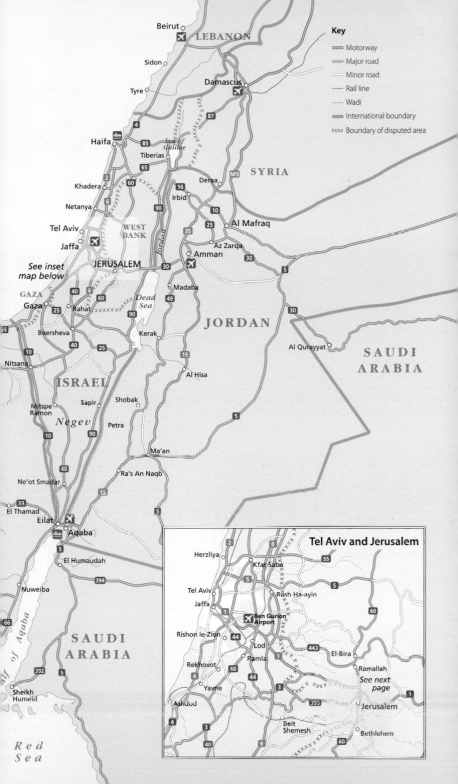

Key

- Motorway
- Major road
- Minor road
- Rail line
- Wadi
- International boundary
- xxxx Boundary of disputed area

Beirut

LEBANON

Sidon

Tyre

Damascus

Haifa

85

4

Sea of Galilee

Tiberias

87

SYRIA

Khadera

2

60

65

Deraa

M5

Netanya

6

16

Irbid

Al Mafraq

Tel Aviv

90

WEST BANK

35

25

Jaffa

Az Zarqa

Amman

30

See inset map below

JERUSALEM

Jordan

30

5

GAZA

40

6

Madaba

Gaza

25

60

49

Dead Sea

JORDAN

Rahat

90

Beersheva

Kerak

30

Nitsana

10

40

25

15

Al Qurayyat

SAUDI ARABIA

ISRAEL

Al Hisa

Mitspe Ramon

Sapir

Shobak

Negev

90

Petra

5

10

Ma'an

40

Ne'ot Smadar

Ra's An Naqb

15

El Thamad

33

5

Eilat

Aqaba

El Humaudah

394

66

Nuweiba

SAUDI ARABIA

392

5

Sheikh Humeid

Red Sea

Tel Aviv and Jerusalem

Herzliya

2

6

55

Kfar Saba

5

5

Tel Aviv

Rosh Ha-ayin

Jaffa

1

60

Ben Gurion Airport

Rishon le-Zion

44

Lod

443

El-Bira

1

Rekhovot

40

Ramla

Ramallah

4

44

See next page

Yavne

395

1

Ashdod

Jerusalem

4

3

Beit Shemesh

Bethlehem

40

6

60

Putting Jerusalem on the Map

Jerusalem covers 125 sq km (48 sq miles). In terms of geographical extent, this makes it Israel's largest city. However, despite its surface area, it is less populous than the Tel Aviv urban area. Only 800,000 people live here – 500,000 Jews, 280,000 Muslims and 15,000 Christians. At the core of Jerusalem is the walled Old City, standing 800 m (2,600 ft) above sea level. Dotted on the hilltops around, and strung along the valley floors between, are the ever-expanding modern suburbs. The city limits extend almost to the Palestinian towns of Ramallah in the north and Bethlehem to the south.

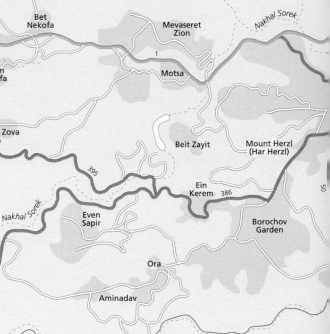

Key

■ Old City
□ Built-up area
═ Motorway
▬ Major road
═ Minor road
— Rail line
-- Wadi

For map symbols *see back flap*

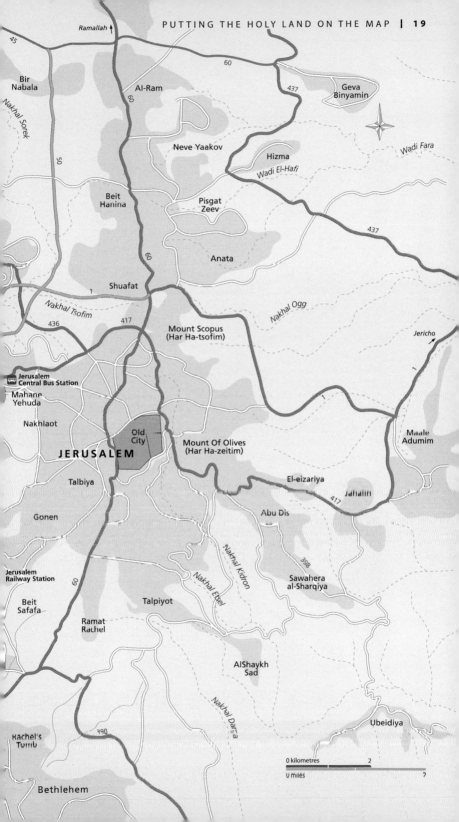

A PORTRAIT OF THE HOLY LAND

A Jew growing up in New York, a Christian in Lisbon and a Muslim in Jakarta will have childhoods as different as can be imagined, but one thing they will share is a common set of reference points, which will include names such as Abraham and Moses, and, above all, Jerusalem and the Holy Land.

For around 2,000 years this narrow corridor of land on the eastern shore of the Mediterranean has exercised an influence on world culture far out of proportion to its modest size. Events that are said to have taken place here in antiquity gave rise to the three great monotheistic religions. As these religions extended their influence throughout the world, so the Holy Land in general, and Jerusalem in particular, became over-burdened with spiritual significance. There is archaeological evidence that Jerusalem is where Solomon built his great temple, Christ was crucified, and the Prophet Muhammad visited on his Night Journey. It comes as a mild shock to some to discover that this spiritual world centre is no bigger than an average city neighbourhood. Those who come to Jerusalem expecting architectural grandeur to match the stature of these spiritual highlights will be disappointed. The city's churches don't begin to compare with the soaring Gothic cathedrals of Europe. The glorious Dome of the Rock aside, the buildings are quite humble. But the effect this has is to bestow on the city an altogether appropriate air of humility and authenticity, pleasingly at odds with the hyperbole and oversell of the new millennium.

While Jerusalem is a city rooted in ancient history, at the same time it lies at the heart of a region which possesses a distinctly youthful nature. Both Israel and Jordan, the two countries which, along with Egypt's Sinai peninsula, make up what we know as the Holy Land, are barely more than half a century old.

Bedouin encampment in the desert scenery of Wadi Rum, southern Jordan

◀ Interior of the Church of the Holy Sepulchre in Jerusalem

A panoramic view of the skyline of Jerusalem

It is a greatly over-used travel cliché, but here it is difficult to avoid commenting on the striking mix of the ancient and modern. In Jerusalem, ultra-Orthodox Jews wearing clothes that were fashionable in Eastern Europe 300 years ago mingle with Christian pilgrims armed with state-of-the-art digital cameras. In the wilderness of the Negev Desert, Bedouin tribesmen

Young boy playing football at the Dome of the Rock, the iconic symbol of Jerusalem

speak nonchalantly on mobile phones, while in Galilee Palestinian farmers lead oxen to fields that lie in the shadow of huge biotechnology plants.

Equally striking is the mix of peoples. The modern state of Israel has drawn its citizens from virtually every continent, embracing a worldwide roll call of Jewry, from Minnesota to Murmansk, Adelaide to Addis Ababa. Side by side with the Jews – and Arabs – are such minority peoples as the Druze, a mysterious offshoot sect of Islam, and the Samaritans, who speak Arabic but pray in Hebrew and number around 600.

In this land of diversity, even the one common element shared by most Israelis, the Jewish faith, is not the uniting factor it might be. The notion of what it is to be Jewish and, more pertinently, what form a Jewish state should take, are subjects of great contention. There are large, and increasingly influential, sections of society that believe Israel should adhere strictly to the laws of the Torah. The greater part of society, however, views the notion of a religious state with horror. The gulf between the two standpoints is best illustrated by the reactions to Dana International. While the transsexual singer's victory at the 1998 Eurovision Song Contest was celebrated by a part of the nation, the religious sector saw it as "the secular sickness of Israel". Gay Pride parades provoke similar feelings: the one in Jerusalem is greeted with harsh criticism from the religious communities, while the one in secular Tel Aviv keeps going from strength to strength.

An even more contentious issue is ownership of the land. Israel bases its right to exist on an ancient covenant with God, related in the Old Testament, in which this land was promised to the descendants of the Jewish patriarch Abraham, as well as the political sovereignty granted to them by the United Nations in 1947. The Palestinian Arabs have their own claims on the territory, based on centuries of occupancy. During the 20th century four major wars were fought between the Arabs and the Jews. The problem is still far from being resolved.

Since the Hebrew tribes first emerged from the desert around the 12th century BC, this has been one of the world's most turbulent neighbourhoods. Every major Near Eastern empire fought here. This has resulted in a fantastic legacy of historical remains, including Roman cities, Byzantine churches and early Islamic palaces. Archaeologists are constantly at work to uncover what other riches this troubled land might yield. Sometimes their aims go far beyond the academic: some expeditions search for evidence to support territorial claims; others seek fabled artifacts such as the Holy Grail or

Divisive Dana International

Souk stall-holder displaying fresh vegetables, a common sight in the local markets of the region

the Ark of the Covenant, which they believe may hold the key to human existence.

Amid all this hullabaloo, one should not forget that the Holy Land is a marvellous region for the visitor. It is not necessary to have an advanced grasp of history to appreciate the magnificence of the region's ancient cities, isolated monasteries and hilltop fortresses, while the desert scenery of Wadi Rum is a setting in which to live out fantasies. The diving in the Red Sea is reckoned by some to be unsurpassed anywhere in the world. Added to this, there is plenty of fine dining and comfortable accommodation. It is quite possible to visit the Holy Land and find that the only issue of concern is getting a decent spot on the beach.

A beach in Tel Aviv, the vibrant cultural and commercial capital of Israel

Old Testament Sites in the Holy Land

Many of the stories told in the Old Testament (known in Judaism as the "Tanakh") are located within Egypt, Sinai and the "Land of Canaan", which corresponds roughly to present-day Israel. The Bible gives plenty of precise geographical references. Some places, such as Jerusalem and Jericho, still exist and have yielded archaeological evidence confirming some, but by no means all, of the references to them in the Old Testament. Other sites were only attached to their biblical episodes much later. Touring these sites, visitors cannot but be aware of the contrast between the importance of the events and the often insignificant and all-too-human scale of the places in which they are said to have occurred.

① The Destruction of Sodom
When Sodom was destroyed by God *(see p206)* only Lot and his family were spared, but his wife looked back and was turned into a pillar of salt.

③ The Tombs of the Patriarchs
Acquired as a burial place for his wife Sarah, the Machpelah cave was the first plot in the Land of Canaan purchased by Abraham (Genesis 23). A mosque/synagogue now occupies the traditional site of the tomb, located in the present-day town of Hebron *(see pp206–7)*.

② The Sacrifice of Isaac
God asked Abraham to sacrifice his son, Isaac. The patriarch was about to obey when an angel stayed his hand and instructed him to slaughter a ram instead (Genesis 22). Tradition identifies the place of sacrifice as Mount Moriah, later a part of Jerusalem, and the site on which Solomon's Temple is said to have been subsequently built *(see p45)*.

Gaza

④ Moses Receives the Ten Commandments
Since the 4th century, Mount Sinai *(see p253)* has been associated with the story of Moses and the Ten Commandments (Exodus 20). The Bible places Mount Sinai in a region called Horeb, but the location of Horeb has never been identified.

④
Mount Sinai

Gulf of Aqaba

⑤ The Death of Moses
Moses is said to have seen the Promised Land from the summit of Mount Nebo and died in the same place. Christian tradition identifies Mount Nebo *(see p219)* as being just southwest of modern-day Amman. As the Bible states, the whereabouts of Moses' tomb is unknown (Deuteronomy 34: 1–7).

| 0 kilometres | 100 |
| 0 miles | 50 |

⑥ Joshua Conquers Jericho

The Old Testament story tells how the walls of Jericho (see pp194–5) fell to the blast of horns (Joshua 6). This ancient oasis was the first city conquered by the Israelites, led by Joshua, after they emerged from their 40 years in the wilderness.

⑦ The Ark of the Covenant

At Shiloh, the Jews built the first temple and placed in it the Ark of the Covenant, the sacred container of the tablets of the Ten Commandments. The Ark is shown here in a 13th-century illumination being carried by two angels.

⑧ Samson and Delilah

The climax of this story, in which Samson pulls down the Philistines' temple, killing himself and his enemies, is described as taking place in Gaza (Judges 14–16).

⑨ David Defeats Goliath

As the champion of the Israelites during the reign of King Saul, David defeated Goliath and routed the Philistines (I Samuel 17). The site of the battle is given as the Ha-Ela Valley, northwest of Hebron.

⑩ Elijah and the Prophets of Baal

Elijah challenged the prophets of the Canaanite god Baal (left). An altar was set up and sacrifices prepared. Only Elijah's offering burst into flames, showing it had been acknowledged and proving who the true God was (I Kings 18). The traditional site of this event is Mount Carmel, at Haifa (see p181).

The Old Testament as History

Unlike Mesopotamia or Egypt, where ancient texts have allowed the development of a detailed historical framework, the Holy Land has yielded few written archives. The only such resource is the Bible. The later books, which describe events not too far removed from the time they were written, may be relatively accurate. For example, events recounted in Kings I and II can be corroborated by contemporary Assyrian inscriptions. However, the historical basis of stories such as those relating to Abraham, Moses or Solomon must be viewed with caution. The Old Testament as we know it was compiled from a variety of sources, no earlier than the 6th century BC. These narratives might well contain kernels of historical reality, but by the time they came to be set down, they were essentially no more than folk tales.

Assyrian obelisk (825 BC) showing Israelite King Jehu (I Kings 19)

Judaism

Jewishness is not just a matter of religion but of belonging to a people. Jews believe themselves to be descended from Abraham, to whom God promised a land "unto thee, and to thy seed after thee". Judaism traditionally passes through the female line or by conversion, with different Jewish movements (Orthodox, Conservative, Reform) having different requirements. Practising Jews conduct their life by the Torah, which can be translated as "instruction" or "guidance". Its core is the Five Books of Moses, but the Torah also includes all the teachings and laws within the Hebrew Bible (Old Testament) and subsequent interpretations by rabbinic scholars. The creation of the State of Israel has presented the Jewish people with new political and religious challenges.

The menorah, a seven-branched candlestick, derives from the candlestick that originally stood in Solomon's Temple.

The Western Wall

This is all that is accessible of the remains of the Jews' great Temple (see pp48–9), built to hold the Ark of the Covenant (see p25). It is the holiest of all Jewish sites and a major centre of pilgrimage (see p89).

The Scrolls of the Torah

The Torah is traditionally inscribed on scrolls. During a synagogue service the scrolls are ceremonially raised to the congregation before being read. It is an honour to read them. A boy of 13 years of age or a girl of 12 is *bar* or *bat mitzvah*, a "child of the commandment". During a *bar/bat mitzvah* service the boys and girls (Reform and Conservative Jews only) read from the scrolls.

The yad ("hand") is a pointer used to avoid touching the sacred text. It is also meant to direct the reader's attention to the precise word and to encourage clear and correct pronunciation.

The scrolls, when not in use, are placed in the ark. They may be kept in an ornamental box (*right*) or else tied with a binder inside a decorated cover, adorned with a breastplate, *yad*, bells or crown.

Traditional Jewish life is measured by the regular weekly day of rest, Shabbat (from sundown Friday to sundown Saturday), and a great many festivals *(see pp40–43)*. The blowing of the *shofar* (a ram's horn trumpet) marks *Rosh ha-Shanah*, the Jewish New Year.

Divisions in Judaism

As a result of their history of dispersion and exile, there are Jewish communities in most countries of the world. Over the centuries, different customs have developed in the various communities. The two main strands, with their own distinctive customs, are the Sephardim, descendants of Spanish Jews expelled from Spain in 1492, and the Ashkenazim, descendants of Eastern European Jews. In Western Europe and the US, some Jews adapted their faith to the conditions of modern life, by such steps as altering the roles of women. This divided the faith into Reform (modernizers) and Orthodox (traditionalists), with Conservative Jews somewhere in between. Israeli Jews are frequently secular or maintain only some ritual practices. The ultra-Orthodox, or *haredim*, adhere to an uncompromising form of Judaism, sometimes living in separate communities.

Yemenite bride in wedding dress

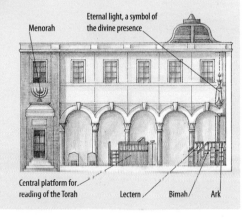

Ultra-Orthodox Jews in Jerusalem's in their distinctive black garb

The Synagogue

Synagogue architecture generally reflects the architecture of the host community, but with many standard elements. There must be an ark, symbolizing the Ark of the Covenant, which is always placed against the wall facing Jerusalem. In front of the ark hangs an eternal light *(ner tamid)*. The liturgy is read from the lectern at the *bimah*, the platform in front of the ark. The congregation sits around the hall, although in most synagogues men and women are segregated. Traditionally, a full service cannot take place without a *minyan*, a group of ten men.

Eternal light, a symbol of the divine presence

Menorah

Central platform for reading of the Torah

Lectern

Bimah

Ark

Christianity

To his followers, Jesus of Nazareth was more than just a prophet, he was the Son of God and bringer of a new covenant replacing the one given by God to Abraham (see p26). His crucifixion in Jerusalem came to be seen as self-sacrifice for the salvation of humankind and inspired a new religious movement based on his teachings. At first this existed as a subset of Judaism; Jesus came to be known as Christ (*Christos*, the anointed one, in Greek), as he was held to be the Messiah of Jewish prophecies. However, the new religion spread far beyond Judaea. It saw persecution, then recognition by the Roman Empire, eventually becoming its dominant religion in the 4th century AD.

The cross is a symbol of the Crucifixion of Christ. An empty cross shows that he has risen from the dead.

The Eucharist (Mass)

Greek Orthodox priests celebrate the Eucharist, the taking of bread and wine, representing the body and blood of Christ. One of the central sacraments of Christianity, it was instituted by Jesus himself at the Last Supper (see p121).

The Christian Bible is in two parts: the Old Testament consists of Jewish sacred texts; the New Testament relates the life and teaching of Jesus and his apostles. The latter was written from the mid-1st century. Most early texts were in Greek; a definitive Latin version by St Jerome (see p199) appeared in about AD 404. This elaborate 15th-century Latin version from France depicts the construction of a temple in Jerusalem.

Icons play a major role in the Greek and Russian Orthodox churches. Usually painted on wood, they are used as aids to devotion, bringing the worshipper into the presence of the subject. This brilliant series of icons decorates the New Jerusalem Monastery in Russia.

The Virgin and Child is a favourite Christian image. Depictions of the baby Jesus emphasize the human side of his nature, while the cult of his mother, the Virgin Mary, allows the faithful to identify with the joys and suffering of motherhood.

A Palm Sunday procession re-creates Christ's entry into Jerusalem. This is a prelude to Holy Week, the most important Christian festival, commemorating the Crucifixion on Good Friday and Christ's Resurrection on Easter Sunday.

Christian Denominations

Almost all the major Christian churches are represented in Jerusalem. The Greek Orthodox (*see p104*) and Syrian churches were the first to be established in the city. Other ancient Christian communities include the Armenians (*see p111*), Copts and Ethiopians. The Roman Catholic Church established its own Patriarchate here in the wake of the Crusades, and the most recent arrivals were the Protestants. The Greek Orthodox, Greek Catholic and Roman Catholic churches have large congregations, mostly of Palestinian Arabs, while priests and officials tend to be Greek and Italian.

Syrian Orthodox Christmas in Bethlehem

Procession of Ethiopian priests in Jerusalem

Armenian priests in their black hooded copes

Churches in the Holy Land

The first churches did not appear in the Holy Land until around AD 200 – the earliest Christians gathered together in each other's homes. Roman suspicion of unauthorized sects kept these churches underground. However, the conversion to Christianity of the Roman emperor Constantine signalled a rash of building on the sites connected with the life of Christ. The usual type of Byzantine church was the basilica, a longitudinal structure with a nave (central aisle) lit by windows in the walls of the side aisles. The apse area, containing the altar, was frequently concealed by an iconostasis, a three-panelled screen adorned with icons.

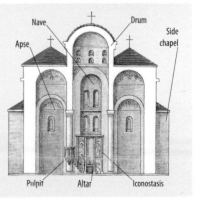

Nave

Drum

Side chapel

Apse

Pulpit

Altar

Iconostasis

Islam

Islam was founded by Muhammad, a former merchant from Mecca in Arabia. Born around AD 570, at the age of 40 he began to receive revelations of the word of Allah. These continued for the rest of his life and were transcribed as the Quran. Muhammad's preachings were not well received in Mecca and in 622 he and his followers were forced to flee for Medina. This flight, or *hejira*, constitutes year zero in the Islamic calendar. Before Muhammad died in 632, he had returned to conquer Mecca. Within a further four years, the armies of Islam had swept out of the Arabian desert and conquered the Holy Land.

The crescent moon, the symbol of Islam, has resonances of the lunar calendar, which orders Muslim religious life.

Dome of the Rock

One of the oldest and most beautiful of all mosques, the richly decorated Dome *(see pp76–7)* is the third most holy site of Islam after the Prophet's cities of Mecca and Medina.

The Quran, the holy book of Islam, is regarded as the exact word of Allah. Muslims believe that it can never be truly understood unless read in Arabic: translations into other languages can only ever paraphrase. The Quran is divided into 114 chapters, or *suras*, covering many topics, including matters relating to family, marriage, and legal and ethical concerns.

The Five Pillars of Faith

Islam rests on what are known as the "five pillars of faith". The first of these, known as the *Shahada*, is a simple declaration that "There is no god but Allah and Muhammad is his Prophet". The second pillar is the set daily prayers, performed in the direction of Mecca five times a day. The third pillar is the fasting during daylight hours that takes place for the whole of the holy month of Ramadan, and the fourth is the giving of alms. The fifth pillar is Haj: at least once in their lifetime all Muslims must, if they are able, make the pilgrimage to Mecca, birthplace of Muhammad.

Muslim at prayer

House decorated with pilgrimage scenes, indicating the owner has made the Haj

Muslim festivals are relatively infrequent, with just four major dates in the calendar *(see p42)*. The most important of these are Eid el-Adha (which commemorates Abraham's covenant with God), marking the time of the pilgrimage, or Haj, and Eid el-Fitr, which marks the end of Ramadan. Celebrations tend to be communal.

The imam is an Islamic teacher, usually attached to a particular mosque. He delivers the *khutba*, or sermon, at the midday prayers on Friday. These prayers are always the best attended of the week.

The Night Journey was one of the defining episodes in the life of the Prophet Muhammad. He was carried during the night from Mecca to Jerusalem and from there made the *Miraj*, the ascent through the heavens to God's presence, returning to Mecca in the morning.

The Mosque

Mosques come in many shapes and sizes but they all share some common characteristics. Chief of these is the mihrab, the niche that indicates the direction of Mecca. Most mosques also have a *minbar*, from which the imam delivers his Friday sermon. A dome usually covers the prayer hall. The minaret serves as a platform for the delivery of the call to prayer, once made by a *muezzin*, but these days more often a prerecorded broadcast through a loudspeaker.

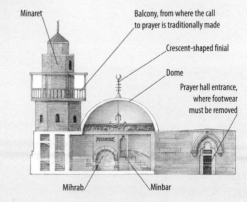

Minaret

Balcony, from where the call to prayer is traditionally made

Crescent-shaped finial

Dome

Prayer hall entrance, where footwear must be removed

Mihrab

Minbar

Sites of the New Testament

The life of Jesus Christ, as narrated in the gospels, was played out in a relatively small geographical arena. He was born in Bethlehem; he grew up in Nazareth; his baptism took place at the Jordan River near Jericho; most of his public activity was carried out around the shores of the Sea of Galilee, where he preached, narrated parables and worked miracles; and his crucifixion, resurrection and ascension all occurred in Jerusalem. Unlike the sites of the Old Testament, those of the New Testament saw the rise of sanctuaries, churches and chapels built within two or three centuries of the death of Jesus. For this reason, a number of these sites have some claim to authenticity, although, as with so much in the Holy Land, nothing is beyond dispute.

① The Annunciation
At Nazareth Mary was visited by the angel Gabriel and told of her forthcoming child (Luke 1: 26–38). The episode is commemorated by the Basilica of the Annunciation (see p185).

② The Birth of Jesus
In Bethlehem Jesus was born in a grotto and an angel appeared to shepherds in nearby fields, telling them of the birth (Luke 2: 1–20). A church was first built on the site in the 4th century (see pp198–9) and a star marks the alleged site of the Nativity.

③ The Wedding at Cana
Jesus performed his first miracle at this small village near Nazareth, at a wedding where he turned water into wine (John 2: 1–11).

Joppa (Jaffa) •

④ The Baptism of Christ
John the Baptist, a cousin of Jesus, baptized and preached the coming of the Messiah on the shores of the Jordan River. John recognized Jesus as the "Lamb of God" (Matthew 3). Two sites are traditionally identified with the baptism – Qasr el-Yehud, east of Jericho on the Jordanian border (see p195), and Bethany Beyond the Jordan, a few kilometres north of the Dead Sea (see p201). Both lie in a military zone but are open to pilgrims throughout the week.

⑤ The Temptations
Following his baptism, Jesus went into the desert, where the Devil tried to tempt him from his 40-day fast (Matthew 4: 1–11). The Greek Orthodox Monastery of the Temptation on Mount Quarntal, just north of Jericho, marks the site of the supposed encounter (see p194–5).

⑥ The First Disciples
Christ's first Disciples were fishermen he encountered on the banks of the Sea of Galilee. He persuaded them to leave their nets to become "fishers of men" (Matthew 5: 18–22). In the mid-1980s a fishing boat was discovered in the mud of the lake. It dates back to the 1st century AD, roughly the time of Christ, and is on display at Kibbutz Ginosar (see p186).

Tabgha ⑦ ⑧
⑥ Sea of Galilee
Cana ③
Nazareth ①

Caesarea
•Beth Shean

GALILEE

SHARON

DECAPOLIS

Jordan River

SAMARIA

④ River Jordan
⑤ Mount Quarntal

• Jerusalem
② Bethlehem

Dead Sea

JUDAEA

⑦ The Multiplication of the Loaves and Fishes
The gospels locate this famous miracle, more colourfully known as the "feeding of the 5,000" (Matthew 15: 32–39), on the shores of the Sea of Galilee. The episode is commemorated in a church at Tabgha on the lake shore (see p188), which has a mosaic in front of the altar showing a basket of bread flanked by fish.

⑧ The Sermon on the Mount
The longest and one of the key sermons in the teachings of Jesus, the Sermon on the Mount, begins with the Beatitudes: "Blessed are the meek for they shall inherit the earth…" (Matthew 5–7). Tradition has it delivered on a small rise at Tabgha. It is celebrated by the nearby octagonal Church of the Beatitudes (see p188).

Jesus in Jerusalem

In what was to be the last week of his life, Jesus made a triumphal entrance into Jerusalem shortly before the Jewish feast of Passover. He proceeded to the Temple where he drove out the moneychangers (Matthew 21: 12–13). He gathered his Disciples to eat a Passover meal; this was to be the Last Supper. After the meal they went to the Garden of Gethsemane (see p118), where Jesus was arrested (Matthew 26: 36–56). Condemned by the Jewish authorities, he was put on trial before Pontius Pilate, possibly in the Antonia Fortress or the Citadel (see pp106–9). After being paraded through the city (see pp34–5) he was crucified and buried at Golgotha, traditionally identified with the site of the Holy Sepulchre church. Following his Resurrection, Jesus departed earth with his Ascension from the Mount of Olives (see pp114–5).

The Last Supper (Matthew 26: 18–30), traditionally associated with a room on Mount Zion (see p121)

Via Dolorosa

The Via Dolorosa in Jerusalem traditionally traces the last steps of Jesus Christ *(see pp68–9)*, from where he was tried to Calvary, where he was crucified, and the tomb in the Church of the Holy Sepulchre, where he is said to have been buried. There is no historical basis for the route, which has changed over the centuries. However, the tradition is so strong that countless pilgrims walk the route, identifying with Jesus's suffering as they stop at the 14 Stations of the Cross. The walk is not done the week after Easter or Christmas.

Locator Map

  Via Dolorosa

Sixth Station
Veronica wipes away Jesus's blood and sweat, and her handkerchief reveals an impression of his face. The Chapel of St Veronica commemorates the story, which is not recorded in the gospels.

Seventh Station Jesus falls for the second time. A large Roman column in a Franciscan chapel indicates this station.

Eighth Station Jesus consoles the women of Jerusalem (Luke 23: 28). The spot is marked by a Latin cross on the wall of a Greek Orthodox Monastery.

Fourteenth Station
The last Station of the Cross is the Holy Sepulchre itself. The tomb belonged to Joseph of Arimathea, who asked Pilate for Jesus's body.

Ninth Station Jesus falls for the third time. The place is marked by part of the shaft of a Roman column at the entrance to the Ethiopian Monastery *(see p97 & p99)*.

Steps to Ninth Station

Tenth to Thirteenth Stations
These four stations (Jesus is stripped of his clothes; he is nailed to the cross; he dies; he is taken down from the cross) are all in the place identified as Golgotha (Calvary) within the Church of the Holy Sepulchre *(see pp96–9)*.

First Station

Jesus is condemned to death. The traditional site of the Roman fortress where this took place lies inside a Muslim college, the Madrasa el-Omariyya (see p72). Franciscan friars begin their walk along the Via Dolorosa here every Friday.

Second Station Jesus takes up the cross, after being flogged and crowned with thorns. This station is in front of the Franciscan Monastery of the Flagellation (see p68).

Ecce Homo Arch is where Pontius Pilate is said to have uttered the words "Behold the man" (see p68).

0 metres		50
0 yards		50

Fourth Station

Jesus meets his mother Mary. This point is in front of the Armenian Church of Our Lady of the Spasm, which is built over an earlier Crusader church. This sculpture above the door shows the grief of Mary as she sees her son walking to his death.

Third Station

Jesus falls beneath the weight of the cross for the first time. This is commemorated by a small chapel with a marble relief above the door.

Fifth Station

Simon of Cyrene is ordered by the Roman soldiers to help Jesus carry the cross (Mark 13. 21). A Franciscan oratory marks this point on the Via Dolorosa, which is the start of the ascent to Calvary. This painting also shows St Veronica (see Sixth Station).

Celebrated Visitors

As a spiritual or utopian concept, Jerusalem has, over the centuries, been celebrated by poets and artists who have never been there, and who would perhaps hardly have known where it was on the map. However, the Holy City and the Holy Land have also been the subject of a no less impressive number of accounts, journals and paintings by a great many well-known travellers, writers and artists who did visit. From the early 19th century, the region also became a magnet for a steady flow of archaeologists and biblical scholars.

Early Pilgrims and Travellers

The establishment of Christianity as the religion of the Roman Empire in the 4th century AD triggered a wave of visitors, drawn by the region's biblical associations. One of the first pilgrims we know of is a nun named Egeria, who was perhaps Spanish, and visited the Holy Land from AD 380 to 415. An 11th-century manuscript found in Italy in 1884 contained a copy of her travel diary, which makes frequent mention of places such as Sinai and Jerusalem. Present-day writer William Dalrymple used a similar historical account (the journal of John Moschos, a 6th-century monk who wandered the Byzantine world) as the basis for his own Holy Land travels recounted in *From the Holy Mountain* (1996).

Early travellers also visited the Holy Land for trade. The most famous of the merchants was Marco Polo who, in the course of his extensive travels, was entertained by the Crusaders in their halls at Akko.

The works of early Muslim travellers include some lively descriptions of the Holy City. The 10th-century historian El-Muqaddasi described Jerusalem as "a golden basin filled with scorpions". The Moroccan scholar Ibn Batuta who, in the 14th century, travelled over 120,000 km (75,000 miles), also visited Palestine. His journals describe the Tombs of the Prophets in Hebron (see p206–7) and Jerusalem's Dome of the Rock (see pp76–7), of which he wrote, "It glows like a mass of light and flashes with the gleam of lightning."

Rediscovering the Holy Land

In the wake of Napoleon's invasion of Egypt (1798) and subsequent expedition into Palestine, and the interest it generated in the Orient, Europeans began to visit the Holy Land. First to arrive were the explorers and adventuring archaeologists, typified by Johann Ludwig Burckhardt (see p227), who was one of the first Westerners ever to visit Jerash, and who discovered Petra in 1812. Lady Hester Stanhope was an eccentric British aristocrat who escaped from her high-society existence to live in Palestine. Although she did conduct some haphazard excavations in Ashkelon (north of Gaza) in 1814, she is more famous for wearing men's clothing in order to avoid wearing the veil.

In 1838, Edward Robinson, an American Protestant clergyman with an interest in biblical geography, was the first to make a proper critical study of supposed holy sites; his name is commemorated in Robinson's Arch south of the Western Wall (see p90). In 1867–70, excavations south of the Haram esh-Sharif were carried out by Lieutenant Charles Warren of the Royal Engineers, a man who, some 20 years later, would lead the investigations into the infamous Jack the Ripper serial murders in London.

Lady Hester Stanhope

Pilgrims in Jerusalem from the *Book of Marvels* on Marco Polo's travels

Jerusalem from the Mount of Olives (1859) by Edward Lear

The Artists

With the writers came the artists, the best-known and most prolific of whom was David Roberts, a Scot who visited the Holy Land in 1839. He produced an enormous volume of very precise lithographs, collected and published in 1842, which ensured him fame in his own lifetime. His work remains ubiquitous today, adorning almost every book published on the Holy Land *(see pp8–9)*. Better known for his whimsical verse, artist, writer and traveller Edward Lear (1812–63) spent time in the Holy Land, painting a fine series of watercolours.

The English evangelical painter William Holman Hunt, who belonged to the Pre-Raphaelite movement, settled on Ha-Neviim Street in Jerusalem in 1854, where he painted several of his most famous works. In the 20th century, Russian-born Jewish artist Marc Chagall (1887–1985) became closely identified with Jerusalem. His naïve-styled work, with its strong Jewish themes, can be seen at the Israel Museum *(see pp136–41)*, in tapestry form at the Knesset *(see p135)*, and in stained glass windows at the synagogue of the Hadassah Hospital *(see p143)*.

He is remembered in Jerusalem today through "Warren's Shaft", the popular name for the Jebusite well at the City of David archaeological site *(see p119)*.

The Writers

As the ground was broken by the early explorers, a steady stream of adventurous travellers followed in their wake, recording their experiences for eager audiences back in the West. François René de Chateaubriand's brief sojourn in Jaffa, Jerusalem, Bethlehem, Jericho and the Dead Sea area, as related in his *Journey from Paris to Jerusalem* (1811), initiated the fashion for travel journals and descriptions of the Holy Land among 19th-century literati. The French poet Alphonse de Lamartine followed in his tracks in 1832, recording his experiences in *Remembrances of a Journey to the East*. In 1850 the creator of Madame Bovary, Gustave Flaubert, visited Palestine and Egypt, but found Jerusalem oppressive, writing in his diary, "It seems as if the Lord's curse hovers over the city." American authors Herman Melville and Mark Twain, both visiting in the mid-19th century, were hardly any more enamoured. Melville, author of *Moby-Dick*, thought the Holy Sepulchre church "a sickening cheat". Twain was even more caustic, commenting in his 1895 book *The Innocents Abroad*, "There will be no Second Coming. Jesus has been to Jerusalem once and he will not come again." The tradition of scathing comment continued in the 20th century, with George Bernard Shaw advising Zionists in the 1930s to erect notices at popular holy sites stating, "Do not bother to stop here, it isn't genuine." Other writers have been kinder: Nobel laureate Saul Bellow produced a warm-hearted account of the city in *To Jerusalem and Back* (1976).

Mark Twain

The Finding of the Saviour in the Temple (1854–60) by William Holman Hunt

The Landscape and Wildlife of the Holy Land

From the life-giving Jordan River in the north to the scattered oases of the Negev and Sinai deserts in the south, water is precious in the Holy Land. In Israel it is rare to see water that is not used for irrigating land or creating fish ponds. Away from the cultivated areas of Galilee and the coast, visitors will encounter a great variety of environments: mountains in the Golan Heights, green hills in Galilee, stony desert in the Negev and sandy desert in southern Jordan. Then there are the strange lifeless waters of the Dead Sea *(see p201)* and the astonishing abundance of life on the reefs of the Red Sea *(see pp244–5)*.

The Jordan River, which flows from the Golan Heights to the Dead Sea

The Desert

Much of the Holy Land is desert. South of the Dead Sea, the landscape changes from scrubby steppe to rocky desert with spectacular craters such as Makhtesh Ramon *(see p208)*. The one common tree is the hardy acacia. Animals such as gazelles, ibexes and hyraxes are found at wadis and oases, but the predators that hunted them, the striped hyena and the wolf, are now extremely rare. A more common sight is that of a wheeling vulture or eagle.

Acacia trees growing in the Negev Desert

The fleet-footed Dorcas gazelle is found in the southern part of Israel and the Sinai peninsula, but in dwindling numbers.

A rock hyrax basks in the hot sun. Hyraxes are hard to spot as they remain hidden among the rocks if it is overcast or cold.

Oases are rare in the deserts of this region. Those with plentiful water, like this one in Azraq, Jordan, are exploited to the full. Others act as magnets for the wildlife of the region.

Wadis are riverbeds, dry for much of the year. After spring rains, they can fill rapidly with torrents of water, causing a brief explosion of flowers and grasses. Trees that manage to survive in these unpredictable conditions include the acacia and terebinth.

Ice plants are succulents that thrive in desert conditions, surviving drought by storing water in their fleshy leaves.

Mountains, Hills and Cliffs

The highest mountains in the region are those on the Sinai peninsula and Mount Hermon in the Golan Heights. Trees on the lower slopes in the Golan include Aleppo pine and Syrian juniper. Vegetation in Sinai is very sparse, as it is in the spectacular rocky cliffs and gorges in the Judaean Hills and around the Dead Sea.

Egyptian vultures are found in many of the wilder areas, such as the Negev and the mountains of northern Israel and northwestern Jordan.

Ibexes live high in the mountains, descending, in the cool of the morning and late afternoon, to wadis and oases to graze and drink.

The Golan Heights

The Madonna lily's beautiful white flowers symbolize purity. A number of Holy Land plants have names inspired by the Bible.

Prickly pears thrive in the hot dry climate. Introduced originally from the Americas, they are much appreciated for their sweet refreshing fruit.

Oranges are one of many fruits grown in the fertile areas; they constitute a major export for Israel.

Cultivated Areas

Israel makes maximum use of the land available for agriculture, even using irrigation to create artificial oases in the desert. There are extensive plantations of oranges and other citrus fruits, avocados, bananas and dates. Jordan is less fortunate, its only fertile area being along the eastern side of the Jordan Valley. In Sinai there are only rare oases such as Feiran (see p253).

The laughing dove, so called for its rising and falling, laughing cry, has spread dramatically since the 1930s in the cultivated regions of Israel and western Jordan.

Neatly cultivated fields at Migdal on the western shore of the Sea of Galilee

Birdwatching in the Holy Land

Israel lies on one of the most important routes for migratory birds that winter in Africa then return to Europe and Asia to nest in the spring. Larger species include both black and white storks and many birds of prey. In terms of the number of species that can be seen, the area around Eilat (see p209) on the Gulf of Aqaba is reckoned the best place for watching migrating birds in the world. Another popular destination for birdwatchers is the Hula Reserve, an area of protected wetlands north of the Sea of Galilee.

Migrating stork

White pelicans with the distinctive yellow underside of their beaks

THE HOLY LAND THROUGH THE YEAR

Shared as it is by Jews, Christians and Muslims, Jerusalem has an overabundance of religious holidays. Add to these secular holidays, commemorations and cultural festivals, and rarely a week passes in which some significant event is not taking place. While visitors may want to time their visit to coincide with some of these events, they may equally want to avoid others. During religious holidays such as Passover (and Ramadan in Israel's Arab areas and in Jordan) many shops, restaurants and museums close for the duration or open only for limited hours, and lodging is hard to find and pricey. The dates of religious and other holidays vary each year so you should check these when planning holidays. The Holy Land has year-round warm weather, but the heat in July and August can be extreme.

Spring

Spring in Jerusalem usually arrives in the latter part of March. This coincides with the Christian Easter and Jewish Passover celebrations, when the city is filled with pilgrims. The religious festivities are accompanied by cultural events, which increase in frequency as summer approaches. The weather is mild, and this is the best time for trips to Israel's many parks – though around the Dead Sea the thermometer is already regularly above 30° C (86° F).

March

Jerusalem Marathon. One of the major sports events in Israel, with routes around the city and hundreds of Israelis and foreigners participating. **Easter** falls from late March to April for Catholics and Protestants; the Orthodox and Armenian churches celebrate a week later. Jerusalem's Easter week begins with a Palm Sunday procession from the Mount of Olives to St Anne's *(see p71)*. The most striking ceremony is the Holy Fire *(see p97)*, held on the Saturday of the Orthodox Easter.

April

Passover, or Pesach, falls sometime from late March to late April. It celebrates the liberation from slavery under the pharaohs. During the week of the festival, restaurants generally remain open.
Boombamela Festival *(1st week)*, Ashkelon, Israel. An alternative arts festival held on the beach.
Armenian Holocaust Day *(24 Apr)*, Jerusalem. Marked with a procession, then a service at St James's Cathedral in

Palm Sunday procession in Jerusalem moving along the Via Dolorosa

memory of the Turkish massacres *(see p110)*.
Mimouna is celebrated the day after Passover ends by North African Jews, with festivities throughout Israel.
Holocaust Day. In the morning, sirens signal for two minutes' silence in remembrance of the victims of the Holocaust.
Remembrance Day. In the same fashion as Holocaust Day, this day honours the Israeli dead from past wars. Sirens signal twice, at sunset and the next morning.
Independence Day. Israeli statehood is commemorated with parades and concerts.
South Sinai Camel Festival *(Apr/May)*, Sharm el-Sheikh, Egypt. The Bedouin tribes of Sinai bring their camels to this huge desert race meeting.

May

Israel Festival *(May/Jun)*. The most important cultural event in Israel: three weeks of music,

Spring in Israel, the perfect time for exploring the countryside

Average daily hours of sunshine in Jerusalem

Hours

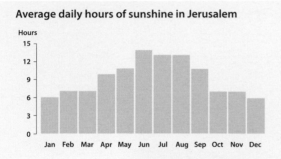

| | Jan | Feb | Mar | Apr | May | Jun | Jul | Aug | Sep | Oct | Nov | Dec |

Sunshine Chart
Even during the winter, most days have some sunshine. The summer sun can be very fierce and adequate precautions against sunburn and sunstroke should be taken. Sunscreen, a hat and sunglasses are recommended. Drinking plenty of water reduces the risk of dehydration.

dance, theatre and visual arts in Tel Aviv, Jerusalem, Haifa and the Roman theatres at Caesarea *(see p180)* and Beth Shean *(see p189)*.
Music Festival *(Passover)*, Jaffa *(see pp178–9)*. This classical music festival takes place from May to July.

Summer

With fewer religious festivals, the attention over summer shifts to the coast, where the soaring temperatures are tempered by sea breezes, and to the towns of Galilee, where the altitude partially counteracts the heat.

June

Ascension falls 40 days after Easter. It celebrates Christ's ascent to Heaven and in Jerusalem it is marked by prayers on the Mount of Olives *(see pp114–15)*.
White Night *(late Jun)*, Tel Aviv *(see pp172–7)*. A celebration with free concerts, street theatre, candle-lit tours and parties. Many shops and attractions stay open all night.

Crowds watch an Independence Day fireworks display in Jerusalem

July

Film Festival *(early Jul)*, Jerusalem. Held at the Cinematheque *(see p154–5)*, this features the work of Israeli and foreign directors.
Jazz Festival *(Jul–Aug)*, Eilat. Held on the shores of the Red Sea, this festival draws international musicians.
Jordan Festival *(late Jul and Aug)*, Jerash. Jordan's most important festival is held in the spectacular setting of the Roman ruins *(see pp214–15)*. It includes folk dance, ballet, opera, poetry competitions, theatre, classical music and displays of local handicrafts.

August

Jaffa Nights, Tel Aviv. Two weeks of open-air concerts and shows in the setting of Old Jaffa *(see pp178–9)*.
Puppet Festival, Jerusalem. This is a festival aimed at the young, with shows in various venues, notably the Train Theatre in the Liberty Bell Gardens.
Klezmer Festival, Safed *(see p185)*. A festival devoted to traditional Eastern European Jewish music.

Jewish Holidays

The Jewish calendar is lunar, meaning that each month begins and ends at the new moon. Jewish holidays therefore fall on a different date each year compared to the Western calendar; however, they do remain roughly fixed about a certain time of the year.

Jewish girl dressed for Mimouna

Performance by the dance troupe Enana at the Jordan Festival

Average monthly temperature in Jerusalem

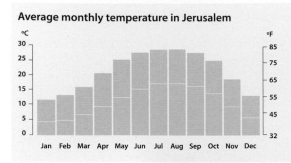

Temperature
Summers in Jerusalem are hot, temperatures frequently climbing to over 30° C (86° F). In winter, the thermometer can drop to near freezing, with even the occasional snowfall. The chart *(left)* shows average daily maximum and average daily minimum temperatures for each month.

Autumn

In terms of the weather, autumn is the ideal time to visit Jerusalem. However, several major Jewish holidays occur in September and October, seriously disrupting public transport and reducing opening hours for shops and restaurants. It is also necessary to make hotel reservations well in advance.

September

Rosh ha-Shanah. The Jewish New Year. It marks the start of ten days of prayer that end with Yom Kippur. On the penultimate day, Jews used to perform Kaparot, a ceremony in which a live fowl is waved over the head to absorb sins; today this practice is confined to the ultra-Orthodox community. The *shofar*, ram's horn, is sounded at services.
Yom Kippur. The Day of Atonement, the holiest day of the year, which Jews observe by fasting for 25 hours and

Sukkoth booths, in which meals are taken for the feast's duration

spending most of the day in intensive prayer at their synagogue. The whole country comes to a virtual standstill.
Sukkoth. Commemoration of the Israelites' 40 years in the wilderness after leaving Egypt. Makeshift "booths" are built outside where meals are eaten for seven days. Orthodox Jews even sleep in them.
Haifa International Film Festival, Haifa, Israel. Held

annually during the holiday of Sukkoth *(see above)*, the biggest and most important film event in Israel hosts more than 200 screenings over eight days.

October

Fringe Theatre Festival, Akko *(see pp182–3)*. This festival in the ancient city of Akko involves local and international avant-garde groups performing in various venues.

November

Jerusalem International Oud Festival *(mid-Nov)*. This important festival of ethnic music attracts artists from all over Israel and abroad.

Winter

Christmas is obviously a good time to visit Bethlehem and Nazareth, especially if you can attend one of the special church services. It does occasionally snow in Jerusalem, and snow on the Golan Heights sees the ski-lifts operating.

Muslim Festivals

Eid el-Fitr and Eid el-Adha are the major feasts, both lasting two or three days and celebrated by the slaughter of sheep. Eid el-Fitr marks the end of Ramadan, the month of fasting, observed by all devout Muslims. Eid el-Adha (Festival of Sacrifice) commemorates Abraham's willingness to sacrifice his son for Allah. Other significant days include the Prophet's Birthday (Moulid en-Nabi) and Islamic New Year (Ras el-Sana). The Islamic year is lunar and 11 days shorter than the Western year. This means that in terms of the Western calendar, Islamic festivals fall 11 days earlier each year.

Muslim at prayer

Average monthly rainfall in Jerusalem

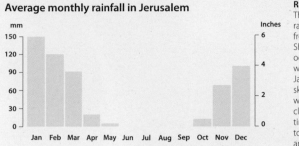

Rainfall
There is virtually no rainfall in Jerusalem from April to October. Showers begin to occur in autumn and winter, and during January and February skies are often filled with threatening grey clouds. Visitors at this time would be wise to go armed with an umbrella.

December
Hanukkah. The Jewish Festival of Lights, this commemorates the reconsecration of the Temple in 164 BC *(see p46)*. It lasts eight days and is celebrated by the lighting of candles in a special eight-branched menorah.

Christmas *(24–25 Dec)*. A Christmas Eve procession from Jerusalem arrives in Bethlehem for midnight mass at the Church of the Nativity *(see pp198–9)*. To attend this service you must book in advance at the Christian Information Centre in Jerusalem *(see p259)*. The mass is also projected on a huge screen in Manger Square. The service at Abu Ghosh *(see p143)* is also impressive. In Nazareth a procession is held on the afternoon of Christmas Eve, which ends with services held in the town's six churches.

Hanukkah candles

Midnight Mass during Christmas at the Church of the Nativity in Bethlehem

International Choir Festival *(26 Dec)*, Nazareth. In the days following the choir festival, the town plays host to sacred music concerts.

Tiberias Marathon *(Dec–Feb)*. Less well-known than the Jerusalem Marathon, this attracts many runners because of the scenery along the route *(see pp186–7)*.

January
Orthodox Christmas *(7 Jan)*, Jerusalem. This is celebrated on Christmas Eve with a service at the Holy Trinity Church in the Russian Compound *(see p128)*.

Armenian Christmas *(19 Jan)*, Jerusalem. This is celebrated with a Christmas Eve mass at St James's Cathedral in the Old City *(see pp110–11)*.

February
Purim. Celebrating the salvation of the Jews in Persia from threatened genocide (related in the Book of Esther). The Scroll of Esther is read publicly in the morning and on the evening of Purim. Adults give gifts to the poor and to friends, while children wear fancy dress costumes.

International Book Fair, Jerusalem. This biennial event culminates with the awarding of the Jerusalem Prize.

Jewish children dressed up as part of Purim festivities

THE HISTORY OF THE HOLY LAND

Since prehistoric times the fertile plains and scattered oases between the Nile and the rivers of Mesopotamia have been colonized by countless different peoples. The ebb and flow of nations continues to this day; as independent countries, both Israel and Jordan are barely half a century old, with the Jewish state composed of a great many nationalities, all united by their shared faith.

Much of our knowledge of the early prehistory of the Holy Land comes from the site of Jericho, just north of the Dead Sea. Excavations have uncovered a series of settlements dating back to about 10,000 BC, when Stone Age hunters first abandoned their nomadic way of life. In settling, these people took the all-important step which led to cultivating crops and domesticating animals – a process known as the "Neolithic revolution". During the following 3,000 years small farming villages sprang up all over the region.

In the 3rd millennium BC the coastal plains witnessed the rise of a fairly uniform culture, known as the Canaanite civilization. There may never have been a single Canaanite nation; rather the Canaanites were probably organized in a series of city-states. A Canaanite army was defeated at Megiddo by the pharaoh Thutmose (1468 BC) and all the city-states were then subject to Egypt. The Canaanites nevertheless survived for two millennia – during which time they developed the world's first alphabet – until their culture was brought to an end by the rise of two new peoples. The first were invaders who came from the sea around

1200 BC; these were the Philistines, after whom the area was called Palestine ("land of the Philistines"). The second were the Hebrew tribes, who, between about 1200 and 1000 BC, coalesced into a political entity known as Israel.

There are several theories as to how the Hebrews came to control Palestine: through hard-won battles, or possibly by peaceful infiltration. There are no historical sources to verify events, but the Old Testament tells how these tribes formed a confederation that eventually led to the birth of a united kingdom whose first sovereign was Saul. His successors, David (whose rule is traditionally given as from around 1010 to 970 BC) and Solomon (c.970–930 BC), laid the foundations for the Jewish nation. It was David, according to the Bible, who captured Jerusalem and made it the Israelite capital, and Solomon who built the Jews' First Temple there.

Babylonian Captivity

According to the Bible, after Solomon died, conflicts led to the division of the Jewish nation into two separate parts: the Kingdom of Israel in the north and the Kingdom of

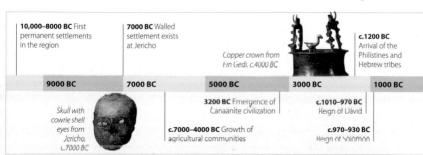

10,000–8000 BC First permanent settlements in the region	7000 BC Walled settlement exists at Jericho	Copper crown from Ein Gedi, c.4000 BC		c.1200 BC Arrival of the Philistines and Hebrew tribes
9000 BC	**7000 BC**	**5000 BC**	**3000 BC**	**1000 BC**
Skull with cowrie shell eyes from Jericho, c.7000 BC		3200 BC Emergence of Canaanite civilization	c.1010–970 BC Reign of David	
		c.7000–4000 BC Growth of agricultural communities	c.970–930 BC Reign of Solomon	

◀ Medieval European map, showing the Holy City of Jerusalem as the centre of the world

Judaea in the south. Two centuries later, the Assyrians conquered the north, and many of the Jews of Israel were deported. When Judaea withheld tribute, it too was invaded and defeated at the battle of Lachish. The Assyrians, in turn, were defeated by the Babylonians who, in 587 BC, captured Jerusalem and destroyed Solomon's Temple, forcing the Jews of Judaea into exile. During the brief period of Babylonian captivity, the Jews maintained and even strengthened their cultural and religious identity. Defeated by the Persians under Cyrus the Great in 538 BC, the Babylonians disappeared from history and the Jews were allowed to return to their land.

The Second Temple

Returning to Jerusalem, in the 6th century BC the Jews built a new temple on the same site as the first. This event in the history of Jerusalem marks the beginning of what is referred to as the "Second Temple" period.

The Persians remained dominant in the region until their empire was torn apart by the armies of Alexander the Great. Judaea was swallowed up in the wake of the Macedonian's triumphant progress into Egypt. On the death of Alexander, his empire was split between three generals; the dynasties they founded proceeded to fight over the spoils, with Palestine eventually going to the Syria-based Seleucids. The culture of the Greeks spread throughout the region. This era saw the rise of the Decapolis ("ten cities"

in Greek), a loose grouping of Hellenistic city-states in an otherwise Semitic landscape, which included Philadelphia (Amman), Gerasa (Jerash) and Scythopolis (Beth Shean). But Jerusalem resisted. The response of the Seleucid king Antiochus IV Epiphanes (175–164 BC) was to rededicate the Jews' temple in Jerusalem to Zeus and make observance of Hebrew law punishable by death. Led by Judas Maccabeus, a priest of the Hasmonean family, the Jews rebelled in 164 BC. They defeated the Seleucids, took complete control of Jerusalem and reconsecrated their Temple.

Rule of Judaea was assumed by the Hasmoneans. However, independence for the Jews did not ensure peace. There was bitter conflict between the Hasmoneans and the Pharisees, a religious sect that demanded that the Hasmonean kings relinquish the High Priesthood. In the ensuing struggle for influence, both factions asked for help from the new political and military power of the period – Rome.

The recapture of the Temple by Judas Maccabeus in his successful revolt against the Seleucids, 164 BC

722 BC Assyria conquers the Kingdom of Israel and sends the Israelites into exile

587 BC The Babylonians conquer Jerusalem and destroy the First Temple

515 BC The founding of the Second Temple

Alexander the Great whose successors Hellenized Palestine

| 800 BC | 700 BC | 600 BC | 500 BC | 400 BC |

The seal of Jeroboam, a 9th-century Jewish king

538 BC Cyrus the Great frees the Jews in exile in Babylon

332 BC Alexander the Great conquers Palestine

The Romans and Jewish Uprisings

The Romans lost no time in taking advantage of this opportunity: in 63 BC their legions took Jerusalem. The Hasmoneans were superseded by a series of Roman governors, known as procurators. Anxious not to offend local religious sensibilities, the Romans had the Jewish Herod (the Great) rule as a client king in Palestine (37–4 BC). Allowed a relatively free hand in domestic affairs, the ambitious Herod expanded his frontiers and promoted architectural projects such as the Masada and Herodion fortress complexes, the port-city of Caesarea and the grand reconstruction of the Jews' Second Temple in Jerusalem.

On Herod's death his kingdom was ruled for a brief period by his three sons, before being governed directly by the Romans. A heavy tax burden, insensitive administration and the imposition of Roman culture were responsible for growing discontent among the Jews. Large numbers of Messianic claimants, revolutionary prophets and apocalyptic preachers only served to inflame the situation further. This was the political climate into which Jesus Christ was born, as described in the biblical New Testament. Jewish clashes with Rome broke out repeatedly, culminating in a full-scale revolt in AD 66. It took the Romans four years to gain victory in this First Jewish War. When in AD 70 they finally captured Jerusalem,

Jerash, a former Decapolis city which flourished under the Romans

they destroyed the city and demolished the Temple *(see pp48–9)*. The final subjugation of the Jews occurred three years later at Masada. Judaea once again became a Roman province, but the Jews refused to be subdued and before long, a second major revolt broke out.

The Exile of the Jews

After the Second Jewish War (AD 132–5), Hadrian rebuilt Jerusalem as Aelia Capitolina, a Roman city, which Jews were forbidden to enter. Their communities were broken up and great numbers were sold into slavery and sent to Rome. Others fled, south into Egypt and across North Africa, or east to join the existing Jewish community in Babylon, who had settled there after the destruction of the First Temple. This great scattering of the Jews is known as the Diaspora.

Hadrian, builder of Aelia Capitolina

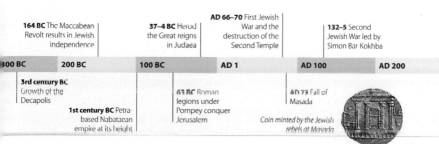

The Destruction of the Second Temple

During the Jewish Revolt of AD 66, the Romans suffered early defeats until the emperor Vespasian sent his son Titus to Jerusalem with four legions. The siege of the city was bitterly fought. Eventually, after five months, on 29 August AD 70, the city's defenders were forced to surrender. In *The Jewish War*, historian Flavius Josephus describes how the Temple was set ablaze in the heat of battle. "When the flames rose up," he writes, "the Jews let out a terrific cry and, heedless of mortal danger, ran to put it out." But it was in vain, and the Second Temple was razed to the ground.

Roman Empire AD 117

▨ Maximum extent of the Empire

Arch of Titus
The Romans built the triumphal Arch of Titus in the Forum in Rome, with friezes showing the victorious troops with their booty from the destroyed Temple.

The Antonia Fortress was built by Herod the Great around 37–35 BC to protect the Temple, and named for his patron, Mark Antony. It was the last stronghold of the Jewish rebels in AD 70.

Portico

The Court of the Gentiles was as far into the Temple complex as non-Jews could venture.

The Causeway linked the Temple with the main city gate to the west. Evidence of it remains today in Wilson's Arch (*see p89*).

Ossuary of Caiaphas
Carved from limestone, ossuaries held the bones of the dead. This particular ossuary bears the name Caiaphas, which was the name of the Temple High Priest at the time of the Crucifixion of Jesus.

The Western Wall
Herod's engineers created the Temple platform by building four walls around a natural hill and filling in. The Western Wall (*see p89*) is part of one of those retaining walls.

Destruction and Sack of the Temple of Jerusalem
Painted by Nicolas Poussin in 1625–6, and now in the collection of the Israel Museum *(see pp136–41)*, this shows Roman soldiers, directed by Titus on his white horse, emerging from the Inner Temple carrying the Jewish menorah and other treasures.

The Inner Temple contained the Holy of Holies, an empty chamber meant for the Ark of the Covenant, which was lost when the First Temple was destroyed.

Bronze Helmet
Archaeologists' finds such as this legionary's helmet (c.AD 100) indicate that Rome maintained a strong military presence after the Jewish Revolt.

The Hulda Gates

The Royal Stoa was a covered colonnade, 162 columns in length, used for teaching.

The Lower City Steps led to the area known as the City of David. Evidence of them exists in Robinson's Arch *(see p90)*.

"Judaea Capta" Coin
A commemorative coin issued after the defeat of the Jewish rebels depicting, on one side, Vespasian and, on the other, Rome standing triumphant over a subdued Judaea.

The Second Temple

Built in the 6th century BC on the same site as the First Temple, which was destroyed by the Babylonians in 587 BC, the Second Temple was greatly expanded by Herod the Great (37–4 BC). He nearly doubled the size of the Inner Temple.

Constantine the Great, the first Christian Roman emperor, who unified the Roman Empire under his rule

Palestine Under Roman Rule

Despite the Jews being banned from Jerusalem, during the 2nd and 3rd centuries their religion and traditions remained very much alive in Palestine, and scholars and religious schools were active throughout Galilee. This was the period in which the academies wrote down Jewish oral law and the commentaries on it, known collectively as the Talmud.

In the early 4th century, the Christians, who had also suffered Roman persecution, were granted freedom of worship by the emperor Constantine (306–37), himself a convert to the religion. Constantine moved his capital from Rome to Byzantium, which was renamed Constantinople.

This turn of events opened the doors of the Holy Land to pilgrims – first and foremost the devout Helena, mother of Constantine – and Jerusalem regained its former importance. The first Christian churches were built on the sites connected with the life of Christ, and monasticism spread both in the towns and in the deserts of Palestine and Egypt. The first Holy Sepulchre church was dedicated in Jerusalem in 335.

During the rule of Theodosius (379–95), Christianity became the official state religion. Not long after, the Roman Empire was divided in 395 between Theodosius's two sons. The Latin-speaking Western Empire fell to Germanic invaders but the Greek-speaking Eastern Empire, thereafter known as the Byzantine Empire, survived.

The Byzantine Era

Despite a long series of schisms within the Eastern Church over the nature of Christ (see p104), the Byzantine period was an age of relative stability and prosperity in the Holy Land. The flow of pilgrims continued and monastic life drew ever more adherents. The construction of two important religious buildings, St Catherine's Monastery (see pp250–52) in Sinai and the enormous Nea Basilica (see p84) in Jerusalem, reflected the confidence of the era. The Holy Land became the land we can see on the early medieval mosaic map at Madaba (see pp220–21). However, upheaval was to arrive in 614 in the form of an invading Persian army. Welcomed and supported by the Jews, who hoped for

Byzantine icon of the Madonna and Child, 6th century

AD 313 Constantine grants freedom of worship to Christians in the Edict of Milan

527–65 Reign of Byzantine emperor Justinian

661 Omayyad dynasty established in Damascus

AD 300   400   500   600

395 The Roman Empire splits into East and West

638 Battle of Yarmuk River; beginning of Arab dominion in the Holy Land

Coin of Constantine, AD 320

691 Dome of the Ro completed in Jerusale

greater religious freedom, the Persians massacred the Christians and desecrated their holy sites before being driven off in 628 by the forces of the Byzantine Empire.

In the same year that the Byzantines reconquered Palestine, in neighbouring Arabia an army led by the Prophet Muhammad conquered Mecca, marking the emergence of a new force in the Near East which, in a little over ten years, would change the face of the Holy Land.

Pilgrimage scroll showing the Haram esh-Sharif

The Arabs and Islam

In AD 638, only six years after Muhammad's death, the troops of his successor, or *caliph*, Omar defeated the Byzantines at the Yarmuk River, in modern-day Syria. The Muslims became the new rulers of Palestine.

Islam recognizes many of the prophets of the Old Testament, such as Abraham (Ibrahim), and so the Arabs regarded Jerusalem as holy in the same way as the Jews and Christians. The Arabs also believed that the Prophet Muhammad had ascended to Heaven on his Night Journey *(see p31)* from the same rock in Jerusalem on which, according to the Bible, Abraham had been about to sacrifice his son, and over which the Jews had built their temples. Consequently, the rubble in the Temple area was cleared and construction of two mosques began there: the Dome of the Rock (691) and El-Aqsa (705). Access to this "sacred precinct" *(Haram esh-Sharif)* was forbidden to non-Muslims, but Christians and Jews were permitted to live in the city of Jerusalem on payment of an "infidels" tax.

Groups of Christian pilgrims regularly arrived in the Holy Land from Byzantium and Europe and were given safe passage under the successive Arab dynasties of the Omayyads (661–750), Abbasids (750–974) and, initially, the Fatimids (975–1171). This happy state of affairs ended in 1009 when the third Fatimid caliph El-Hakim initiated the violent persecution of non-Muslims and destroyed the Holy Sepulchre. The situation became critical in 1071 when Jerusalem fell to the Seljuk Turks, who forbade Christians access to the Holy City

The outraged response of Christian Europe was to take up arms and set off on the first of a series of Crusades spread over almost 200 years to recapture the Holy City and biblical sites of Palestine *(see pp52–3)*.

Triumphant group of the feared Muslim cavalry

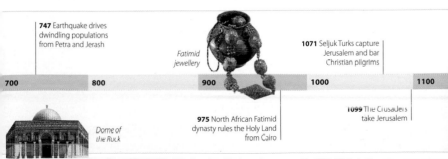

747 Earthquake drives dwindling populations from Petra and Jerash

Fatimid jewellery

1071 Seljuk Turks capture Jerusalem and bar Christian pilgrims

| 700 | 800 | 900 | 1000 | 1100 |

Dome of the Rock

975 North African Fatimid dynasty rules the Holy Land from Cairo

1099 The Crusaders take Jerusalem

The Crusades

"God wills it!" With these words, on 27 November 1095 at the Council of Clermont, Pope Urban II launched an appeal to aid the Byzantines in their wars with the Seljuk Turks and so free the Holy Land. His preachings inspired more than 100,000 men and women from all over Europe to join the armies heading east. They succeeded in creating a Latin kingdom of Jerusalem, but a series of further Crusades meant to reinforce the Western Christian presence in the east were ever less successful. Within 200 years the Crusaders were gone, leaving a legacy of fine ecclesiastical and military architecture.

The Holy Land
▨ Crusader domains 1186

Church of the
Holy Sepulchre

Scenes from the
life of Christ

The First Crusade
Passing through Constantinople, the Crusaders first engaged the Muslim Seljuks in Anatolia (Turkey). They conquered Nicaea and Antioch before marching down through Syria to Palestine.

Stylized Gothic gates
of Jerusalem

The Second Crusade
Most of the Second Crusaders never made it to the Holy Land. Those that did launched a disastrous attack on Damascus and had to withdraw.

The Capture
of Jerusalem

On 7 June 1099, the Crusaders laid siege to Jerusalem. The Muslims held out for five weeks until, on 15 July, the Christian troops breached the walls, unleashing a massive slaughter in the streets.

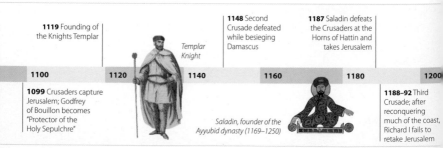

1119 Founding of
the Knights Templar

*Templar
Knight*

1148 Second
Crusade defeated
while besieging
Damascus

1187 Saladin defeats
the Crusaders at the
Horns of Hattin and
takes Jerusalem

1100	1120	1140	1160	1180	1200

1099 Crusaders capture
Jerusalem; Godfrey
of Bouillon becomes
"Protector of the
Holy Sepulchre"

*Saladin, founder of the
Ayyubid dynasty (1169–1250)*

1188–92 Third
Crusade; after
reconquering
much of the coast,
Richard I fails to
retake Jerusalem

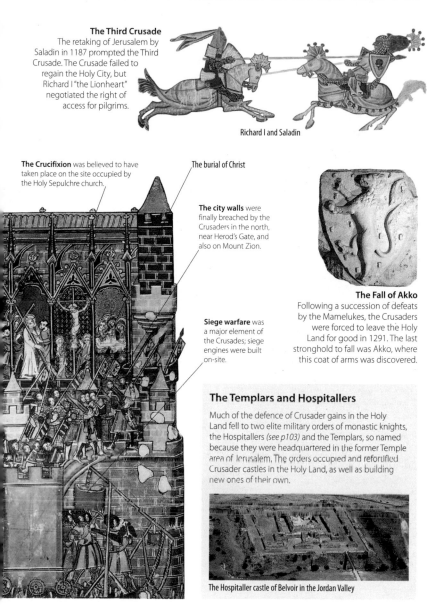

The Third Crusade
The retaking of Jerusalem by Saladin in 1187 prompted the Third Crusade. The Crusade failed to regain the Holy City, but Richard I "the Lionheart" negotiated the right of access for pilgrims.

Richard I and Saladin

The Crucifixion was believed to have taken place on the site occupied by the Holy Sepulchre church.

The burial of Christ

The city walls were finally breached by the Crusaders in the north, near Herod's Gate, and also on Mount Zion.

Siege warfare was a major element of the Crusades; siege engines were built on-site.

The Fall of Akko
Following a succession of defeats by the Mamelukes, the Crusaders were forced to leave the Holy Land for good in 1291. The last stronghold to fall was Akko, where this coat of arms was discovered.

The Templars and Hospitallers

Much of the defence of Crusader gains in the Holy Land fell to two elite military orders of monastic knights, the Hospitallers (see p103) and the Templars, so named because they were headquartered in the former Temple area of Jerusalem. The orders occupied and refortified Crusader castles in the Holy Land, as well as building new ones of their own.

The Hospitaller castle of Belvoir in the Jordan Valley

1244 Jerusalem falls to Muslim mercenaries in the employ of Egypt

1270 Last major Crusade, led by Louis IX, ends in his death in Tunis

Louis IX embarking on the last Crusade

1220	1240	1260	1280	1300

1217–21 Fifth Crusade

1249–50 Louis IX of France leads unsuccessful invasion of Egypt

1260 Mamelukes defeat invading Mongols; Baybars becomes Sultan of Egypt

1291 Last Latin strongholds in Holy Land, including Akko, fall to Mamelukes

Mameluke horsemen training for battle, from a
15th-century manuscript

Palestine Under the Mamelukes

In the wake of the Crusades, Jerusalem
slowly declined to the status of a provincial
city. The Mamelukes (former slave guards of
Saladin's Ayyubid dynasty) ruled the Holy
Land from Egypt, and the Holy City became
a place of banishment for officials who fell
from court favour in Cairo.

While the Mamelukes had driven the
Christian knights from the Holy Land, they
did make allowance for Christian pilgrims.
In 1333 the Franciscan Friars were permitted
a presence in Jerusalem, living in the
supposed Hall of the Last Supper. In
1342 Pope Clement VI ratified this
mission, which took on the name of the
Franciscan Custody of the Holy Land.

The following century saw the
beginning of a flow of Jews into
Palestine escaping persecution
in Europe, a movement that
continued through into the
20th century. In this case, the
defeat of the Moors in Spain had

given way to the Inquisition and the
resultant expulsion of some 100,000 Jews
from the country, accused of having too
close ties with the vanquished Arabs.

The Ottoman Empire

Mameluke control of Palestine ended
in 1516 with defeat at the hands of the
Ottoman army. Originating in northwest
Turkey, the Ottoman Turks had captured
Constantinople in 1453, renaming it
Istanbul. Under the rule of their greatest
sultan, Suleyman the Magnificent
(1520–66), vast architectural projects were
carried out in Jerusalem, most notably the
construction of the city walls and gates.

However, a series of weak sultans meant
that by the 18th century the enormous
Ottoman empire was no longer so secure,
particularly in the provinces where
corruption was often a system of
administration. This was the case in
Palestine, where the people frequently
suffered heavy taxes and poor government.
But the Jews continued to return, largely
because they were safer under Turkish rule
than they were in Europe. Many chose to
settle in Galilee, around Tiberias and
Safed, joining the Sephardic Jewish
communities that had fled Spain several
centuries earlier. At the same time,
Europe was making its first real
entry into the region since the
Crusades; Napoleon landed in
Egypt in 1798 and the following
year he had to be repelled from
invading at Akko by the
Ottoman governor,
Ahmed Pasha el-Jazzar.

Suleyman I, the Magnificent, Ottoman
sultan 1520–66

14th century Development of
the area round the Haram esh-
Sharif in Jerusalem

1492 Edict signed by
King Ferdinand
expelling all professing
Jews from Spain

1516 Ottomans defeat
the Mamelukes and
seize control of Palestine
and Egypt

1300   **1400**   **1500**

1333 Franciscans
permitted to settle
in Jerusalem

1400 Mamelukes halt
westward advance
of Mongol ruler
Tamerlane

*Jaffa Gate, one of
seven gates built by
Suleyman's engineers*

1537 Suleyman the
Magnificent orders
the construction of
the walls of Jerusalem

Akko in northern Israel, rebuilt by successive Ottoman governors (see 182–3)

Jerusalem and the Colonial Powers in the 19th Century

With the continuing decline of the Ottoman Empire, the European nations, newly empowered by their Industrial Revolution, began to follow in Napoleon's wake – unsuccessful though he had been. When in 1831 the Egyptian ruler Muhammad Ali, the supposed vassal of Istanbul, seized Palestine, it was only with British military help that the Turks regained the territory. A British consul arrived in Jerusalem in 1838, followed closely by diplomatic representatives of France and Prussia. One of the causes of the Crimean War (1854) was a dispute between France and Russia over guardianship of the Holy Places.

All the while, Jewish immigration continued, propelled by virulent anti-Semitism and pogroms in eastern Europe and throughout the Russian Empire. A result of this influx was that in the mid-19th century, Jerusalem overspilled the bounds of its medieval walls with the establishment of a series of small Jewish settlements outside the city gates. The city began to emerge from the lethargy that had characterized it in the preceding centuries.

Over in Europe there had been a growing, but not yet unified, Jewish national movement. In 1839, the British Jew Sir Moses Montefiore had first called for the creation of a Jewish state. This culminated in 1896 with the publication by an Austro-Hungarian Jewish journalist named Theodor Herzl of *Der Judenstat (The Jewish State)*, which proved a rallying cry for Jews worldwide. The following year saw the formation of the World Zionist Organization, with Herzl at its head. Its stated aim was "to create for the Jewish people a home in Palestine". A Jewish National Fund was set up to purchase land for settlement.

However, the Zionist immigrants were laying the foundations for conflict; slogans such as "A land without a people for a people without a land" ignored the large indigenous Arab population of Palestine and the Arab nations' resistance to any form of autonomous Jewish presence there.

The American Colony, one of a great many Western outposts established in 19th-century Jerusalem

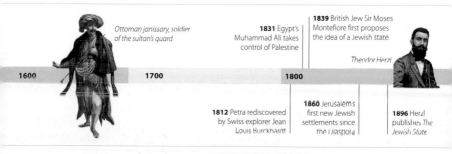

Ottoman janissary, soldier of the sultan's guard

1831 Egypt's Muhammad Ali takes control of Palestine

1839 British Jew Sir Moses Montefiore first proposes the idea of a Jewish state

Theodor Herzl

1600   1700   1800

1812 Petra rediscovered by Swiss explorer Jean Louis Burckhardt

1860 Jerusalem's first new Jewish settlements since the Diaspora

1896 Herzl publishes *The Jewish State*

The Collapse of the Ottomans and the British Mandate

Turkish rule in Palestine ended in 1917, during World War I, when British troops under the command of General Allenby took Jerusalem. The Arabs, under their leader Faisal, had fought alongside the British and expected Palestine in return. However, with the Balfour Declaration of 1917 the British had let it be known that "His Majesty's government favourably views the creation of a national Jewish home in Palestine". In the event, peace talks in 1920 put Palestine under British authority and this was ratified by the League of Nations on 24 July 1922.

General Allenby making his entry through Jaffa Gate

The following year, in order to placate Arab discontent, the British recognized Trans-Jordan as an autonomous Arab emirate, ruled by the emir Abdullah, the eldest brother of Faisal, with Amman as its capital. Initially under the supervision of the British in Jerusalem, the territory became totally independent in 1946, with Abdullah confirmed as its king.

Arab-Jewish Conflict

At the time of World War I, some 500,000 Palestinian Arabs and about 85,000 Jews were living in the Holy Land. In the 20 years between then and the outbreak of World War II, about 250,000 more Jews arrived at the ports of Jaffa and Haifa to settle in Palestine. Each new wave of immigrants served to increase the tension between the Palestinian and Jewish communities. In 1929, Palestinian riots culminated in a series of pogroms in Jerusalem, Hebron and Safed. An Arab "revolt" proclaimed in 1936 led to a six-month general strike that brought the country to a standstill.

The *Theodor Herzl* about to dock at Haifa, decks crowded with Jewish immigrants, 1947

T E Lawrence "of Arabia"

1916 Faisal and the Arabs, encouraged by T E Lawrence, join the British in a desert war against the Turks

24 July 1922 League of Nations ratifies British mandate in Palestine

1900	1905	1910	1915	1920	1925

1904 Second Aliyah, which continues until 1914, sees the arrival of large numbers of Jewish immigrants

1909 Founding of Tel Aviv and first kibbutz in Palestine

1914 War breaks out in Europe; the Ottoman Turks side with Germany

1917 General Allenby captures Jerusalem from the Ottoman Turks

General Allenby

Proposals for Partition

By this time, the British were finding rule in Palestine extremely uncomfortable. In 1937, following the deliberations of the Peel Commission, they proposed ending the Mandate and partitioning the country. The Jews accepted but the Arabs refused, claiming that the proposed Jewish homeland occupied the region's most fertile zones.

Allenby Street, in the rapidly expanding Jewish Tel Aviv of the 1930s

Elsewhere, the world was much more concerned with developments in Europe, where war seemed inevitable. In a brazen attempt to improve relations with its potential allies, the Arabs, in 1939, on the eve of war, Britain published a "White Paper" drastically limiting Jewish immigration to Palestine. However, faced with the dangers of Nazism, tens of thousands of Jews continued to arrive, often sneaking in clandestinely by sea. British attempts to check the immigration were, for the most part, in vain.

One effect of this new post-war situation was to inspire extremists to attacks on the British. On 22 July 1946 the Jewish military organization Irgun – one of whose leaders was the future prime minister Menachem Begin – bombed British headquarters at the King David Hotel in Jerusalem, killing more than 80 and wounding hundreds more.

The departure of British troops from Haifa port in 1948

Trapped in a no-win situation, the British placed the "Palestine question" before the newly formed United Nations. On 29 November 1947 the UN voted for the partition of the Holy Land into an Arab state and a Jewish state, with Jerusalem under international administration. Britain announced its intention to pull out of Palestine on 15 May 1948 and leave the Arabs and Jews to fight among themselves.

The Creation of Israel

Skirmishing between the Palestinians and Jews escalated as both sides manoeuvred to control as much territory as possible before the end of the Mandate. Jewish extremists attacked Palestinian villages (most infamously at Deir Yassin, on the road between Tel Aviv and Jerusalem), while armed Palestinians made similar raids against Jewish settlements.

As the British prepared to leave, the Jews were ready to replace them. On 14 May 1948, the eve of departure, David Ben Gurion declared the birth of the State of Israel.

1934 Jews flee central Europe and the threat of Hitler's Germany

1936 Arab Revolt in Palestine

1939 Great Britain publishes the "White Paper"

1947 Discovery of the Dead Sea Scrolls at Qumran

1930   **1935**   **1940**   **1945**   **1950**

1929 Arab attacks on Jews in Jerusalem, Hebron and Safed

1937 Peel Commission proposes partition of Palestine

14 May 1948 State of Israel declared in Tel Aviv

One of the Dead Sea Scrolls

Refugees crossing the border into Jordan in 1967 during the Six-Day War

The 1948 War

The Arab reaction to the creation of Israel was swift. Lebanon, Syria, Iraq, Jordan and Egypt launched a combined attack with the avowed aim of casting the new-born state into the sea. Fighting continued until an armistice was signed in December 1949. At the cease of hostilities, the Israelis had made great territorial gains at the expense of the Palestinians. Prior to 1948 the Jews owned less than seven per cent of Palestine but at the war's end they occupied about 80 per cent. As a result, some 500,000 to 750,000 Palestinians were made refugees in neighbouring Arab countries and in camps in the Egyptian-controlled Gaza Strip and in the Jordanian-held territories on the west bank of the Jordan River.

Israeli's building defences during the war of 1973.

One of the main objectives of the opposing sides had been the capture of Jerusalem. Neither side had achieved this; the Israelis held the modern quarters of West Jerusalem, the Jordanians held the Old City and East Jerusalem. The city was to remain divided, along what came to be known as the Green Line, for almost 20 years.

The Arab-Israeli Wars after 1949

After the violent birth of Israel, the infant state sought to strengthen its position by passing the Law of Return. This extended to all Jews throughout the world the right to live in Israel. The first to heed the invitation were communities of Jews from the Arab world, followed by displaced Jews from Europe. Those that followed came from everywhere, from the then-Soviet Union to South America.

Relations with the Arabs remained on a war footing. In 1956, the Israeli army swept into Sinai as part of the French and British plan to seize the Suez Canal, nationalized by Egypt's President Nasser. On this occasion, under pressure from the United States and the United Nations, they were forced to retreat. Eleven years later, in 1967, Israeli tanks rolled into Sinai once again. Alarmed by a build-up of Egyptian forces on the border, Israel launched a pre-emptive attack. Despite then facing the combined forces of all its Arab neighbours, in six days Israel's army had taken the Golan Heights from Syria, the Gaza Strip and Sinai from Egypt, and the West Bank from Jordan. The Israelis also captured the whole of

1951 Assassination of King Abdullah of Jordan in Jerusalem by Palestinian extremists

1956 Suez crisis

Golda Meir, Israeli prime minister 1969–74

6 October 1973 Yom Kippur War breaks out

1982 Sinai returned to the Egyptians

1950 · 1955 · 1960 · 1965 · 1970 · 1975 · 1980

14 May 1948 On the declaration of the State of Israel, war breaks out with the Arabs

Hussein, crowned king of Jordan in May 1953

5–11 June 1967 Six-Day War results in reunification of Jerusalem under the Israelis

1979 Camp David peace treaty signed between Egypt and Israel

The contentious Israeli-built security fence, designed to stop Palestinian attacks

Jerusalem. In what amounted to a face-saving exercise, on 6 October 1973, the Jewish fast of Yom Kippur, Egypt and Syria launched a surprise attack on Israeli positions. Caught off guard, the Israelis suffered initial losses but they counter-attacked and reversed early Arab gains. At the cease of hostilities the action had not altered the territorial state of affairs set six years previously.

The 1973 war did, however, pave the way for the first talks between Egypt and Israel. In 1979 the two countries formally agreed to peace by signing the Camp David agreement. In 1982 Sinai was returned to Egypt.

The Quest for Peace

The peace treaty was not welcomed by all parties. The Palestinians saw it as undermining their campaign for self-rule. Groups such as the Palestine Liberation Organisation (PLO) stepped up their anti-Israel guerrilla war. Their tactics won them little sympathy with the international community. That changed in late 1987 with the beginning of the *intifada* ("shaking off"), a grass-roots Palestinian revolt against Israeli occupation in the Gaza Strip and West Bank.

Television screens worldwide were filled with images of the ensuing confrontations. In the wake of 1991's Gulf War, the Americans brokered a meeting between Israeli and Palestinian delegations in Madrid. This seemed to achieve little, but in 1993 it was revealed that the two parties had been meeting in Norway where agreement had been reached. The signing of the "Oslo Accords" was capped that year by a handshake between Israeli prime minister Yitzhak Rabin and PLO president Yasser Arafat on the lawns of the White House. The following year saw Jordan and Israel formally end the state of war that had existed between the two countries since 1948.

Since then, Rabin has been assassinated by a Jewish extremist and Arafat has died. Israel has experienced 60 years of statehood, but the Palestinians remain stateless. The Israelis have built a giant wall between themselves and the Palestinians in an attempt to halt the terror bombings that were a fact of daily life in the 1990s. The cycle of violence continues, but so do the attempts to find a solution that will bring a lasting peace to the region.

Thousands of Israeli Jew and Arab activists unite to demonstrate for peace

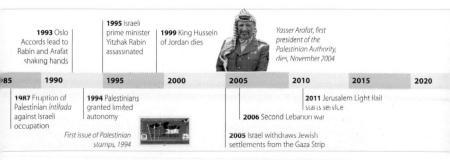

1993 Oslo Accords lead to Rabin and Arafat shaking hands

1995 Israeli prime minister Yitzhak Rabin assassinated

1999 King Hussein of Jordan dies

Yasser Arafat, first president of the Palestinian Authority, dies, November 2004

85   1990   1995   2000   2005   2010   2015   2020

1987 Eruption of Palestinian *intifada* against Israeli occupation

1994 Palestinians granted limited autonomy

First issue of Palestinian stamps, 1994

2011 Jerusalem Light Rail starts service

2006 Second Lebanon war

2005 Israel withdraws Jewish settlements from the Gaza Strip

JERUSALEM AREA BY AREA

Jerusalem at a Glance

The old city of Jerusalem has a history that stretches back more than 3,000 years, although the present street plan dates largely from Byzantine times, and the encircling walls are from the 16th century. Within the walls, the Old City divides into four vaguely defined quarters – one each for the Christians, Jews and Muslims, and the fourth occupied by the Armenians. East and south of the Old City are the Mount of Olives and Mount Zion, both places traditionally linked with the last acts of Jesus Christ. To the north and west is modern Jerusalem, liberally endowed with fine examples of late 19th-century architecture.

The Church of the Holy Sepulchre *(see pp96–9)* is the most important of the Holy Land's Christian sites. Tradition has it that the church occupies the site of Golgotha, where Jesus Christ was crucified and buried.

The Citadel *(see pp106–9)* is an impressively restored, fortified complex, which has its origins in the 2nd century BC. It now houses an excellent museum devoted to the history of Jerusalem. There are also splendid views of the city from its ramparts.

Modern Jerusalem *(See pp122–31)*

The Christian and Armenian Quarter *(See pp92–111)*

The Israel Museum *(see pp136–41)* was purpose-built in the 1960s to house the country's most significant archaeological finds, including the Dead Sea Scrolls, some of which are displayed in this uniquely shaped hall. The museum was renovated in 2007–10 and is a short distance west of the city centre.

◄ An overview of the Old City of Jerusalem at sunset

Yemin Moshe *(see pp124–5)* is one of several attractive old quarters in modern Jerusalem, developed in the mid-19th century to ease overcrowding in the Old City. It is distinguished by its windmill and by this communal housing block, known as Mishkenot Shaananim.

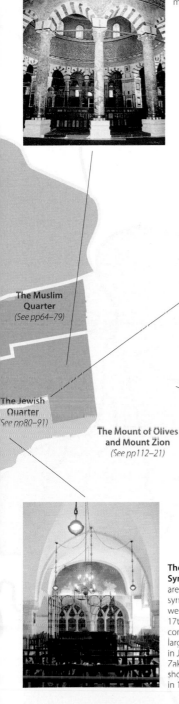

The Haram esh-Sharif *(see pp72–7)* is the focus of the Muslim faith in Jerusalem. A large plateau on the eastern edge of the Old City, it contains some fine Islamic buildings, including the 8th-century El-Aqsa Mosque and the magnificent Dome of the Rock, with its dazzling interior.

The Western Wall *(see p89)* is one of Judaism's holiest sites. It is believed to be part of the great Temple enclosure built by Herod in the 1st century BC. The plaza in front is busy, day and night, with supplicants at prayer.

| 0 metres | 500 |
| 0 yards | 500 |

The Muslim Quarter
(See pp64–79)

The Jewish Quarter
See pp80–91)

The Mount of Olives and Mount Zion
(See pp112–21)

The Sephardic Synagogues *(see p86)* are a group of four synagogues which were at the heart of the 17th-century Sephardic community, once the largest Jewish group in Jerusalem. The Ben Zakkai Synagogue, shown here, was built in 1610.

The Mount of Olives *(see pp112–21)* has several fine churches, including the richly decorated Russian Orthodox Church of St Mary Magdalene.

THE MUSLIM QUARTER

This is the largest and most densely populated quarter of the Old City. It was first developed under Herod the Great and delineated in its present form under the Byzantines. In the 12th century it was taken over by the Crusaders, hence the quarter's wealth of churches and other Christian institutions, such as the Via Dolorosa

(see pp34–5). In the 14th and 15th centuries the Mamelukes rebuilt extensively, especially in the areas abutting the Haram esh-Sharif. The quarter has been in decay since the 16th century. Today it contains some of the city's poorest homes. It is also one of the most fascinating and least explored parts of Jerusalem.

Sights at a Glance

Historic Streets, Buildings and Gates
- ❷ Ecce Homo Arch
- ❸ Via Dolorosa
- ❹ Lady Tunshuq's Palace
- ❻ Chain Street
- ❽ Damascus Gate
- ❾ Herod's Gate
- ⓫ Lions' Gate

Souks and Markets
- ❺ Cotton Merchants' Market
- ❼ Central Souk

Holy Places
- ❶ Monastery of the Flagellation
- ❿ St Anne's Church
- ⓬ *Haram esh-Sharif pp72–7*

☐ **Restaurants** *p270*
1 Abu Shukri
2 Viennese Café

See also Jerusalem Street Finder, map 4

0 metres   150
0 yards   150

HARAM ESH-SHARIF

◀ A visitor at the Dome of the Rock, centrepiece of the Haram esh-Sharif

Street-by-Street: The Muslim Quarter

The main routes through this busy quarter are along the Via Dolorosa and up and down El-Wad. Both streets are lined with a gaudy array of shops, whose salesmen eagerly press on visitors all manner of ornaments and kitsch, from plastic crucifixes to glass-bowled water pipes. Few people stray from the main thoroughfares, but those who do are richly rewarded. The quiet, winding back alleys contain a wealth of fine medieval Islamic architecture, much of it dating from the Mameluke era (1250–1516). Not all of it is in good condition, but many of these buildings still perform the functions for which they were intended.

The Austrian Hospice was built in 1869 to accommodate Christian pilgrims.

Damascus Gate

VIA DOLOROS

EL-WAD

❸ Via Dolorosa
Crossing the quarter from east to west, this street is revered by Christian pilgrims as the route taken by Christ as he was led to his crucifixion.

Holy Sepulchre church and the Christian Quarter

Abu Shukri restaurant *(see p270)*

El-Takiya Street
A narrow, stepped street at the heart of the quarter, El-Takiya contains some of the city's finest examples of Mameluke architecture.

❹ Lady Tunshuq's Palace
The banding of different coloured stone and panels of intricate marble inlay typify the decorative style of the Mamelukes.

Key

— Suggested route

0 metres	50
0 yards	50

1 ★ Monastery of the Flagellation
Built on the site traditionally associated with the flogging of Christ, this Franciscan complex includes two attractive chapels and the Studium Museum.

Locator Map
See Jerusalem Street Finder, map 4

Lions' Gate and the Mount of Olives →

RQUA

ALLAH-E-DIN

BAB

EL-HADID

Jewish Quarter

Convent of the Sisters of Zion
The convent, which runs a pilgrims' hospice, dates from the 19th-century Christian building boom.

2 ★ Ecce Homo Arch
The arch, which spans the Via Dolorosa, is the main section of a Roman triple arch. One of the smaller, flanking arches *(left)* is incorporated into the structure of the Convent of the Sisters of Zion.

Madrasa el-Araghonia (1358)

Bab el-Hadid Street
Though badly neglected, this street has a number of *madrasas (see p75)* from the 14th and 15th centuries.

Monastery of the Flagellation, with the Via Dolorosa behind

❶ Monastery of the Flagellation

Via Dolorosa. **Map** 4 D2. **Tel** (02) 627 0444. **Open** 7:30am–5pm daily. Studium Museum: **Open** 9am–1pm & 4–6pm Tue–Sat (phone for appt).

Owned by the Franciscans, this complex embraces the simple and striking Chapel of the Flagellation, designed in the 1920s by the Italian architect Antonio Barluzzi, who was also responsible for the Dominus Flevit Chapel on the Mount of Olives (see p117). It is located on the site traditionally held to be where Christ was flogged by Roman soldiers prior to his crucifixion (Matthew 27: 27–30; Mark 15: 16–19).

On the other side of the courtyard is the Chapel of the Condemnation, which also dates from the early 20th century. It is built over the remains of a medieval chapel, on the site popularly identified with the trial of Christ before Pontius Pilate.

The neighbouring monastery buildings house the Studium Biblicum Franciscanum, a prestigious institute of biblical, geographical and archaeo-logical studies. Also part of the complex, the **Studium Museum** contains objects found by the Franciscans in excavations at Capernaum, Nazareth, Bethlehem and various other sites. The most interesting exhibits are Byzantine and Crusader objects, such as fragments of frescoes from the Church of Gethsemane, precursor of the present-day Church of All Nations (see p118), and a 12th-century crozier from the Church of the Nativity in Bethlehem (see pp198–9).

❷ Ecce Homo Arch

Via Dolorosa. **Map** 4 D2. Convent of the Sisters of Zion: **Tel** (02) 627 7292. **Open** 8am–5pm daily. 🎨 🎫

This arch that spans the Via Dolorosa was built by the Romans in AD 70 to support a ramp being laid against the Antonia Fortress, in which Jewish rebels were barricaded (see p48). When the Romans rebuilt Jerusalem in AD 135 in the wake of the Second Jewish

The span of the Ecce Homo Arch, bridging the Via Dolorosa

War (see p47), the arch was reconstructed as a monument to victory, with two smaller arches flanking a large central bay. It is the central bay that you see spanning the street.

One of the side arches is also still visible, incorporated into the interior of the neighbouring **Convent of the Sisters of Zion**. Built in the 1860s, the convent also contains the remains of the vast Pool of the Sparrow (Struthion), an ancient reservoir which collected rainwater directed from the rooftops. The pool was originally covered with a stone pavement (lithostrothon) and it was on this flagstone plaza, Christian tradition has it, that Pilate presented Christ to the crowds and uttered the words "Ecce homo" ("Behold the man"). However, archaeology refutes this, dating the pavement to the 2nd century AD, long after the time of Christ. Within a railed section you can see marks scratched into the stone. Historians speculate that they may have been carved by bored Roman guards as a kind of street game.

Crusader-era angel's head, Studium Museum

❸ Via Dolorosa

Map 3 C3 & 4 D2.

The identification of the Via Dolorosa (see pp34–5) with the ancient "Way of Sorrows" walked by Christ on the way to his crucifixion has more to do with religious tradition than historical fact. It nevertheless continues to draw huge numbers of pilgrims every day. The streets through which they walk are much like any others in the Muslim Quarter, lined with small shops and stalls, but the route is marked out by 14 "Stations of the Cross", linked with events that occurred on Christ's last, fateful walk. Some of the Stations are commemorated only by wall plaques, which can be difficult to spot among the religious souvenir stalls. Others are located inside buildings.

The last five Stations are all within the Holy Sepulchre church (see pp96–9).

Friday is the main day for pilgrims, when, at 4pm in summer and 3pm in winter, the Franciscans lead a procession along the route.

In fact, the more likely route for the original Via Dolorosa begins at what is now the Citadel (see pp106–9) but was at the time the royal palace. This is where Pontius Pilate resided when in Jerusalem, making it a more likely location for the trial of Christ. From here, the condemned would probably have been led down what is now David Street, through the present-day Central Souk (see p70), out of the then city gate and to the hill of Golgotha, the presumed site of which is now occupied by the Holy Sepulchre church.

Stalactite stone carvings above a window on Lady Tunshuq's Palace

❹ Lady Tunshuq's Palace

El-Takiya St. **Map** 4 D3.
Closed to public.

Lady Tunshuq, of Mongolian or Turkish origin, was the wife, or mistress, of a Kurdish nobleman. She arrived in Jerusalem some time in the 14th century and had this edifice built for herself. It is one of the loveliest examples of Mameluke architecture in Jerusalem. Unfortunately the narrowness of the street prevents you from standing back and appreciating the building as a whole, but you can admire the three great doorways with their beautiful inlaid-marble decoration. The upper portion of a window

An unusually quiet Via Dolorosa, leading down from Ecce Homo Arch to El-Wad Road

recess also displays some fine carved stone, stalactite-like decoration, a form known as *muqarnas*. The former palace now serves as an orphanage and is not open to the public.

When Lady Tunshuq died, she was buried in a small tomb across from the palace. The fine decoration on the tomb includes panels of different coloured marble, intricately shaped and slotted together like a jigsaw – a typical Mameluke feature known as "joggling".

If you head east and across El-Wad Road, you will enter a narrow alley called Ala ed-Din, which contains more fine Mameluke architecture. Most of the façades are composed of bands of different hues of stone, a strikingly beautiful Mameluke decorative technique known as *ablaq*.

❺ Cotton Merchants' Market

Off El-Wad Rd. **Map** 4 D3.

Known in Arabic as the Souk el-Qattanin, this is a covered market with next to no natural light but lots of small softly lit shops. It is possibly the most atmospheric street in all the Old City. Its construction was begun by the Crusaders. They intended the market as a free-standing structure but later, in the first half of the 14th century, the Mamelukes connected it to the Haram esh-Sharif (see pp72–7) via a splendidly ornate gate facing the Dome of the Rock. (But note, non-Muslims are not allowed to enter the Haram esh-Sharif by this gate, although you can depart this way.)

As well as some 50 shop units with living quarters above, the market also has two ornate bathhouses, the Hammam el-Ain, built in the 14th century by the Mamelukes, and the Hammam el-Shifa. Both of these are undergoing restoration with a view to eventually opening them to the public. Between the two bathhouses is a former merchants' hostel called Khan Tankiz, which has been restored.

Less than 50 m (160 ft) south of the Cotton Merchants' Market on El-Wad Road is a small public drinking fountain, or *sabil*, one of several such erected during the reign of Suleyman the Magnificent.

The tunnel-like interior of the Cotton Merchants' Market

❻ Chain Street

Map 4 D4.

The Arabic name for this street is Tariq Bab el-Silsila, which means "Street of the Gate of the Chain". The name refers to the magnificent entrance gate to the Haram esh-Sharif (see pp72–7) situated at its eastern end. The street is a continuation of David Street, and together the two streets run the width of the Old City from Jaffa Gate to the Haram esh-Sharif.

Chain Street has several noteworthy buildings commissioned by Mameluke emirs in the 14th century. Heading eastwards from David Street, the first is the Khan el-Sultan caravanserai, a restored travellers' inn. Further along on the right is Tashtamuriyya Madrasa, with its elegant balcony. It houses the tomb of the emir Tashtamur and is one of many final resting places built here in the 14th and 15th centuries in order to be close to the Haram esh-Sharif. On the same side of the street is the tomb of the brutal Tartar emir Barka Khan, father-in-law of the Mameluke ruler Baybars, who drove the Crusaders out of the Holy Land (see pp52–3). This building, with its intriguing façade decoration, now houses the Khalidi Library.

Opposite the Khalidi Library are two small mausoleums. Of the two, that of emir Kilan stands out for its austere, well-proportioned façade. Further

Some of the many and varied spices on sale at the Central Souk

along on the same side is the tomb of Tartar pilgrim Turkan Khatun, easily recognizable by the splendid arabesques on its façade. Opposite the Gate of the Chain is the impressive entrance to the 14th-century Tankiziyya Madrasa. In the inscription, three symbols in the shape of a cup show that emir Tankiz, who built the college, held the important office of cupbearer. Nearby is a drinking fountain, or sabil, from the reign of Suleyman the Magnificent, which combines Roman and Crusader motifs.

Window on Khalidi Library

❼ Central Souk

David St/Chain St. **Map** 3 C4.
Open 8am–7pm Sat–Thu.

The Central Souk consists of three parallel covered streets at the intersection of David Street and Chain Street. They once formed part of the Roman Cardo (see p84). Today's markets sell mostly clothes and souvenirs, although the section

called the Butchers' Market (Souk el-Lakhamin in Arabic), restored in the 1970s, still offers all the excitement of an eastern bazaar. It is not for the faint-hearted, however, as the pungent aromas of spices and freshly slaughtered meat can be overwhelming.

❽ Damascus Gate

Map 3 C1. 🚌 1, 2. Roman Square Excavations: **Open** 9am–5pm (winter: 4pm) Sat–Thu. 🅿

Spotting this gate is easy, not only because it is the most monumental in the Old City, but also because of the perpetual bustle of activity in the area outside the gate.

Arabs call it Bab el-Amud, the Gate of the Column. This could refer to a large column topped with a statue of the emperor Hadrian (see p47) which, in Roman times, stood just inside the gate. For Jews it is Shaar Shkhem, the gate which leads to the biblical city of Shechem, better known by its Arabic name – Nablus.

The present-day gate was built over the remains of the original Roman gate and parts of the Roman city. Outside the gate and to the west of the raised walkway, steps lead down to the excavation area. In the first section are remains of a Crusader chapel with frescoes, part of a medieval roadway and an ancient sign marking the presence of the Roman 10th Legion. Further in, metal steps lead down to the single surviving arch of the Roman gate, which gives access to the

Crowds of visitors and market traders outside Damascus Gate

For hotels and restaurants in this area see p260 and p270

Roman Square Excavations. Here, the fascinating remains of the original Roman plaza, the starting point of the Roman Cardo, include a gaming board engraved in the paving stones. A hologram depicts Hadrian's column in the main plaza. It is possible to explore the upper levels of the gate as part of the ramparts walk (see pp146–7).

❾ Herod's Gate

Map 4 D1.

The Arabic and Hebrew names for this gate, Bab el-Zahra and Shaar ha-Prakhim respectively, both mean "Gate of Flowers", referring to the rosette above the arch. It came to be known as Herod's Gate in the 1500s, when Christian pilgrims wrongly thought that the house inside the gate was the palace of Herod the Great's son. It was via the original, now closed, entrance further east that the Crusaders entered the city and conquered it on 15 July 1099 (see pp52–3).

❿ St Anne's Church

2 Shaar ha-Arayot St. **Map** 4 E2. **Tel** (0/2) 628 3285. **Open** 8am–noon & 2–6pm (winter: 5pm) daily. 🅿️

This beautiful Crusader church is a superb example of Romanesque architecture. It was constructed between 1131 and 1138 to replace a previous Byzantine church, and exists today in more or less its original form. It is traditionally believed that the church stands on the spot where Anne and Joachim, the parents of the Virgin Mary, lived. The supposed remains of

Visitors outside the Lions' Gate, in the Old City's eastern wall

their house are in the crypt, which is also noted for its remarkable acoustics.

Shortly after the church was built, it was made larger by moving the façade forwards by several metres. The connection with the original church can still be seen in the first row of columns. In 1192, Saladin (see pp52–3) turned the church into a Muslim theological school. There is an inscription to this effect above the church's entrance. Later abandoned, the church fell into ruins, until the Ottomans donated it to France in 1856 and it was restored.

Next to the church are two cisterns that once lay outside the city walls. They were built in the 8th and 3rd centuries BC to collect rainwater. Some time later, under Herod the Great, they were turned into curative baths. Ruins of a Roman temple, thought to have been to the god of medicine, can be seen here, as can those of a later Byzantine church built over the temple. It is also widely believed that this is the site of the Pool of Bethesda, described in St John's account of Christ curing a paralysed man (John 5: 1–15).

⓫ Lions' Gate

Map 4 F2.

Suleyman the Magnificent built this gate in 1538. Its Arabic name, Bab Sitti Maryam (Gate of the Virgin Mary), refers to the Tomb of the Virgin in the nearby Valley of Jehoshaphat (see p119). The Hebrew name, Shaar ha-Arayot, or Lions' Gate, refers to the two emblematic lions on either side of the gateway, although one school of thought insists that they are panthers. There are many different stories to explain the significance of the lions. One is that Suleyman the Magnificent had them carved in honour of the Mameluke emir Baybars and his successful campaign to rid the Holy Land of Crusaders. Also known as St Stephen's Gate, this name was adopted in the Middle Ages by Christians who believed that the first Christian martyr, St Stephen, was executed here. Prior to that, it was thought that St Stephen had been stoned to death outside Damascus Gate.

Lion detail from Lions' Gate

The gate is also significant because of its more recent history, for it was through it that the Arab Legion penetrated the Old City in 1948 (see p58) and where Israeli paratroopers entered in 1967 (see p58). It is an excellent starting point for the walk along the Via Dolorosa (see p68).

Archaeological site in front of St Anne's Church

⑫ Haram esh-Sharif

Haram esh-Sharif, the "Noble Sanctuary" or Temple Mount, is a vast rectangular esplanade in the southeastern part of the Old City. Traditionally the site of Solomon's Temple, it later housed the Second Temple, enlarged by Herod the Great and destroyed by the Romans *(see pp48–9)*. Left in ruins for more than half a century, the site became an Islamic shrine in AD 691 with the building of the Dome of the Rock. Over the centuries other buildings have been added to this, the third most important Islamic religious sanctuary.

★ Dome of the Rock
This is the crowning glory not just of the Haram esh-Sharif but of all Jerusalem *(see pp76–7)*.

Grammar College
Also known as "The Dome of Learning", this still serves as a Quranic teaching school. The doorway on the north side is flanked by some unusual barley-sugar columns dating from the Ayyubid era (1169–1250).

KEY

① **Moors' Gate** (Bab el-Maghariba) is one of only two gates that non-Muslims may use to enter the Haram.

② **Western Wall** *(see p89)*

③ **Chain Gate** (Ha-Shalshelet)

④ **Sabil of Qaitbey**, the public fountain, was built on the order of the Mameluke sultan Qaitbey (ruled 1468–98). It has a superb carved stone dome, the only one of its kind in the Holy Land.

⑤ **Cotton Merchants' Gate** is a strikingly decorated Mameluke portal giving access to the market of the same name *(see p69)*.

⑥ **Madrasa el-Omariyya** is one of several Mameluke-era schools on the Haram.

⑦ **Madrasa el-Isardiyya**

⑧ **Dome of the Rock**

⑨ **Asbat Minaret**

⑩ **Gate of the Tribes** (Bab el-Asbat) leads to the Via Dolorosa.

⑪ **Golden Gate** is one of the original city gates *(see p75)* but was sealed up by the Muslims in the 16th century. The area is out of bounds.

⑫ **Crusader-built tower**

⑬ **Women's mosque**

Museum of Islamic Art
This engraved Mameluke vessel is part of a collection of artifacts, largely from the Middle Ages, that includes Qurans, textiles, ceramics and weaponry *(see p74)*.

★ Dome of the Chain
This small dome *(see p75)* stands at the approximate centre of the Haram esh-Sharif, which, according to one theory, equated to the centre of the world. The 13th-century tiling on the interior surpasses even that of the Dome of the Rock.

VISITORS' CHECKLIST

Practical Information
Entrance via Mugrabi Gate only. **Map** 4 E3. **Open** summer: 7:30–11am & 1:30–2:30pm Sun–Thu; winter: 7:30–10am & 12:30–1:30pm Sun–Thu. **Closed** Fri, Sat, Muslim hols. 🔲 for the Museum of Islamic Art 🔄 inside Dome of the Rock and El-Aqsa Mosque. Check security with tourist office before visiting. Currently non-Muslims cannot enter the El-Aqsa Mosque and the Dome of the Rock.

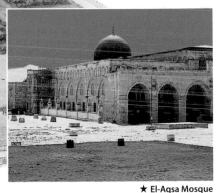

Qanatir
Each of the eight flights of steps up to the platform of the Dome of the Rock is topped by a *qanatir*, or freestanding arcade *(see p74)*. Some of the column capitals were recycled from Roman-era buildings.

★ El-Aqsa Mosque
Originally built in the early years of the 8th century *(see p74)*, El-Aqsa remains the main place of Islamic worship in Jerusalem and draws huge crowds of devout Muslims each Friday for noon prayer.

El-Kas Fountain
Carved from a single block of stone and dating from 1320, this is the largest of the Haram's many old but still functioning ablutions fountains.

Exploring the Haram esh-Sharif

Although the undoubted main attraction is the Dome of the Rock, the Haram esh-Sharif has a great many other features that are worthy of attention. The esplanade acts as a virtual museum of Islamic architecture, beginning with the Dome, which dates back to the Omayyad era and is the earliest structure, and running through the Ayyubid (Grammar College), Mameluke (numerous *madrasas*) and Ottoman periods. Visitors should be aware that certain parts of the Haram esh-Sharif are out of bounds, notably the area south of the Gate of the Tribes and east of El-Aqsa.

Antiquity-strewn area in front of the Museum of Islamic Art

The much reconstructed interior of the El-Aqsa Mosque

El-Aqsa Mosque

Construction of El-Aqsa was begun less than 20 years after the completion of the Dome of the Rock. However, unlike the Dome, whose structure and interior have remained intact over the centuries, El-Aqsa has undergone great changes. In the first 60 years of its existence the mosque was twice razed to the ground by earthquakes. Its present form dates from the early 11th century. When the Crusaders captured Jerusalem in 1099, El-Aqsa became the headquarters of the Templars *(see p53)*; their legacy remains in the three central bays of the main façade. As it appears today, the façade has seven bays; in the mid-14th century the Mamelukes added an extra two on either side of the original Crusader porch.

The interior is dominated by mid-20th-century additions, notably ranks of marble columns donated by Benito Mussolini, and an elaborately painted ceiling paid for by King Farouk

of Egypt. Older elements include the mihrab, decorated in 1187 under the patronage of Saladin, and the mosaics above the central aisle arch and around the drum of the dome, dating from 1035. Until 1969, the mosque had a fine carved pulpit *(minbar)*, also dating from the time of Saladin, but this was lost in a fire started by a deranged visitor.

Museum of Islamic Art

Housed in the Crusader-era refectory of the Knights Templar, this sparsely filled museum

contains objects donated to the Haram esh-Sharif over the centuries, as well as architectural remnants from many of the Haram's buildings. Worthy of mention are the precious large Qurans, with pages adorned by fine Islamic calligraphy; part of a carved cypress-wood ceiling from El-Aqsa, dating from the 7th century and removed in 1948; and fine 15th-century copper doors from the Dome of the Rock. Admission to the museum is included in the fee for the Dome of the Rock and El-Aqsa Mosque. However, it is currently closed to the public.

Visitors with an interest in Islamic art should also visit the LA Mayer Museum in the New City *(see p134)*.

The Qanatirs

Eight short flights of steps lead up to the platform on which the Dome of the Rock sits. All these stairways are of different sizes and lengths, and they all date from different periods. The flight opposite the Sabil of Qaitbey, leading up to the main entrance of the Dome, is unique in that it is carved out of the stone of the platform. Each flight is crowned by a slender arcade known as a *qanatir*. An alternative name for the arches is *mawazin*, or scales, because according to a widely accepted Muslim belief, on the day of the Last Judgment the scales used by God to weigh the souls of humankind will be hung from these arches on the Haram.

A *qanatir*, topping a flight of steps up to the Dome

Dome of the Chain

Beside the Dome of the Rock, the Haram has many other, smaller domes. The most impressive is the Dome of the Chain, immediately to the east of the Dome of the Rock. It is a simple structure of a domed roof supported on 17 columns. It originally had 20 columns but was remodelled to its current form by the Mameluke emir Baybars in the 13th century. The interior tiling is splendid *(see p73)*. Some mystery exists over the purpose of the dome, but it is likely that it was once a treasury. Its name derives from the legend that a chain once hung from the roof, and whoever told a lie while holding it would be struck dead by lightning.

The Madrasas

Most of the buildings fringing the Haram are *madrasas* – Islamic colleges. Of these, the **Ashrafiyya** on the western side of the Haram, built in 1482 by Sultan Qaitbey, is a masterpiece of Islamic architecture. It has an especially ornate doorway exhibiting all the best elements of Mameluke design, including bands of different coloured stone, stalactite carvings above the doorway and, on the benches on either side, intricate, interlocking stones known as "joggling". Adjoining the Ashrafiyya to the north, close to the

Sabil of Qaitbey, is another *madrasa*, the **Uthmaniyya**. Its upper section has beautiful wheel-shaped decorations formed by inlays of yellow and red stone. Along the northern edge of the Haram are two more, the triple-domed **Isardiyya** and adjacent **Malekiyya**. Both of them date from the 14th century. West of these two, in the corner, is the **Omariyya** college, which is held to contain the First Station of the Cross, but can only be entered from the Via Dolorosa *(see pp34–5)*.

Jerusalem and Islam

The Dome of the Rock and neighbouring El-Aqsa Mosque represent the first great religious complex in the history of Islam. Although Muslims venerate many of the same prophets as the Jews and Christians, notably Abraham (Ibrahim to the Muslims), Jerusalem itself is never mentioned in the Quran. The choice of this site was more likely a political issue. In locating his mosque on the site of the Temple, the caliph Abd el-Malik meant to reinforce the idea that the new religion of Islam, and its worldly empire, was the successor and continuation of those of the Jews and the Christians.

The brilliant dome of the El-Aqsa Mosque in Jerusalem

It was only later that Jerusalem came to be tied into Islamic tradition through the story of the Night Journey *(see p31)*. In this, Muhammad visits *el-masjid el-aqsa*, which means literally "the most distant mosque", and this name was retroactively applied to the whole Haram esh-Sharif before later being restricted to the mosque only.

Golden Gate

Also known as the Gate of Mercy (Bab el-Rahma), the Golden Gate was one of the original Herodian city gates. According to Jewish tradition, the Messiah will enter Jerusalem through this gate, which is said to be the reason why the Muslims walled it up in the 16th century. The existing structure dates to the Omayyad period and is best viewed from outside the city walls.

The domed fountain, the Sabil of Qaitbey, with part of the Ashrafiyya Madrasa in the background

Dome of the Rock

One of the first and greatest achievements of Islamic architecture, the Dome of the Rock was built in AD 688–91 by the Omayyad caliph Abd el-Malik. Intended to proclaim the superiority of Islam and provide an Islamic focal point in the Holy City, the majestic structure now dominates Jerusalem and has become a symbol of the city. More a shrine than a mosque, the mathematically harmonious building echoes elements of Classical and Byzantine architecture, including the rotunda of the Holy Sepulchre (see pp96–9).

View of the Dome of the Rock with the Muslim Quarter in the background

★ **Tilework**
The multicoloured tiles that adorn the exterior are faithful copies of Persian tiles that Suleyman the Magnificent added in 1545 to replace the badly damaged original mosaics.

KEY

① **The octagonal arcade** is adorned with original mosaics (AD 692) and an inscription inviting Christians to recognize the truth of Islam.

② **Marble panel**

③ **Quranic verses**

④ **The drum** is decorated with tiles and verses from the Quran which tell of Muhammad's Night Journey.

⑤ **Green and gold mosaics** create a scintillating effect on the walls below the dome.

⑥ **Outer ambulatory**

⑦ **Stained-glass window**

⑧ **Each outer wall** is 20.4 m (67 ft) long. This exactly matches the dome's diameter and its height from the base of the drum.

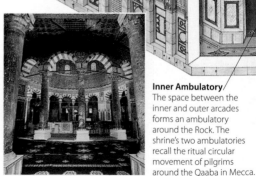

Inner Ambulatory
The space between the inner and outer arcades forms an ambulatory around the Rock. The shrine's two ambulatories recall the ritual circular movement of pilgrims around the Qaaba in Mecca.

Dome
The dome was originally made of copper but is now covered with gold leaf thanks to the financial support of the late King Hussein of Jordan.

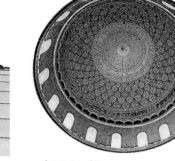

★ Interior of Dome
The dazzling interior of the cupola has elaborate floral decoration as well as various inscriptions. The large text commemorates Saladin, who sponsored restoration work on the building.

Well of Souls
This staircase leads down to a chamber under the Rock known as the Well of Souls. The dead are said to meet here twice a month to pray.

The Rock
The Rock is variously believed to be where Abraham was asked to sacrifice Isaac, where Muhammad left the Earth on his Night Journey (see p31), and the site of the Holy of Holies of Herod's Temple (see pp48–9).

South entrance

THE JEWISH QUARTER

In Herodian times this area abutted the Temple enclosure *(see pp48–9)* and was occupied by the priestly elite. In the late Roman period, Jews were forbidden from living in Jerusalem, but under the more tolerant Arab rule a small community was re-established here. The district became predominantly Jewish during Ottoman rule, when it acquired its present name. By the 16th century, pilgrimage to the Western Wall – the only surviving remnant of the Temple – had become a strong tradition.

After the destruction wrought in the 1948 War and the subsequent years of Jordanian occupation, the Jewish quarter was liberated by Israeli troops in 1967, and reconstruction work began soon afterwards. A great many ruins from ancient periods were uncovered below more recent buildings. These remains were made accessible to the public, so that the Jewish Quarter of today stands as a fascinating, living mix of more than 3,000 years of Jerusalem Jewry.

Sights at a Glance

Archaeological Sites
1 The Cardo
2 The Broad Wall
13 St Mary of the Germans
15 *Jerusalem Archaeological Park (pp90–91)*

Museums
6 Wohl Archaeological Museum
9 Old Yishuv Court Museum
10 The Temple Institute Museum
11 Ariel Centre for Jerusalem in the First Temple Period
12 The Burnt House

Holy Places
4 Ramban Synagogue
8 The Sephardic Synagogues
16 The Western Wall

Streets and Squares
3 Hurva Square
5 Tiferet Yisrael Street
7 Batei Makhase Square
14 Dung Gate

See also Jerusalem Street Finder, maps 3 and 4

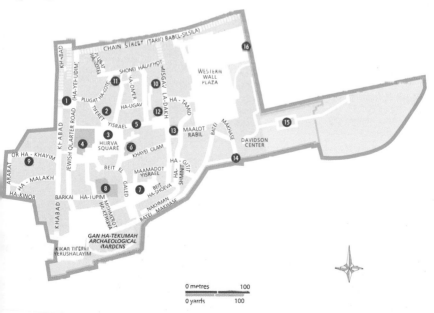

◀ Men praying at the Western Wall, a key site for Jewish prayer and pilgrimage

Street-by-Street: Around Hurva Square

Extensively reconstructed since 1967 and largely residential, the Jewish Quarter is noticeably more orderly than the rest of the Old City, though it is also frequented by large groups of tourists. The focal point for the local community is Hurva Square. This has a few small shops and cafés with outdoor seating. Most of the interesting sights in the quarter are just a few minutes' walk from here. Another hub of the district is the Cardo and Jewish Quarter Road area, which is filled with souvenir shops and more places to eat.

Looking towards Hurva Square from Jewish Quarter Road

Cardo shopping arcade

The Sidna Omar minaret is all that remains of a 14th-century mosque.

1 ★ The Cardo
This is an excavated and partially reconstructed section of the main street of Byzantine-era Jerusalem.

8 The Sephardic Synagogues
Two of these four synagogues date back to the early 17th century. They all contain much ornate decoration.

Rothschild House

7 Batei Makhase Square
A small secluded square, this is favoured by local children as a play area. Its most notable feature is the elegant 19th-century Rothschild House, with its arcaded façade.

Shelter Houses *(see p86)*

Remains of Nea Basilica *(see p86)*

MISHMEROT HA-KEHUNA

GALED

BATE MAKHA SQUA

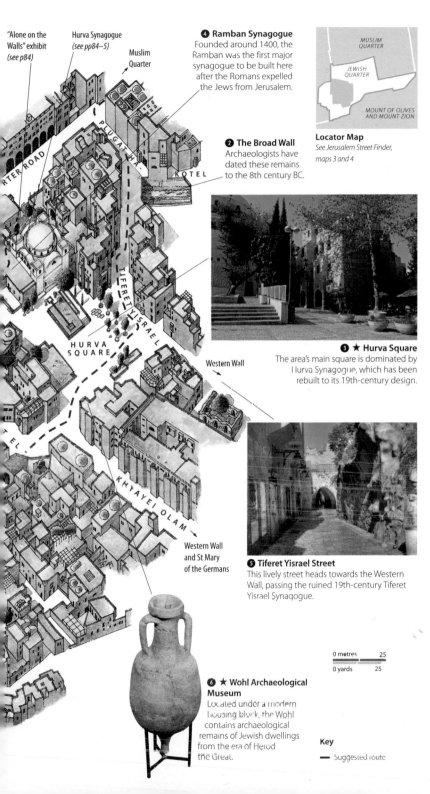

④ Ramban Synagogue
Founded around 1400, the Ramban was the first major synagogue to be built here after the Romans expelled the Jews from Jerusalem.

② The Broad Wall
Archaeologists have dated these remains to the 8th century BC.

Locator Map
See Jerusalem Street Finder, maps 3 and 4

"Alone on the Walls" exhibit (see p84)

Hurva Synagogue (see pp84–5)

Muslim Quarter

③ ★ Hurva Square
The area's main square is dominated by Hurva Synagogue, which has been rebuilt to its 19th-century design.

Western Wall

Western Wall and St Mary of the Germans

⑤ Tiferet Yisrael Street
This lively street heads towards the Western Wall, passing the ruined 19th-century Tiferet Yisrael Synagogue.

⑥ ★ Wohl Archaeological Museum
Located under a modern housing block, the Wohl contains archaeological remains of Jewish dwellings from the era of Herod the Great.

| 0 metres | 25 |
| 0 yards | 25 |

Key
— Suggested route

❶ The Cardo

Map 3 C4.

Now in part an exclusive shopping arcade, the Cardo was Jerusalem's main thoroughfare in the Byzantine era. It was originally laid by the Romans, then extended in the 4th century as Christian pilgrims began to flock to Jerusalem and the city expanded accordingly. The Byzantine extension, which remains in evidence today, linked the two major places of worship of the time, the Church of the Holy Sepulchre *(see pp96–9)* in the north and the long-since-vanished Nea Basilica *(see p86)* in the south.

The central roadway of the Byzantine Cardo was 12.5 m (41 ft) wide. This was flanked by broad porticoed pavements and lined with shops. You can visit a reconstructed section, which runs for almost 200 m (650 ft) along Jewish Quarter (Ha-Yehudim) Road.

The Cardo's continued importance during the reign of Justinian in the 6th century is attested to by its prominent appearance on the famous Madaba map *(see pp220–21)*. Some 500 years later, in the Crusader era, the Cardo was converted into a covered market; the northern section is now preserved as an arcade of smart galleries and boutiques.

An exhibition on Jewish Quarter Road entitled "Alone on the Walls" displays photographs that document the fall of the Jewish Quarter to a regiment of the Arab Legion in 1947–8, in which 68 residents lost their lives.

The Broad Wall, part of the city's 8th-century-BC fortifications

❷ The Broad Wall

Plugat ha-Kotel St. **Map** 3 C4.

The Jewish Quarter was largely destroyed during the 1948 War and allowed to deteriorate further under Jordanian occupation. Following the 1967 Israeli victory, a vast reconstruction programme resulted in many significant archaeological finds. One of these was the unearthing of the foundations of a wall 7 m (22 ft) thick and 65 m (215 ft) long. This was possibly part of fortifications built by King Hezekiah in the 8th century BC to enclose a new quarter outside the previous city wall. The need for expansion was probably brought about by a flood of refugees after the Assyrian invasion of 722 BC. On the

building next to the exposed wall, a clearly visible line indicates what archaeologists think was the original height of the wall. Also visible are the remains of housing from the same period, demolished to make way for the wall, as described in the Book of Isaiah (22: 10), "And ye have numbered the houses of Jerusalem, and the houses have ye broken down to fortify the wall."

❸ Hurva Square

Map 3 C4.

This is the heart and social centre of the present-day Jewish Quarter. In the maze of narrow, winding streets which, though modern, follow the topography of the quarter before its destruction, Hurva Square is one of the few open spaces in the area. It has cafés, souvenir shops and a few snack bars that have small tables outside when the weather is good. Also here is the **Jewish Students' Information Centre**, which provides help with accommodation and invitations to Shabbat (Sabbath) dinners for visiting young Jews.

On the west side of the square is the minaret of the long-since-vanished, 14th-century Mameluke **Mosque of Sidna Omar**, along with the historic Hurva and Ramban synagogue complexes. Hurva means "ruins" and the history of the **Hurva Synagogue** more than justifies its name. In the 18th century a group of a few hundred Ashkenazi Jews from Poland came to Jerusalem and founded a synagogue on this site. However, it was burned down by creditors angered by the community's unpaid debts. The synagogue was rebuilt in 1864 in a Neo-Byzantine style. However, during the fighting that took place in 1948 between the Arab and Jewish armies, the synagogue was destroyed. After the Israelis

Sidna Omar minaret

The Cardo, the main street of Byzantine-era Jerusalem

Hurva Square, the social and commercial hub of the Jewish Quarter

recaptured the Old City in 1967, a single arch of the synagogue's main façade was reconstructed. The structure underwent further renovation and has now been reconstructed in the same style as the 1864 Neo-Byzantine building.

❹ Ramban Synagogue

Hurva Square. **Map** 3 C4. **Open** for morning and evening prayers. ♿

When the Spanish rabbi and scholar Moses Ben Nahman (Nahmanides) arrived in Jerusalem in 1267, he was shocked to find only a handful of Jews in the city. He dedicated himself to nurturing a Jewish community and bought land near King David's Tomb on Mount Zion in order to build a synagogue. Some time around 1400, the synagogue was moved to its present site. It was perhaps the first time there had been a Jewish presence in this quarter of the Old City since the exile of the Jews in AD 135. The synagogue had to be rebuilt in 1523 after it collapsed. It is believed that, at this time, it was probably the only Jewish place of worship in what was then Ottoman-controlled Jerusalem. In 1599 the authorities banned the Jews from worship in the synagogue and the building became a workshop. It was not until the Israelis took control of the Old City in 1967 that it was restored as a place of worship.

❺ Tiferet Yisrael Street

Map 4 D4.

This is one of the busiest streets in the Jewish Quarter. It connects Hurva Square with the stairs that descend towards the Western Wall. Partway along is the shell of the ruined **Tiferet Yisrael Synagogue**, destroyed in the 1948 War and left gutted as a memorial. Sectarian feelings run high around here, and local souvenir shops stock contentious items such as Israeli Army T-shirts and postcards of the Haram esh-Sharif with its mosques replaced by the "future Third Temple". The street ends in an attractive tree-shaded square which has several snack bars and cafés, including the

Tiferet Yisrael Street, one of the liveliest thoroughfares in the Jewish Quarter

popular Quarter Café, which serves kosher food and offers great views of the Haram esh-Sharif and Dome of the Rock from its terrace.

❻ Wohl Archaeological Museum

1 Ha-Karaim St. **Map** 4 D4. **Tel** (02) 626 5922. **Open** 9am–5pm Sun–Thu, 9am–1pm Fri. ♿ ✦

In the era of Herod the Great (37–4 BC), the area of the present-day Jewish Quarter was part of a wealthy "Upper City", occupied for the most part by the families of important Jewish priests. During post-1967 redevelopment, the remains of several large houses were unearthed here. This rediscovered Herodian quarter now lies from 3 to 7 m (10 to 22 ft) below street level, underneath a modern building, and is preserved in the Wohl Archaeological Museum.

The museum is remarkable for its vivid evocation of everyday life 2,000 years ago. All the houses had an inner courtyard, ritual baths, and cisterns to collect rain, which was the only source of water at the time. The first part of the museum, called the Western House, has a mosaic in the vestibule and a well-preserved ritual bath *(mikveh)*. Beyond this is the Middle Complex, the remains of two separate houses where archaeologists found a maze-pattern mosaic floor covered in burnt wood; this, they surmised, was fire damage from the Roman siege of Jerusalem in AD 70. The most complete of all the Herodian buildings is the Palatial Mansion, with more splendid mosaic floors and ritual baths. The entrance fee to the Wohl Museum also covers admission to the Burnt House *(see p88)*.

❼ Batei Makhase Square

Map 4 D5.

This quiet square is named after the so-called Shelter Houses (Batei Makhase), which lie just south of it. They were built in 1862 by Jews from Germany and Holland for destitute immigrants from central Europe. Severe damage in the 1948 and 1967 wars made restoration necessary.

The work brought to light the first remains of the Nea (New) Basilica, whose existence had previously been known only from the Madaba map (see pp220–21) and literary sources. Built by Byzantine emperor Justinian in AD 543, it was at the time the largest basilica in the Holy Land. The remains of one of the apses can be seen near the square's southwest corner. Archaeologists have now traced the basilica's full extent – an enormous 116 m (380 ft) by 52 m (171 ft). More impressive remains can be found in the cellar of a house to the north of the square.

The handsome, arcaded building on the western side of the square was built for the Rothschild family in 1871. In front of it are parts of Roman columns, whose original provenance is unknown.

The 17th-century Ben Zakkai Synagogue

❽ The Sephardic Synagogues

Ha-Tupim St. **Map** 3 C5. **Tel** (02) 628 0592. **Open** 9:15am– 3:45pm Sun–Thu, 9am–12:45pm Fri. Visits must be booked in advance. 🅿

The four synagogues in this group became the spiritual centre of the area's Sephardic community in the 17th century. The Sephardim were descended from the Jews expelled from Spain in 1492 and Portugal in 1497. They had first settled in the Ottoman Empire and then moved to Palestine when the latter was conquered by the Turks in 1516. When the first two synagogues were built, the Sephardim formed the largest Jewish community in Jerusalem. The synagogue floors were laid well below street level to allow sufficient height for the buildings, as

Bimah **from the Istambuli Synagogue**

Ottoman law stated that synagogues should not rise above the surrounding houses.

The **Ben Zakkai Synagogue** was built in 1610. Its courtyard, with a matroneum, or gallery for women worshippers, was converted into the **Central Synagogue**, whose present form dates from the 1830s. The **Prophet Elijah Synagogue**, created from a study hall built in 1625, was consecrated in 1702. Legend has it that during prayers to mark Yom Kippur, Elijah appeared as the tenth adult male worshipper needed for synagogue prayer – hence the building's name. The **Istambuli Synagogue** was built in 1857 and, like the other three, contains furnishings salvaged from Italian synagogues damaged in World War II.

❾ Old Yishuv Court Museum

6 Or ha-Khayim St. **Map** 3 C5. **Tel** (02) 627 6319. **Open** 10am–5pm Sun–Thu (winter: 3pm), 10am–1pm Fri. 🅿 🈂

This small museum, devoted to the history of the city's Jewish community from the mid-19th century to the end of Ottoman rule in 1917, occupies one of the oldest complexes of rooms in the Jewish Quarter. Of Turkish construction, thought to date from the 15th or 16th centuries, it was once part of a private home. The exhibits, consisting largely of reconstructed interiors, memorabilia and photographs, also include the Ari Synagogue on the ground floor. This was used by a Sephardic congregation during most of the Ottoman period. Badly damaged in the fighting of 1936, it fell into disuse until 1967, when it was restored. On the top floor is the 18th-century Or ha-Khayim Synagogue, used by Ashkenazi Jews in the 19th century. Closed between 1948 and 1967, it is now a functioning synagogue once more.

Rothschild House and a Roman column base and capital in Batei Makhase Square

Menorah on display at the exhibition in the Temple Institute Museum

⑩ The Temple Institute Museum

19 Misgav La-Dakh St. **Map** 4 D4.
Tel (02) 626 4545. **Open** 9am–5pm
Sun–Thu, 9am–noon Fri. 🎧 📷
compulsory. 11:30am & 3:15pm
Sun–Thu (in English); extra charge;
must be booked in advance. 📷
W templeinstitute.org/treasures-
of-the-temple.htm

Near the steps leading down
to the Western Wall Plaza is an
enormous golden menorah
measuring more than 2 m
(6 ft) in height. This is perhaps
the best-known creation of
the Temple Institute, a small,
eccentric organization whose
long-term goal is achieving
readiness for the day when
the Messiah builds a Third
Temple. Until that time,
the organization is dedicated
to the study and re-creation
of ritual items according to
biblical specifications, as
well as promoting awareness
of its work. To this end, it
runs an exhibition called
"Treasures of the Temple" in
a small museum near the
Western Wall.

The exhibition displays a
range of golden and silver
vessels, musical instruments,
altars and priestly vestments.
The collection of kitsch oil
paintings depicting the
rebuilt Temple is of less
interest, but the scale model
of the Second Temple, made
with real marble and gold,
is a sight to behold.

⑪ Ariel Centre for Jerusalem in the First Temple Period

Bonei Hahomah St. **Map** 4 D4.
Tel (02) 628 6288. **Open** 9am–4pm
Sun–Thu. Visits must be booked in
advance. 🎧 **W** ybz.org.il

The principal exhibit here is a
model of all the archaeological
remains of First Temple Period
Jerusalem (around the 8th
century BC). It illustrates the
relationship between remains,
which can be difficult to
interpret when they are seen
on the ground surrounded by
other buildings. It also shows
the original topography of the
area before valleys were filled in
and occupation layers built up.
An audiovisual show describes
the city's history from 1000 to
586 BC.

There is also a display of
finds from a secret dig carried
out in 1909–11 by English
archaeologist Captain Montague
Parker. His team of excavators
penetrated underneath the
Haram esh-Sharif in search of
a chamber that reputedly
contained King Solomon's
treasure. When news of the dig
got out, violent demonstrations
by Jews and Muslims, united
in their opposition to the
desecration of their holy site,
forced Parker to flee the city.

Jewish Quarter Architecture

Heavily damaged during the 1948
War, the Jewish Quarter has been
almost totally reconstructed. While
there is no distinct "Jewish style",
the quarter's modern architecture
belongs to a well-defined Jerusalem
tradition. First and foremost,
everything is constructed of the
pale local stone. Use of this stone
has been mandatory in Jerusalem
since a law to this effect was
passed by the British military
governor, Ronald Storrs, in 1917.
Buildings and street patterns are
deliberately asymmetrical to evoke

Modern additions harmonize with traditional styles

haphazard historical development. Streets are also narrow and cobbled, with many small
courtyards and external staircases to upper levels. Buildings make great use of traditional Middle
Eastern elements such as arches, domes and oriels (the high bay windows supported on brackets,
much favoured by Mameluke builders). A jumble of different heights means that the roof of one
building is often the terrace of another. The result is a very contemporary look, which is at the same
time firmly rooted in the past.

⑫ The Burnt House

Tiferet Yisrael St. **Map** 4 D4. **Tel** (02) 626 5900. **Open** 9am–5pm Sun–Thu, 9am–1pm Fri.

In AD 70 the Romans took Jerusalem and destroyed the Temple and Lower City to the south. A month later they rampaged through the wealthy Upper City, setting fire to the houses. The charred walls and a coin dated to AD 69 discovered during excavations show that this was one of those houses.

A stone weight found among the debris bears the inscription "son of Kathros", indicating that the house belonged to a wealthy family of high priests. They are known from a subsequent reference to them in the Babylonian Talmud, written between the 3rd and 6th century AD.

The rooms on view, introduced by a moving sound-and-light show with commentary, comprise a kitchen, four rooms that may have been bedrooms and a bathroom with a ritual bath. It is believed that these formed part of a much larger residence, but further excavations cannot be undertaken as the remains lie beneath present-day neighbouring houses.

The entrance fee also discounts the Wohl Archaeological Museum (see p85).

Surviving walls of the Crusader-built St Mary of the Germans

⑬ St Mary of the Germans

Misgav la-Dakh St. **Map** 4 D4. **Open** daily.

Immediately below the terrace of Tiferet Yisrael's Quarter Café are the original walls of St Mary of the Germans. This early 12th-century Crusader church was part of a complex that included a pilgrims' hospice (no longer in existence) and a hospital. It was built by the Knights Hospitallers (see p53) and run by their German members. This was in response to the influx of German-speaking pilgrims unfamiliar with French, the lingua franca, or Latin, the official language, of the new Latin Kingdom of Jerusalem. Activity ceased when Jerusalem fell to the Muslims in 1187, but the church and the hospital were again used during the brief period when Jerusalem was once more under Christian rule (1229–44). Today the church is roofless. However, the walls survive to a considerable height, showing clearly the three apses of the typical basilica plan so widely used in the Holy Land from early Byzantine times. Beside the church is a flight of steps down to the Western Wall Plaza. These provide wonderful views of the Western Wall, the Dome of the Rock and the Mount of Olives behind.

⑭ Dung Gate

Map 4 D5.

In old photographs the Dung Gate is shown to be hardly any larger than a doorway in the average domestic house. Its name in Hebrew is Shaar ha-Ashpot, and it is mentioned in the Book of Nehemiah (2: 13) in the Old Testament. It is probably named after the ash that was taken from the Temple to be deposited outside the city walls. The Arab name is Bab Silwan, because this is the gate that leads to the Arab village of Silwan.

Dung Gate, leading to the Western Wall

The gate was enlarged by the Jordanians in 1948 to allow vehicles to pass through. It is now the main entrance and exit for the Jewish Quarter, but it still remains the smallest of all the Old City gates. It retains its old Ottoman carved arch with a stone flower above.

⑮ Jerusalem Archaeological Park

See pp90–91.

The outline of rooms and some of the artifacts unearthed at the Burnt House

⑯ The Western Wall

Western Wall Plaza. **Map** 4 D4.
🚌 1, 2, 38. 🚻 📷 on Sabbath.
Chain of the Generations Centre:
Tel (02) 627 1333. **Open** 8am–8pm
Sun–Thu, 8am–noon Fri. Visits must
be booked in advance. **Closed** Jewish
hols. 🚻 📷 compulsory. Western
Wall Tunnel: **Tel** (02) 627 1333.
Open 7am–midnight Sun–Thu, 7am–
noon Fri. Visits must be booked in
advance. **Closed** Jewish hols. 🚻
📷 compulsory. Tickets can also be
booked online. **W** thekotel.org

A massive, blank wall built
of huge stone blocks, the
Western Wall (Ha-Kotel in
Hebrew) is Judaism's holiest
site, and the plaza in front
of it is a permanent place of
worship. The wall is part of the
retaining wall of the Temple
Mount and was built by Herod
the Great during his expansion
of the Temple enclosure
(see pp48–9). The huge, lower
stones are Herodian, while
those higher up date from
early Islamic times.

During the Ottoman period,
the wall became where Jews
came to lament the destruction
of the Second Temple. For
this reason it was for centuries
known as the Wailing Wall.

Houses covered most of
what's now the Western Wall
Plaza until relatively recently.
When the Israelis gained
control of the Old City after
the 1967 war, they levelled
the neighbouring Arab district

Worship at the Western Wall

The Western Wall Plaza
functions as a large,
open-air synagogue
where groups gather
to recite the daily,
Shabbat (Sabbath)
and festival services
of the Jewish faith.
Special events are
also celebrated here,
such as the religious
coming of age of a

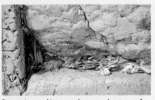

Prayers inserted into gaps between the stones of
the Western Wall

boy or girl (bar or bat mitzvah). Some worshippers visit the wall
daily to recite the entire Book of Psalms; others, who believe
that petitions to God made at the wall are specially effective, insert
written prayers into the stones. On Tisha B'Av, the
ninth day of the month of Av, which falls in either
July or August, a fast is held commemorating
the destruction of both Temples (see pp46–9).
People sit on the ground reciting the Book of
Lamentations and liturgical dirges called kinot.
Since the plaza is essentially a public space, conflicts
arise over such issues as the relative size of
the men's and women's sections and the
wish of non-Orthodox groups to hold
services in which men and women
participate together.

Orthodox Jew at prayer
beside the Western Wall

Non-Jews can approach the
wall, provided they dress
appropriately and cover their
heads (see p293).

At the left-hand corner of the
men's prayer section is Wilson's
Arch (named after a 19th-century
archaeologist). Now contained
within a building that functions
as a synagogue, it originally
carried the Causeway to
the Temple. From the arch,

archaeologists have dug the
Western Wall Tunnel to explore
the wall's foundations. It follows
the base of the outside face of
the Temple wall along a Herodian
street, below today's street level,
and emerges on the Via Dolorosa.
The **Chain of the Generations
Centre** tells the story of the
Jewish people. Access to this
and the Tunnel is by tour only;
book well in advance.

The Western Wall Plaza, with the men's prayer section to the left and woman's to the right

⓯ Jerusalem Archaeological Park

The area south of the Western Wall and Haram esh-Sharif is one of the most important archaeological sites in all Jerusalem. Excavations, ongoing here since 1968, have uncovered remains dating back to the First and Second Temple periods *(see pp45–7)*, and through Byzantine times to the Omayyad era. In this one small, L-shaped site, the entire sweep of the history of the ancient city is revealed. The Davidson Center provides a multimedia introduction to the site and contextualizes the archaeologists' findings.

The Western Wall Plaza *(see p89)*

Robinson's Arch
A row of stones projecting from the wall is the remains of an arch that once supported a flight of stairs, as shown in this model at the Tower of David Museum *(see pp106–9)*.

Ritual Bath (Mikveh)
The baths are where worshippers purified themselves before approaching the Temple. The divider, running down the centre of the stairs, ensured the separation of the clean and the unclean.

Herodian Street
At the base of the Temple Mount is a flagged street dating from the time of the Second Temple. It would have been lined with shops – four small doorways have been reconstructed.

★ Davidson Center
This subterranean exhibition centre contains artifacts from the site and screens two informative films, plus a computer-animated re-creation of the Second Temple.

Early Excavators

Before the archaeologists, the Temple Mount area drew the attentions of 19th-century biblical scholars. The American Edward Robinson (1794–1863) was the first to identify the huge arch that is now named after him. The first serious excavations were made by the British officer Captain Charles Warren, who discovered a series of underground tunnels, as well as the nearby water shaft that carries his name *(see p119)*.

Charles Warren, 1840–1927

Temple Mount
The great retaining wall of the Temple Mount dates from the reign of Herod (37–4 BC). To see what the complex would have looked like at this time, turn to pages 48–9.

★ Hulda Gates
At the top of a monumental flight of steps, a Double Gate and Triple Gate (together known as the Hulda Gates) provided access to the precincts of the Second Temple. They were later walled up by the Romans.

KEY

① **Dung Gate**

② **The Western Wall** is a part of the retaining wall of the Temple Mount, which runs south into the Archaeological Park.

③ **El-Aqsa Mosque**

④ **The Crusader-era tower** partially obscures the Double Gate *(see right)*.

⑤ **The Old City walls** date from the reign of Suleyman the Great.

Omayyad Palace
A canopy covers what was the central courtyard of an Omayyad-era palace. The building would have filled the area between the Temple Mount and the city walls.

THE CHRISTIAN AND ARMENIAN QUARTERS

Under Byzantine rule, the Christian community of Jerusalem expanded rapidly. Settlement was concentrated in the northwest corner of the city, in the shadow of the great basilica of the Holy Sepulchre. Bounded by Souk Khan el-Zeit and David Street, the modern quarter remains filled with the churches, patriarchates and hospices of the city's many Christian denominations. To the south is the area traditionally inhabited by the Armenians, who have a long history in Jerusalem. It is one of the quietest parts of the Old City.

Sights at a Glance

Museums
7 Museum of the Greek Orthodox Patriarchate
9 *The Citadel (Tower of David) pp106–9*
14 Gulbenkian Library

Churches
1 *Church of the Holy Sepulchre pp96–9*
2 Alexander Hospice
3 Lutheran Church of the Redeemer

5 Church of St John the Baptist
12 St Mark's Church
13 St James's Cathedral

Historic Areas, Streets and Gates
4 Muristan
6 Christian Quarter Road

8 Jaffa Gate
10 Omar ibn el-Khattab Square
15 Zion Gate

Walks
11 A Walk on the Roofs

See also Jerusalem Street Finder, map 3

0 metres 150
0 yards 150

Street-by-Street: The Christian Quarter

The most visited part of the Old City, the Christian Quarter is a head-on collision between commerce and spirituality. At its heart is the Church of the Holy Sepulchre, the most sacred of all Christian sites. It is surrounded by such a clutter of churches and hospices that all one can see of its exterior are the domes and entrance façade. The nearby streets are filled with shops and stalls that thrive on the pilgrim trade. Respite from the crowds can be found in the cafés of Muristan Road.

The Christian Quarter, centred on the Holy Sepulchre

⑤ Church of St John the Baptist
The founding of the Crusader Knights Hospitallers is connected with this small church. A carved stone cross echoes the order's historic emblem.

⑥ Christian Quarter Road
Along with David Street, this is the quarter's main shopping thoroughfare. It specializes in religious items and quality handicrafts.

CHRISTIAN QUARTER ROAD

David Street
From the Jaffa Gate area, David Street is the main route down through the Old City. This cramped, stepped alley doubles as a busy tourist bazaar.

Jaffa Gate

DAVID STREET

MURISTAN R

④ ★ Muristan
The intersecting avenues of the Muristan were created when the Greek Orthodox Church redeveloped the area in 1903.

❶ ★ Church of the Holy Sepulchre
The Stabat Mater Altar is one of numerous chapels and shrines that fill the church, which commemorates the Crucifixion and burial of Christ.

Locator Map
See Jerusalem Street Finder, map 3

Omar Mosque
(see p103)

Khanqa Salahiyya
(see p103)

Souk el-Dabbagha
With the Holy Sepulchre church at the end of the street, the few shops here have no shortage of customers for their religious souvenirs.

Ethiopian Monastery
(see p99)

Pillars of original Byzantine Holy Sepulchre church *(see p102)*

Zalatimo's is a famed confectionery shop; its storeroom contains remains of the doorway of the original 4th-century Holy Sepulchre church.

❷ Alexander Hospice
Belonging to the Russian Orthodox Church, the hospice is built over ruins of the early Holy Sepulchre church.

SOUK EL-DABBAGHA

SOUK KHAN EL-ZEIT

Key

— Suggested route

| 0 metres | 30 |
| 0 yards | 30 |

❸ ★ Lutheran Church of the Redeemer
This church has an attractive medieval cloister, but most people visit for the views from the bell tower.

❶ Church of the Holy Sepulchre

Built around what is believed to be the site of Christ's crucifixion, burial and Resurrection, this complex church is the most important in Christendom. The first basilica here was built by Roman emperor Constantine between AD 326 and 335 at the suggestion of his mother, St Helena. It was rebuilt on a smaller scale by Byzantine emperor Constantine Monomachus in the 1040s following its destruction by Fatimid sultan Hakim in 1009, but was much enlarged again by the Crusaders between 1114 and 1170. A disastrous fire in 1808 and an earthquake in 1927 necessitated extensive repairs.

The mosaic of roofs and domes of the Church of the Holy Sepulchre

★ Christ's Tomb
For Christians, this is the most sacred site of all. Inside the 1810 monument, a marble slab covers the rock on which Christ's body is believed to have been laid.

Stone of Unction
This is where the anointing and wrapping of Christ's body after his death has been commemorated since medieval times. The present stone dates from 1810.

Courtyard
The main entrance courtyard is flanked by chapels. The disused steps opposite the bell tower once led to the Chapel of the Franks, the Crusaders' ceremonial entrance to Golgotha.

The Holy Fire

On the Saturday of Orthodox Easter, all the church's lamps are put out and the faithful stand in the dark, a symbol of the darkness at the Crucifixion. A candle is lit at Christ's Tomb, then another and another, until the entire basilica and courtyard are ablaze with light to symbolize the Resurrection. Legend says the fire comes from heaven.

The Easter ceremony of the Holy Fire

VISITORS' CHECKLIST

Practical Information
Entrance from Souk el-Dabbagha.
Map 3 C3. **Tel** (02) 626 7011.
Open summer: 5am–9pm daily;
winter: 4am–7pm daily.

Catholikon Dome
Rebuilt after the 1927 earthquake and decorated with an image of Christ, this dome covers the central nave of the Crusader church. This part of the building is now used for Greek Orthodox services.

★ Golgotha
Through the glass around the Greek Orthodox altar can be seen the outcrop of rock venerated as the site of the Crucifixion.

KEY

① **Chapel of the Franks**

② **The main entrance** is early 12th century. The right-hand door was blocked up late in the same century.

③ **The Crusader bell tower** was reduced by two storeys in 1719.

④ **The Rotunda**, heavily rebuilt after the 1808 fire, is the most majestic part of the church.

⑤ **The Seven Arches** of the Virgin are the remains of an 11th-century colonnaded courtyard.

⑥ **The Centre of the World**, according to ancient map-makers (see p44), is marked here by a stone basin.

⑦ **Rock of Golgotha** (see p98)

⑧ **Chapel of Adam** (see p98)

⑨ **The Chapel of St Helena** is now dedicated to St Gregory the Illuminator, patron of the Armenians

⑩ **Stairs to the Inventio Crucis Chapel** (see p99)

Ethiopian Monastery
A cluster of small buildings on the roof of the Chapel of St Helena is inhabited by a community of Ethiopian monks.

Exploring the Church of the Holy Sepulchre

The reconstructions and additions that have shaped this church over the centuries make it a complex building to explore. Its division into chapels and spaces allotted to six different denominations adds a further sense of confusion. The interior is dimly lit, and queues often form at Christ's Tomb, so that the time each person can spend inside the shrine may be limited to just a few minutes. Nonetheless, the experience of standing on Christianity's most hallowed ground inspires many visitors with a deep sense of awe.

The Roman Catholic altar on Golgotha

Golgotha

Just inside the church's main entrance, on the right, two staircases lead up to Golgotha, which in Hebrew means "Place of the Skull" and was translated into Latin as Calvary. The space here is divided into two chapels. On the left is the Greek Orthodox chapel, with its altar placed directly over the rocky outcrop on which the cross of Christ's crucifixion is believed to have stood. The softer surrounding rock was quarried away when the church was built and the remaining, fissured, so-called Rock of Golgotha can now be seen through the protective glass around the altar. It can be touched through a hole in the floor under the altar. The 12th Station of the Cross (see p34) is commemorated here.

To the right is the Roman Catholic chapel, containing the 10th and 11th Stations of the Cross. The silver and bronze altar was given by Ferdinand de Medici in 1588.

The 1937 mosaics encircle a Crusader-era medallion of the Ascension on the ceiling. The window looks into the Chapel of the Franks (see pp96–7).

Between these altars is the Altar of the Stabat Mater, commemorating Mary's sorrow as she stood at the foot of the cross. It marks the 13th Station of the Cross. The wooden bust of the Virgin is 18th century.

Archaeological evidence that the church rests on a possible site of the Crucifixion is scant, but positive. Excavations show that the site lay outside the city walls until new ones encompassed it in AD 43; that in the early 1st century it was a disused quarry in which an area of cracked rock had been left untouched; and that rock-hewn tombs were in use here in the 1st centuries BC and AD. This all tallies with Gospel accounts of the Crucifixion.

Chapel of Adam

Immediately beneath the Greek Orthodox chapel on Golgotha, this chapel is built against the Rock of Golgotha. It is the medieval replacement of a previous Chapel of Adam that was part of Constantine's 4th-century basilica. It was so called because tradition told that Christ was crucified over the burial place of Adam's skull – a tradition first recorded by the Alexandrian theologian Origen (c.AD 185–245).

The crack in the Rock of Golgotha, clearly visible in the apse, is held by believers to have been caused by the earthquake that followed Christ's death (Matthew 27: 51).

11th-century apse, Chapel of Adam, built against the Rock of Golgotha

The Status Quo

Fierce disputes, lasting centuries, between Christian creeds (see p104) over ownership of the church were largely resolved by an Ottoman decree issued in 1852. Still in force and known as the Status Quo, it divides custody among Armenians, Greeks, Copts, Roman Catholics, Ethiopians and Syrians. Some areas are administered communally. Every day, the church is unlocked by a Muslim keyholder acting as a "neutral" intermediary. This ceremonial task has been performed by a member of the same family for several generations.

Coptic priest in ceremonial vestments

Christ's Tomb

The present-day shrine around the tomb of Christ was built in 1809–10, after the severe fire of 1808. It replaced one dating from 1555, commissioned by the Franciscan friar Bonifacio da Ragusa. Before that, there had been a succession of shrines replacing the original 4th-century one destroyed by the sultan Hakim in 1009. Constantine's builders had dug away the hillside to leave the presumed rock-hewn tomb of Christ isolated and with enough room to build a church around it. They had also had to clear the remains of an AD 135 Hadrianic temple from the site, as well as the material with which an old quarry had been filled to provide the temple's foundations. In so doing, the Rock of Golgotha was also found.

Today the shrine, owned by the Greek Orthodox, Roman Catholic and Armenian communities, contains two chapels. The outer Chapel of the Angel has a low pilaster incorporating a piece of the stone said to have been rolled from the mouth of Christ's Tomb by angels. It serves as a Greek Orthodox altar. A low door leads to the tiny inner Chapel of the Holy Sepulchre with the 14th Station of the Cross. A marble slab covers the place where Christ's body was supposedly laid. The slab was installed in the 1555 reconstruction and purposely cracked to deter Ottoman looters.

People queuing to enter the shrine containing Christ's Tomb in the church's Rotunda

Site of Christ's Tomb

In the 1st century AD, this site consisted of a small, rocky rise just outside the city walls and a disused stone quarry into whose rock face tombs had been cut.

The hillside was dug away in the 4th century to allow a church to be built around the tomb.

Burial chambers existed here in the 1st centuries BC and AD.

Christ's tomb

Present church

Rock of Golgotha

In the Coptic chapel behind the shrine, a piece of polished stone is shown as being part of the tomb itself, but it is granite and not limestone, as the tomb here is known to be.

Rotunda and Syrian Chapel

The Rotunda is built in classical Roman style. The outer back wall (now hidden by interior partitions) survives from the 4th-century basilica up to a height of 11 m (36 ft). The 11th-century dome was replaced after the 1808 fire and the two-storey colonnade built. The first two columns on the right, standing with your back to the nave, are replicas of two that survived the fire, but were judged unstable. The originals were made in the 11th century from the two halves of a single, gigantic Roman column – from either the 4th-century basilica or the previous Hadrianic temple. In the Rotunda's back wall is the chapel used by the Syrians. It contains Jewish rock tombs (c.100 BC–AD 100), marking the limit to which the hillside was dug away when the first church was built

Carvings in St Helena's Chapel

Chapels of St Helena and the Finding of the Cross

From the ambulatory in the Crusader-period apse, now the choir in the Greek Catholikon, steep steps lead down to St Helena's Chapel. The crosses on the walls were carved by pilgrims. Although this crypt was built by the Crusaders, who reused Byzantine columns, the side walls are foundations of the 4th-century basilica. More stairs go down to the Finding of the Cross (Inventio Crucis) Chapel, a former cistern in which St Helena is said to have found the True Cross. The statue of her is 19th century.

Ethiopian Monastery

This simple monastery is approached either through the Ethiopian chapel in the corner of the courtyard, to the right of the main entrance, or from Souk Khan el-Zeit (see p95), up steps beside Zalatimo's, a famous pastry shop.

It occupies a series of small buildings on the roof of St Helena's Chapel, among the ruins of the former Crusader cloister. The Ethiopians were forced here in the 17th century, when, unable to pay Ottoman taxes, they lost ownership of their chapels in the main church to other communities.

❷ Alexander Hospice

Souk el-Dabbagha. **Map** 3 C3.
Tel (02) 627 4952. Excavations:
Open 9am–6pm daily.

Home to St Alexander's Church, the central place of worship for Jerusalem's Russian Orthodox community, the Alexander Hospice also houses some important excavations. When the hospice was founded in 1859, the site was already known to contain ruins of the original church of the Holy Sepulchre, built in AD 335. However, in 1882, excavations revealed remains of a Herodian

Alexander Hospice doorway

city wall. This finally proved that the site of the Holy Sepulchre church was outside the ancient city walls, which added credence to the claim that it was on the true site of Christ's crucifixion (see pp96–9). Also preserved here are remnants of a colonnaded street and, in the church, part of a triumphal arch from Hadrian's forum, begun in AD 135. The excavations are open to the public, but only parts of the church can be visited.

❸ Lutheran Church of the Redeemer

24 Muristan Rd. **Map** 3 C3. **Tel** (02) 627 6111. **Open** 10am–5pm (winter: 4pm) Mon–Sat. for bell tower only.
W elcjhl.org

This Neo-Romanesque church was built for the German Kaiser Wilhelm II, and completed in 1898. Renewed interest in the Holy Land by Europe during the late 19th century had ushered in a period of restoration and church building, with many nations wanting to establish a religious presence in Jerusalem. The Lutheran Church of the Redeemer was constructed over the remains of the 11th-century church of St Mary of the Latins, built by wealthy merchants from Amalfi in Italy. An even earlier church is thought to have existed on the site from the 5th century. Many details from the medieval church have been incorporated into the new building, and the entrance way, decorated with the signs of the zodiac and symbols of the months, is largely original. The attractive cloister, which is inside the adjacent Lutheran hospice, has two tiers of galleries and dates from the 13th–14th centuries. Perhaps the most interesting part of the church, though, is the bell tower. After climbing the 177 steps, visitors are rewarded with some great views over the Old City.

One of the many souvenir shops in the Muristan

❹ Muristan

Muristan Rd. **Map** 3 C3.

The name Muristan derives from the Persian word for a hospital or hospice for travellers. For centuries the area known as the Muristan, south of the Holy Sepulchre, was the site of just such a hospice for pilgrims from Latin-speaking countries. It was built by Charlemagne in the early 9th century, with permission from the caliph Haroun el-Rashid. Partly destroyed in 1009 by the Fatimid caliph El-Hakim, it was restored later in the 11th century by merchants from Amalfi. They also built three churches here: St Mary Minor for women, St Mary of the Latins for men and St John the Baptist for the poor.

St John the Baptist still stands today, and was where the Knights of the Hospital of St John (or the Knights Hospitallers) were founded. They were to take over much of the Muristan area as their

The dominating tower of the Lutheran Church of the Redeemer

The fountain square, at the heart of the Muristan

headquarters, later building their own huge hospital to the north of the church. During the Crusades it was reported that there could often be up to 2,000 people under their care here at any one time.

By the 16th century the Muristan had fallen into ruins and Suleyman the Magnificent had its stones used to rebuild Jerusalem's city walls.

Today the Muristan is very different from how it once looked, most traces of the original buildings having long since disappeared. It is now characterized by its quiet lanes and attractive pink-stone buildings. The lanes converge at the ornate fountain in the main square – site of the original hospice. The surrounding streets are packed with small shops selling souvenirs, handicrafts and antiques. Along the nearby Muristan Road you will also find a number of outdoor cafés where you can sit and absorb the atmosphere.

The distinctive dome of the Church of St John the Baptist

❺ Church of St John the Baptist

Christian Quarter Rd. **Map** 3 C4. **Closed** to the public.

The silvery dome of the Church of St John the Baptist is clearly visible above the rooftops of the Muristan, but the entrance is harder to spot among the hordes of people along busy Christian Quarter Road. A small doorway leads into a courtyard, which in turn gives access to the neighbouring Greek Orthodox monastery and the church proper. Founded in the 5th century, the Church of St John the Baptist is one of the most ancient churches in Jerusalem. After falling into ruin, it was extensively rebuilt in the 11th century, and aside from the two bell towers which are a later addition, the modern church is little changed.

Glassware on sale on Christian Quarter Road

In 1099 many Christian knights who were wounded during the siege of Jerusalem were taken care of in this church. After their recovery they decided to dedicate themselves to helping the sick and protecting the pilgrims visiting Jerusalem. Founding the Knights of the Hospital of St John, they later developed into the military order of the Hospitallers and played a key role in the defence of the Holy Land (see pp52–3).

❻ Christian Quarter Road

Map 3 B3.

Together with David Street, which runs from Jaffa Gate towards the Muristan, Christian Quarter Road is one of the main streets in the Christian Quarter. Marking off the Muristan zone, it passes by the western side of the Holy Sepulchre, and parallel to Souk Khan el-Zeit. This busy road is lined with shops selling antiques, Palestinian handicrafts (embroidery, leather goods and Hebron glass) and religious articles (icons, carved olive-wood crucifixes and rosaries).

Midway up the road on the right, down an alley signposted for the Holy Sepulchre, a short stairway descends to the modest **Omar Mosque**, with its distinctive square minaret. Its name commemorates the caliph Omar, the person generally credited with saving the Holy Sepulchre from falling into Muslim control after Jerusalem passed under Muslim dominion in February 638. Asked to go and pray inside the church, which would almost certainly have meant its being converted into a mosque, he instead prayed on the steps outside, thus allowing the church to remain a Christian site. The Omar mosque was built later, in 1193, by Saladin's son Aphdal Ali, beside the old Hospital of the Knights of St John.

The unassuming **Khanqa Salahiyya** is at the top of Christian Quarter Road. Built by Saladin between 1187 and 1189 as a monastery for Sufi mystics, it is on the site of the old Crusader Patriarchate of Jerusalem. Its ornate entrance way may be as close as you are allowed, however, as it is not open to non-Muslims. Along the north side of the mosque is El Khanqa Street. This attractive, old, stepped street is lined with interesting shops, and runs up one of the Old City's many hills.

❼ Museum of the Greek Orthodox Patriarchate

Greek Orthodox Patriarchate Rd.
Map 3 B3. **Tel** (02) 627 4941.
Closed for restoration.

Tucked away in the back alleys of the Christian Quarter, this museum houses a collection of ecclesiastical items that includes icons, embroidered vestments, mitres, chalices and filigree objects. It also has a fine array of archaeological finds.

Of most interest are two white-stone sarcophagi found at the end of the 19th century in a tomb near the present-day King David Hotel (see p126). They are considered to belong to the family of Herod the Great, and are covered in wonderfully elaborate floral decoration, which represents some of the finest Herodian-era funerary art ever found.

The museum also displays Crusader objects, including a 12th-century carved capital from Nazareth, and artifacts found in the tomb of Baldwin I (king of Jerusalem, 1100–18) in the Church of the Holy Sepulchre. Other treasures include a 12th-century mitre carved from rock crystal, with bands of copper around the base and set with gems, which may once have contained relics of the Holy Cross.

Among a collection of historical firmans (imperial edicts), is one that purports to have been issued by the caliph Omar in AD 638, granting the Greek Orthodox Church custody of Jerusalem's holy places.

Codex from the Greek Patriarchate Museum

❽ Jaffa Gate

Map 3 B4. 🚌 1, 13, 20.

This is the busiest of the seven Old City gates. It is the main gate for traffic and pedestrians coming from modern West Jerusalem via Mamilla. Despite the gate's great size, the entrance tunnel is

Jaffa Gate, the main way into the Old City from West Jerusalem

narrow; it is also L-shaped – both measures intended to thwart attackers. It was constructed during the reign of Suleyman the Magnificent – an exact date of 1538 is given in a dedication within the arch on the outside of the gate. The breach in the wall through which cars now pass was made in 1898, in order to allow the visiting Kaiser Wilhelm II of Germany to enter the city in his carriage.

Immediately inside the gate, set into the wall behind some railings on the left, are two graves. Tour guides like to tell how these belong to Suleyman's architects, executed because they failed to incorporate Mount Zion within the city walls. An alternative legend has it that they were killed to prevent them ever building such grand walls for anyone else. In fact, they are the graves of a prominent citizen and his wife.

Jaffa Gate is one of the places where visitors can access the ramparts to walk along the city walls (see pp146–7). To the Arabs this gate is known as Bab el-Khalil, from the Arabic name for Hebron (El-Khalil). The old road to the town started here.

Eastern Christianity and the Patriarchates

Jerusalem's Greek Orthodox Patriarch

There are no fewer than 17 churches represented in Jerusalem, a result of a great many historical schisms. As Christianity spread in the 2nd and 3rd centuries, patriarchates were established in Alexandria, Antioch, Constantinople, Jerusalem and Rome. Their heads, the patriarchs, claimed lineage from the Apostles, which gave them the authority to pronounce on correct doctrine. The first major schism came when the Council of Chalcedon (AD 451) proclaimed the dual "divine and human" nature of Christ, and in so doing estranged the Armenian, Ethiopian, Coptic and Syrian churches from the Roman Catholic and mainstream Orthodoxy. Eastern and Western Christianity split in 1054, when the Eastern churches refused to acknowledge the primacy of the Pope and the Roman church. Today there are four patriarchs (a position akin to that of an archbishop) resident in Jerusalem: those of the Greek Orthodox, Armenian, Greek Catholic and Latin (Roman Catholic) churches. The Ethiopians and Copts have a building called a patriarchate, but without the figure of the patriarch.

Syrian Orthodox priest

Armenian priest

Omar ibn el-Khattab Square, just inside Jaffa Gate

❾ The Citadel (Tower of David)

See pp106–9.

❿ Omar ibn el-Khattab Square

Map 3 D4.

Not so much a square as a widening of the road as it passes around the Citadel, this area just inside Jaffa Gate is a focal point of Old City life. Arab boys selling street food solicit black-garbed Orthodox Jews heading for the Western Wall, and priests in cassocks pose for the cameras of the tourist groups who pick up their tour guides here.

The square takes its name from the caliph Omar, who captured Jerusalem for Islam in AD 638. The Muslim name is misleading, as most of the property around the square is owned by the Greek Orthodox Patriarchate. In the late 19th century, the Patriarchate built the hotels and shops on the north side, including the Neo-Classical **Imperial Hotel**. These days the hotel suffers badly from neglect and has appeal only for those who value atmosphere over comfort

At a street junction behind the hotel is a **Roman column**, erected around AD 200 in honour of the prefect of Judaea and commander of the 10th Legion. This was one of the legions that participated in the recapture of

Jerusalem in AD 70 *(see p47)*, and was subsequently quartered in the city. The column now supports a street light.

Several cafés with pavement tables fringe the east side of the square. Next to the cafés is the Christian Information Centre, and, opposite the entrance to the Citadel, the Anglican Christ Church compound. Its Neo-Gothic church (1849) was the first Protestant building in the Holy Land.

⓫ A Walk on the Roofs

Map 3 C4.

At the corner of St Mark's Road and Khabad Street, in an area where the Jewish, Christian and Muslim quarters overlap, an iron staircase leads up to the Old City rooftops. From here it is possible to walk above the central souk area, peering down through

ventilation grilles at the bustling street below. It is possible to walk for some distance, between satellite dishes and dividing walls. There is even a ramshackle children's playground up here. Locals use the rooftops as a short cut; for visitors, the appeal is in the views the terrace affords of the Church of the Holy Sepulchre and Dome of the Rock. It is also worth coming up here in the evening to see the rooftop skyline thrown into silhouette by moonlight. A second set of stairs leads down past a *yeshiva* (Jewish religious school) onto El-Saraya Street in the Muslim Quarter.

⓬ St Mark's Church

5 Ararat St. **Map** 3 C4. **Tel** (02) 628 3304. **Open** 9am–1pm & 3–5pm (winter: 4pm) Mon–Sat.

This small church is the centre of the Syrian Orthodox community in Jerusalem. It is a place rich in biblical associations, albeit of suspect authenticity. According to tradition, the church was built on the site of the house of Mary, mother of St Mark the Evangelist. A stone font in the church is supposedly that in which the Virgin Mary was baptized, and the church also has a painting on parchment of the Virgin and Child that is often attributed to St Luke. Of course, historians identify it as dating from a much later period. Some scholars do believe, however, that a small cellar room here was the true site of the Last Supper, not Mount Zion *(see p121)*.

Orthodox Jews cross the rooftops of the Old City

⊙ The Citadel (Tower of David)

The Tower of David Museum of the History of Jerusalem *(see pp108–9)* stands in the Citadel, an imposing bastion at the entrance to the walled city. The present-day structure dates mainly from the Middle Ages and includes additions made in 1532 by Suleyman the Magnificent. However, excavations have revealed remains dating back to the 2nd century BC, and indicate that there were fortifications here from Herodian times. Some believe this supports the view that this is the most likely site of Christ's trial and condemnation.

★ **Ramparts**
As with most other fortresses of the Middle Ages, the Citadel is surrounded by an upper walkway. It is possible to walk almost the whole circuit, taking in views of the city in all directions.

Tower of David
The Citadel is also commonly known as the Tower of David. The misnomer dates back to Byzantine confusion over the geographical layout of the city. Today the name "Tower of David" is also applied to this minaret, added in 1655.

Arched Gateway
In 1917, General Allenby proclaimed the capture of Jerusalem by British forces *(see p57)* right in front of this gate built in the 16th century.

The Night Spectacular
This sound-and-light show allows spectators to immerse themselves in the history of Jerusalem as the streets of the Citadel come alive with images and music.

View of the Citadel and the Dome of the Rock behind, from the New City

VISITORS' CHECKLIST

Practical Information
Jaffa Gate. **Map** 3 B4. **Tel** (02) 626 5333. **Open** 9am–4pm Sat–Thu (to 2pm Fri); Aug: 9am–5pm Sat–Thu (to 4pm Fri).
w tod.org.il

★ **Phasael's Tower**
This defensive tower, built by Herod the Great and named after his brother, was decorated in the Greco-Roman style and partly rebuilt in the 1300s. The top offers spectacular views.

KEY

① **The entrance** was built with an L-shaped hallway to impede the progress of attackers.

② **Open-air mosque**

③ **East Tower**

④ **Southeast Tower**

⑤ **Base of an early Islamic tower**

⑥ **The mosque** was built by the Mamelukes above a Crusader hall.

⑦ **The Hasmonean city wall** (2nd century BC) is one of the oldest finds. Part of the same wall can be seen in the Jewish Quarter.

⑧ **An 1873 model of Jerusalem** is on display in an underground cistern.

⑨ **The courtyard** was built by the Mamelukes above a Crusader hall.

⑩ **Entrance to café**

⑪ **Traces of the Byzantine city wall** can be seen at the base of this section of wall.

⑫ **Moat**

Mameluke Cupola
This small cupola and the hexagonal room beneath are part of the Mameluke rebuilding that took place around 1310. The tour of the museum starts on this rooftop.

Exploring the Citadel

There is a lot to see in the Citadel's Tower of David Museum. To help the visitor, there are three well-signposted routes: the Observation Route runs along the ramparts for the best panoramic views of the city, both Old and New; the Excavation Route concentrates on the archaeological remains in the courtyard; and the Exhibition Route takes visitors through a series of rooms tracing the history of the city. This takes the form of displays, dioramas and models, rather than a collection of historical artifacts. Visitors can join a free English tour of the route departing at 11am Sunday to Friday, and lasting one and a half hours.

Three-dimensional representation of the Second Temple

Phasael's Tower

The Exhibition Route begins in Phasael's Tower with a short, animated film. From here, exit to the roof of the octagonal entrance chamber, where there is the first in a series of models placed throughout the museum that depict Jerusalem at various stages during its history. This one shows the topography of the site before the founding of the city. If you then ascend Phasael's Tower, you can see the pattern of hills and valleys for yourself.

The Canaanites and the First Temple

Heading clockwise from Phasael's Tower, the first two sections deal with the origins of Jerusalem, covering the period from 3150 to 587 BC, the year the First Temple was destroyed. The Canaanite era is explained in three display boards outside the East Tower, while the First-Temple-era

exhibits are inside the tower. These include a replica of a 19th-century-BC Egyptian statuette bearing the first written reference to Jerusalem. There is also a model of the 10th-century City of David, prior to the building of the Temple, a hologram of the Temple itself and an informative animation showing how the ancient city's water system worked. The latter is very useful for anyone who intends visiting Hezekiah's Tunnel and the Pool of Siloam (see p119).

Return to Zion and the Second Temple

The next series of rooms, in a lower level of the East Tower, traces the return of the Jews to Jerusalem from exile in Babylon – illustrated in the form of

interpretative reliefs in Babylonian and Persian style. One room features a three-dimensional portrait of the Second Temple, which is worth studying closely by anyone who intends visiting the Jerusalem Archaeological Park (see pp90–91). There is also an illustration of the three original Herodian towers – one of these forms the base of Phasael's Tower, visited at the start of this route, which still has some of the stone used to build the lower part of the 2nd-century-BC structure.

The destruction of the Temple is represented by a reproduction of a frieze from the Arch of Titus, erected in Rome in AD 81 to celebrate the triumph over the Jews 11 years earlier. It shows Roman soldiers carrying off Jewish treasures, including a menorah and trumpets.

Between here and the next exhibition room is a bronze copy of Verrochio's David, a Renaissance sculpture of the young king. David, in fact, had nothing to do with the Citadel or the tower that bears his name (see p106), as the fortress dates from the time of Herod, a thousand years after the time of David. The statue was a gift to Jerusalem from the city of Florence in Italy.

Verrochio's statue of David

Phasael's Tower (left) seen across the Citadel's courtyard

Late Roman and Byzantine Periods

A small room in the Southeast Tower deals with the creation of Aelia Capitolina, the Roman city, built on the ruins of Second-Temple-era Jerusalem. The room has floors based on mosaics from Hadrian's Villa in Rome and the St Martyrius Monastery near Jerusalem. There is also a splendid model, 1.5 m (5 ft) long, of the Church of the Holy Sepulchre as it is thought to have looked when it was first built in the 4th century, on the orders of Helena, mother of the emperor Constantine.

The *sabil* of Suleyman in a finely detailed model in the Ottoman room

The prayer niche and pulpit in the Citadel's former mosque

Early Islam and the Crusades

Appropriately enough, the early Islamic exhibits are housed in the Citadel's former mosque. This is the most striking room in the whole Citadel complex, with a still intact mihrab (niche indicating the direction of Mecca) and *minbar* (pulpit). At the centre of the room is a large, detailed, sectioned model of the Dome of the Rock. The model apparently took two years to construct. An aluminium model at the

Members of Saladin's retinue

centre of the room shows that by this time the Old City had taken on the form in which it appears today. There is also a diorama of the Crusader Church of St Anne's and life-size statues of the Western knights, as well as a brightly coloured diorama depicting the famed conqueror of the Crusaders, Saladin (Salah al-Din in Arabic), in his tent outside the city walls.

The Mamelukes and Ottomans

The final exhibition rooms are housed in the large, northwest tower. The Mamelukes (1260–1516), a dynasty of former slaves who ruled from Egypt, endowed Jerusalem with some of its most distinctive and beautiful buildings. Their contribution is represented by drawings and a scale reconstruction of a street of distinctive striped-stone (*ablaq*) architecture. You can see similar examples today at Lady Tunshuq's Palace in the Old City (*see p69*). Illustrating Ottoman Jerusalem is a large-scale model of a fountain (*sabil*) erected by Suleyman the Magnificent – the real thing survives today on Chain Street in the Muslim Quarter.

End of the Ottomans and the British Mandate

This last room is a brief race through the city's more recent history. The story it tells is of the mass influx of Christian pilgrims and Jewish immigrants who began to settle for the first time outside the security of the walls of the Old City and, in doing so, established what is now the modern city of Jerusalem. A video wall with nine screens depicts 30 years of British mandate from 1917 until 1948. There is also some rare 1896 Lumière brothers footage of the Jerusalem–Jaffa railway.

In a separate hall is a vast and superb model of late 19th-century Jerusalem, made by a Hungarian artist in 1873. It was exhibited throughout Europe before going into storage and being forgotten for a century until its rediscovery and removal here in the early 1980s.

Detail of the enormous model of Jerusalem constructed in 1873

Wrought-iron gate framing the ornate main entrance to St James's Cathedral

⓭ St James's Cathedral

Armenian Patriarchate Rd. **Map** 3 B5.
Tel (02) 628 2331. **Open** 6–7:30am & 3–3:30pm daily.

The Armenian Cathedral is one of the most beautiful of all Jerusalem's sacred buildings. It was originally constructed in the 11th and 12th centuries over the reputed tomb of St James the Great, the Apostle, killed by Herod Agrippa I (AD 37–44). Many alterations and additions have since been made, most notably in the 18th century, when much of the existing decoration was added.

Entrance to the cathedral is via a small courtyard with a 19th-century fountain. On the western wall of the courtyard are inscriptions in Armenian, one of which dates from 1151. Hanging in the vaulted porch are wooden bars. Each afternoon a priest strikes these with a wooden mallet known as a *nakus*, to signal the start of the service.

The cathedral interior is enchanting. It is only dimly illuminated by a forest of oil lamps hung from the ceiling. There are no seats; instead the floors are thickly laid with Oriental rugs. Four great square piers divide the main space into three aisles. These piers, along with the walls, are covered in blue-and-white tiles with floral and abstract patterns. In the apses at the end of each of the three aisles are altars, separated from the rest of the church by the iconostasis screen. Two thrones stand in the choir; the one nearest the pier is said to be that of St James the Less, traditionally held to have been a step-brother of Christ and the first bishop of Jerusalem. It is used only once a year, in early January, on the occasion of his feast day. The other throne is the one normally used by the patriarch.

The cathedral contains many small shrines and chapels. The third on the left as you enter is the most important: it supposedly holds the head of St James the Great. Off to the right, the Etchmiadzin Chapel has some beautiful tiling.

⓮ Gulbenkian Library

Armenian Patriarchate Rd. **Map** 3 B5.
Tel (02) 628 2331. Egged bus 38.
Open 2–6pm Mon–Fri. call ahead. **W** armenian-patriarchate.com/home/gulbenkian-library

Located in the complex of St James's Cathedral, the Gulbenkian Library is one of the largest and most important resource centres dedicated to the history and culture of the Armenian people. It first opened in 1932 and has a growing collection of more than 100,000 works, both historical and contemporary, a large number of which are in Armenian. The library also contains the third largest collection of Armenian newspapers, along with an extensive stock of periodicals and magazines.

A separate room houses rare and early imprints. Significant among these is a copy of the inaugural issue of the official publication of the Armenian Patriarchate. Other interesting objects are examples of the first books printed in the first print shop in Jerusalem, which has been active since 1833 inside the Armenian monastery.

The Patriarchate also curates an extraordinary collection of 4,000 ancient manuscripts, housed in the Church of St Toros, close to the Cathedral.

Battle-scarred Zion Gate, which leads to the Jewish and Armenian quarters

⓯ Zion Gate

Map 3 C5.

Zion Gate was constructed by Suleyman the Magnificent's engineers *(see p54)* in 1540. It allowed direct access from the city to the holy sites on Mount Zion. Fighting was particularly fierce here in 1948, when Israeli soldiers were desperate to breach the walls to relieve the Jewish Quarter inside, under siege by the Jordanians. The outside of the gate is terribly pockmarked by bullet holes. A short distance to the west of the gate there is conspicuous damage to the base of the wall where soldiers tried to blast their way through with explosives.

In Arabic, the gate is known as Bab el-Nabi Daud (Gate of the Prophet David), because of its proximity to the place traditionally known as King David's Tomb *(see p121)*.

The Armenians in Jerusalem

The kingdom of Armenia was the first country to make Christianity the state religion, when in AD 301 its king was converted. Armenian pilgrims began to visit the Holy City soon after. In the 12th century they purchased St James's Cathedral from the Georgians, and this became the focal point of their community in Jerusalem. The Armenian Quarter grew to its current size in the 17th and 18th centuries, during the rule of the Turks. In the early 20th century Armenian numbers were swollen by refugees who had fled from the 1915 persecution in Turkey, a terrible genocide in which some one and a half million Armenians were exterminated. But from a peak of around 16,000 in 1948, the Armenian population of Jerusalem has since dwindled to less than 2,000, largely due to emigration. After the 1967 war, the Jews also started to encroach into the area, and the fear now is that, other than in name, the Armenian Quarter may one day disappear altogether.

Tiling adorns the interior of St James's Cathedral. The tiles were made in the early 18th century in Kütahya, a town around 125 km (75 miles) southeast of Constantinople, and renowned as the foremost Armenian ceramic centre in the Ottoman Empire.

The Armenian Church (above) is one of the three major guardians of the Christian places in the Holy Land. Among the sites they have at least partial jurisdiction over are the Church of the Holy Sepulchre, the Tomb of the Virgin Mary at the foot of the Mount of Olives, the Church of the Nativity in Bethlehem and St James's Cathedral.

Mosaics represent the finest legacy of ancient Armenian art. This 5th- or 6th-century example was unearthed just outside Damascus Gate.

Armenian-language manuscripts, such as this 13th-century example, are held in huge numbers at the Gulbenkian Library, next to St James's Cathedral.

The Gulbenkian Library preserves a vast array of resources on Armenian history, religion, language and culture (see p110).

THE MOUNT OF OLIVES AND MOUNT ZION

The Mount of Olives is the hill that rises to the east of the Old City. Its slopes have been used as a place of burial since the 3rd millennium BC. The hill is also dotted with sites connected with the last days of Jesus Christ, but the highlight for many visitors is the superb view of the Old City from the summit. Between the city walls and the hill is the Valley of Jehoshaphat, with several tombs from the 1st and 2nd centuries BC. At the southern end of the valley is the site of the 3,000-year-old settlement that was to become Jerusalem (the City of David). The land rises again to the west to Mount Zion, an area of the city traditionally linked with the Last Supper.

Sights at a Glance

Holy Places

1 Russian Church of the Ascension
2 Mosque of the Ascension
3 Church of the Paternoster
5 Dominus Flevit Sanctuary
6 Church of St Mary Magdalene
7 Basilica of the Agony
8 Tomb of the Virgin
11 St Peter in Gallicantu
13 Church of the Dormition
14 Hall of the Last Supper

Archaeological Sites

10 City of David

Historic Areas

12 Mount Zion

Tombs

4 Tombs of the Prophets
9 Valley of Jehoshaphat
15 King David's Tomb
16 Schindler's Tomb

See also Jerusalem Street Finder, map 2

◀ Basilica of the Agony, with the Mount of Olives and Church of St Mary Magdalene behind

The Mount of Olives

Rising on the eastern side of Jerusalem, the Mount of Olives offers magnificent views of the Dome of the Rock and the Old City. Now best known as the scene of Christ's Agony and betrayal in the Garden of Gethsemane and his Ascension into Heaven, this prominent hill has always been a holy place to the inhabitants of the city. The Jebusites dug tombs here as early as 2400 BC, as later did Jews, Christians and Muslims. To take in all the sights it is wisest to start at the top, near the Mosque of the Ascension, and walk downhill to the Tomb of the Virgin. The Old City views are best in the morning.

⑤ Dominus Flevit Sanctuary
The west window here frames a stunning view of the Old City.

⑧ ★ Tomb of the Virgin
An impressive flight of Crusader steps leads into the cruciform underground church. Tradition says this is where the Virgin Mary was laid to rest.

⑦ ★ Basilica of the Agony
Mosaics, predominantly in blues and greens, decorate the 12 domes of this church, built in 1924 with donations from many countries.

KEY

① **Jericho Road**

② **Garden of Gethsemane**

③ **The Cave of Gethsemane** is the traditional site of Christ's betrayal by Judas.

④ **Benedictine convent**

⑤ **This road** leads to Bethphage, the village from which Christ rode in triumph to Jerusalem on Palm Sunday.

⑥ **Village of El-Tur**

⑦ **Seven Arches Hotel**

⑥ Church of St Mary Magdalene
This Russian Orthodox Church, with typically Muscovite gilded onion domes, was built by Tsar Alexander III in memory of his mother, whose patron saint was Mary Magdalene.

2 Mosque of the Ascension
Sacred to Muslims and Christians, this medieval chapel, now part of a mosque, is on the supposed site of Christ's Ascension.

Locator Map
See Jerusalem Street Finder, map 2

3 ★ Church of the Paternoster
Its name meaning "Our Father", this church was built above a grotto where Christ is believed to have taught the Lord's Prayer.

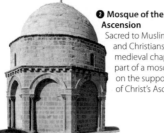

4 Tombs of the Prophets
Revered as the burial place of three Old Testament prophets, this catacomb in fact dates from a much later period, the 1st century AD.

Jewish Cemeteries
Many Jews wish to be buried on the Mount of Olives so as to be close to the Valley of Jehoshaphat, where it is said mankind will be resurrected on the Day of Judgment.

Russian Church of the Ascension's bell tower in the quiet convent gardens

❶ Russian Church of the Ascension

Off Ruba el-Adawiya St, Mount of Olives. **Map** 2 F3. **Tel** (02) 628 4373. **Open** summer: 9am–noon Tue & Thu; winter: 10am–1pm Tue & Thu.

This is the church of a still active Russian Orthodox convent built between 1870 and 1887. The bell tower, a prominent landmark on the Mount of Olives, was built tall enough to allow pilgrims too infirm to walk to the River Jordan to see it from afar. The 8000-kg (8-tonne) bell was hauled from Jaffa by Russian pilgrims.

Two Armenian mosaics were found during construction. A small museum was built over the most beautiful, which is fragmentary and dates from the 5th century AD; the other, complete and made slightly later, is in the Chapel of the Head of John the Baptist, inside the church. An iron cage on the floor shows where John's head was supposedly found.

❷ Mosque of the Ascension

Off Ruba el-Adawiya St, Mount of Olives. **Map** 2 F3. **Open** 8am–5pm (winter: 2:30pm) daily (if closed, ring bell).

Poemenia, a Christian noble-woman, built the first chapel here around AD 380 to commemorate Christ's Ascension. It had three concentric porticoes around an uncovered space, where the dust miraculously formed the image of Christ's footprints.

The Crusaders rebuilt the chapel as an octagon and the column bases of a surrounding Crusader portico are still visible outside. By this time, the footprints, now set in stone, were venerated here, and the right imprint remains to this day. The capitals were carved in the 1140s and the two depicting animals and leaves are particularly beautiful.

The chapel became a Muslim shrine after Saladin's conquest in 1187. In 1200 it was roofed with a dome, the arches were walled in, a mihrab added and a surrounding wall built. The outer wall today is largely rebuilt. The adjacent minaret and mosque are 17th century.

The underground tomb near the entrance is venerated by Jews as belonging to the Old Testament prophetess Huldah, by Christians as St Pelagia's and by Muslims as that of the holy woman Rabia el-Adawiya.

❸ Church of the Paternoster

Mount of Olives. **Map** 2 F4. **Tel** (02) 626 4904. **Open** 8:30am–noon & 2:30–5pm Mon–Sat.

This church stands next to the partly restored ruins of one commissioned by the emperor Constantine, who sent his mother, St Helena, to supervise construction in AD 326. Called

Site of Christ's footprint in the Mosque of the Ascension

Eleona (*elaion* in Greek meaning "of olives"), it was sited above a grotto where the Ascension was commemorated. By Crusader times, the church had been rebuilt three times and the grotto was known as the place where Christ had taught the Disciples the Paternoster (meaning "Our Father"), or Lord's Prayer.

The present church and a Carmelite monastery were built nearby between 1868 and 1872 by the French Princesse de la Tour d'Auvergne. Excavations of the Byzantine church in 1910–11 unearthed a marble plaque engraved in Latin with the Paternoster. In 1920, the grotto was restored, but plans to reconstruct the Byzantine church were never realized, through lack of funds.

Today, the 19th-century church and its cloister are famous for the tiled panels inscribed with the Paternoster in more than 60 languages.

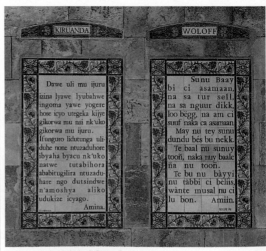

Panels inscribed with the Lord's Prayer, Church of the Paternoster

❹ Tombs of the Prophets

Mount of Olives. **Map** 2 F4.
Open 9am–3:30pm Mon–Fri.

The southwestern slope of the Mount of Olives, facing the Kidron Valley – also known along this stretch as the Valley of Jehoshaphat *(see p119)* – is densely occupied by Jewish cemeteries. At the top of the slope, an unusual, fan-shaped catacomb containing *kokhim* (oven-shaped) graves is held by Christian and Jewish tradition to enclose the tombs of the 5th-century-BC prophets Haggai, Malachi and Zechariah. The graves actually date from the 1st century AD and were reused in the 4th or 5th.

❺ Dominus Flevit Sanctuary

Mount of Olives. **Map** 2 F4.
Tel (02) 626 6450. **Open** 8–11:45am & 2:30–5pm daily.

Its name meaning "The Lord Wept", this chapel stands where medieval pilgrims identified a rock as the one on which Jesus sat when he wept over the fate of Jerusalem. The chapel was designed in the shape of a teardrop by Italian architect Antonio Barluzzi and built in 1955 over a 7th-century chapel. Part of the original apse is preserved in the new one. The view of the Dome of the Rock from the altar window is justly famous. A mosaic floor preserved in situ outside is from a 5th-century monastery. The graves on view nearby

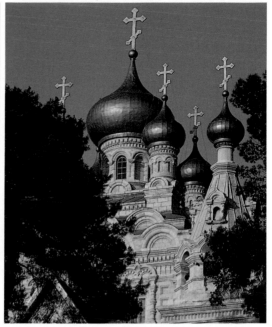

Russian Church of St Mary Magdalene, built in Muscovite style

show the types found in the 1950s in a vast cemetery here, in use periodically from 1600 BC to AD 70. Also on show are some carved stone ossuaries.

❻ Church of St Mary Magdalene

Mount of Olives. **Map** 2 F4.
Tel (02) 628 4371. 99.
Open 10am–noon Tue & Thu.

In 1885, Tsar Alexander III had this Russian Orthodox church built in memory of his mother, Maria Alexandrovna. It is pleasantly set among

trees, and the seven gilded onion domes are among the most striking features of Jerusalem's skyline when viewed from the Old City. The domes and other architectural and decorative features are in 16th- to 17th-century Muscovite style.

The church was consecrated in 1888 in the presence of Grand Duke Sergei Alexandrovich (Tsar Alexander III's brother) and his wife, Grand Duchess Elizabeth Feodorovna. In 1920, after her murder during the Russian Revolution, her remains were buried here.

The Russians in Jerusalem

Russia's Christians belong to the Eastern Orthodox Church, the centre of which was once Constantinople. In the 19th century, when the European powers were competing to stake their claims on pieces of the crumbling Ottoman Empire, the Russians thus presented themselves as the successors to the Byzantine Empire and the true "defenders of Christianity and the Holy Places". At this time some 200,000 Russian pilgrims

Russian Orthodox nuns embroidering vestments, Church of the Ascension

were visiting Jerusalem each year. The Russian government purchased land on a grand scale, notably on the Mount of Olives and just west of the Old City, where they built a great cathedral, a consulate, a hospital and several hospices, all enclosed in a walled compound *(see p120)*. In World War I Britain captured Jerusalem and confiscated all Russian property as "enemy institutions". Some White (Tsarist) Russians did remain after the war.

Mosaic-decorated, vaulted ceiling in the Basilica of the Agony

❼ Basilica of the Agony

Jericho Rd. **Map** 2 E3. **Tel** (02) 626 6444. 🚍 99. **Open** 8am–noon & 2–5pm (summer: 6pm) daily.

The Basilica of the Agony, also known as the Church of All Nations, was named for the rock in the Garden of Gethsemane on which it is believed Christ prayed the night before he was arrested.

The 4th-century church built here was destroyed in an earthquake in 747. The Crusaders built a new one, aligned differently to cover three outcrops of rock, recalling Christ's three prayers during the night. It was consecrated in 1170, but fell into disuse after 1345.

After excavation of the site in the early 20th century, the present church was designed by Antonio Barluzzi and built in 1924 with financial contributions from 12 nations – hence the church's other name and its 12 domes decorated with national coats of arms. In the centre of the nave is the rock of the Byzantine church, surrounded by a wrought-iron crown of thorns. The mosaic in the apse represents Christ's agony, while others depicting his arrest and Judas's kiss are at the sides. The plan of the Byzantine church is traced in black marble on the floor, and sections of Byzantine mosaic pavement can also be seen.

Outside, the gilded mosaic scene decorating the pediment also depicts the Agony. Next to the church is the surviving part of the Garden of Gethsemane, with its centuries-old olive trees.

❽ Tomb of the Virgin

Jericho Rd. **Map** 2 E3. **Tel** (02) 628 4054. 🚍 99. **Open** 6am–12:30pm & 2:30–6pm daily. Cave of Gethsemane: **Open** 6am–12:30pm & 2–6pm daily.

Believed to be where the Disciples entombed the Virgin Mary, this underground sanctuary in the Valley of Jehoshaphat is one of the most intimate and mystical holy places in Jerusalem. The façade, the impressive flight of 47 steps

The 12th-century entrance to the atmospheric Tomb of the Virgin

and the royal Christian tombs in side niches halfway down, all date from the 12th century. The tomb on the right, going down, was originally the burial place of Queen Melisande of Jerusalem, who died in 1161. Her remains were moved into the crypt in the 14th century and the tomb has been venerated since about that time as that of St Anne and St Joachim, Mary's parents.

The first tomb was cut in the hillside here in the 1st century AD. The cruciform crypt as seen today, much of it cut into solid rock, is Byzantine. By the 5th century, an upper chapel had also been built. This was destroyed by the Persians in 614, rebuilt by the Crusaders, but again destroyed by Saladin in 1187. He left the crypt, however, largely intact.

The Tomb of Mary stands in the eastern branch of the crypt, which is decorated with icons and sacred ornaments typical of Orthodox Christian tradition. Today, religious services are held here by Greek, Armenian, Coptic and Syrian Christians.

In the southwestern wall beside the Tomb of Mary is a mihrab installed after Saladin's conquest. The place was sanctified by Muslims because, according to the 15th-century scholar Mujir al-Din, Muhammad saw a light over the tomb of his "sister Mary" during his Night Journey to Jerusalem *(see p31)*. In the opposite wall, a 1st-century tomb is evidence of the site's earliest use for burials.

Outside, to the right of the façade, is the **Cave of Gethsemane**, or Cave of the Betrayal, the traditional place of Judas's betrayal. It was once used for oil pressing, but fragments of 4th- to 5th-century

The Basilica of the Agony in the Garden of Gethsemane

The Tomb of Bnei Hezir (left) and the pyramid-roofed Tomb of Zechariah in the Valley of Jehoshaphat

mosaics bear witness to its transformation into a place of worship. The stars on the vaults were painted in Crusader times.

❾ Valley of Jehoshaphat

Map 2 E3.

The Kidron Valley separates the Old City from the Mount of Olives. Near Gethsemane the valley is also known by its Old Testament name, the Valley of Jehoshaphat (meaning "Yahweh judges", Yahweh being the Hebrew name for God), where it was believed the dead would be resurrected on the Day of Judgment (Joel 3: 1–17). For this reason, the valley sides are densely covered with Christian, Jewish and Muslim cemeteries.

At the southern end are several Jewish rock-hewn tombs of the 1st and 2nd centuries BC. Four are particularly fine. Absalom's Tomb, like an inverted funnel, was ascribed in medieval times to King David's rebellious son, Absalom. The so-called Tomb of Jehoshaphat (the 9th century-BC king of Judah) behind it has a carved frieze above the doorway. The pyramid topped Tomb of Zechariah is actually the above-ground monument of the adjacent Tomb of Bnei Hezir. The latter has a rectangular opening with two Doric columns and was identified by an inscription referring to the "sons of Hezir", a Jewish priestly family.

❿ City of David

Maalot Ir David. **Map** 2 D4. **Tel** (02) 626 8700. **Open** winter: 8am–5pm Sun–Thu, 8am–2pm Fri & holiday eves; summer: 8am–7pm Sun–Thu, 8am–4pm Fri & holiday eves. Last adm: 2 hrs before closing. 🗺 📷 phone for times. 🌐 **cityofdavid.org.il**

South of the Temple Mount (Haram esh-Sharif) a rocky ridge runs beside the Kidron Valley. Its summit was already settled by the Jebusites, a Canaanite (see p45) people, in the 20th century BC, making this the oldest part of Jerusalem. It was from them that David supposedly took the city for his capital in about 1000 BC (2 Samuel 5: 6–17).

On the site are remains of buildings up to the city's capture by the Babylonians in 586 BC. They include 13th-century-BC walls belonging to the Jebusite acropolis, fragments of a palace attributed to David and houses burned in the Babylonian attack. About 100 m (330 ft) from the entrance to the acropolis

The Pool of Siloam, which stored the City of David's water supply

excavations is **Warren's Shaft**, named after Charles Warren, its 19th-century English discoverer. A sloping tunnel, reached by spiral stairs, leads to the vertical shaft, at the bottom of which is a pool fed by the Gihon Spring. The system was built by the Jebusites to ensure a water supply during sieges. Nearby is their 18th-century-BC city wall, identified by the large, uncut stone blocks used in its construction. It was sited to bring the entrance to Warren's Shaft within the confines of the city.

In the 10th century BC a tunnel, later attributed to Solomon, was dug to take water from the Gihon Spring to fields in the Kidron Valley. In the face of Assyrian invasion in about 700 BC, King Hezekiah had a new tunnel built to bring the spring water right into the city, so concealing the source of the supply. **Hezekiah's Tunnel** ran 533 m (1,750 ft) from the spring to a large, new storage pool – the Pool of Siloam – in the south of the city. Not far from the Siloam end an inscription, carved by the engineer, describes the tunnel's construction. The pool is now smaller than it was originally and was rebuilt after the Romans sacked Jerusalem in AD 70 and burned it "as far as Siloam", as told by contemporary historian Flavius Josephus.

Visitors can wade through the tunnel in thigh-deep water from the Gihon Spring – wear shoes and bring a flashlight.

The beautifully painted interior of St Peter in Gallicantu

⓫ St Peter in Gallicantu

Malki Tsedek Rd. **Map** 2 D5. **Tel** (02) 673 4812. 🚍 38. **Open** 8:30am–5pm Mon–Sat. 🚻 🅿

Standing to the east of Mount Zion, on the slopes overlooking the City of David *(see p119)* and the Kidron Valley, this church commemorates the traditional site of St Peter's reported denial of Christ which fulfilled the prophecy, "Before the cock crows twice, thou shalt deny me thrice" (Mark 14: 72). Built in 1931, the church has a modern appearance. In the crypt, however, are ancient caves where, it is said, Christ spent the night before being taken to Pontius Pilate. The remains of some Herodian architecture have been discovered under the church and, in the garden, there still exists part of a Hasmonean stairway, which was in use in Christ's time and once connected the city with the Kidron Valley. Mosaics from a previous 5th- to 6th-century Byzantine church and monastery have also been unearthed.

⓬ Mount Zion

Map 1 C5. 🚍 1, 2.

A short walk from Zion Gate is the hill synonymous with biblical Jerusalem and the Promised Land. Believed by many to be the site of King David's tomb and associated with the final days of Christ,

Mount Zion is revered by Jews, Muslims and Christians alike.

The hill is bounded to the east by the Kidron Valley, to the south and west by the Hinnom Valley, and to the north by the city walls. This makes it seem like an island outside the confines of the Old City. This was not always the case, however, for on the Madaba mosaic map in Jordan *(see pp220–21)* it is shown inside the walls. It appears to have been excluded in 1542 when the walls were rebuilt. Legend has it that Suleyman the Magnificent's architects left it outside by mistake.

Christians began assembling here some time after Christ's death to worship in the Hall of the Last Supper and later at the stone where the Virgin Mary is said to have died. Now the site of the Church of the Dormition, this point marked the ceasefire border from 1949 to 1967 *(see p58)*.

⓭ Church of the Dormition

Mount Zion. **Map** 1 C5. **Tel** (02) 565 5330. 🚍 38, 20. **Open** 8:30am–5pm Mon–Sat, 11:30am–5pm Sun (closed noon–1pm for prayer). 🚻

Crowned by a tall bell tower and a dome with four small corner turrets, the Neo-Romanesque Church of the Dormition dominates the Mount Zion hilltop. The large, airy, white-stone church stands on the site where the Virgin Mary is said to have fallen into an "eternal sleep". After Christ's death, according to Christian tradition, his mother went to live on Mount Zion until she herself died.

The hill soon became a holy site, available information suggesting that there may have been a church here as early as the 4th century AD. It is known with more certainty that around the 6th century a large basilica was built on the site, which later fell into ruins. When the Crusaders came, they too erected a church with chapels devoted to the Dormition of the Virgin and the Last Supper.

The present-day church, which includes the Chapel of the Dormition and Dormition Abbey, was built in the early 20th century for Kaiser Wilhelm II and was inspired by the Carolingian cathedral in Aachen, Germany.

During the 1948 and 1967 wars the church was used as a strategic outpost by Israeli soldiers and was damaged in the crossfire of several battles. The main part of the church boasts a fine mosaic floor

The conical dome and bell tower of the Church of the Dormition

The Crusader-built Hall of the Last Supper, with fine Gothic details

featuring zodiac symbols and the names of saints and prophets. In the crypt is a wood and ivory sculpture of the "sleeping" Virgin, while the walls are adorned with images of women from the Old Testament, including Eve, Judith, Ruth and Esther. In the rooms on the mezzanine are some of the remains from the site's previous churches.

⓮ Hall of the Last Supper

Mount Zion. **Map** 1 C5.
Open 8am–6pm daily.

On the first floor of a Gothic building – all that remains of the large church constructed by the Crusaders to commemorate Mary's Dormition and over-shadowed slightly by the more recent Church of the Dormition – is the Hall of the Last Supper, or Coenaculum. Christian tradition maintains that it is on the site of Christ's last meal with his Disciples. The room is unadorned apart from the Gothic arches dividing it.

In the Middle Ages it became part of the adjacent Franciscan monastery, while in the 15th century it was turned into a mosque by the Turks, who added a mihrab and some stained-glass windows.

⓯ King David's Tomb

Mount Zion. **Map** 1 C5. **Tel** (02) 671 9767. 🚌 1, 2, 3, 38. **Open** 8am–9pm Sat–Thu & hols, 8am–2pm (winter: 1pm) Fri. 🕎 Sat.

Beneath the Hall of the Last Supper, on the lower floor of the Crusader building, are some small chambers venerated as King David's Tomb. The main chamber is bare apart from a cenotaph covered by a drape. The site was first identified as David's tomb in the 11th century AD, and in the 15th century was incorporated into a mosque by the Muslims, who consider David one of the true prophets. In spite of doubts about the tomb's authenticity, it is one of the most revered

Jewish holy sites. It was particularly so between 1948 and 1967, when the Old City was under Jordanian control. As the Western Wall was inaccessible to Jews, they came here to pray. Today the entrance hall is still used as a synagogue, where there is separate seating for men and women. From the 4th to the 15th centuries, the tomb was associated with Pentecost and the death of the Virgin and, according to tradition, it was here that Christ washed his Disciples' feet after the Last Supper (John 13: 1–17).

⓰ Schindler's Tomb

Mount Zion. **Map** 1 C5. 🚌 1, 2.

Straight down the hill from Zion Gate, the path forks left past the Chamber of the Holocaust, a small museum commemorating the thousands of Jewish communities wiped out by the Nazis. Across the road at the end of the path is a Christian cemetery. It is here that the grave of German-born Oskar Schindler is located.

Schindler was an industrialist who, during World War II, went out of his way to use Jewish prisoners as labourers in his factory. By doing this, he saved over 1,000 people from the death camps. He became a symbol of the fight against the Holocaust and before he died, in 1974, he asked to be buried in Jerusalem. The story of his courageous stand against the Nazis was told in Steven Spielberg's successful 1993 movie, *Schindler's List*.

Schindler's tomb in the Christian cemetery on Mount Zion

MODERN JERUSALEM

By the 1860s the Old City had become overcrowded, and the need for more space gave rise to a period of unrestricted building activity outside the walls. The earliest developments, such as Yemin Moshe, Nakhalat Shiva and Mea Shearim, were Jewish community projects or, like the Russian Compound, intended to cater

for Holy Land pilgrims. The architecture of the New City became increasingly eclectic as colonial builders imported their own national styles. As a result, exotic features such as Muscovite domes and Florentine towers form the backdrop to the equally multicultural bustle on the streets of the modern city.

Sights at a Glance

Historic Districts
④ Ben Yehuda and Nakhalat Shiva
❽ Russian Compound
❾ Ha-Neviim Street
⓫ Mea Shearim

Holy Places
❺ Italian Synagogue
⓮ St Etienne Monastery
⓯ St George's Cathedral

Tombs
⓭ Garden Tomb
⓰ Kings' Tombs

Museums and Historic Buildings
❶ YMCA
❷ King David Hotel
❸ Jerusalem Time Elevator
❻ Ticho House
❼ City Hall
❿ Italian Hospital
⓱ American Colony Hotel
⓲ Rockefeller Museum

Archaeological Site
⓬ Solomon's Quarries

☐ Restaurants *pp270–71*
1 Adom
2 Arabesque
3 Cavelier
4 Chakra
5 Darna
6 Dolphin Yam
7 The Garden Restaurant
8 Lavan
9 Link
10 Little Jerusalem
11 Mona
12 Philadelphia
13 Rooftop at Mamilla
14 Sakura
15 Te'enim
16 Tmol Shilshom
17 Village Green

See also Jerusalem Street Finder, map 1

0 metres	500
0 yards	500

◀ The charming houses in Yemin Moshe in Modern Jerusalem

For map symbols *see back flap*

Street-by-Street: Yemin Moshe

Sir Moses Montefiore, a rich British Jewish philanthropist, was so shocked by the living conditions in the squalid Old City that he decided to improve the Jews' lot by building new homes outside the walls. The first project was Mishkenot Shaananim ("Dwellings of Tranquillity"), a communal block of 16 apartments, completed in 1860. Initially, people were afraid to move outside the security of the walls because of bandits, but by the end of the century a small community called Yemin Moshe had been established nearby and was thriving. From this core, the vast spread of modern Jerusalem has grown. Yemin Moshe survives as its beautifully renovated historic heart.

Public Sculptures
Outdoor sculptures, such as these buried cubes, are found all around Yemin Moshe.

Jaffa Road

❶ ★ YMCA
Even if a room is beyond your budget, as one of Jerusalem's most elegant and beautiful buildings, both inside and out, the YMCA is well worth looking around.

ABA SIKRA

KING DAVID STREET (DAVID HA-MELEKH)

KING DAVID HOTEL

BLOOMFIEL

KING DAVID STREET (DA

❷ King David Hotel
Still the premier hotel in Jerusalem, and all Israel, the King David has been hosting royalty, politicians and international celebrities since it first opened its doors in the 1930s.

Key

— Suggested route

| 0 metres | 100 |
| 0 yards | 100 |

Herod's Family Tomb
The splendour of this 1st-century-BC tomb, discovered in 1892, suggests that it may be that of Herod's family. The king himself was supposedly buried at the Herodion *(see p196)*.

For hotels and restaurants in this area see p260 and pp270–71

★ **Yemin Moshe**
Built on the slope of the valley facing the Old City walls, these early, attractive Oriental-style houses are now some of the most sought-after and exclusive residences in all Jerusalem.

Locator Map
See Jerusalem Street Finder, map 1

★ **Montefiore's Windmill**
Montefiore meant Mishkenot Shaananim to be self-sufficient, hence a windmill to grind the settlement's own flour. Unfortunately, there was rarely enough wind to turn the sails.

Mishkenot Shaananim
In the earliest days, lodging in this block had to be offered rent-free in order to attract tenants. Now the place serves as a guesthouse for artists and writers. Saul Bellow, Marc Chagall and Simone de Beauvoir have all been accommodated here.

Bloomfield Gardens
Grassy parks fringe Yemin Moshe. Attractive in their own right, and dotted with ornament, such as the Lion Fountain *(right)*, the parks also afford great views across the valley to the Old City.

❶ YMCA

26 King David St. **Map** 1 A4. **Tel** (02) 569 2692. 🚌 7, 8, 30, 38. Tower: **Open** 8am–8pm daily. 🅿️

Built in 1926–33 by Arthur Loomis Harmon, who also created New York's Empire State Building, Jerusalem's YMCA is one of the city's best-known landmarks. It consists of three sections – the central body, dominated by a bell tower offering extraordinary views of the city, and the two side wings. The stone and wrought-iron decorative elements on the outside of the building, including the 5-m (16.5-ft) bas-relief of one of the six-winged seraphim described in the Old Testament (Isaiah 6: 2–3), reflect a stylized form of Oriental Byzantine design, combined with elements of Romanesque and Islamic art.

Yet the exterior, splendid as it is, does not prepare the visitor for the fabulously elaborate decor on the inside. Here design elements from three different cultures are woven through with symbols from the three main monotheistic religions. In the concert hall, the dome's 12 windows represent the 12 Tribes of Israel, the 12 Disciples of Christ and the 12 Followers of Muhammad, while depicted on the chandelier are the Cross, Crescent and Star of David. The entire decor has a kind of Art Deco gloss, while the ethos of its eclectic design is one of peace and tolerance between faiths and cultures.

Inside the elegant lobby of the King David Hotel

The distinctive high-domed bell tower of Jerusalem's YMCA

❷ King David Hotel

23 King David St. **Map** 1 B4. **Tel** (02) 620 8888. 🚌 7, 8, 30, 38.

Eye-catching not least for its pink stone walls and green windows, this impressive 1930s hotel (see p260) is a grandiose display of colonial architecture. It was designed by Swiss architect Emile Vogt for the Jewish-Egyptian Mosseri family. Inside, the spacious lobbies and exotic public areas, with their period wooden furnishings and discreet motifs, reflect a sense of splendour from an altogether different era. The richly ornamental style includes Egyptian, Phoenician, Assyrian and Greek elements, as well as aspects of Islamic art. The hotel boasts an impressive list of former guests, including Winston Churchill and Haile Selassie, and for a long time, part of the British Mandate administration (see p56) was housed here. In 1946 it was the target of a bomb attack perpetrated by the Zionist paramilitary terrorist group Irgun, led by Menachem Begin (see p57). It was rebuilt and the two top floors were added later. Nearby is the Alrov Mamilla complex, with a number of exclusive shops, cafés and restaurants.

❸ Jerusalem Time Elevator

Beit Agron, 37 Hillel St. **Map** 1 A3. **Tel** (02) 624 8381. **Open** 10am–5pm Sun–Thu, 10am–2pm Fri, noon–6pm Sat. 🅿️ 🌐 time-elevator.co.il

On the southern edge of the neighbourhood of Nakhalat Shiva, this is a theme-park-style ride through 3,000 years of Jerusalem's often-turbulent history. The audience is belted into their seats and given surround-sound headphones for an audio-visual journey enhanced by computer-generated animation and other special effects.

It begins in the times of King David and Solomon, and rattles through dramatic highlights of conquest, destruction, earthquake and fire, ending with the Six-Day War of 1967 and reunification.

The special "motion" seats jolt and sway through the experience, which culminates in an "aerial" ride over the Jerusalem of today. The ride lasts about 30 minutes, with shows at 40-minute

The square-set form of the King David Hotel, the choice of many rich and famous visitors to Jerusalem

For hotels and restaurants in this area see p260 and pp270–71

The Italian Synagogue and Museum of Italian-Jewish Art in a quiet square

intervals, and it is a useful introduction to the city's complicated chronology. The Time Elevator ride is not recommended if you do not enjoy rollercoasters.

One of the popular streetside cafés and restaurants in Ben Yehuda

❹ Ben Yehuda and Nakhalat Shiva

Map 1 A3. 🚍 20, 23, 27.

At the heart of modern Jerusalem are the pedestrianized precincts of Ben Yehuda Street and Nakhalat Shiva. They constitute one of the liveliest parts of the city, with shops, restaurants, street vendors and musicians coming together to create a rich and varied atmosphere. In the minds of local people, Ben Yehuda Street and Nakhalat Shiva are the embodiment of secular Jerusalem. The contrast with the Orthodox city, just a short distance to the north in Mea Shearim *(see p129)*, is clear.

Ben Yehuda Street was built in the 1920s, and has since been the traditional meeting place for Jewish intellectuals, politicians and journalists. South of Ben Yehuda Street is a series of narrow lanes, with low houses and connecting courtyards. These are collectively known

as Nakhalat Shiva, meaning "the Domain of the Seven", which refers to the seven families who built them. Dating back to 1869, this area was the third Jewish residential quarter to appear outside the Old City walls. Despite being threatened with demolition on more than one occasion, the area was finally renovated in the 1980s. Today it is filled with shops, workshops, bars, restaurants and cafés, and is invariably busy until the early hours.

Other streets in this locality also have much to interest the visitor. Buildings of varied architectural styles reflect the diverse cultural influences that have shaped the city.

❺ Italian Synagogue

27 Hillel St. **Map** 1 A3. **Tel** (02) 624 1610. 🚍 18, 21, 22, 30 **Open** 10am–5pm Sun, Tue & Wed, noon–9pm Thu, 10am–1pm Fri. **Closed** Mon, Sat & Jewish hols. 🅿 ♿
🅦 ijamuseum.org

Originally a German college constructed in the late 19th century, this building now houses an 18th-century synagogue from Conegliano Veneto, near Venice in Italy. In 1952, with no more Jews living there, the synagogue had fallen into disuse. It was decided to dismantle the interior and bring it here. It is arguably the most beautiful synagogue in Israel, and on Saturdays and Jewish holidays the Italian-Jewish community worships here. The building also houses

the Museum of Italian-Jewish Art, which has some fascinating items, such as medieval ritual objects. On the lower floor is the Centre of Studies on Italian Judaism and a library on the same subject.

❻ Ticho House

9 Ha-Rav Kook St. **Map** 1 A2. **Tel** (02) 624 4186. 🚍 13, 18, 20. Museum: **Open** 10am–5pm Sun, Mon, Wed & Thu, 10am–10pm Tue, 10am–2pm Fri. **Closed** Jewish hols. 🅿

Built in the 19th century as the luxurious residence of a wealthy Jerusalem family, this is one of the city's loveliest examples of an Arab mansion. Its large central drawing room is the focal point of both the architecture and the social life of the building. In the early 20th century the house was bought by Dr Abraham Ticho, a famous Jewish ophthalmologist who used to give the poor free treatment, irrespective of their ethnic origin or religion. Dr Ticho's wife, Anna, who grew up and studied in Vienna, was an artist. By day the house was a clinic and by night it was the centre of Jerusalem's social and intellectual life.

Nowadays the house is administered by the Israel Museum *(see pp136–41)*, to which Anna Ticho left more than 2,000 watercolours and drawings. Some of these are exhibited here. The house also has a charming restaurant overlooking a lovely garden.

View over the beautiful garden at the back of Ticho House

❼ City Hall

Jaffa Rd. **Map** 1 B3. **Tel** (02) 629 5363. 6, 13, 18, 20. **Open** not generally open for visitors. 10am Mon, call ahead for times Sun–Thu (in English).

Completed in 1993, the City Hall complex is sited just outside the Old City walls, where Jewish West Jerusalem meets Arab East Jerusalem. Its architecture displays an appropriate spirit of synthesis – the complex includes ten renovated historical buildings, along with two modern blocks that refer subtly to historical models (for example, the banding of different coloured stone echoes the Mameluke buildings of the Old City).

One of the renovated buildings, on Jaffa Road, is the old City Hall. It is still pocked with bullet holes from its days as a frontline Israeli army post when, between 1948 and 1967, the city was divided *(see p57)*.

❽ Russian Compound

1 Mishol Hagevura St. **Map** 1 B3. 13, 18, 20. Underground Prisoners' Museum 1917–48: **Tel** (02) 623 3166. **Open** 9am–5pm Sun–Thu. Cathedral of the Holy Trinity: **Open** 9am–1pm Tue–Fri, 9am–noon Sat & Sun.

The Russians were some of the first people to settle outside the Old City in the 19th century *(see p117)*. The process began around 1860 when a few acres of land were acquired a short distance outside the city walls. The Russians built a self-contained compound to provide lodgings for the city's growing number of Russian

City Hall, seen through the palms of Safra Square

pilgrims, and erected a cathedral for services. Consecrated in 1864, the **Cathedral of the Holy Trinity** is fashioned in an unmistakably Muscovite style, with eight drums topped by green domes. Across the plaza, under a pavement grille, is what is known as Herod's Column, a 12-m (40-ft) stone pillar, which historians believe is from the Byzantine period or was intended for the Second Temple before it cracked and was abandoned.

These days the Russians own only the cathedral, as many of the other buildings belonging to the compound were sold off by the Soviet Union in exchange for shipments of Israeli oranges. The building with the crenellated tower – the grandest of the former pilgrims' hostels – is now home to the Agriculture Ministry. The street on which it stands, Heleni ha-Malka, is one of the city's nightlife centres, filled with bars and cafés. The former women's hostel, behind the cathedral, now

Royal lion above the door, Ethiopian Church

houses the **Underground Prisoners' Museum 1917–48**, which is dedicated to Jewish underground movements, some members of which were jailed here during the British Mandate *(see pp56–7)*.

❾ Ha-Neviim Street

Map 1 B2. 1.

One of the oldest streets outside the Old City, Ha-Neviim (Street of the Prophets) marks the dividing line between the religious and secular halves of modern Jerusalem (ultra-Orthodox Mea Shearim lies just to the north; the drinking and dining scene of the Russian Compound is to the south). Once a prestigious address, Ha-Neviim is lined with some grand buildings. At No. 58 is Thabor House, the self-designed home of Conrad Schick, a German who arrived in the Holy Land a Protestant missionary and became the city's most renowned architect of the late 19th century. The house now belongs to the Swedish Theological Institute, but visitors can admire the eccentric fortress-like main gate. Someone will usually answer the bell and admit the curious into the courtyard to admire the building's façade, complete with embedded archaeological finds.

A few steps west at No. 64 is the house once occupied by the Victorian painter William Holman Hunt *(see p37)*. It is

The Cathedral of the Holy Trinity, in the Russian Compound

now a private residence and closed to the public. A couple of minutes' walk to the north, along narrow, leafy Etyopya Street, is Ben Yehuda House, named after the man responsible for reviving popular usage of the Hebrew language. This was his residence in the early years of the 20th century.

A little further up the lane is the striking, round form of the Ethiopian Church, which sits in beautifully tended gardens. It was built between 1873 and 1911 and is modelled after churches in Ethiopia, with its sanctuary clearly separated from the main body of the church. Just five minutes' walk away, back on Ha-Neviim Street, the Ethiopians also have their consulate. It is notable for a vivid blue and gold mosaic on the façade depicting the Lion of Judah.

⑩ Italian Hospital

Corner of Ha-Neviim and Shivtei Yisrael Sts. **Map** 1 B2. 🚌 1, 50. **Closed** to public.

The grandest building of all on Ha-Neviim Street is the Italian Hospital. It was built just before World War I to underscore Italian presence in the Holy City, at a time when the colonial powers were using architecture to assert their influence and status. Designed by prolific architect Antonio Barluzzi, the hospital is clearly inspired by the Palazzo Vecchio in Florence. The building now houses the Ministry of Education.

The extravagant, Renaissance-style building of the Italian Hospital

Mea Shearim, heartland of the ultra-Orthodox community

⑪ Mea Shearim

Map 1 A1. 🚌 1, 4, 71, 72.

Possibly the most unusual district in all Jerusalem, Mea Shearim is a perfectly preserved, living model of 18th-century Jewish Eastern Europe. It is a quarter inhabited exclusively by the insular ultra-Orthodox Jews, where the influence of the outside world is kept to an absolute minimum. Dress is traditional in the extreme; many men wear black stockings and long black coats, and women keep their hair covered beneath a snood. The streets either side of main Mea Shearim

Street are narrow alleyways, which squeeze between long, narrow two-storey dwellings, occasionally opening out into washing-strewn communal courtyards. The area is completely self-contained, with its own bakeries, markets, synagogues and, although no longer in use, its own huge cistern.

Mea Shearim was founded in the late 19th century and built in three stages, to a design by Conrad Schick, for Jews from Poland and Lithuania. Until well into this century the quarter was shut off from the rest of the city each night by six gates.

The gates are gone but visitors should bear in mind that this is still a very insular community. Skirts should reach below the knee, and men must not wear shorts or T-shirts. Discretion is advised when taking photographs.

Northwest of Mea Shearim is the Bukharan Quarter, founded in the late 19th century by wealthy Central Asian Jews. Traces of its former grandeur remain in some elegant, if dilapidated, mansions.

Ultra-Orthodox Jews

The life of the ultra-Orthodox (haredim) is grounded in rigorous observance of Judaic law and study of the Torah. Their lifestyle involves an uncompromising rejection of modern life and all its trappings, which means no television, no cars and minimum intrusion by technology. The ultra-Orthodox live and dress strictly according to traditions practised in Eastern Europe several centuries ago. This lifestyle means that they segregate themselves from less observant Jews. More radical factions are opposed to the common use of Hebrew, the "Holy tongue", and instead speak Yiddish; some do not recognize the State of Israel or its laws, even refusing to pay taxes. They claim that there can be no true Jewish state until the coming of the Messiah.

Ultra-Orthodox Jews dressed in everyday attire

⑫ Solomon's Quarries (Zedekiah's Cave)

Sultan Suleyman St. **Map** 4 D1.
Tel (02) 627 7550. 1. **Open** 9am–2pm Sun–Thu. **Closed** Jewish hols.

This is an enormous empty cave stretching under the Old City, with its entrance at the foot of the wall between Damascus and Herod's gates. Despite the popular name, historians are not convinced that the cave has any connection with Solomon, but it is likely that Herod took stone from here for his many building projects, including his modification of the Second Temple.

The quarry is also known as Zedekiah's Cave, after the last king of Judaea who, legend has it, hid here during the Babylonian conquest of Jerusalem in 586 BC.

⑬ Garden Tomb

Conrad Schick St. **Map** 3 C1.
Tel (02) 627 2745. 1, 3.
Open 8:30am–noon & 2–5:30pm Mon–Sat. **W** gardentomb.org

Towards the end of the 19th century, the British general Charles Gordon, of Khartoum fame, was visiting Jerusalem and started a dispute among archaeologists. He argued that this skull-shaped hill was the Golgotha referred to in the New Testament (Mark 15: 22) and that the real burial site of Jesus Christ was here and not at

The simple Neo-Romanesque chapel at St Etienne Monastery

Tourists visiting the ancient Garden Tomb in its attractive setting

the Holy Sepulchre (see pp96–9). Excavations carried out in 1883 did in fact unearth some ancient tombs, but further study found them to date back to the 9th–7th century BC, with an entirely different configuration from those in use in Christ's time. However, regardless of its authenticity, this place is well worth a visit, if only for the lovely garden.

⑭ St Etienne Monastery

Nablus Rd. **Map** 1 C2. **Tel** (02) 626 4468. 23. **Open** 8am–noon & 12:30–6pm Mon–Sat.

The name of this site relates to the belief that in AD 439 Cyril of Alexandria interred the remains of St Stephen (St Etienne in French), the first Christian martyr, in a basilica built on this spot. The basilica was destroyed by the Persians in AD 614, and a subsequent 7th-century chapel on the same site was also destroyed, this time by the Crusaders holding Jerusalem, who feared Saladin would use it as a base for assaults on the city.

The present monastery was built between 1891 and 1901 by the French Dominicans. Its eclectic design includes an Oriental tower, Romanesque walls and Neo-Gothic flying buttresses. Within are remains of the mosaic floor of the original Byzantine church, as well as the Ecole Biblique, the Holy Land's first school of biblical archaeology.

⑮ St George's Cathedral

30 Nablus Rd. **Map** 1 C1. **Tel** (02) 627 1670. 6, 23. **Open** not generally open for visitors so call first.

This Archetypal Middle England church, with its pretty, cloistered courtyard and connotations of vicars, tweeds and cucumber sandwiches, stands in startling contrast to the chaotic Arab streets of its East Jerusalem neighbourhood.

The cathedral dates from 1910 and is named for the patron saint of England, who was actually a Palestinian conscript in the Roman army, executed in AD 303 for tearing up a copy of the emperor Diocletian's decree forbidding Christianity. He is supposedly buried at Lod (ancient Lydda), now better known as the site of Ben Gurion airport.

In World War I the cathedral was the local headquarters of the Turkish army, and the 1917 truce sanctioning British presence in Palestine was signed in the bishop's quarters.

St George's Cathedral, part of Jerusalem's colonial heritage

🄰 Kings' Tombs

Salah al-Din St. **Map** 1 C1. 🚌 23.
Open currently closed. 🏛

Despite the name, this single but elaborate tomb is thought to have been that of Queen Helena of Adiabene. In the 1st century AD she converted to Judaism and moved to Jerusalem from her kingdom in Mesopotamia. The tomb was named by early explorers who believed that the magnificent tomb housed members of the dynasty of David. A small entrance, an easily missed, plain door in a wall, leads down into a dimly lit maze of chambers with stone doors.

The tomb is currently closed to the public.

Well-worn steps leading to the deceptively named Kings' Tombs

🄱 American Colony Hotel

23 Nablus Rd. **Map** 1 C1.
Tel (02) 627 9777. 🚌 23.

This elegant hotel (see p260), built in 1865–76, has long been a favourite of diplomats and journalists. It started life as the home of a rich Turkish merchant. The name American Colony came about in the late 19th century, when Anna and Horatio Spafford of Chicago bought the building and made it the centre of an American religious community dedicated to good works. When the community broke up in the early 20th century, a Baron Ustinov, related to the actor Peter Ustinov, suggested converting the building to accommodate pilgrims to the Holy Land. Soon after, it was

The central courtyard of the Rockefeller Museum, designed by Austin Harrison

turned into a beautiful hotel, which it remains today. If you cannot afford to stay here, it is definitely worth coming for lunch, taken out in the tree-shaded courtyard.

🄲 Rockefeller Museum

27 Sultan Suleyman St. **Map** 2 D2.
Tel (02) 628 2251. 🚌 1, 2
Open 10am–3pm Mon, Wed, Thu & Sun, 10am–2pm Sat. ♿ 🌐 **english. imjnet.org.il/page_1684**

This museum was made possible by a substantial financial gift made in 1927 by the American oil magnate John D Rockefeller. British architect Austin Harrison designed the building along Neo-Gothic lines. It is vaguely reminiscent of the Alhambra in Spain and runs around a central courtyard. Constructed from the white stone typical of Jerusalem buildings, the Rockefeller has Byzantine- and Islamic-type decorative motifs. It was once one of the most important museums in the Middle East and the first to make a systematic collection of finds from the Holy Land. These days, it is a branch of the Israel Museum (see pp136–41), but still houses a very impressive collection.

Among its many remarkable objects are the stuccowork from Hisham's Palace in Jericho, beams from the Holy Sepulchre church and wooden panels from El-Aqsa mosque. Other exhibits worth seeing include a fascinating portrait modelled on an 8,000-year-old cranium discovered in Jericho; a lovely Bronze Age bull's head; a Canaanite vase in the shape of a human head; sculptures from the time of the Crusades; and Hellenistic and Roman objects found in Judaean Desert caves.

The delightfully secluded courtyard of the American Colony Hotel

FURTHER AFIELD

Since the creation of the state of Israel in 1948, the boundaries of Jerusalem have greatly expanded in all directions. The city has also been endowed with many significant modern buildings. Two stand out as being of particular importance: the Israel Museum, a world-class institution that incorporates several collections of priceless treasures, including the famous Dead Sea Scrolls; and the Knesset, the seat of national government.

Another cornerstone in the psyche of Israeli society is Yad Vashem, the moving – and, in parts, harrowing – memorial complex that honours the more than six million Jews who died at the hands of the Nazis during the Holocaust. The site of this memorial is Mount Herzl, named after Theodor Herzl, the founding father of Zionism *(see p55)*. The grassy slopes here are also home to an extensive military cemetery, in which many figures of national importance are buried.

As Jerusalem has expanded, what, not too long ago, were small, isolated villages are now virtually suburbs of the city. They have not, however, lost their character. Places such as Ein Kerem, nestled in the valley below Mount Herzl, and Abu Ghosh, further to the northwest, have a great deal of rural charm, as well as several attractive religious buildings linked with biblical events.

Sights at a Glance

Museums
1 LA Mayer Museum of Islamic Art
3 *The Israel Museum, Jerusalem pp136–41*
4 Bible Lands Museum
8 Biblical Zoo
10 Mount Herzl and Herzl Museum

Memorials
9 Yad Vashem

Holy Places
2 Monastery of the Cross

Modern Buildings
6 Knesset
5 Supreme Court

Districts
7 Mahane Yehuda and Nakhlaot
12 Hadassah Hospital Synagogue

Towns and Villages
11 Ein Kerem
13 Abu Ghosh

Key
- Major sightseeing area
- Motorway
- Motorway under construction
- Major road
- Minor road

0 kilometres 2
0 miles 2

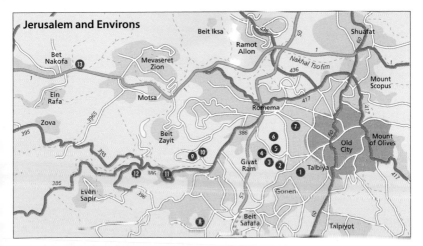

Jerusalem and Environs

Beit Iksa · Shuafat · Ramot Allon · Nakhal Tsofim · Bet Nakofa 13 · Mevaseret Zion · Mount Scopus · Ein Rafa · Motsa · Zova · Romema · Beit Zayit · Mount of Olives · 9 10 · 6 · 7 · Old City · Givat Ram 3 5 2 · Talbiya · 1 · 12 11 · Gonen · Even Sapir · 8 · Beit Safafa · Talpiyot

Yad Vashem, established in 1953 as a memorial to the Jewish victims of the Holocaust

The refectory at the 11th-century Monastery of the Cross

❶ LA Mayer Museum of Islamic Art

2 Ha-Palmakh St, Talbiya. **Tel** (02) 566 1292. 🚌 13. **Open** 10am–3pm Mon, Wed & Sun, 10am–7pm Tue & Thu, 10am–2pm Fri, 10am–4pm Sat. 🅿 🅲 🌐 **islamicart.co.il**

While the cream of Islamic artifacts collected in the Holy Land are to be found in the Rockefeller Museum (see p131) and the Museum of Islamic Art on the Haram esh-Sharif (see p74), this modern, purpose-built museum offers a beautifully presented collection of pieces from the greater Islamic world. There are especially attractive examples of Persian tiling and Indian Mughal miniatures, plus an Arabic calligraphy section.

❷ Monastery of the Cross

Shalom St, Neve Granot. **Tel** (052) 221 5144. 🚌 32. **Open** 10am–4:30pm Mon–Sat. 🅿 🅴

Stranded in the middle of a large area of scrubland, ringed at its outer perimeters by main roads and modern buildings, this solitary Byzantine monastery has the look of a place that time forgot and urban planners ignored. Its high, buttressed walls emphasize still more its seclusion and reflect its once precarious position outside the Old City.

There was a church here in the 5th century, but it was destroyed by the Persians in 614. Part of its mosaic floor can still be seen on one side of the main altar in the present church. The monastery which exists today was built in the 11th century by monks from Mount Athos, with financial backing from King Bagrat of Georgia. According to tradition, it marks the spot where the tree grew that was used to make Christ's cross.

In the 13th century the Georgian poet Shota Rustaveli lived here and commissioned the frescoes in the main church. They were repainted in the 17th century respecting the original style.

By the 14th century the monastery had become the centre of Jerusalem's Georgian community and a major centre of Georgian culture in the region. Gradually, however, their standing declined and, by 1685, the monastery had been taken over by the Greek Orthodox Patriarchate.

The church is largely in its original, 11th-century form, while many other parts of the complex have been altered or added to. The court-yard and the late Baroque bell tower display clear signs of 19th-century changes. In the late 1990s large-scale restoration was undertaken. The simple dome is one of the church's most beautiful features. Also remarkable are the frescoes, which show an unusual combination of Christian, pagan and worldly images. Visitors are permitted to wander freely around the complex. Particularly evocative of monastic life are the refectory on the upper floor and the kitchen.

❸ Israel Museum

See pp136–41.

❹ Bible Lands Museum

25 Avraham Granot St, Givat Ram. **Tel** (02) 561 1066. 🚌 9, 17, 24, 99. **Open** 9:30am–5:30pm Sun–Tue & Thu, 9:30am–9:30pm Wed, 10am–2pm Fri, Sat & eves of Jewish hols. **Closed** Jewish hols. 🅿 🅴 🅾 🖵 🗨 🎥 English-speaking guides available. 🌐 **blmj.org**

Babylonian tablet, Bible Lands Museum

Opposite the Israel Museum is this rather unremarkable building, which houses an outstanding collection of archaeological finds that reflect the different cultures of the Holy Land region in biblical times. The museum was inaugurated in 1992 with the private collection of Elie Borowski, a passionate scholar of ancient Middle Eastern civilizations. The collection features many finely crafted objects from ancient Egypt, Syria, Anatolia, Mesopotamia and Persia. Among these are a great number of artifacts that shed light on the culture of the Mesopotamian region in the

The Bible Lands Museum, covering the early history of the Middle East

millennia before the Christian era. The many fascinating objects include ancient inscriptions, jewellery, mosaics, seals, ivory carvings and scarabs.

The exhibits are displayed in a way that enables the visitor to build a clear and illuminating picture of the cultural context in which the biblical texts were written. The items are arranged according to both chronology and region. The result is a clear illustration of the way in which different cultures influenced each other and new societies evolved.

The sculpted menorah near the entrance to the Knesset

❺ Knesset

1 Kaplan, Givat Ram. **Tel** (02) 675 3333. 9, 24, 99. **Open** 8:30am–2pm Sun & Thu. compulsory (ring in advance or contact tours@knesset. gov.il to book; bring passport and dress modestly).

The Knesset (Assembly) is the seat of the Israeli Parliament. It takes its name from the Knesset ha-Gedola (Great Assembly) of 120 men that governed the political and civic life of Jews in the Second Temple period (see p46). The building, inaugurated in 1966, was designed by Joseph Klarwin. His design is inspired by the Parthenon in Athens and various reconstructions of the Temple.

Opposite the entrance is a large, seven-branched menorah (candelabrum), symbol of the State of Israel. It is the work of British sculptor Benno Elkan and was a gift from the British parliament. The relief work on its branches depicts crucial

moments in Jewish history and is accompanied by biblical quotations. Nearby is a monument with an eternal flame, commemorating the dead of the Holocaust and Israel's wars (see pp57–9).

The reception area inside the Knesset was designed and decorated by the Russian-Jewish artist Marc Chagall (see p37). It is adorned with his mosaics and a triple tapestry which depicts the creation of the world, the exodus of the Israelites from Egypt and the city of Jerusalem. The main chamber ends in a stone wall that is a very clear reference to the Western Wall (see p89).

❻ Supreme Court

Shaarei Mishpat St, Givat Ram. **Tel** (02) 675 9612. 9, 24, 99. **Open** 8:30am–2:30pm Sun–Thu. noon daily in English (groups must ring in advance to book).

In the absence of a formal constitution, Israel's Supreme Court plays a pivotal role in the lives of ordinary citizens. Its significance is reflected in the building's design – by Ram Karmi and Ada Karmi-Melamed – which manages to depict the concept of justice in architectural terms. The two copper pyramids on the roof are powerful symbols of the immutable nature of the principles of law. The long sweeping stairway seems to represent the accessibility of the law to ordinary people, and at the top it offers an all-embracing view of Jerusalem.

The Supreme Court, one of the city's architectural highlights

Motifs from the past, such as the Islamic elements in the inner courtyard and the Byzantine-era mosaic outside the entrance, recall Israel's cultural and historical influences. They are given a modern context to link the past with the present and reflect the universality of justice.

❼ Mahane Yehuda and Nakhlaot

6, 7, 8, 13, 14, 18, 21, 74, 75.

The district of Mahane Yehuda, which means Field of Judah, was built in 1929 to house Jewish immigrant workers. It is famous for its vibrant and very colourful market, selling mainly foodstuffs. During the night from Friday to Sunday, the market becomes a fashionable meeting place, with music and food. The district is also home to a large number of popular local restaurants, which specialize in Middle Eastern salads and kebabs. To the south of Mahane Yehuda is the older district of Nakhlaot. This lively, warren-like jumble of low houses and narrow alleyways is fascinating to explore.

Displays of fruit and vegetables at the market in Mahane Yehuda

❸ The Israel Museum, Jerusalem

Built in 1965 on a ridge overlooking West Jerusalem, the Israel Museum contains some of the country's finest art and archaeological finds. It was designed by Israeli architects Alfred Mansfeld and Dora Gad as a modernist reference to traditional Arab hilltop villages. A major renovation was completed in 2010, and the expanded collections include synagogue interiors and the world-famous Dead Sea Scrolls.

★ Shrine of the Book
This innovatively designed underground hall displays some of the Dead Sea Scrolls. It is the most visited part of the museum *(see pp140–41)*.

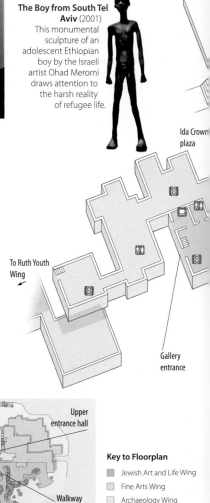

The Boy from South Tel Aviv (2001)
This monumental sculpture of an adolescent Ethiopian boy by the Israeli artist Ohad Meromi draws attention to the harsh reality of refugee life.

Ida Crown plaza

Suriname Synagogue
The Tzedek ve-Shalom Synagogue was a Neo-Classical wooden structure founded in 1736 by immigrant Jews in Paramaribo, Suriname. After it became disused, the interior was transferred to the Israel Museum.

To Ruth Youth Wing ←

★ The Nuremberg Mahzor (1331)
This massive, illuminated Hebrew prayer book contains the Ashkenazi yearly cycle of prayers, with commentaries. It also includes a rare collection of liturgical poems.

Gallery entrance

Plan of Museum

Key

- ▣ Entrance pavilion
- ▢ Main museum block
- ▣ Ruth Youth Wing for Art Education
- ▣ Billy Rose Art Garden
- ▣ Shrine of the Book
- ▢ Tour group entrance/ exit pavilion

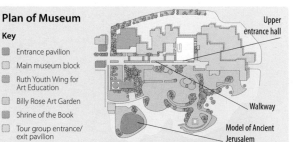

Upper entrance hall

Walkway

Model of Ancient Jerusalem

Key to Floorplan

- ▣ Jewish Art and Life Wing
- ▢ Fine Arts Wing
- ▢ Archaeology Wing
- ▢ Temporary exhibitions gallery
- ▣ Non-exhibition space

Gold-Glass Bases (4th century AD)
These vessel bases were found in
Roman catacombs. They were made
by encasing gold leaf between
two layers of translucent glass. The
medallions feature Jewish motifs,
including the ark, the menorah
and the *shofar* (ram's horn).

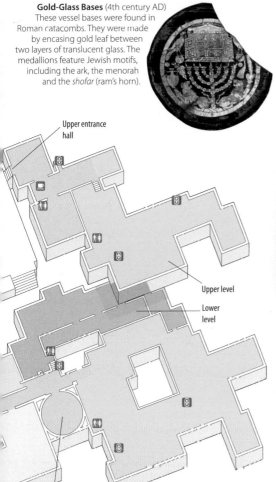

Upper entrance
hall

Upper level

Lower
level

Auditorium

*St Peter in Prison (The Apostle
Peter Kneeling)* (1631)
Rembrandt's painting expertly
uses light and shadow to portray
the apostle in his prison cell in
Jerusalem following his arrest.

★ **Mask, Horvat Duma**
(Neolithic Period)
This forms part of a fascinating
exhibition of rare 9,000-year-old
stone masks, discovered in the
Judaean Desert and Hills. These
masks are considered to be the
most ancient human portraits.

Museum Guide

*The museum's sizeable campus
has extensive gallery space for
archaeology, fine arts and Jewish
art and life collections. It also
includes a large outdoor sculpture
garden, a Youth Wing, which
organizes educational programmes
and exhibitions, and the Shrine of
the Book and a Model of the Second
Temple of Jerusalem complex.*

The Cliff of Aval, Etrétat (1885)
Part of a series by Claude Monet, in which he painted the
same subject in different lights, at different hours of the day,
and through changes of weather and season.

Exploring the Israel Museum

Thanks to its wide variety of sources, the collection is extraordinarily eclectic. Its core was inherited from the Bezalel School and Museum (Israel's first arts academy) and the Israel Antiquities Authority, and this has been supplemented by gifts, loans and acquisitions from around the globe. The biggest draw, though, for most visitors is the Shrine of the Book, which houses some of the Dead Sea Scrolls *(see pp140–41)*.

Jeanne Hebuterne, Seated (1918), by Amedeo Modigliani

Jewish Art and Life Wing

The museum's collection of Judaica and Jewish Ethnography spans the period from the Middle Ages to the present, and has exhibits from as far afield as Spain and China. Five main sections integrate the sacred and secular dimensions of Jewish life from different cultures. Among the most precious objects are the medieval illuminated manuscripts.

The Rothschild Miscellany

These include a 14th-century German *Haggadah* (the story read at Passover of the Israelites' liberation from Egypt) and the Rothschild Miscellany, a 15th-century collection of biblical, legal and other pieces. Elaborate silverwork includes *hadassim* (spiceboxes used during the ceremony of separation between the Sabbath and the start of the week) and the *rimonim* (pomegranates that decorate Torah scrolls in the synagogue). Another highlight is the large collection of *Hannukkiot* – the oil lamps that are lit for Hanukkah *(see p43)*. There are also four beautiful, complete synagogue interiors, from Italy, Germany, India and Suriname. The daily life of Jewish communities from around the world is also represented in textiles, clothing, jewellery, reconstructions of rooms and ritual articles connected with life events such as birth, circumcision and marriage.

Fine Arts Wing

The museum's various art collections cover a wide range of periods and artistic disciplines. Visitors can take in Chinese porcelain, African figurines, Impressionist masterpieces and even an entire 18th-century French salon.

The modern art collection has international works from the 1890s to the 1960s. These include paintings by figures such as Gauguin, Cézanne, Chagall, Matisse and Modigliani. Twentieth-century sculpture is also represented, both here and outdoors in the Billy Rose Art Garden *(see p140)*.

The Rothschild Room, an 18th-century Parisian salon donated by Baron Edmond de Rothschild

Other rooms are devoted to design, architecture and contemporary art.

One of the largest collections of Israeli art in the country is also exhibited here on both floors. It begins with paintings and drawings produced in the 19th century, at the beginning of Jewish resettlement (see p55). The 1920s and 30s are represented by figurative pieces by artists such as Reuven Rubin and Yitzhak Danziger. The contemporary Israeli art on display mirrors, and sometimes anticipates, tendencies seen elsewhere in the world.

Other rooms are devoted to prints and drawings, Old Master paintings – including a depiction of the sacking of the Second Temple by Poussin (see p49) – Islamic and East Asian art, and the art of Africa, the Americas and Oceania. Pieces from the Levine Photography Collection are incorporated into the other exhibitions in this wing and build on the museum's long history of collecting photographs.

Anthropoid sarcophagi, a highlight of the archaeology collection

Archaeology Wing

The archaeology collection constitutes the largest section of the museum. Most pieces are on loan from the Israel Antiquities Authority and come from excavations carried out all over the country, which has the highest concentration of digs in the world. The digs cover a vast period of history – from as far back as 1.5 million BC – and have revealed artifacts from an impressive number of civilizations, from Palaeolithic flint utensils, through Canaanite

and Israelite figurines, to Byzantine mosaics and Islamic jewellery. The museum's collection represents most aspects of this cultural spectrum, and visitors will require at least two hours to fully appreciate the range of pieces on display.

The artifacts are arranged chronologically within the renovated gallery, as seven "chapters" of an archaeological timeline. Objects to look out for in the first section (Palaeolithic to Chalcolithic periods, 1.5 million–3500 BC) include the jewellery and sculpted figures of the Natufian culture (10th–9th millennium BC), the 6,000-year-old, house-shaped ossuaries at the end of the first gallery and the elegant copperware of the so-called Judaean Desert Treasure (5th millennium BC). Highlights from the Canaanite Period (3500–1200 BC) are the sophisticated gold jewellery and the anthropoid sarcophagi found in a cemetery at Deir el-Balah, in the Gaza Strip.

The Israelite Period (1200 –586 BC) starts with the rise of the Israelites in the region and ends with the destruction of Solomon's Temple. Look out for the beautiful Philistine pottery, the ivory pomegranate inscribed with ancient Hebrew (believed to be the only object ever found relating to worship in Solomon's Temple) and the priestly benediction written on a tiny silver amulet – the earliest known fragment of biblical text (7th century BC).

Mosaic from floor of 6th-century-AD synagogue at Gaza, showing King David playing the lyre

Finds from the next 300 years are relatively scarce but the Hellenistic, Roman and Byzantine periods (332 BC–AD 636) offer fascinating objects, such as the sarcophagi and ossuaries from various Jewish catacombs, the bronze statue of the emperor Hadrian and the beautiful mosaics from Tsipori (Sepphoris), Kisufim, Gaza and Beth Shean.

The last room focuses on "Muslims and Crusaders" and "Neighbouring Cultures", with artifacts such as Egyptian cult and game objects, Assyrian and Babylonian reliefs, Greek vases and Roman jewellery. This wing also houses exhibitions on glass, early Hebrew writing and coins.

Throughout the section are interesting models and reconstructions of some of the most important sites in this part of the world. The permanent exhibitions are flanked by temporary displays based on historical themes or particular archaeological sites.

Jewish Art of the Diaspora

During the many centuries of the Diaspora, Jews around the world directed their artistic talents primarily to ritual objects connected with the life cycle and synagogue liturgy. They produced fine examples of applied art, especially in the fields of gold- and silverware, other metalwork and manuscript decoration. Naturally, the motifs and techniques reflect the place and time in which the objects were produced, but many elements, both functional and iconographic, recur again and again. These recurring themes and local variations can be appreciated among the many exhibits in the museum's Judaica section.

18th-century silver spicebox from Germany

Ruth Youth Wing for Art Education

This section is devoted to interactive art activities. The idea behind it was to introduce children to art and culture. The largest of its kind in the world, the centre has now extended its reach to adults. With ten classrooms, an auditorium, library, recycling workshop and exhibition space, it provides a stimulating environment in which to learn about creative processes. There are regular "hands on" exhibitions, art courses and summer schemes for all ages, as well as tours for groups with special needs.

Children participating in creative activities in the Ruth Youth Wing

Billy Rose Art Garden

The garden was designed by the Japanese-American sculptor Isamu Noguchi. It is an extraordinary combination of elements from local history and landscape, motifs from the traditional Zen garden and significant works of modern sculpture. It is laid out as a series of semicircular terraces echoing those made for centuries by farmers in the Judaean Hills. Indigenous plants such as olive trees, cypresses and rosemary bushes are dotted around the garden.

The garden offers an overview of sculpture through the 20th century. There are stunning early works by Rodin, Maillol, Picasso and Bourdelle. Henry Moore's curvaceous pieces stand alongside Roxy Paine's inverted tree sculpture made of stainless steel, *Inversion* (2008). Contemporary sculptures include James Turrell's intriguing installation with a large rectangular opening in the top for observing the sky, and Robert Indiana's iconic sculpture, *Ahava* ("love", 1977).

Shrine of the Book

Built to house the Dead Sea Scrolls and other important artifacts, the intriguingly shaped Shrine of the Book has become a symbol of the whole museum. The unusual design, by American architects Frederick Kiesler and Armand Bartos, is inspired by the scrolls themselves. The distinctive dome is intended to imitate the lids of the jars in which the scrolls were found. Near the entrance is a black granite wall. The contrast between the black of the wall and the white of the dome is a reference to the decisive battle between the Children of Darkness and the Children of Light, described in the scroll known as the War Scroll. This final confrontation between good and evil would, the authors believed, herald the coming of the Messiah.

Inside, a long, subtly lit passageway, designed to evoke the catacomb-like environment in which the scrolls were found, has a permanent exhibition on life in Qumran at the time the scrolls were written. It leads into the main chamber under the dome. The imposing showcase directly beneath the dome contains a facsimile of the Great Isaiah Scroll, the only biblical book that survived in its entirety. Its 66 chapters were written on several strips of parchment, which were then sewn together, making it more than 7 m (23 ft) long. One of the surrounding display cases contains part of the real scroll. Also on show are the Psalms

Magdalena Abakonowicz's *Negev* (1987), Billy Rose Art Garden

Scroll, 28 columns of text consisting of psalms, hymns and a prose passage about the psalms; the War Scroll; the Manual of Discipline; and the Temple Scroll.

On the Shrine's lower level are 2nd-century-AD articles, such as keys and baskets, found in the Cave of Letters, south of Ein Gedi *(see p201)*. Also on display here is the 10th-century Aleppo Codex – not one of the Dead Sea Scrolls, but the oldest complete Bible in Hebrew.

Adjacent to the Shrine of the Book is a Second Temple-era model of Jerusalem. Originally constructed on the grounds of the Holyland Hotel on the outskirts of the city, this large-scale model offers visitors a three-dimensional view of the landscape of Jerusalem during the 1st century. Mainly built from local limestone, the model was constructed at a scale of 1:50, with 2 cm of the model representing 1 m of the city.

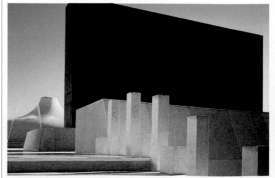

Symbolic clash of darkness and light at the Shrine of the Book entrance

For hotels and restaurants in this area see p261 and p271

The Dead Sea Scrolls

In 1947, a Bedouin shepherd, in search of a lost goat near the Dead Sea, entered a cave and discovered jars containing seven ancient scrolls. Over the next two decades fragments of some 800 more were found in 11 caves. At the same time, archaeologists, looking for signs of habitation, uncovered the nearby settlement of Qumran *(see p200)*. The scrolls had been written in the Late Second Temple period, between the 3rd century BC and AD 68. Some contain the oldest existing versions of biblical scriptures. Others are tracts on history, daily life and the messianic predictions of a Hebrew sect generally identified with the separatist and monastic Essenes. Since the discovery of the scrolls, their interpretation, the identity and mission of their authors and the significance of nearby Qumran have been the subject of passionate academic and theological debate.

The Shrine of the Book is dominated by a dramatic display case, which contains a copy of the Great Isaiah Scroll. It was designed to look like the wooden rods around which the Torah scrolls are rolled for readings at synagogue services.

Inkwell found at Qumran

The reconstruction of thousands of scroll fragments is still being carried out by researchers hoping to unravel the mysteries surrounding the scrolls.

The parchment on which the scrolls were written was made from sheepskin. Inkwells found near a table at Qumran suggest a scriptorium – a room for copying manuscripts.

The Great Isaiah Scroll is the largest and best-preserved of the scrolls. Written around 100 BC, it is 1,000 years older than the oldest biblical manuscript known before the finds at Qumran.

Qumran was excavated by Roland de Vaux, a French Dominican friar. He believed that the settlement was a communal retreat used by the Essenes.

❽ Biblical Zoo

Manahat. **Tel** (02) 675 0111. 🚌 26, 33, 99. **Open** 9am–5pm (to 7pm Jun–Aug) Sun–Thu, 9am–4:30pm Fri, 10am–5pm (to 6pm Jun–Aug) Sat. Last entry: 1 hour before closing. 🅿️ ♿ 🌐 **jerusalemzoo.org.il**

The Jerusalem Biblical Zoo, also known as the Tisch Family Zoological Gardens, is famous for its collection of wildlife featured in the Bible. This group of animals, many of which are no longer naturally present in the Holy Land, includes bears, lions, Arabian oryx and Nile crocodiles. There are also other endangered species from around the world. The zoo occupies an attractive site in the southwestern suburbs of the city. You can gain an overview of the zoo on a train ride around the grounds.

❾ Yad Vashem

Mount Herzl. **Tel** (02) 644 3400. 🚌 13, 21, 23, 27. **Open** 9am–5pm Sun–Wed, 9am–8pm Thu, 9am–2pm Fri & hols. 🎟️ ♿ 🌐 **yadvashem.org**

Yad Vashem, meaning "a memorial and a name" (from Isaiah 56: 5), is an archive, research institute, museum and, above all, a monument to perpetuate the memory of the more than six million Jews who were killed in the Holocaust. More than 20 monuments occupy this hillside site.

Entrance to Yad Vashem is along the Avenue of the Righteous Among Nations, which is lined with plaques bearing the names of Gentiles who helped Jews and, in doing so, put their own lives at risk. Some 23,000 people are recognized, including Oskar Schindler *(see p121)*. The avenue leads to the Historical Museum, which was designed by Jewish architect Moshe Safdie. The museum is one long corridor, carved into the mountain, with ten exhibition halls, each dedicated to a different chapter of the Holocaust. Its exhibits include some 2,500 personal items donated by survivors, adding a harrowing first-person dimension to the horrors that began with the rise of the Nazis in 1933 and culminated in the death camps.

The Hall of Remembrance beside the museum is a stark, tomb-like chamber that bears the names of 21 of the main camps on flat, black basalt slabs. At the centre of the vast chamber is a casket of ashes from the cremation ovens; above it is an eternal flame. The Hall of Names inside the Historical Museum records the names of all those Jews who perished, along with as much biographical detail as possible. Yad Vashem also has a museum of Jewish art and a visual centre where films related to the Holocaust may be viewed. Visitors must dress appropriately – no shorts or miniskirts.

Janusz Korczak Memorial, Yad Vashem

Grave of Israel's fifth prime minister, Yitzhak Rabin, Mount Herzl

❿ Mount Herzl and Herzl Museum

Mount Herzl. **Tel** (02) 632 1515. 🚌 13, 14, 18, 20, 21, 27, 33. **Open** 8:30am–6pm Sun–Wed (to 7pm Thu, to 1pm Fri). Last tour: 1 hr before closing. Arrange visits in advance. 🅿️ 🎟️ ♿ 🌐 **herzl.org**

Mount Herzl (in Hebrew *Har Hertzel*) is a high hill north of central Jerusalem, named after Theodor Herzl, the man considered to be the founder of Zionism *(see p55)*. The slopes serve as a large cemetery, and Herzl's tomb lies at the top of the hill. At the entrance to the site is the Herzl Museum, which offers a crash course in Zionist history, with audiovisual presentations and re-creations of the founding father's study and library. Mount Herzl is also the burial place of three of Israel's prime ministers and the country's presidents, and is the site of Israel's main military cemetery.

⓫ Ein Kerem

7 km (4 miles) W of central Jerusalem. 🚌 17, 184.

A picturesque village, Ein Kerem ("the vineyard spring") has strong biblical associations. According to Christian tradition, John the Baptist was born and

Memorial to Holocaust victims at the Yad Vashem museum

lived here. The village boasts several fine churches and monasteries connected with his life. Recognizable by its tall, thin tower, the Franciscan **Church of St John the Baptist** dates from the 17th century, but is built over the ruins of earlier Byzantine and Crusader structures. Steps inside the church lead down into a natural cave, known as the Grotto of the Nativity of St John, which tradition connects with the birth of the Baptist.

The other church of note is the two-tiered **Church of the Visitation**, completed in 1955 to a design by Antonio Barluzzi, architect of the Dominus Flevit Sanctuary (see p117) and the Chapel of the Flagellation (see p68). It commemorates the Virgin Mary's visit to Elizabeth, mother of John the Baptist, who was then pregnant, an episode depicted in mosaic on the church's façade. Within is a natural grotto, in front of which are the remains of Roman-era houses. According to tradition, the grotto is where Elizabeth hid with her infant son to escape from the Massacre of the Innocents (the killing of all first-born sons, ordered by King Herod). The courtyard walls are lined with tiled panels inscribed with the *Magnificat* (Luke 1: 46–55), Mary's hymn of thanks, in 42 languages.

At the bottom of the hill below the church is a small, abandoned mosque. Beside it surfaces the spring (popularly known as the Spring of the Virgin) from which the village takes its name.

One of the other pleasures to savour in Ein Kerem is its tranquil, wooded, valley setting. This can be best appreciated on a beautiful scenic walk that starts beside the sculpture at the beginning of the access road to Yad Vashem, and winds through the trees.

Church of St John the Baptist, Ein Kerem

⓬ Hadassah Hospital Synagogue

Ein Kerem. **Tel** (02) 677 6271. 🚌 19, 27. **Open** 8am–3pm Sun–Thu. Call ahead to check availability. 🅿️ 📷 ♿

A splendid cycle of 12 stained-glass windows decorates the synagogue at the otherwise unremarkable Hadassah Hospital. The windows were created in 1960–61 by the Russian-Jewish artist Marc Chagall (see p37), and installed the following year for the inauguration of the building. Each of the windows represents one of the 12 tribes of Israel (Genesis 49). Tradition associates each of the tribes with a symbol, a precious stone and a social role, and these elements are all represented in Chagall's imagery and choice of colour.

Several of the windows were damaged by shrapnel during the 1967 War (see p58) and had to be repaired by the artist. However, one of the windows (a green one) bears a small symbolic bullet hole in the lower half, deliberately left there as testimony to the fighting.

⓭ Abu Ghosh

13 km (8 miles) W of central Jerusalem. 🚌 185, 189.

This Arab village just north of the main Jerusalem–Tel Aviv highway was considered by the Crusaders to be Emmaus, where Christ appeared to two Disciples in the days after his Resurrection. The beautiful Romanesque **Crusader Church** was built in the early 12th century by the Knights Hospitallers and stands almost complete in its original form. Its 12th-century frescoes are lovely, but in a poor state of repair. The adjacent early 20th-century monastery belongs to French Olivetan Benedictine monks, who produce pottery. Up on the hill above the village stands the **Church of Notre Dame de l'Arche de l'Alliance**, built in 1924 over the remains of a 5th-century church, whose mosaics are still visible. It is said to occupy the site of the house of Abinadab, where the fabled Ark of the Covenant (see p25) rested for 20 years (1 Samuel 7: 1–2) until David took it to Jerusalem.

The modern Church of Notre Dame de l'Arche de l'Alliance, Abu Ghosh

THREE GUIDED WALKS

Jerusalem is a perfect city to explore on foot: it is small and compact, and there are plenty of sites to see and places to sit and rest. This is particularly true in the Old City, which, with the exception of just one or two roads, doesn't allow for motor vehicles at all, so dodging traffic is rarely an issue, though pavements may be crowded. Most streets are simply too narrow and meandering for motorized traffic, and there are too many steps. It is a place perfectly described by the overused adjective "labyrinthine"; a place in which getting lost is inevitable. However, this is no bad thing because wandering aimlessly around the Old City is a highly pleasurable activity. For that reason, we have avoided describing any walks within Jerusalem's ancient fortified walls. Instead, we suggest you get up on the walls themselves, which is something few visitors do, largely because they remain unaware that the opportunity exists.

Similarly, few visitors spend any time exploring the more modern parts of the city and so miss out on some attractive old quarters and some fine architecture. Much of this is non-indigenous, raised at the end of the 19th century, when the great powers of Europe were all vying for political influence in the Holy City. This was expressed through ostentatious examples of their own national architectures. Muscovite churches, English Gothic cathedrals, German hospices and Italian insurance offices all serve as reminders of the central role Jerusalem has always played in the Western consciousness.

CHOOSING A WALK

Three Walks

The routes of the three walks are marked on this map, which shows the main areas of Jerusalem.

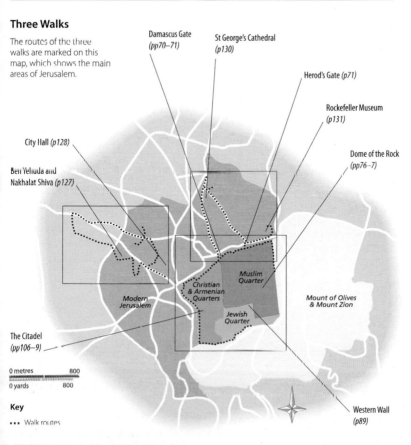

Damascus Gate
(pp70–71)

St George's Cathedral
(p130)

Herod's Gate (p71)

Rockefeller Museum
(p131)

City Hall (p128)

Dome of the Rock
(pp76–7)

Ben Yehuda and
Nakhalat Shiva (p127)

Muslim
Quarter

Christian
& Armenian
Quarters

Mount of Olives
& Mount Zion

Modern
Jerusalem

Jewish
Quarter

The Citadel
(pp106–9)

0 metres   800
0 yards   800

Western Wall
(p89)

Key

••• Walk routes

◀ The ancient stone ramparts in the Old City of Jerusalem

A 90-Minute Walk around the Old City Walls

The Old City of Jerusalem may occupy a relatively small area geographically, but its compactness and uneven topography make it a frequently confusing place to explore. One good way to gain an overview is to take to the ramparts and view the crush of alleys, domes and towers from the top of the walls that enclose them. Visitors can walk along two sections of wall: from Jaffa Gate clockwise to Lions' Gate, and from Jaffa Gate anti-clockwise to the Dung Gate. The section between Lions' Gate and the Dung Gate is closed to the public. Many steep flights of steps mean that this is not a walk for the elderly or infirm.

Clockwise from Jaffa Gate

Jerusalem's walls were built in the first half of the 16th century (in part on the line of earlier walls) on the order of the Ottoman sultan Suleyman the Magnificent. They are pierced by eight gates, of which seven remain in use. Until as recently as 1870, the gates were all closed from sunset to sunrise.

② A section of the ramparts just east of New Gate

Tips for Walkers

Starting point: Jaffa Gate.
Length: Jaffa Gate to Lions' Gate 2.4 km (1.5 miles); Jaffa Gate to Dung Gate 1.2 km (0.75 miles).
Open: summer: 9am–5pm daily; winter: 9am–4pm Sat–Thu, 9am–2pm Fri (south side open Sat only). Admission fee.
Stopping-off points: There are several small cafés on Omar ibn el-Khattab Square, just inside the Jaffa Gate. Otherwise, when you descend at Lions' Gate, walk west along the Via Dolorosa and then left onto El-Wad Road for Abu Shukri (p270), which serves the best houmous in town.

Start the walk by climbing the steps that are immediately inside the **Jaffa Gate** ① (see p104), to your left as you enter the Old City. After paying admission, you pass through a gate and ascend a steep flight of steps leading to the top of the gatehouse. Heading north brings you to the first of some 35 watchtowers that punctuate the circuit of the walls. This one has a raised platform which allows walkers to step up for a view of the Mamilla Mall, a large shopping and office development outside the city walls. Looking into the Old City, you will see the backs of buildings belonging to the Latin Patriarchate, the centre of Roman Catholicism in Jerusalem.

A short distance on and you'll notice that the third watchtower along has been reinforced with side walls; this was done by the Jordanians when they were in occupation of the Old City between 1948 and 1967, and Jerusalem was divided between Arabs and Jews. After skirting around three sides of a crescent-topped dome, the ramparts pass over **New Gate** ②. This was added in 1889 to allow pilgrims in the compounds outside the walls direct access to the Christian Quarter.

From here the ramparts drop, following the slope of the land. Notice the profusion of aerials and satellite dishes inside the

The city walls wrap around the Tower of David

Key

••• Walk route

walls, evidence of the large number of people who continue to live in the Old City. At a certain point the level of the rooftops falls below that of the ramparts, affording a fine view of the golden Dome of the Rock.

Damascus Gate to Lions' Gate

The ramparts now climb over **Damascus Gate** ③ *(see p70)*, the grandest of all the Old City gates. From up here you can survey the vaulted roof over the gate's defensive dogleg entrance tunnel and the crowds on El-Wad Road. Continuing east, you will encounter a rapid succession of towers, because

The view from the ramparts between New Gate and Damascus Gate

attacks on Jerusalem have traditionally always come from the north, where the approach is flattest (the approaches to the east, south and west are protected by deep valleys).

It was the north wall, just east of the next gate, **Herod's Gate** ④ *(see p71)*, that the Crusader army breached on 15 July 1099 to capture Jerusalem from the Muslims. Look outwards from the gate and you are facing down Salah al-Din Street, the main street of Arab East Jerusalem.

At Storks' Tower ⑤, with its views to the northeast of the Hebrew University's Mount Scopus campus, the wall swings through 90° to run due south. From the ramparts here, you overlook the tombs that fill the Kidron Valley below and the slopes of the Mount of Olives *(pp114–15)*. As you approach the final gate, to your right, just inside the walls, are the remains of the complex of the biblical Pool of Bethseda and, beside them, the Crusader-built St Anne's Church *(see p71)*.

③ Crenellations on Damascus Gate

The walk ends at **Lions' Gate** ⑥ *(see p71)*, built by Suleyman the Magnificent, where you descend to street level. The beginning of the Via Dolorosa *(see pp31–5)* is just ahead, which, if followed, leads back towards the Jaffa Gate area. Energy permitting, you can then embark on another short ramparts walk.

③ The modern amphitheatre outside Damascus Gate

Anti-clockwise from Jaffa Gate

The access to this section of the ramparts is from outside the city walls, just south of the **Citadel** ⑦ *(see pp106–9)*.

The initial stretch southwards is like a trench, with a high stone wall on either side of the walkway. This arrangement was fashioned by the Jordanian army between 1948 and 1967. Occasional vantage points allow you to look out across the Hinnom Valley below to the red rooftops of the early Jewish settlement of Mishkenot Shaananim *(see p125)* and the cliff-like bulk of the King David Hotel *(see p126)*. At the southwestern corner you have a good view of Sultan's Pool, an ancient reservoir, now dry and used as an outdoor concert venue.

As the ramparts run east, they pass close by the Church of the Dormition *(see p120)* before passing over the **Zion Gate** ⑧ *(see p110)*. The gate is riddled with bullet holes from the fighting in 1948, although, of course, you can't see this from above.

The final stretch affords wonderful views of the Arab village of Silwan, before the rampart walk ends on Batei Makhase Street, which you can follow down to the **Dung Gate** ⑨ *(see p88)*. This is the smallest of the city gates, despite being widened for cars by the Jordanians. The name indicates that what is now the main access to the Western Wall was probably once the site of a refuse tip.

A 90-Minute Walk around West Jerusalem

The heart of West Jerusalem, centred on Jaffa Road, was largely developed during the years of the British Mandate (1917–48). So, while it is nowhere near as ancient as the Old City, it does carry a weight of modern history related to the founding of the Jewish state of Israel. Aside from the scattering of historic buildings and monuments, this is also the heart of the modern city, with pedestrianized streets of cafés, restaurants and shops, cultural centres and busy markets. It is a highly rewarding area to explore.

② Water sculpture on Safra Square at the City Hall complex

Jaffa Road

Until Tel Aviv got its own port in the 1930s, Jews arriving in Palestine would disembark at Jaffa, entering Jerusalem on the Jaffa Road. It ran right up to the Old City and the correspondingly named Jaffa Gate. The road now ends just short of the city walls, which is where this walk begins, at the rounded façade of the **Former Barclays Bank** ① (look for the "BB" in the iron window grilles). The building was on the line that divided Arabs and Jews between 1948 and 1967 and still bears the scars left by

bullets. Walk west, and almost immediately you come to palm-filled Safra Square, forecourt to the **City Hall complex** ② *(see p128)*, also home to the main tourist information office. Cross to the left-hand side of the road at the next junction to pass **Feingold House** ③, built in 1895, with its series of arched shopfronts and one arched entrance to a passageway containing the fine bar-restaurant Barood *(see p154)*. Look back to spot the winged lion on top of the Generali Building, trademark of the Italian insurance company that once had its offices here.

Continue along Jaffa Road, taking the next left into Rivlin Street and **Nakhalat Shiva** ④ *(see p127)*. This is one of the oldest parts of the modern city (founded 1869) but also one of the liveliest. Its attractive two-storey buildings are home to trendy eateries and late-night bars. At the bottom of Rivlin turn right, then head up

⑤ Passing time on the pedestrianized Ben Yehuda Street

```
Key
• • • Walk route
```

④ A balcony in the historic neighbourhood of Nakhalat Shiva

Salomon to Zion Square, the traditional gathering point for protests and demonstrations. Running west from here, **Ben Yehuda Street** ⑤ *(see p127)* is one of the city's main shopping streets. Take the third right into Ben Hillel, cross over main King George V Street and you will be standing in front of Felafel & Shawarma King, which makes supposedly the best falafels in the city.

Mahane Yehuda

Continue west along **Agrippas Street** ⑥, passing on the right a passage that leads to top restaurant Arcadia. This has traditionally been a poor area with cheap rents that have proved attractive to recent immigrants, hence all the signs in Cyrillic. Agrippas is also the southern boundary of **Mahane Yehuda Market** ⑦, the city's colourful prime source of fresh produce, from fruit and vegetables to fish and meat *(see p152)*.

Exit the market back onto Jaffa Road, now returning east. Pass by a building on your right that has a doorway flanked by two lions on pillars – the former residence of the British Consul, 1863–90 – before arriving

⑪ The garden terrace at Ticho House, open daily for lunch

at a major junction marked by a small monument of a mortar on a plinth; this is a **Davidka** ⑧, a weapon that played a large role in the 1948 War. The Hebrew inscription is from the Old Testament Book of Isaiah and reads, "For I will defend this city to save it".

Fork left at the monument to follow historic **Ha-Neviim Street** ⑨ *(see p128)*, which during the 19th century was one of Jerusalem's main avenues. It is lined by some notable buildings, including at No. 64 a fine house once occupied by the English Victorian painter William Holman Hunt and, at No. 58, Thabor House, designed and once occupied by the German Conrad Schick, one of the city's foremost early architects.

Just past Thabor House, a pretty, high-walled lane on the left leads to the **Ethiopian Church** ⑩, a modest basilica with an interior painted in nursery blues and pinks, and filled with glittery, golden icons and smoky incense.

Return to Ha-Neviim and cross over to head south down Ha-Rav Kook Street looking for the signs for **Ticho House** ⑪ *(see p127)*. This is an historic Arab residence that has been turned into a lively

⑩ Decorative panel, Ethiopian Church

cultural centre hosting art exhibitions and regular jazz, folk and classical recitals; it also has a pleasant garden terrace.

Returning to Ha-Neviim, take the next right and walk straight over the roundabout; the end point of the walk is visible ahead in the form of the three Muscovite-styled domes of the **Cathedral of the Holy Trinity** ⑫ *(see p128)*. Consecrated in 1872, the church was built to cater to Russian pilgrims, who at the time far outnumbered pilgrims from any other country. From here, it's just a short step back to Jaffa Road and the start of the walk.

Tips for Walkers

Starting point: Jaffa Road.
Length: 3 km (2 miles).
Best time to walk: Any time, but avoid Friday afternoon and Saturday, when everything is closed.
Stopping-off points: In addition to the places mentioned in the walk, there are dozens of food stalls around Mahane Yehuda Market, including some selling "meorav Yerushalmi," literally "Jerusalem meats," a mix of chopped livers, kidneys, hearts and beef, fried and served in pockets of bread. At the end of the walk, there are two good cafés at the junction of Heleni Ha-Malka and Jaffa Road, and many more cafés and restaurants in Nakhalat Shiva, which is just across Jaffa Road.

⑦ A stall in one of the covered lanes of Mahane Yehuda Market

A 90-Minute Walk around East Jerusalem

East Jerusalem is the Palestinian Arab part of the city. It lies
north of the Old City and east of the main north–south road
Derekh Ha-Shalom, swelling over the Mount of Olives and
down the other side. The main street is Salah al-Din Street,
which is visited as part of this walk. High-profile tourist sights
are few, but it is a vibrant area with many points of interest,
including Christian pilgrimage sights and the Holy Land's
most atmospheric old hotel.

A fruit stall on the corner of the
traditional Nablus Road

Nablus Road

The walk starts at **Damascus
Gate** ① *(see pp70–71)*, the largest
and one of the busiest of
the Old City gates. Taking
advantage of the perpetual
crowds, small traders
spread their wares
on sheets around
the amphitheatre-like
space in front of
the gate so that it
operates as a small
makeshift market.
Cross the busy road
that runs parallel with
the city walls to the
junction with Nablus
Road, which is also busy
with street traders selling
breads and fruit. Some
of these traders stand
in the shadow of **Schmidt's
Girls' College** ②, part of
the St Paul's Hospice complex,
designed in fine Germanic
style by the same architect
responsible for Mount Zion's
Church of the Dormition
(see p120).

Walk north up Nablus Road
and shortly you come to an
alley enclosed between high
walls off to the right: this
leads to the **Garden Tomb** ③
(see p130). The claims for it
as the burial place of Jesus
Christ have been dismissed by

An elderly
Palestinian

archaeologists, but that does
not seem to deter the coach-
loads of Christian pilgrims who
flock here each day to engage
in open-air prayer sessions
in what is, admittedly,
a lovely garden setting.
Stroll on, passing on your
left the Arab bus station
for services to West
Bank towns and
Ramallah. At the
next traffic junction,
marked by the
modest little Sadd and
Said Mosque, continue
north as Nablus Road
becomes a narrow, leafy
lane squeezed beside the
fortified bulk of the local
US Consulate. On your
right at No. 14 is
Palestinian Pottery
④, founded on
this site back in 1922
by the Balians, one of
three Armenian families
brought over by the
British authorities
from Kuthaya, Turkey, to
renovate the ceramic tiles
on the Dome of the Rock.
Ring the bell to enter and
visit the showrooms and a
small museum on the history
of ceramics in Jerusalem. You
can also watch the craftspeople
at work hand-painting designs
onto the ceramic tiles
or pottery prior to firing.
Further along, on
the left, are several fine
examples of late 19th-
and early 20th-century
buildings, including a
villa that houses the
East Jerusalem offices of
the British Council. On
the right is the high wall
that rings St George's
Cathedral, which is
visited later in the walk.

Key

••• Walk route

Nablus Road now joins with
Salah al-Din Street, but continue
on, taking the second right,
Louis Vincent Street, a short cul-
de-sac leading to the **American
Colony Hotel** ⑤ *(see p131)*.
Originally built (1865–76) as

④ Hand-painting at the Palestinian Pottery workshop

a home by a wealthy Arab merchant, the building was subsequently sold to pilgrims from Chicago, hence the name, before later becoming a hospice and then a hotel. It boasts a beautiful courtyard café and an equally welcoming cellar bar. Opposite the main entrance to the hotel, beside an attractive little giftshop, steps lead up to the excellent Munther's Bookshop at the American Colony Hotel (see p153).

Salah al-Din Street
Return the way you came, taking a quick detour left down

⑤ Lobby area of the historic American Colony Hotel

0 metres	250
0 yards	250

KHALED IBN EL-WALID
AKHWAN EL-SAFA
EL-YAQUBI
BATUTA
ZAHRA
EL-HARIRI
FAHANI
HARUN EL-RASHID
NUR EL-DIN
EL-AKHTAL
EL-MUQDASI
SULTAN SULEYMAN

⑦ The Gothic bell tower of the Anglican St George's Cathedral

Abu Ubaida Street to take a look at **Orient House** ⑥, an elegant 1897 villa that served as the headquarters of the Palestinian Authority in Jerusalem until it was shut down by the Israeli government in 2001.

Back on Salah al-Din Street, pass the Kings' Tombs (see p131) and then cross over the street to the main gate of **St George's Cathedral** ⑦ (see p130) and buzz for admittance. Visitors are usually free to wander the gardens and courts of what is a surprisingly large compound. It is worth finding your way into the cathedral for its admirably restrained interior, which contains the royal arms formerly displayed in Government House during the time of British rule and deposited here when the Mandate came to an end in 1948. Services are still held throughout the week, although the language of mass these days is Arabic.

South of the cathedral, **Salah al-Din Street** ⑧ becomes a busy high street with a clutter of low-rise shops, moneychangers, pharmacies and snack joints. Although vibrant, the scene is very visibly poorer than the corresponding main streets over in West Jerusalem. At its southern end Salah al-Din Street terminates opposite the city walls and **Herod's Gate** ⑨, which to the Arabs is the far more poetic Bab

el-Zahra, or "Flower Gate". At this point you can enter the Old City; or turn left and follow the walls down to the very worthwhile **Rockefeller Museum** ⑩ (see p131) and its archaeological finds from the Holy Land; or bear right and follow Sultan Suleyman Street, past rows of small clothes and jewellery shops and eateries, back to the Damascus Gate area.

⑩ Decorative sarcophagus at the Rockefeller Museum

Tips for Walkers
Starting point: Damascus Gate.
Length: 1.5 miles (2.4 km).
Palestinian Pottery: Open 9am–4pm Mon–Sat.
Stopping-off points: The American Colony Hotel serves lunch in the courtyard garden or indoors in Val's Brasserie Lounge. Café Europe, at 9 El-Zahra Street, just off Salah al-Din, offers good-value Western-style cuisine, including ham and eggs, in premises that resemble an English tearoom.

Shops and Markets

When it comes to shopping, the main attractions in Jerusalem are the souks (markets) of the Old City. In comparison with the great bazaars of Istanbul or Cairo, Jerusalem's souks are perhaps a little small, and the array of goods on offer is largely limited to souvenir items such as T-shirts and religious articles, but they still reward exploration. There is better shopping elsewhere, however, notably in the modern centre of West Jerusalem, where you'll find high-street shops and malls, and areas of trendy boutiques: see Where to Shop, below. For more information on methods of payment and bargaining, see pp276–7.

Sacks of spices at a shop on the Old City's Souk Khan el-Zeit Street

Religious souvenirs are popular throughout the Old City

Opening Hours

Shops in the Muslim Quarter of the Old City and in East Jerusalem are open daily except for Friday morning. Many shops and stalls in the souks of the Old City are also closed all day Sunday, as many of the shop owners are Christian. Shops in the Jewish Quarter of the Old City and throughout West Jerusalem are open Sunday to Thursday from around 9am to 7pm, Friday from 9am to 3pm, and closed Saturday. Beware of local religious holidays (see pp40–43): during the holy month of Ramadan, Muslim shops close 30 minutes to one hour before sunset. All Jewish-owned businesses close for Jewish holidays.

Where to Shop

Away from the Old City, visit King George V Street around the intersection with Jaffa Road for general high-street shopping. For boutique shopping, visit nearby Ben Hillel and Bezalel streets, while the Mamilla Mall, which runs west from Jaffa Gate, is a pleasant pedestrianized stretch of cafés and smart shops. For the most diverse selection of interesting shops, go to Emek Refa'im Street in the German Colony (it is just five minutes from the King David Hotel/YMCA), which boasts a long stretch of chic boutiques and cafés.

Markets

The streets in the Muslim and Christian Quarters of the Old City form a single large market, or souk. In the traditional Middle Eastern manner, different areas specialise in specific wares. David Street, for example, which runs east from the Jaffa Gate area, is almost entirely devoted to tourist trinkets and is the place to buy Christian-themed kitsch. Christian Quarter Road, off David Street, is more upmarket and, in addition to more religious souvenirs, also sells items such as richly coloured Palestinian rugs, covers and dresses. Many of the shops in the Muristan (see p94) specialize in leather, while the Via Dolorosa is strong on religious items. Most diverse of all is Souk Khan el-Zeit, where stores sell everything from DVDs and clothes to live chickens and honey-drenched Arabic pastries.

West Jerusalem has an excellent covered central market in **Mahane Yehuda**, which runs between Agrippas Street and Jaffa Road. Many stalls sell fruit and vegetables, but there are also fishmongers, butchers, and sellers of dairy produce, olives, nuts and dried fruits. There are a handful of cafés and cool bars, and even a couple of small jewellery and designer apparel boutiques. The market is open Sunday to Thursday from 9am to 8pm, and Friday 9am to one hour before Shabbat. The **First Station** complex, in the attractively renovated old station, sells fresh produce and has some excellent restaurants and casual eateries that are open daily, besides holding events for children and adults.

Antiques

In Jerusalem (and Israel in general), unlike other parts of the Holy Land, you may buy

A typical antiques shop in the Christian Quarter of the Old City

antiques and objects from excavations, but to take them out of the country you must obtain a permit from the Israeli Antiquities Authority *(see p277)*. Only certain shops are authorized to deal in antiques of this kind; buy from a non-accredited source and there is a chance that you may be buying looted goods. **Zadok** in West Jerusalem is an authorized specialist that often has items for sale garnered from recent digs. Founded in 1938, **Baidun** is one of the better-known antique dealers along the Via Dolorosa. It sells pieces from the Chalcolithic era to early Islamic times. There are many antique stores along this street, but it is advisable to check a store is authorized before you commit to buying anything.

Books

Israel's oldest and largest bookstore chain is **Steimatzky**, founded in Jerusalem in 1925. It still has several branches in the city (including on Jaffa Road, Ben Yehuda Street and King George V Street), all of which sell English-language newspapers and magazines, fiction and non-fiction, and books about Jerusalem and Israel. However, the best selection on the history and politics of the city, and the Middle East in general, is found

at **Munther's Bookshop**, in the American Colony Hotel. It also carries a well-chosen selection of English-language literature.

Ceramics

Distinctive items of pottery are sold in shops throughout the Old City, but for the best quality visit **Palestinian Pottery** *(see p150)*. Its showrooms are filled with displays of the company's trademark hand-painted cups, bowls, tiles and vases, with prices starting from a few dollars.

In West Jerusalem, the narrow lanes of Nakhalat Shiva are full of pottery-stocked gift stores, including **Gilda Ceramics Gallery Shop**, which has different collections of unique pieces by a variety of Israeli artisans.

Distinctive items of hand-painted ceramics at Palestinian Pottery

Jewellery

Israeli jewellery designer **Michal Negrin**, whose whimsical designs are sold in her own-brand boutiques across the world, has several stores in Jerusalem; the most central of these is located in Nakhalat Shiva. **Goldtime** is another respected local chain store with several branches in Jerusalem. For more one-off and highly decorative designs visit **Poenta**, which is also in Nakhalat Shiva.

Religious Articles

For Christian religious items there is a plethora of shops along the Old City's David Street and the Muristan area of the Christian Quarter, specializing in crucifixes, rosaries and biblical scenes crafted from olive wood. Shops selling items of Judaica are found all throughout the Old City's Jewish Quarter, particularly on the ancient Cardo, which is where you'll find **The Cardo Charm**, where artist/owner Galit Ben-Yeheskiel produces delicate silver-filigree work. In the New City, Judaica shops cluster on King David Street, near the King David Hotel and YMCA. However, the best place in town for handmade Judaica is **Yad LaKashish**, which consists of several workshops creating everything from *mezuzot* to Hanukkah lamps.

DIRECTORY

Markets

First Station
4 David Ramez Street,
West Jerusalem. **Map** 1 B5.
Tel (02) 653 5239.
W firststation.co.il

Mahane Yehuda
120 Jaffa Road, West
Jerusalem.

Antiques

Baidun
28 Via Dolorosa, Muslim
Quarter, Old City.
Map 4 D2. **Tel** (02) 626
1469. **W** baidun.com

Zadok
18 King David Street, West
Jerusalem. **Map** 1 B4.
Tel (02) 625 8039.

Books

Munther's Bookshop
23 Nablus Road, East
Jerusalem. **Map** 1 C1.
Tel (02) 627 9731.

Steimatzky
33 Jaffa Road, West
Jerusalem. **Map** 1 A3.
Tel (02) 627 0155.

Ceramics

Gilda Ceramics Gallery Shop
27 Yoel Salomon Street,
Nakhalat Shiva, West
Jerusalem. **Map** 1 A3.
Tel (02) 624 4065.
W gildaceramics.com

Palestinian Pottery
14 Nablus Road, East
Jerusalem. **Map** 1 C2.
Tel (02) 628 2826.
W palestinianpottery.com

Jewellery

Goldtime
8 King George V Street,
West Jerusalem.
Map 1 A3. **Tel** (02) 625
5003.

Michel Negrin
Mamilla Mall, 9 King
Solomon Street, West
Jerusalem. **Map** 1 B4.
Tel (02) 624 2112.
W michalnegrin.com

Poenta
21 Yoel Salomon Street,
Nakhalat Shiva, West
Jerusalem. **Map** 1 A3.
Tel (02) 624 0383.

Religious Articles

The Cardo Charm
23 Cardo, Jewish Quarter,
Old City. **Map** 3 C4.
Tel (02) 626 2988.
W mysilverart.com

Yad LaKashish
14 Shivtei Yisrael Street.
Map 1 B2.
Tel (02) 628 7829.
W lifeline.org.il

Entertainment

For a relatively small city, Jerusalem offers a wide range of high-quality entertainment, especially in the fields of theatre and classical music. It enjoys several months of dynamic artistic and cultural activity a year, focused on summer and the Christmas season. Every May and June there is the Israel Festival, the country's most important cultural jamboree, and in April/May there is the Jerusalem Arts Festival. The Jerusalem Film Festival is in July and there is an annual Jewish Film Festival. For information on what's on, consult the daily *Jerusalem Post* or the free monthly *Time Out*, available at hotels and tourist offices.

The Armenian Tavern, a lone drinking spot in the Old City

Bars and Pubs

Apart from a small but characterful bar in the corner of the **Armenian Tavern** restaurant, just south of the Citadel, there is nowhere to drink in the Old City. You need to go to West Jerusalem and, specifically, the district of narrow lanes known as Nakhalat Shiva. This small neighbourhood has become the centre of nightlife in the city, with dozens of bars, whose patrons spill outside in the warmer months. Among them, **Barood** stands out for its superb selection of spirits and liqueurs, including shelves of absinthes, schnapps and home-made flavoured vodkas. Near the Russian Compound, the super-cool **Uganda** bar is the place to enjoy Taybeh beer, with live music or DJs every night.

Also in West Jerusalem, just off King George V Street, is **Link**, a bar-restaurant with a pleasant garden terrace. One block north and west in the premises of the Bezalel Art School, **Mona** is a bar-restaurant beloved of the city's secular population for being one of the few places open on Shabbat. The First Station complex, bordering Emek Refaim and Yemin Moshe, is also a popular meeting spot, with dozens of bars and eateries.

Predominantly Muslim, East Jerusalem is naturally thin on venues serving alcohol, but getting a drink is possible at the **Cellar Bar** of the American Colony Hotel, which is the place to meet UN officials, international correspondents and Palestinian entrepreneurs. Otherwise, the **Kan Zaman** garden restaurant at the Jerusalem Hotel serves Palestinian beers, wine and *nargilehs* (water pipes).

Children

The **Jerusalem Biblical Zoo** *(see p142)* brings together all the animals that the Bible mentions as living in the Holy Land. It is beautifully designed and kids love it. The **Bloomfield Science Museum** is devoted to acquainting children with science via lots of interactive exhibits. It's fun for adults too. In the Liberty Bell Gardens (Ha-Pa'amon), just south of the Bloomfield Gardens *(see p125)*, is the **Train Theater**, with a permanent repertoire of puppetry, plays and annual productions. The park itself is also very child friendly, with basketball courts, ping-pong tables and a rollerblade rink.

Cinema

Jerusalem's cinemas screen both local Israeli films plus international and Hollywood hits. Non-Hebrew films are usually screened in the original language with subtitles. Cinema City, on Sderot Yitschak Rabin, is Jerusalem's largest cinema complex and has 19 screens that show a range of films for all ages, along with a cinema museum and a surrounding mall. **Globus Cinema**, in Binyanei Ha'uma, near the Central Bus Station, is also good for mainstream fare. The **Jerusalem Cinematheque**, on the slopes of the Hinnon Valley just outside the Old City walls, screens seasons of classics and retrospectives, as well as recent world cinema releases. Every July it hosts the Jerusalem Film Festival. **Lev Smador** in the German Colony is another quality art-house cinema.

Music

The **Henry Crown Concert Hall** at the Jerusalem Theatre is the major venue for classical performances and home to the

Creative advertising for the Cinematheque Film Festival

Jerusalem Symphony Orchestra. Organ and choral concerts are held regularly at the **Church of the Dormition** (see p120) on Mount Zion, while the **YMCA** and **Ticho House** host regular classical recitals by soloists and ensembles. In East Jerusalem, the **Kan Zaman** restaurant has Friday night performances of classical Arabic music.

Rock, Pop and Jazz

The city's premier live music venue is **Yellow Submarine**, which features nightly acts performing blues, jazz, rock and folk. It is in an industrial district south of the centre, but it's only a short taxi ride from the Jaffa Road area. For world and ethnic music and festivals head to

Confederation House on Emile Botta Street. When the occasional big name plays in town, the venue is the **Sultan's Pool** on Hebron Road, a now-dry ancient reservoir, which, when not in use, resembles an abandoned quarry, just outside the city walls.

Theatre and Dance

The **Jerusalem Theatre** is the city's largest and most active cultural centre. In addition to the main Sherover Theatre, it has three other concert spaces and is a busy venue for both local and foreign productions. Smaller, but housed in a beautifully renovated old Ottoman structure, the **Khan Theatre** has two

performance spaces, kept busy with a lively programme of international productions.

The **Gerard Bahar Performance Centre**, just west of King George V Street, hosts regular theatre and dance events (it's the home of the respected Vertigo and Kombina dance companies), as well as occasional music concerts. The **Zappa Club** enterprise puts on live gigs featuring new local talent and international acts. Over in East Jerusalem you'll find **El-Hakawati Palestinian National Theatre**, featuring performances in Arabic that are often of a political nature. Hora Jerusalem, a folk ensemble specializing in traditional Jewish dancing, also performs new pieces by Israeli choreographers at **Efron Dance Centre**.

DIRECTORY

Bars & Pubs

Armenian Tavern
79 Armenian Patriarchate Road, Armenian Quarter, Old City. **Map** 3 B4.
Tel (02) 627 3854.

Barood
31 Jaffa Street, Nakhalat Shiva, West Jerusalem.
Map 1 A3.
Tel (02) 625 9081.

Cellar Bar
American Colony Hotel, 2 Louis Vincent Street, off Nablus Road, East Jerusalem. **Map** 1 C1.
Tel (02) 627 9777.

Kan Zaman
Jerusalem Hotel, Nablus Road, East Jerusalem.
Map 1 C1.
Tel (02) 628 3282.

Link
3 Hama'alot Street, West Jerusalem.
Tel (02) 625 3446.

Mona
12 Shmuel Ha-Nagid, West Jerusalem.
Tel (02) 622 2283.

Uganda
4 Aristobulus Street, West Jerusalem. **Map** 1 A3.
Tel (02) 623 6087.
w ugandajlm.com

Children

Bloomfield Science Museum
Hebrew University, Givat Ram, West Jerusalem.
Tel (02) 654 4888.
w mada.org.il

Jerusalem Biblical Zoo
Manahat, West Jerusalem.
Tel (02) 675 0111.
w jerusalemzoo.org.il

Train Theater
Liberty Bell Park, West Jerusalem. **Map** 1 B5.
Tel (02) 561 8514
w traintheater.co.il

Cinema

Globus Cinema
1 Shazar Blvd, Binyanei Ha'uma. **Tel** (02) 622 3685 or *2235. **w** globusmax.co.il

Jerusalem Cinematheque
11 Hebron Road, West Jerusalem. **Map** 1 B5.
Tel (02) 565 4333.
w jer-cin.org.il

Lev Smadar
4 Lloyd George Street, German Colony, West Jerusalem. **Tel** *5155.
w lev.co.il

Music

Church of the Dormition
Mount Zion, Old City.
Map 1 C5.
Tel (02) 565 5330.

Henry Crown Concert Hall
20 David Marcus Street, Talbiye, West Jerusalem.
Tel (02) 561 1498.
w jso.co.il

Kan Zaman
See Bars and Pubs.

Ticho House
9 Ha-Rav Kook Street, West Jerusalem. **Map** 1 A2.
Tel (02) 624 4168.

YMCA
26 King David Street, West Jerusalem. **Map** 1 A4.
Tel (02) 569 2692.

Rock, Pop & Jazz

Confederation House
12 Emile Botta St, Yemin Moshe. **Map** 1 B4. **Tel** (02) 624 5206. **w** confederationhouse.org

Yellow Submarine
13 Ha-Rechavim Street, Talpiot, West Jerusalem.
Tel (02) 679 4040.
w yellowsubmarine.org.il

Theatre & Dance

Efron Dance Centre
19 Yehosha Yevin, Emek Hamatzleva.
Tel (02) 679 6552.
w horajerusalem.org

El-Hakawati Palestinian National Theatre
El-Nuzha Street, East Jerusalem. **Map** 1 C1.
Tel (02) 628 0957.
w pnt-pal.org

Gerard Bahar Performance Centre
11 Bezalel Street, Nakhla'ot, West Jerusalem.
Tel (02) 625 1139.

Jerusalem Theatre
20 David Marcus Street, Talbiye, West Jerusalem.
Tel (02) 560 5755.
w jerusalem-theatre.co.il

Khan Theatre
2 David Remez Square, West Jerusalem.
Tel (02) 671 8281.
w khan.co.il

Zappa Club
28 Hebron Road, West Jerusalem. **Map** 1 B5.
Tel (03) 762 6666 or *9080. **w** zappa-club.co.il

JERUSALEM STREET FINDER

The map references that are given throughout the Jerusalem chapters of this guide refer to the maps on the following pages only. References are also given in the listings for hotels *(see pp260–63)* and restaurants *(see pp270–75)*. Some of the many small streets and alleys may not be named on the maps. Many streets and monuments have two or even three names: one in Hebrew, one in Arabic and, occasionally, a commonly used English-

language form, too. What we call Damascus Gate is also known as Shaar Shkhem to Israelis and Bab el-Amud to Arabs. In this guide and on the following maps, where there is a sufficiently well-recognized English name, we have used it; otherwise, we have used the Arabic names for predominantly Arab areas (for example, the Muslim Quarter of the Old City) and Hebrew names for Jewish areas. Spellings in this guide may vary from those you see on street signs.

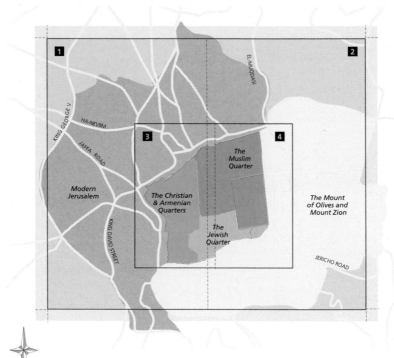

Key to Jerusalem Street Finder

- Major sight
- Other sight
- Other important building
- Bus station
- Light Rail stop
- *i* Tourist information
- Synagogue
- Church
- **C** Mosque
- ···· Route of Via Dolorosa
- **IV** Station of the Cross

- Hospital with casualty unit
- Pedestrian street
- Covered street
- 25» Street number

Scale of Map above

| 0 metres | 1000 |
| 0 yards | 1000 |

Scale of Maps 1 – 2

| 0 metres | 250 |
| 0 yards | 250 |

Scale of Maps 3 – 4

| 0 metres | 100 |
| 0 yards | 100 |

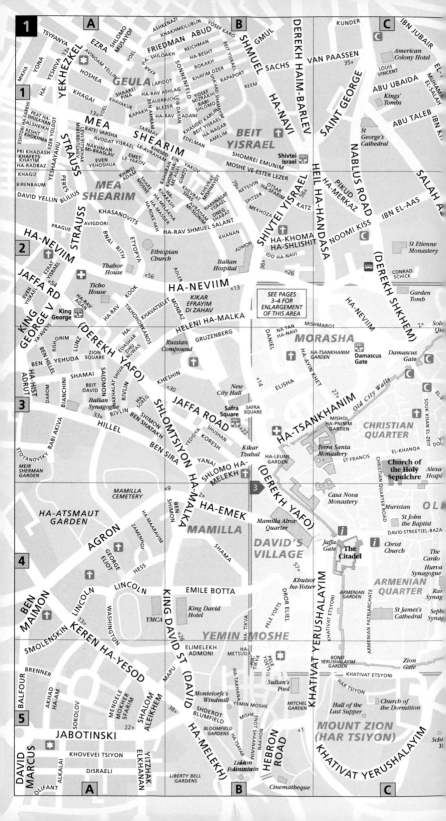

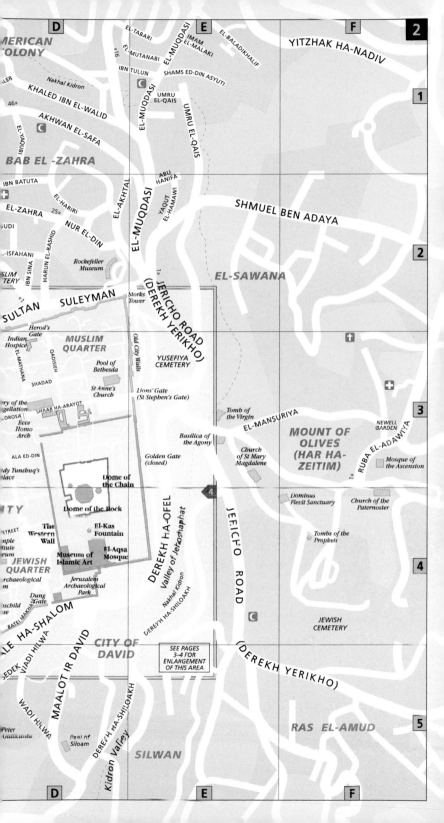

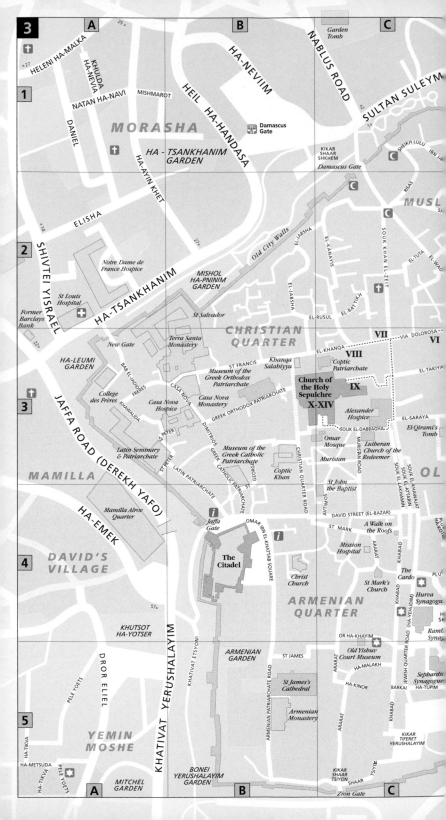

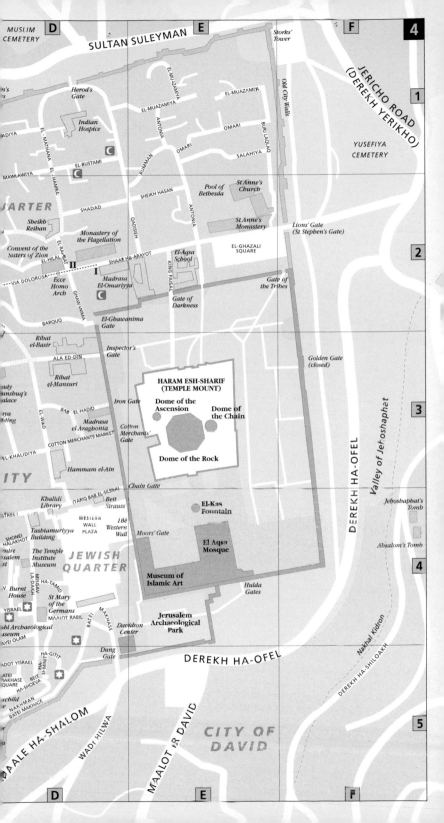

MUSLIM CEMETERY

D · E · F · 4

SULTAN SULEYMAN

Storks' Tower

JERICHO ROAD (DEREKH YERIKHO)

1

Herod's Gate
EL-MUZAMIYA
EL-MUAZAMIYA
EL-MUAZAMIYA

Indian Hospice

ANTONIA
OMARI
OMARI
BURJ LAQLAQ
SALAHIYA

Old City Walls

YUSEFIYA CEMETERY

'ADIYA
EL-MATHANA
EL-HAMRA

C
EL-BUSTAMI

RUMMAN

MAWLAWIYA

JARTER

SHEIKH HASAN

SHADAD

Pool of Bethesda

St Anne's Church

Sheikh Reiban

ANTONIA

St Anne's Monastery

Lions' Gate (St Stephen's Gate)

2

Convent of the Sisters of Zion

Monastery of the Flagellation

EL-GHAZALI SQUARE

EL-HILAL
EL-RAHBAT

QADISEH

SHAAR HA-ARAYOT

El-Aqsa School

II
VIA DOLOROSA
Ecce Homo Arch

I

Madrasa El-Omariyya

C

KING FAISAL

Gate of the Tribes

BARQUQ

GHAWANIMA

Gate of Darkness

El-Ghawanima Gate

Ribat el-Basir

Inspector's Gate

ALA ED-DIN

Ribat el-Mansuri

'ady
umshuq's
alace

BAB EL HADID

Iron Gate

Golden Gate (closed)

3

aya
ding

EL-WAD

Madrasa el Aragbonia

Cotton Merchants' Gate

HARAM ESH-SHARIF (TEMPLE MOUNT)

Dome of the Ascension

Dome of the Chain

EL-KHALIDIYA

COTTON MERCHANTS MARKET

Dome of the Rock

Valley of Jehoshaphat

EL-KHALIDIYA

Hammam el-Ain

Chain Gate

Khalidi Library

(TARIQ BAB EL-SILSILA)

Beit Strauss

El-Kas Fountain

Jehoshaphat's Tomb

STREET

WESTERN WALL PLAZA

The Western Wall

Absalom's Tomb

SHONE HALAKHOT

Tashtamuriyya Building

entre
salem
st

The Temple Institute Museum

JEWISH QUARTER

Moors' Gate

El Aqsa Mosque

4

MISGAV
LA-DAKH

HA-TAMID

Museum of Islamic Art

Burnt House

St Mary of the Germans

MAALOT RABIL

Hulda Gates

YISRAEL

BATEI

MAKHASE

shl Archaeological
useum
AYEI OLAM

Davidson Center

Jerusalem Archaeological Park

NAKHMAN

ADOT YISRAEL

HA-GITIT

Dung Gate

DEREKH HA-OFEL

schild
e

ATEI
MAKHASE
QUARE

HA-SHOEVA

BEIT

BATEI MAKHASE

Nakhal Kidron

PAALE HA-SHALOM

WADI HILWA

MAALOT IR DAVID

CITY OF DAVID

DEREKH HA-SHILOAKH

D · E · F

DEREKH HA-OFEL

ISRAEL, PETRA & SINAI REGION BY REGION

Israel, Petra & Sinai at a Glance

The Holy Land is rich in historical sights far beyond its biblical associations. In Petra it has one of the most unusual and magical ruined cities in the world, and the Roman-era remains at sites such as Jerash in Jordan and Beth Shean in northern Israel are similarly stunning. The scenery that the visitor encounters while travelling can also be dramatic, especially in the region of the Dead Sea (a geographic marvel in itself) and in the Sinai peninsula. Off the coast of Sinai, the Red Sea conceals underwater scenery every bit as spectacular as that on dry land.

Waterfront at Jaffa, a virtual suburb of Tel Aviv and a favourite place for city-dwellers to dine at weekends

Beautiful sandstone cloisters at the Church of the Nativity in Bethlehem

St Catherine's Monastery, Sinai, one of the world's oldest continuously functioning monasteries

◀ A mesmeric view of sunrise at the Dead Sea

Netanya

Tel Aviv

Jerus

Gaza

THE DEAD
AND THE
NEGEV DES
(see pp190–20

Eilat

Aqaba

THE RED SEA
AND SINAI
(see pp240–53)

Sharm
el-Sheikh

E COAST
O GALILEE
e pp168–89)

● Amman

PETRA AND
WESTERN
JORDAN
(see pp210–39)

● Ma'an

View from the shore of the Sea of Galilee, rich in associations with the miracles and teachings of Jesus Christ

The ruined main street of Jerash, the best-preserved Roman city in the Holy Land

The mountaintop fortress of Masada on the Dead Sea, the most visited site in Israel after Jerusalem

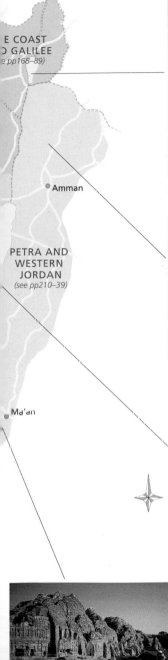

The incredible shaping of the landscape in the carved rock façades of Petra

| 0 kilometres | 50 |
| 0 miles | 50 |

THE COAST AND GALILEE

A fertile corridor squeezed between the sea and the desert, this is the Promised Land of the Old Testament. The green hills and fresh waters of Galilee provided the setting for many episodes in the early life and ministry of Christ. Beside all its religious associations this is very much a secular paradise too, the heartland of modern Israel and a sun-drenched scenic magnet for tourists.

The wealth of ancient sites along this stretch of coast bears witness to the fact that for centuries this has been an important land corridor connecting Africa, Europe and Asia. The great empires of ancient Egypt to the south and Assyria and Babylon to the east met here in trade and battle. Later, the Romans exploited this coastline with the laying of a great highway, the Via Maris, and Herod built a magnificent port in Caesarea (see p180), one of the grandest and most important in the eastern Mediterranean. Ports such as this formed the nuclei of the Latin Kingdoms when the Crusaders came conquering in the Middle Ages. The Muslim Arabs eventually drove out the Christian knights but their legacy remains in some superb muscular

architecture, especially at Akko, which retains one of the most charming old towns in the whole of the Holy Land. When in the 19th century the first major waves of Jewish immigrants began arriving, it was on the fertile coastal plains and rolling hills of Galilee that they chose to settle. They planted wheat and cotton in the fields, orange groves and vineyards on the slopes, and cities overlooking the sea. The capital they founded, Tel Aviv, has become a vibrant centre of culture and commerce, while Haifa, attractively tumbling down Mount Carmel to the sea, is a thriving economic powerhouse. Inland Galilee remains rural and idyllic, equally pleasing to pilgrims on the trail of Christ and to seekers of relaxation and the picturesque.

Lush green fields next to the sea in Galilee

◀ An aerial view of the Tel Aviv cityscape at sunset

Exploring the Coast and Galilee

Northern Israel is arguably the most attractive region in the Holy Land. The coast has long white sandy beaches, while Galilee is a landscape of rolling green hills, forested valleys and clear freshwater lakes. The Golan even has mountains that are capped with snow for part of each year. Places of interest include the hilltop Jewish holy town of Safed, Nazareth, traditionally held to be where Jesus spent his childhood, and many fine archaeological sites, including Crusader castles and Roman towns. With such a concentration of beauty spots and picturesque vistas, this is an area ideally explored by car.

Sights at a Glance

Herod the Great's port of Caesarea, now an impressive set of ruins beside the sea

Getting Around

Jerusalem and Tel Aviv are linked by a good motorway. Buses depart roughly every 15 minutes and the journey takes less than an hour. Northbound services along the coastal highway from Tel Aviv to Caesarea and Haifa are only slightly less frequent. Trains link Tel Aviv and Jerusalem, and there is a coastal line from Tel Aviv to Nahariya. A fast train connecting Tel Aviv and Jerusalem, taking less than 30 minutes, is due to be in place by 2018.

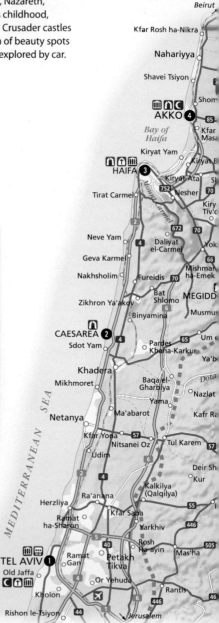

The Sea of Galilee viewed from the Church of the Beatitudes, Tabgha

Key

 Motorway

── Major road

⋯⋯ Minor road

── Scenic route

⌐⌐ Railway

━━ International border

▪ ▪ Disputed border/Ceasefire line

```
0 kilometres            20
0 miles         10
```

Old Jaffa, where the Gan ha-Pisga Gardens crown a hilltop with splendid views of seafront Tel Aviv

❶ Tel Aviv

Tel Aviv represents the modern face of the Jewish state – a brash, confident centre of commerce and contemporary culture. It is also a true Mediterranean resort city, with a long, sandy beach fringed by cafés, bars and shops. Away from the seafront are gracious palm-filled avenues, lined with elegant buildings in the international Bauhaus style *(see p175)*. All this has been created since 1909, when the Jewish National Fund purchased land among the dunes north of the old Arab port of Jaffa *(see pp178–9)* on which to build a new city, to be called Tel Aviv ("Hill of the Spring").

Mosaic flooring at the Eretz Israel Museum in northern Tel Aviv

🏛 Beit Hatfutsot (Museum of the Jewish People)
University Campus, Gate 2, Klausner St, Ramat Aviv. **Tel** (03) 745 7808. **Open** 10am–4pm Sun–Tue, 10am–7pm Wed & Thu, 9am–1pm Fri. 🅿 🌐 **bh.org.il**

When it opened in 1978, this was regarded as one of the world's most innovative museums. It is still worth setting aside several hours to visit. Instead of showing historical artifacts, it uses thematically arranged dioramas, interactive displays and short videos to illustrate aspects of life in the Jewish diaspora, past and present, throughout the world, and the influence of Jewish arts and literature on other cultures. One of the highlights is a display of beautifully made scale models of synagogues from various countries. The permanent collection is supplemented by temporary exhibitions. There is also a genealogy centre, where Jews from around the world can trace their lineage.

Beit Hatfutsot exhibit

🏛 Eretz Israel Museum
2 Haim Levanon, Ramat Aviv. **Tel** (03) 641 5244. **Open** 10am–4pm Sun–Wed, 10am–8pm Thu, 10am–2pm Fri & Sat. 🅿 🌐 **eretzmuseum. org.il**

Built around the site of Tel Qasile, where excavations have revealed layers of human habitation dating back to 1200 BC, this museum depicts the history and culture of the land of Israel. It comprises a number of themed pavilions, all containing permanent exhibitions. One has a very fine collection of ancient and Islamic-era glass; others are devoted to coins, ancient pottery, Judaica, copper mining, postal history and philately, and to ancient crafts. Additionally there's a square with a collection of beautiful mosaic floors from early synagogues, churches and mosques; an old olive oil press; a reconstructed flour mill; and a 1925 fire engine given by the city of New York to Tel Aviv's volunteer fire brigade in 1947.

Historical Jewish personages, part of a display at Beit Hatfutsot

Tel Aviv Marina
Gordon Swimming Pool
Ben Gu House
BEN GU
Gordon Beach
GORDON S
FRISHMAN
Ba
Beachfront Promenade ④
HERBERT SAMUEL ESPLANADE
HAYARKON STREET
BEN YEHUDA STREET
Old Cemete
Trumpeldor Beach
Opera Towers
ALLENBY ST
Geula Beach
GEULA ST
⑨ Carme Marke
YEMENITE QUARTER
Hassan Bek Mosque
Charles Clore Park
MANSHIYE
Shalon Tower
⑫
HA-CARMEL
PINES STREET
Indepe
Etzel Museum
KAUFMAN STREET
NEVE TZEDEK
⑬
HaTachana
Suzanne Dellal Centre
EILAT STREET
Old Jaffa
③

0 metres		600
0 yards		600

Sights at a Glance

1. Beit Hatfutsot (Museum of the Jewish People)
2. Eretz Israel Museum
3. Old Port
4. Beachfront Promenade
5. Dizengoff Street
6. Rabin Square
7. Tel Aviv Museum of Art
8. Bialik Street
9. Yemenite Quarter
10. Shalom Tower
11. Rothschild Avenue
12. Manshiye
13. Neve Tzedek

A café on the boardwalk in the fashionable Old Port area

VISITORS' CHECKLIST

Practical Information
Road map B3. 404,400.
46 Herbert Samuel Rd,
(03) 516 6188. Beach Festival
(Jul & Aug). daily.

Transport
Ben Gurion, 22 km (14 miles)
SE. Arlosoroff Station,
Arlosoroff Rd, *5770. New
Central Bus Station, Levinsky St,
(03) 639 4444 or *2787.

bigger facilities were created in Ashdod to the south, and lay neglected for around 30 years until the site was revitalized in the 1990s. It is now a lively area of cafés, bars, night-clubs, restaurants and shops. (Check www.namal.co.il for events and other details.) There is even an antiques market on Saturdays. Many of the businesses are on the boardwalk facing the sea; some also have a view of the old power plant just across the river. The promenade continues past the power station, north along the beachfront.

Beachfront Promenade

A white-sand beach stretches right along the seafront of central Tel Aviv, backed by a long promenade, modern hotels and Miami-style condo-miniums. It is possible to walk all the way from the Old Port in the north down to Jaffa in the south (see pp178–9) along the promenade. At its northern end this takes the form of a big, rolling wooden deck, which in parts gently undulates like sand dunes. This is a favourite area for fishermen and for wedding couples, who have their photographs taken with the Mediterranean Sea as a backdrop.

Further south, in the vicinity of **Independence Park** (Gan Ha-Atzmaut), there's a small children's playground. Beside this, a section of beach is screened off for the use of Orthodox Jews (men and women on different days).

The city-centre stretch of beach is dominated by the huge, pink **Opera Towers**, with shops and restaurants at street level and a distinctive stepped profile. The beach here is crowded all summer with sun-seekers and, after dark, with open-air concert- and discn-goers. Strong sea currents mean that you should swim only where you see white flags. Red flags mean that it is dangerous, black flags that it is forbidden.

Old Port

North of the centre, at the point at which the Yarkon River empties into the Mediterranean, Tel Aviv's port (known as the Namal) was developed in the late 1930s to lessen Jewish dependence on the Arab port of Jaffa. It was decommissioned in 1965, when

The beachfront parade in central Tel Aviv, part of a promenade that stretches the length of the city

For map symbols see back flap

Exploring Tel Aviv

North central Tel Aviv is where the money is. Visit Basel Street for chic cafés and boutiques. The real heart of the city, however, lies south of Ben Gurion Avenue, which is named for Israel's first prime minister *(see p57)*; his former home at No. 17 is now a museum. The main streets run north–south and are Ben Yehuda Street and Dizengoff Street *(see below)*, both of which run almost the whole length of the city centre. South again is the Yemenite Quarter and the districts of Manshiye and Neve Tzedek, which are some of the oldest parts of Tel Aviv.

Dizengoff Square with a performing fountain at its centre

🚇 Dizengoff Street
The city's main shopping street is named after Tel Aviv's first mayor, Meir Dizengoff. It is at its liveliest around the junction with Frishmann Street, where there are plenty of street cafés with pavement seating and a large branch of the Israeli chain bookstore Steimetzky's. Also here is the **Bauhaus Center**, which is dedicated to raising awareness of Tel Aviv's unique architectural heritage *(see p175)*. To this end, the Center runs two-hour English-language tours at 10am each Friday, visiting some of the city's Bauhaus buildings.

One block south of the Bauhaus Center is **Dizengoff Square**, an irregularly shaped concrete platform raised above a traffic underpass. It sports a drum-like fountain by Israeli artist Yaacov Agam that has water jets programmed to perform hourly light and music shows. On Tuesdays and Fridays, the square is host to a flea market. On the east side are two beautifully renovated Bauhaus buildings, one of which is now the **Hotel Cinema Eden**;

it's possible to take the elevator up to the fifth-floor roof terrace to enjoy the city views.

🏛 Bauhaus Center
99 Dizengoff St. **Tel** (03) 522 0249. **Open** 10am–7:30pm Sun–Thu, 10am–2:30pm Fri, noon–7:30pm Sat.
Ⓦ bauhaus-center.com

🚇 Rabin Square
A large, rectangular plaza in the eastern part of central Tel Aviv, Rabin Square is overlooked by **City Hall**, a brutal concrete block that is only slightly softened by having its windows painted in

Modern large-scale sculpture outside the Tel Aviv Museum of Art

different colours. The square is a venue for demonstrations, celebrations and concerts. It was at one such gathering – a peace rally on 4 November 1995 – that the then Israeli prime minister Yitzhak Rabin was assassinated. The basalt stones of the **Rabin Memorial** on Ibn Givrol Street, beside City Hall, occupy the very spot where he was shot. Nearby is a wall covered with graffiti drawn by mourning citizens and now preserved behind glass.

At the centre of the square is another memorial, the **Monument of Holocaust and Resistance**, a huge glass-and-iron structure erected in the 1970s and designed by well-known and often controversial Israeli artist Yigal Tumarkin. An eco pool was added next to it after renovation.

There are some good shops on the west side of the square, notably Tola'at Seferim, a bookshop with a pleasant café, and Mayu, a youthful fashion boutique. Across on the east side is Brasserie, an excellent Art Deco, French-style restaurant.

🏛 Tel Aviv Museum of Art
27 Ha-Melekh Shaul Ave. **Tel** (03) 607 7000. **Open** 10am–4pm Mon & Wed, 10am–8pm Tue & Thu, 10am–2pm Fri, 10am–4pm Sat.
Ⓦ tamuseum.org.il

Israel's most important collection of 19th- and 20th-century art includes works representing the major trends of Modernism: Impressionism (Degas, Renoir, Monet), Post-Impressionism (Van Gogh, Gauguin, Cézanne), Cubism (Braque, Leger, Metzinger) and Surrealism (Miró), as well as key pieces by Pablo Picasso. Other works range from 17th-century Flemish to modern Israeli. In addition to the permanent collections, there are excellent temporary exhibtions. A ticket also covers entrance to the **Helena Rubenstein Pavilion** on Habima Square, where additional contemporary art shows are held.

Tel Aviv's Bauhaus Architecture

Tel Aviv has the world's largest assemblage of buildings in the International Modern style, also known as Bauhaus. Altogether there are some 4,000 examples within the city. These buildings, largely erected in the 1930s and 1940s, were designed by immigrant architects trained in Europe, particularly in Germany, home of the modernist Bauhaus School between 1919 and 1933. The simplicity and functionality of the style, which aimed to unify art with technology, was considered highly appropriate to the socialist ideals of Zionism that underpinned the founding of the new city. In 2003, Tel Aviv's unique and bountiful Bauhaus legacy was recognized by the United Nations cultural agency UNESCO, who declared the "White City" on the Mediterranean a World Heritage Site.

Horizontals Characteristics of Bauhaus architecture include asymmetrical façades with "ribbons" of windows running horizontally. Balconies are often curbed and have overhanging ledges to provide shade for the rooms below.

Verticals The sole vertical element in the typical Bauhaus building is provided by the internal stairwell this appears on the façade as a ladder-like arrangement of windows.

Ships Some of the most striking buildings were inspired by the superstructure of the ships that brought the Jewish immigrants to Palestine. Windows shaped like maritime portholes are a common feature.

Where to look The highest concentration of Bauhaus buildings is on Rothschild Boulevard and neighbouring Ahad Ha'am Street. The Bauhaus Centre, on Dizengoff Street, is a source of books and information on the subject, as well as a place to find some unusual souvenirs.

Rounded forms Although initially Bauhaus buildings were completely rectilinear, later architects began to introduce more rounded forms. This was decried by purists who regarded curves as heretical because of their supposed impracticality: "How do you hang a picture on a curved wall?" they asked.

Olive stall at Carmel Market on Ha-Carmel Street, Tel Aviv

🕮 Bialik Street

Bialik is one of the city's most historic streets. At No. 14 is the **Rubin Museum**, the former residence of one of Israel's most famous painters, Reuven Rubin (1893–1974). It now contains a permanent collection of 45 of his works, as well as a historical archive of his life. Changing exhibits also feature other Israeli artists.

A few doors along, **Bialik House** (Beit Bialik) is the former home of Haim Nahman Bialik (1873–1934), Israel's national poet. The house has been kept as it was during Bialik's time, and includes a library and paintings by some of Israel's best-known artists.

A little south of Bialik, **Bezalel Street** is home to a colourful and popular street market famed for cut-price fashion. There are also numerous food stalls that offer traditional local cuisine. South again, **Sheinkin Street** was a centre of alternative culture in the 1980s. That is no longer the case, but it still boasts many independent shops and some great places to eat.

🏛 Rubin Museum

14 Bialik St. **Tel** (03) 525 5961. **Open** 10am–3pm Mon, Wed & Thu, 10am–8pm Tue, 10am–3pm Fri, 11am–2pm Sat. 🚗 🗎 **rubinmuseum.org.il**

🏛 Bialik House

22 Bialik St. **Tel** (03) 525 4530. **Open** 9am–5pm Mon–Thu, 10am–2pm Fri & Sat. 🚗 📷 (book ahead).

🕮 Yemenite Quarter

A masterplan for Tel Aviv was drawn up by Scottish urban planner Sir Patrick Geddes at the request of Mayor Dizengoff in 1925. This influenced the growth of the city for decades to come. The Yemenite Quarter (Kerem Ha-Temanim), however, predates the Geddes plan, and its maze of small streets contrasts sharply with the orderly layout of the rest of the city. The architecture also predates the arrival of the Bauhaus style that characterizes much of the rest of Tel Aviv. Here, buildings instead employ motifs from Classical, Moorish and Art Nouveau styles. This is most apparent on **Nakhalat Binyamin Street**, which boasts many curious, if slightly faded, examples of this eclectic architecture. The street is especially worth visiting on Tuesdays and Fridays, when it hosts a busy craft market. This is also one of the busiest nightlife streets, in particular the area around the junctions with Rothschild Avenue and Lilienblum Street.

Street performer on Nakhalat Binyamin

The other local landmark is **Carmel Market** (open 9am–6pm Sun–Thu, 9am–3pm Fri), which is on Ha-Carmel Street and is the city's largest and busiest open-air market. It begins near the junction with Allenby Street, with stalls selling cheap clothing and household items, before switching to fresh fish, meat, fruit and vegetables, spices and herbs, breads and biscuits, and nuts and seeds. Many of the side streets off Ha-Carmel specialize in different food produce.

🕮 Shalom Tower

9 Ahad Ha'am St. **Tel** (03) 517 7304. **Open** 9am–6pm Sun–Thu, 9am–2pm Fri. 🗎 **migdalshalom.co.il**

One block west of Nakhalat Binyamin Street, this austere, 1960s office building sits on the former site of Israel's first secular Hebrew school. At the time of its construction, the tower was the tallest structure in Israel. There are impressive mosaics by Nahum Gutman in the lobby area, and a small museum of the city's history on the mezzanine. Also of interest are several small exhibitions that contain models of Tel Aviv and multi-media presentations, plus an art gallery. A free elevator ride to the 29th floor affords a fabulous view of the city.

🕮 Rothschild Avenue

This is one of Tel Aviv's most elegant old thoroughfares, lined with palm trees and some of the city's finest examples of Bauhaus buildings (see p175). **Independence Hall** (Beit Ha-Tanakh) at No. 6 was once the residence of the first mayor, Meir Dizengoff. This is also where Ben Gurion declared

Twice-weekly craft market on Nakhalat Binyamin in the Yemenite Quarter

For hotels and restaurants in this region see pp261–2 and pp271–3

The attractive little Hassan Bek Mosque, founded by a local governor

the independence of Israel on 14 May 1948. The museum's Hall of Declaration remains as it was on that day, with original microphones on the table and a portrait of Herzl, the Zionist leader. Nearby 23 Allenby Street is now the **Haganah Museum**. The Haganah was the clandestine pre-1948 military organization that later became the Israeli army.

Independence Hall
16 Rothschild Blvd. **Tel** (03) 517 3942. **Open** 9am–5pm Sun–Thu, 9am–2pm Fri.

Haganah Museum
23 Rothschild Blvd. **Tel** (03) 560 8624. **Open** 8am–4pm Sun–Thu.

Manshiye
Manshiye is the coastal neighbourhood that acts as a buffer between the twin municipalities of Tel Aviv and Jaffa (see pp178–9). Its most distinguished landmark is the **Hassan Bek Mosque** on the main seafront road, built in 1916 by a governor of Jaffa of the same name. During the 1948 War, Arab soldiers used the mosque's minaret as a firing position; this is one of the episodes recorded in the nearby **Etzel Museum 1947–1948**, which is dedicated to the Israeli defence forces and their role in this particular conflict. Historical documents, photos, newspaper clippings and weapons are exhibited in a purpose-built, black-glass structure in the attractive **Charles Clore Park** on the seafront. The park is a venue for many of the city's big open-air events, including the annual Love Parade.

Etzel Museum 1947–1948
15 Goldman St. **Tel** (03) 528 4001. **Open** 8am–4pm Sun–Thu.

Neve Tzedek
Neve Tzedek is where Tel Aviv began. The settlement was founded on empty sandy flats in the late 1880s by a group of Jewish families keen to escape overcrowding in the port of Jaffa. Today, the area retains the feel of a small village, with narrow lanes lined by high walls and a strange mix of architectural styles. Decades of neglect are currently being reversed by an energetic programme of renovation and restoration.

At the heart of the district is the **Suzanne Dellal Centre** for dance and drama. It boasts four performance halls in a building that was once a local school. The main courtyard, with orange trees and tiled murals, is a popular place to meet and relax.

Nearby, the **Rokach House Museum** occupies the former home of Shimon Rokach, one of the founding fathers of Neve Tzedek. Inside, photos and documents illustrate the daily life of the community at the end of the 19th century.

A few doors away, the **Nahum Gutman Museum** is dedicated to another of Israel's best-known artists, a Russian-born painter who was also admired for his children's books. As well as displaying a small collection of Gutman's work, the galleries are used for temporary exhibitions.

A short walk away is **HaTachana**, an old train station that has been transformed into a modern centre of leisure and culture, to go with attractively restored period buildings, shops and restaurants.

Suzanne Dellal Centre
6 Yehieli St. **Tel** (03) 510 5656.

Rokach House Museum
36 Shimon Rockach St. **Tel** (03) 516 8042. **Open** 10am–4pm Sun–Thu, 10am–2pm Fri & Sat.
W rokach-house.co.il

Nahum Gutman Museum
21 Shimon Rockach St. **Tel** (03) 516 1970. **Open** 10am–4pm Mon–Thu (to 2pm Fri, to 3pm Sat).
W gutmanmuseum.co.il

HaTachana
Parking entrance on Hamered St.
W hatachana.co.il

The history of Neve Tzedek in tiled murals at the Suzanne Dellal Centre

Street-by-Street: Old Jaffa

According to the Bible, Jaffa (then called Joppa) was founded in the wake of the great flood by Noah's son Japheth. Archaeologists have unearthed remains dating back to the 20th century BC, establishing Jaffa as one of the world's oldest ports. However, with the growth of Tel Aviv, Jaffa, which had flourished under the Ottomans, went into decline. Following Jewish victory in the 1948 War, it was absorbed into the new city to the north. The core of the old town has since been revived as an attractive arts, crafts and dining centre.

The seafront of Old Jaffa, with its warehouses reborn as restaurants

Ha-Pisga open-air amphitheatre is used for concerts during the summer.

The Mahmoudiya Mosque dates from 1812 and remains in use by the local Muslim community.

To Flea Market

To Clock Tower

A 19th-century *sabil* (fountain)

Napoleonic cannons

To the Promenade

MIFRAZ SHLOMO

HA-ALIYAH HA-SHNIYA

Clock Tower
Built in 1901 to mark the 25th anniversary of the then Turkish sultan, the clock tower has since been heavily restored and now serves as a symbol of modern Jaffa.

The Sea Mosque was the mosque of local fishermen.

| 0 metres | 50 |
| 0 yards | 50 |

Key

━ Suggested route

Gan Ha-Pisga
Ha-Pisga garden lies on top of the ancient "tel" (mound) of Jaffa. An observation area, marked by the curious *Statue of Faith*, offers good views across to Tel Aviv.

★ Artists' Quarter
This compact area of old Arab houses and narrow stone-flagged alleys has been transformed into residences, studios and galleries for artists and craftspeople.

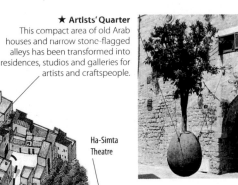

VISITORS' CHECKLIST

Practical Information
2 km (1 mile) S of central Tel Aviv. *i* Kedumim Square, (03) 518 4015. **Open** summer: 9am–8pm Sun–Thu & Sat, 9am–4pm Fri; winter: 9am–5pm Sun–Thu & Sat, 9am–3pm Fri. **W** **oldjaffa.co.il**

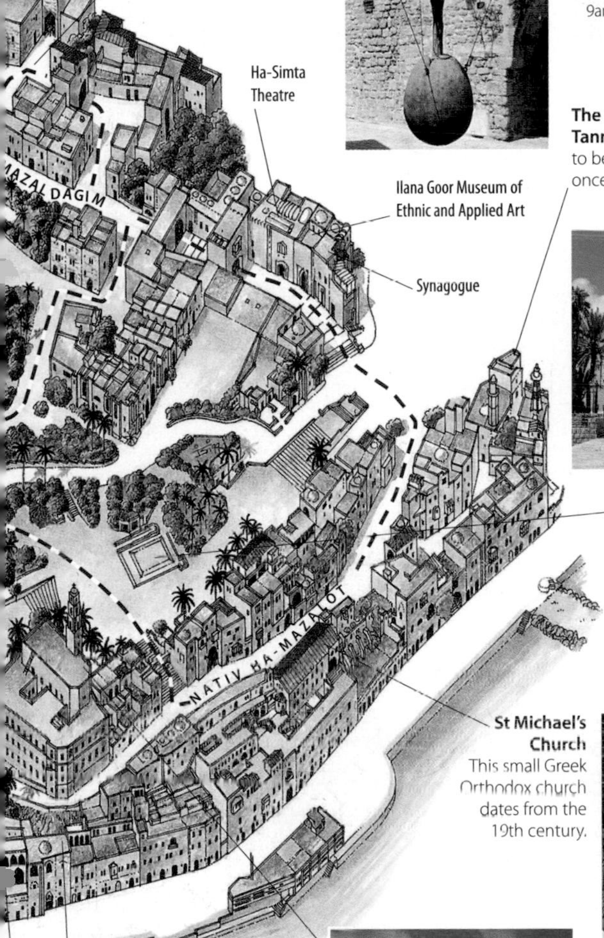

MAZAL DAGIM
NATIV HA-MAZALOT
Ha-Simta Theatre
Ilana Goor Museum of Ethnic and Applied Art
Synagogue

The House of Simon the Tanner is traditionally held to be where the apostle Peter once stayed (Acts 9: 43).

★ Kedumim Square
Underneath the picturesque main square of Old Jaffa is the Visitors' Centre, with exposed Roman-era exhibits and a sound-and-light show about the old city.

St Michael's Church
This small Greek Orthodox church dates from the 19th century.

The Monastery of St Nicholas, built around 1667, still serves Jaffa's Armenian community.

The Wishing Bridge is said to bring true the wish of anyone crossing it if they touch the bronze statue of their zodiac sign while looking at the sea.

Monastery of St Peter
Built in Latin American Baroque style, this Roman Catholic monastery and church was dedicated in 1891. It stands on a site formerly occupied by a Crusader citadel.

The impressive Roman aqueduct at Caesarea

❷ Caesarea

Road map B2. 🚌 76 and 77 from Khadera. 🛈 *6550 (ext. 4).
🌐 caesarea.com

At the height of his power, in 29–22 BC, Herod the Great *(see pp47–9)* built a splendid city over the site of an ancient Phoenician port and dedicated it to Augustus Caesar, the Roman emperor. The splendour of this city is attested to by the lavish description of it by Flavius Josephus in his book *The Jewish War*. Until it was excavated, this had been seen by many scholars as wild exaggeration.

This prosperity lasted in Caesarea until AD 614, after which its history became more unstable. During the early 12th century and the Crusades, Caesarea again became an important city, and was used once more as a port. By the late 13th century, however, it had been destroyed by the Mamelukes and was left to be reclaimed by the sand, with only a small Arab village remaining. The importance of these great hidden ruins was not realized until the 1940s; now Caesarea is one of Israel's major archaeological sites.

Most of the main sights lie in the **Caesarea National Park**.

The magnificent ruins of the Roman theatre at Caesarea

If entering from the south, you will first see the huge Roman theatre. With seats for 4,000 spectators, it has been restored, and hosts summer concerts. A short distance to the west, on a small coastal promontory, a group of half-submerged walls indicate the site of Herod's palace. Further inland are the neglected ruins of one of the largest hippodromes in the Roman Empire. On the coast by the inner harbour is the Crusader citadel, still surrounded by walls which date back to around AD 1250. Enclosing this whole area are the ruins of the much larger

Crusader city walls. Within these ruins lies the unique **Underwater Archaeological Park**. The four diving complexes at this park enable divers to see the techniques used to build the ancient port, as well as remnants of wrecked ships.

North of the ancient city is a Roman aqueduct dating from the Herodian period. Extending for 17 km (11 miles), it carried water from the foothills of Mount Carmel to Caesarea. A short way to the south of the site, the **Caesarea Museum** has interesting artifacts from the Roman city.

🏛 Caesarea National Park
Tel (04) 626 7080. **Open** 8am–4pm (summer: 6pm) daily. Closes 1 hr earlier Fri. 🅿 ♿

🏛 Underwater Archaeological Park
Caesarea Harbour. **Tel** (04) 626 5898. **Open** summer: 9am–5pm Sun–Thu, 7am–5pm Fri & Sat; winter: 10am–4pm Sun–Thu, 7am–4pm Fri & Sat. Visits must be booked in advance. 🅿 ♿

🏛 Caesarea Museum
Kibbutz Sdot Yam. **Tel** (04) 636 4367. **Open** 10am–4pm Sun & Tue–Thu, 10am–1pm Fri. 🅿 📷 ♿

Ruins of Caesarea

① Roman Theatre
② Herod's Palace
③ Hippodrome
④ Byzantine Street
⑤ Crusader Citadel
⑥ Crusader Wall
⑦ Roman Aqueduct
⑧ Underwater Archaeological Park

Map labels:
Byzantine wall
Herodian amphitheatre
Herodian wall
To Modern Caesarea
Entrance
Outline of Herodian harbour
To Khadera
Entrance
To Caesarea Museum

0 metres 300
0 yards 300

❸ Haifa and Mount Carmel

The city of Haifa lies on the Mediterranean coast at the foot of Mount Carmel. Israel's third largest city, it is a major industrial centre. Away from the busy port, steep slopes rise up the mountain, providing quiet, attractive suburbs for the wealthy. A small trading port for most of its history, Haifa was conquered by the Crusaders in the early 12th century *(see pp52–3)*, and later fortified under Ottoman rule. In the late 19th century it became an important refuge for Jewish immigrants. Between 1918 and 1948, Haifa was taken over by the British in the occupation of Palestine. Today it is a mixed, non-religious city, and the only one in Israel where buses run on Saturdays.

Tourists enjoying spectacular views at the Baha'i Shrine and Gardens in Haifa

🏛 Madatech: The Israeli National Museum of Science, Technology and Space
Old Technion, 12 Balfour St.
Tel (04) 861 4444. **Open** daily. 🅿 ♿
🖵 mustsee.co.il

The former Technology Institute in the city centre is one of Haifa's most important buildings. Founded by German immigrants in the early 1900s, it was Israel's first institute of higher education. Renovated many times, it is now home to Madatech, which has many interesting interactive exhibits, exploring the latest innovations in Israeli science.

🅲 Baha'i Shrine and Gardens
Ha-Ziyonut St. **Tel** (04) 831 3131.
Open daily (shrine; am only).
Closed One month in summer (shrine); see website for info. ♿ 📷
🖵 ganbahai.org.il

On the edge of the city centre towards Central Carmel is Haifa's most striking landmark, the impressive golden-domed Baha'i Shrine. Standing imperiously on the hillside, it is surrounded by a splendidly manicured garden and is the headquarters of the Baha'i faith. Its followers believe that no religion has a monopoly on the truth and aim to reconcile the teachings of all holy men. The ornate shrine houses the tomb of the Bab, the herald of Bahaulla. Bahaulla (1817–92) is the central figure of the Baha'i faith and is considered by his disciples to have been the most recent of God's messengers.

Central Carmel
South of the temple, Central Carmel spreads up the slopes of the mountain. A largely wealthy residential area, it manages to resist the onslaught of traffic and busy modern life. Its many parks, cafés and stylish bars make it a relaxing detour.

Bat Galim
Northwest of Central Carmel is the popular coastal area of Bat Galim. Close to the city centre, its beach and busy seafront promenade have made it a favourite with tourists. For those wanting more extensive beaches, however, try the attractive Carmel Beach. This is 6 km (4 miles) to the south, away from the busy city.

🏛 Carmelite Monastery
Stella Maris St. **Tel** (04) 833 7758.
Open daily. **Closed** 12:30–3pm daily, Sun am. ♿

On much of the upper slopes of Mount Carmel are wide stretches of vegetation, the remnants of an ancient forest. On these slopes, to the southwest of Bat Galim, is the Stella Maris Carmelite Monastery, which can be reached by cable car or on foot. Built in an area that for centuries was frequented by hermits, this was a place of worship near where the Carmelite order was founded. The beautiful church here dates from the early 1800s.

🏛 Elijah's Cave
201 Allenby St. **Tel** (04) 852 7430.
Open summer: 8am–6pm Sun–Fri (to 1pm Fri); winter: 8am–5pm Sun–Fri (to 1pm Fri).

Located below the monastery, this is where Elijah is said to have lived and meditated before defeating the pagan prophets of Baal on Mount Carmel. Today it is a synagogue with a Torah Ark and a niche in the ceiling where visitors can place notes.

Dome of the Stella Maris Carmelite Monastery on Mount Carmel

❹ Akko

Outside of Jerusalem, Akko (the historic Acre) has the most complete and charming old town in all of the Holy Land. Its origins date back to the Hellenistic period, but the form in which it survives today was set by the Arabs and their Crusader foes. After the Crusaders took Jerusalem in 1099, they seized Akko as their main port and lifeline back to Europe. Lost at one point to the Muslim armies under Saladin, it was regained by Richard I "the Lionheart". For most of the 13th century, with Jerusalem in the hands of the Muslims, Akko was the Crusaders' principal stronghold. As the Christian armies steadily lost ground, it was the last bastion to fall. Akko's fortunes were revived under a series of Ottoman governors, one of whom, Ahmed Pasha el-Jazzar, successfully defended the city against an invasion by Napoleon in 1799.

The harbour at Akko, in continuous use since Hellenistic times

Exploring Akko

Crusader Akko was destroyed by the victorious Arab armies in 1291, and what can be seen today is largely an 18th-century Turkish town built on the site of the old. The defensive **walls** are rebuildings of the original Crusader walls, fragments of which are still discernible. The warren-like street pattern is interrupted by three great khans, or merchants' inns: the **Khan el-Umdan** (Khan of the Columns), with its distinctive clock tower; the **Khan el-Faranj** (Khan of the Franks or Foreigners); and the **Khan a-Shuarda** (Khan of the Martyrs). While the khans date from the Ottoman era, they echo the fact that in Crusader times Akko had autonomous quarters given over to the merchants of Italy and Provence. Such was the rivalry between these colonies that at one point open warfare erupted between the Venetians and Genoese, who fought a sea battle off Akko in 1256. The khans are no longer in commercial use, but Akko does have a lively **souk** selling fruit, vegetables

and household items. You'll also find plenty of fresh fish, which you can see being brought ashore at the town's picturesque harbour early each morning.

There is also the Ethnographic Museum, which has a beautiful collection that illustrates life in Galilee from the 19th century to the start of the 20th century.

🅲 Mosque of El-Jazzar
El-Jazzar St. **Tel** (04) 991 3039.
Open daily. **Closed** during prayers. 🅿

Akko lay semi-derelict for more than 400 years after its

destruction in 1291. Its rebirth came with the rule of the emir Dahr el-Amr and his successor, Ahmed Pasha El-Jazzar ("the Butcher"), both of whom governed the city for the Ottomans in the second half of the 18th century. El-Jazzar, in particular, was a prolific builder. Among his legacy is the Turkish-style mosque (built 1781) that bears his name and continues to dominate the old town skyline. Its courtyard contains recycled columns from the Roman ruins of Caesarea and, at the centre, a small, elegant fountain used for ritual ablutions. By the mosque are the sarcophagi of El-Jazzar and his son, while underneath are the remains of a Crusader church that El-Jazzar had transformed into a cistern to collect rainwater.

🅲 Crusader City
El-Jazzar St. **Tel** (04) 995 6707.
Open winter: 8:30am–4pm daily; summer: 8:30am–5pm daily. Closes 1 hr earlier Fri. 🅿

When the Ottoman governors rebuilt Akko, they did so on top of the ruins of the Crusader city. The Crusader-era street level lies some 8 m (25 ft) below that of today. Part of it has been excavated, revealing a subterranean wealth of well-preserved examples of 12th- and 13th-century streets and buildings. There are some amazingly grand Gothic knights' halls, built around a broad courtyard. An extensive network of drainage channels has also been excavated. South of the courtyard is a large refectory

Akko's dominant landmark, the Turkish-style Mosque of El-Jazzar

Gothic-arched halls of the former Crusader City in Akko

with huge columns; in two corners you can still see carved lilies that may indicate building work done in the period of Louis VII of France, who arrived at Akko in 1148. Another of Akko's well-known visitors was Marco Polo and it is quite possible that he dined in this very room. Below the refectory is a network of underground passageways that lead to an area known as El-Bosta (from the Arabic for "post office", which is what the Turks used this space for); divided by columns into six

sections, it was originally the crypt of St John's Church.

🏛 Citadel

Off Ha-Hagannah St. **Tel** (04) 991 1375. **Open** 8am–4:30pm Sun–Thu. 🐾
Akko's Citadel was built by the Turks in the 18th century on top of Crusader foundations. During the British Mandate it served as a prison for Jewish activists and political prisoners, some of whom were executed in the gallows room. These events are commemorated in the Citadel's **Museum of Underground Prisoners**.

🏛 Hammam el-Pasha

Off El-Jazzar St. **Tel** (04) 995 1088. **Open** summer: 8:30am–5pm daily; winter: 8:30am–4pm daily. Closes 1 hr earlier Fri. 🐾
This is not a museum as such, but a Turkish bathhouse dating to 1780 and the rule of El-Jazzar (hence the name of Hammam el-Pasha,

Fountain from the Hammam el-Pasha

meaning "Bathhouse of the Governor"). It was in use until the 1940s and remains in an excellent state of repair. The floors and walls are composed of panels of different coloured marble, and the fountain in the "cold room" (where patrons would relax after bathing) retains most of its beautiful majolica decoration. A sound-and-light show introduces visitors to the history of Akko and the life of a typical bathhouse attendant.

The Old City of Akko

① Mosque of El-Jazzar
② Crusader City
③ Hammam el-Pasha
④ Citadel
⑤ El-Jazzar's Wall
⑥ Khan el-Umdan
⑦ Khan el-Faranj
⑧ Khan a-Shuarda
⑨ Souk
⑩ Lighthouse

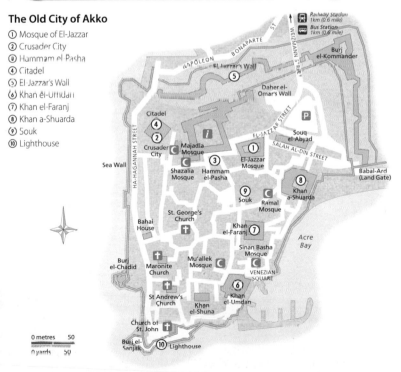

0 metres 50
0 yards 50

Aerial view of the ruined hilltop city of Megiddo

❺ Megiddo

Road map B2. Route 66, 35 km
(22 miles) SE of Haifa. **Tel** (04) 659
0316. 🚌 from Haifa & Tiberias.
Open 8am–5pm (winter: 4pm) daily.
Closes 1 hour earlier Fri. 🖼

This ancient town at the head
of the Jezreel Valley was the
scene of so many battles that
the Book of Revelation in the
New Testament says that it is
where the final battle between
Good and Evil will take place
at the end of the world. The
biblical name of "Armageddon"
derives from "Har Megedon",
or mountain of Megiddo.

The settlement controlled the
main communication routes
between the East and the
Mediterranean, and in the 3rd
millennium BC it was already
a fortified city. In 1468 BC, its
Canaanite fortress was destroyed
by the troops of the Egyptian
pharaoh Thutmose III and it
became an Egyptian stronghold.
Megiddo was subsequently
conquered and again fortified,
possibly by Solomon, and in
the 8th century BC came under
Assyrian rule, after which it fell
slowly into decline.

Extensive excavation of the
spectacular mound (or "tel")
has, over the years, revealed
20 successive settlements, each
built over the other. The visible
remains include defensive
walls, a temple, an enormous
grain silo and the foundations
of many buildings. On the

eastern side of the "tel" is an old
reservoir, at the base of which a
tunnel leads to a spring that lies
outside the city walls. Visitors
can go through the tunnel at
the end of their tour of the site.

In 2005, the site joined
UNESCO's World Heritage
list, reflecting its historical
importance and powerful
influence on later civilizations.

❻ Nazareth

Road map B2. 🏘 75,000. 🚌
ℹ Casa Nova St, (04) 601 1072.
🌐 nazarethinfo.org

Lying on the rise between the
Jordan Valley and the Jezreel
plain, Nazareth consists of two
parts. The old town is inhabited
by Christian and Muslim
Palestinians, and contains all
of the major sights. To the north

Mosaic of Joseph, Basilica of the
Annunciation, Nazareth

is Nazareth Illit, a large Jewish
district founded in 1957 by
colonists as part of the plan
to settle all Galilee.

Famous as the site of
the Annunciation and the
childhood of Jesus, Nazareth
has had a colourful history.
The village suffered at the
hands of the Romans during
the Jewish Revolt of AD 66 (see
p47), then flourished under the
Byzantines and later became
an important Christian site with
the Crusader conquest of
the Holy Land in 1099. After
the resurgence of Muslim
power in the 12th and 13th
centuries, Christians found it
increasingly dangerous to visit.
Improving relations by the 18th
century allowed the Franciscans
to acquire the Basilica, and they
have maintained a Christian
presence here ever since.

Today the town is still a pilgrimage
site, with its many Christian
churches attracting large
numbers of visitors. Restoration
projects and modern hotel
developments have helped
Nazareth to cope with the
crowds. Unfortunately though,
such high levels of tourism have
done little to preserve the city's
magical atmosphere. The old
town is still fascinating however,
with much of its traditional
architecture remaining. The
souk, the heart of local life,
is a maze of narrow alleys
where you can find a wide
range of unusual goods.

Built in 1969 over the ruins of the original Byzantine church, and the successive Crusader one, the **Basilica of the Annunciation** is the major focal point in Nazareth. A bold, modern church, its large dome towers over the town. The crypt includes the Cave of the Annunciation, where the angel Gabriel is said to have appeared to Mary. A peaceful garden leads to **St Joseph's**, a small church rebuilt in 1914 on what is thought to be the site of Joseph's home and workshop.

Environs

The main attraction of the ruined fortified town of **Tsipori** (Sepphoris), northwest of Nazareth, is its splendid 3rd-century-AD mosaics. The hilltop site includes a Roman theatre that seated 5,000, the remains of a Crusader citadel and sections of the ancient water supply. Tsipori is also famous as being the supposed birthplace of the Virgin Mary.

On **Mount Tabor**, 10 km (6 miles) east of Nazareth, is a beautiful basilica, built here in 1924 to commemorate the Transfiguration (Mark 9: 9–13). It lies within the ruins of a 12th-century Muslim fortress.

🏠 Tsipori
Route 79, 3 km (2 miles) NW of Nazareth **Tel** (04) 656 8272. **Open** 8am–4pm (summer: 5pm) daily. Closes 1 hour earlier Fri. 🏠 🚻 (must be booked in advance).

❼ Safed

Road map C2. 🏔 26,000. 🚌
ℹ 100 Ha-Palmach St, (04) 680 1465. 🆆 **safed.co.il**

The highest town in Israel, Safed is also one of the four holy cities of the Talmud, together with Jerusalem, Hebron and Tiberias. In the Middle Ages, Safed became a popular meeting place for many groups of Sephardic Jews who had been driven out of Spain in the course of the Christian Reconquest. Religious schools were founded and many interpreters of the Kabbalah lived in the town. To this day Safed has remained an important centre of Jewish religious studies.

Safed covers a number of small hilltops, with its attractive old town centre located around the slopes of Gan ha-Metusda, once the site of a Crusader citadel. The old quarters of the town centre are best explored on foot, via their narrow streets and steep stairways. The Synagogue Quarter has many interesting Kabbalist synagogues, including those of Itzhak Luria, Itzhak Abuhav and Joseph Caro. The former Arab Quarter (which became Jewish in 1948) is now home to a large colony of artists and is known as the Artists' Quarter. In the narrow streets and alleys between the area's picturesque houses, artists display their paintings and sculptures.

The majestic waters of the Banias Falls, Golan Heights

❽ Golan Heights

Road map C2. 🚌 to Katsrin. ℹ (04) 696 2885. 🆆 **tour.golan.org.il**

This region of long-running historical conflict has nevertheless got much to admire. A high fertile plateau, dominated by Mount Hermon, it borders Israel, Syria, Jordan and Lebanon. This unique geography, aside from making it strategically important, also makes it a spectacular place to visit, with incredible vistas all around.

A major source of the Jordan River, one of the most popular places to visit is **Banias**, 15 km (9 miles) east of Kiryat Shmona. Here a large spring cascades downstream to the attractive Banias Falls nearby. **Nimrud Castle**, a short way to the northeast, originates from biblical times, though it owes its present shape to the rule of the Mameluke sultan Baybars I (1260–77). Nine of the defensive towers remain, along with much of the outer wall, a keep and the moat.

In the south of the Golan is the administrative capital of **Katsrin**. Founded as an Israeli settlement in 1974, the town itself is unremarkable, but is a good base for exploring the beautiful countryside around. This is ideal hiking country, and the spectacular **Yehudiya Reserve** to the south of Katsrin is well worth a visit.

🏠 Nimrud Castle
26 km (16 miles) E of Kiryat Shmona. **Tel** (04) 694 9277. **Open** daily. 🚻

The city of Nazareth with Mount Tabor in the background

❾ Sea of Galilee

Israel's chief source of water, the Sea of Galilee (Lake Tiberias/Kinneret) lies 212 m (696 ft) below sea level and is fed and drained by the Jordan River. It is 21 km (13 miles) long and 9 km (6 miles) wide, and since biblical times has been famous for its abundance of fish. Many of Jesus's disciples were fishermen here, and he did much of his preaching by its shores. Today, this beautiful area is one of Israel's most popular tourist centres, with a mix of fascinating historical and religious sites and a varied selection of hotels and outdoor activities.

Speedboating on the Sea of Galilee, one of many water sports available

Tiberias
The largest town on the Sea of Galilee, Tiberias is a popular resort, with many hotels, bars and restaurants. The busy lakeside offers beaches and water sports.

To Safed

Capern

Tabkha

Kibbutz Ginosar

Migdal

HAR ARBEL

To Nazareth

Tiberias

HAR MENORIM

Poriya

Kibbu Kinnere

KEY

① **Kibbutz Kinneret's cemetery**, with great views of the sea, is resting place to many spiritual leaders of the Zionist movement.

② **The Hammat Tiberias Hot Springs** have long been renowned for their curative properties and are said to date from the time of Solomon.

③ **Kibbutz Ginosar** is home to a fishing boat from Jesus's time, found here in 1986 *(see p33)*.

④ **Church of the Multiplication of the Loaves and the Fishes** *(see p188)*

⑤ **Church of the Primacy of St Peter** *(see p188)*

⑥ **Mount of the Beatitudes** *(see p188)*

⑦ **Kibbutz Ein Gev** is renowned for its fish restaurants, good beaches and its annual international music festival.

Key

━━ Major road
═══ Minor road

Yardenit Baptism Site
The Jordan River has always been an important Christian site since Christ was supposedly baptized here. At Yardenit, large crowds of pilgrims gather to be baptized in the river themselves.

A View of the Sea of Galilee
This view is taken from the hills above the northeastern shore.

To Katsrin

Jordan River

87

92

Ramot

• Kursi

92

Kibbutz Ein Gev

7

Kibbutz Haon •

92

Mevo Khama

98

HAR NIMRON

bbutz
gania

98

eth Shean

Hammat Gader

0 kilometres 4
0 miles 2

VISITORS' CHECKLIST

Practical Information
Road map C2. 🛈 19 Habanim St, Tiberias, (04) 672 5566.
🎭 Kibbutz Ein Gev Music Festival (Apr), Galilee Song Festival (May).

Transport
🚌 from Tel Aviv and Jerusalem.
🚌 for groups only from Tiberias to Kibbutz Ein Gev, phone for times, (04) 665 8008.
🚢 Jesus Boats, Tiberias (all year round), (04) 672 3006,
W jesusboats.com; Lido Kinneret Sailing Co, Tiberias (all year round), (04) 672 1538.

The First Kibbutz – Degania

Conceived by Eastern European Jews, the first kibbutz was founded at Degania in 1909. The guiding ideals behind Israel's kibbutzim are self-sufficiency and equality, with everyone working for the common good. Rural farming communities, they are highly productive, and hold their own plenary meetings to decide on community matters. There are now two kibbutzim here, with the original called Degania Alef (A). By the main gate to the kibbutz is a Syrian tank, stopped here by the kibbutzniks when they famously defeated an entire armoured column during the 1948 War

Typical kibbutz house at Degania

Hammat Gader Alligator Farm
The large alligator farm at Hammat Gader is open to the public. The town is also famous for its ancient Roman hot springs, which have now been largely restored. You can still bathe in their relaxing waters.

⑩ Capernaum

Road map C2. Route 87, 12 km
(7.5 miles) N of Tiberias. 🚌 from
Tiberias. **Tel** (04) 672 1059.
Open 8am–4:30pm daily. 🅿

Capernaum, on the northern
shoreline of the Sea of Galilee,
was an important Roman town
and one of the focal
points of Christ's
teachings in Galilee.
It was also home
to a number of his
Disciples, including
Simon Peter.
In Capernaum's
fascinating archae-
ological precinct
there are surviving
houses from the period, as well
as a church, built over the ruins
of what is said to have been
Simon Peter's house. There are
also the remains of a synagogue
that has been dated to the
4th century AD.

*Carved relief, Church of
the Multiplication*

⑪ Tabgha

Road map C2. Route 87, 10 km
(6 miles) N of Tiberias. 🚌 from Tiberias
to junction of routes 90 and 87.

Just to the southwest of
Capernaum, Tabgha (Ein Sheva)
is one of the most important
sites of Christ's ministry in
Galilee, where he did much
of his preaching. Heading from
the bus stop, a short way along
Route 87, you will come to the
**Church of the Multiplication of
the Loaves and the Fishes**. Built
in the 1980s, it boasts the
remains of a 5th-century
Byzantine basilica and
fragments of splendid
mosaics. This original
church was built over
the supposed spot
from which Christ
fed 5,000 followers
with five loaves and

two fish. Nearby to the east, on
the lakeside, is the **Church of
the Primacy of St Peter**. A
black basalt Franciscan chapel,
it is built on the site where
Jesus Christ is said to have
appeared to the apostles after
his Resurrection. The area has
various other ruins, including
a 4th-century chapel.
On top of the hill
behind, known as
the Mount of the
Beatitudes, is the
modern **Church
of the Beatitudes**.
The hill is so-called
because it is thought
that here, over-
looking the lake,
Christ gave his Sermon on the
Mount. This famously began
with his blessings or "beatitudes".

⑫ Tiberias

Road map C2. 🅰 39,500. 🚌
ℹ Archaeological Garden, Rehov
ha-Banim, (04) 672 5666.

The busy town of Tiberias
(Tverya) is the largest on the
shores of the Sea of Galilee.
It was founded during Roman
times by Herod Antipas, who
dedicated it to the emperor
Tiberius and moved the
regional capital here from
Tsipori. The town has been
home to many notable scholars
and rabbis, and became one of
Israel's holy cities, along with
Jerusalem, Hebron and Safed.
The **Tomb of Maimonides**,
the great medieval Jewish
philosopher, can be found
on Ben Zakai Street.
Today, Tiberias is a popular
tourist centre, with
an attractive lakeside
setting, and in an ideal
location for exploring
Galilee. The town has
a lively atmosphere,

especially along the busy
lakeside promenade. Just off the
promenade is **St Peter's Church**,
built originally by the Crusaders.
The current church has a boat-
shaped nave, reflecting
St Peter's life as a fisherman.
Tiberias is also known for
its curative hot springs, of
which there are several to visit
in the town. There are also some
public beaches to the north of
town, and the popular **Luna Gal
Beach Water Park** is 1 km (half
a mile) to the south of Tiberias.

🏊 **Luna Gal Beach Water Park**
Sederot Eliezer Kaplan. **Tel** (04) 670
0700. **Open** daily. **Closed** Nov–Mar. 🅿

*Ruined arches at Belvoir Castle, from
the 12th century*

⑬ Belvoir Castle

Road map C2. Off Route 90, 27 km
(17 miles) S of Tiberias. 🚌 to Beth
Shean, then taxi. **Tel** (04) 658 1766.
Open 8am–5pm (winter: 4pm) daily.
Closes 1 hour earlier Fri. 🅿

The ruined Crusader fortress
of Belvoir offers incomparable
views of the Jordan Valley.
The impressive fortress is
surrounded by two huge walls,
the outer one pentagonal and
the inner one square. Built by
the Knights Hospitallers in 1168,
Belvoir was besieged many
times by Saladin. It capitulated
only in 1189 after a siege of
more than a year, with the
Muslim leader sparing both the
fortress and its defenders'
lives, in recognition of their
great courage. Belvoir was
finally destroyed by troops
from Damascus in the 13th
century. The area around
the fortress is dotted
with modern sculpture.

The modern Church of the Beatitudes near Tabgha

Detail from 6th-century mosaic at Beth Alpha, showing signs of the zodiac

⑭ Beth Alpha

Road map C2. Off Route 71, 11 km (7 miles) W of Beth Shean. **Tel** (04) 653 2004. ▨ **Open** 8am–5pm (winter: 4pm) daily. Closes 1 hour earlier Fri. ♿ ♿

The remnants of this 6th-century synagogue were found by chance in 1928 by colonists from the nearby Hefzi-Bah kibbutz. The ruined walls give an idea of the original basilica-shaped building, but the main interest is the magnificent mosaic floor, which has survived largely intact. The upper part of the floor depicts the Ark of the Covenant, with cherubs, lions and religious symbols. The large central patterns represent the zodiac and symbols of the seasons. These show the continuing importance of pagan beliefs at the time, and the need for Judaism to try to accommodate them. The lower part relates the story of Abraham and the sacrifice of his son Isaac.

⑮ Beth Shean

Road map C2. ⚃ 18,000. ▨ from Tiberias.

The best-preserved Roman-Byzantine town in Israel, Beth Shean lay on the old trade routes between Mesopotamia and the Mediterranean. First inhabited 5,000 years ago during the Canaanite era, it later became the main city in the region during the period of Egyptian occupation (see p45). Falling to the Philistines in the 11th century BC, it then became part of Solomon's kingdom. After the conquest of Alexander the Great, it was renamed Scythopolis and became a flourishing Hellenistic city. The Roman conquest in the 1st century BC saw Scythopolis further prosper as one of the ten city-states of the Decapolis. It later retained its economic importance under the Byzantines, also becoming a major centre of Christianity. An economic collapse, then an earthquake in AD 749, eventually left only a small remaining Jewish community. The archaeological sites at Beth Shean are in two areas. The main site comprises the Roman-Byzantine city and the archaeological mound, or "tel". These are both within the Beth Shean National Park, 1 km (half a mile) north of the town. The jewel of this site is the Roman theatre, one of the best preserved in Israel, and once capable of seating 7,000. The old Byzantine baths have surviving mosaic and marble decoration, and tall columns from the ruined temples are equally impressive. The "tel" offers a good overview of the site, and consists of 16 or more superimposed towns. It is difficult, however, to understand the details of its complex archaeology.

The other site focuses on the ruined Roman amphitheatre, a short way to the south. Used for gladiatorial contests, it was connected to the main town by a paved street. Some of this street survives today, paved with huge blocks of basalt.

🏛 Beth Shean National Park

Tel (04) 658 7189. **Open** 8am–5pm (to 6pm Jul–Aug, winter: 4pm) daily. Closes 1 hour earlier Fri. ▨

Ruined colonnade along an old Byzantine street, Beth Shean

THE DEAD SEA AND THE NEGEV DESERT

In this, the most arid and inhospitable region of the Holy Land, even the waters of its great lake are incapable of supporting life, hence the name "Dead Sea". But in times past, the harsh remoteness of the hills and desert was prized by reclusive communities and rebels, and so the area is dotted with ancient ruins charged with biblical significance.

Today, the Dead Sea is no longer so remote – just a 20-minute ride from Jerusalem on an air-conditioned bus. Tourists flock to its shores to test its incredibly buoyant waters. The lowest body of water in the world, it has such a high salt content it is impossible to sink. Its mineral-rich mud is also claimed to have therapeutic qualities, and a string of lakeside spas do good business out of the black, sticky silt. Away from the water, high up on the rocky hillsides, are the caves in which the Dead Sea Scrolls were discovered, while on a mountaintop to the south is Herod the Great's fortress of Masada, one of the most stunning attractions in all Israel.

Where the Dead Sea ends, the Negev Desert begins. Here, the only signs of life, apart from the odd convoy of tourists exploring canyons and craters, are a few groups of Bedouin (see p253) tenaciously clinging to traditional nomadic ways.

Over the centuries, there have been many attempts to cultivate the desert. More than 2,000 years ago, the Negev was the final stage for caravans on the spice and incense route from India and southern Arabia to the Mediterranean; the Nabataeans, who controlled the route, perfected irrigation and cultivation techniques and established flourishing cities, such as Ovdat (see p206). More recently, Israel has initiated programmes for the economic development of the region in the form of desert kibbutzim.

In spite of this desire to tame the desert, more and more people these days come in search of all that remains wild and undeveloped. In this respect, the Negev still has much to offer.

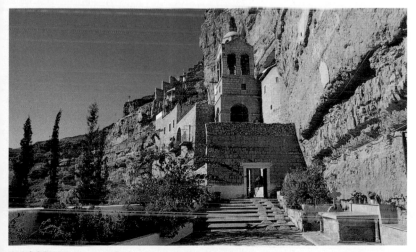

The secluded retreat of St George's Monastery, hidden in a desert canyon near Jericho

◀ A dead tree lying covered with visible flakes of salt in the shallow waters of the Dead Sea

Exploring the Dead Sea and the Negev Desert

All the sites as far south as Masada can be visited in a series of day trips from Jerusalem. Heading south beyond Masada or Beersheva and into the Negev Desert is more of an undertaking. There are only two main routes through this vast wedge of sun-baked wilderness: along the border with Jordan on Route 90; or straight down the centre of the country via Ein Ovdat and Mitspe Ramon. This latter route is by far the more interesting.

The mountaintop fortress of Masada, conveniently visited as a day trip from Jerusalem

Sights at a Glance

1. St George's Monastery
2. Jericho
3. Nebi Musa
4. Mar Saba Monastery
5. Herodion
6. *Bethlehem pp196–9*
7. Qumran
8. Ein Gedi
9. The Dead Sea
10. *Masada pp204–5*
11. Sodom
12. Ein Ovdat
13. Ovdat
14. Hebron
15. Beersheva
16. Makhtesh Ramon
17. Khai Bar Yotvata Wildlife Reserve
18. Timna National Park
19. Eilat

0 kilometres — 25
0 miles — 20

Ein Gedi, where waterfalls and greenery provide respite from the heat and dust

For hotels and restaurants in this region see p262 and p274

Bethlehem and surrounding hills, viewed over the roof of the Church of the Nativity

Getting Around

The easiest way of getting from Jerusalem to Jericho, Bethlehem and Hebron is a shared taxi from Damascus Gate (see p309). You can also take bus No. 163 from Jaffa Road in Jerusalem to Bethlehem. From Bethlehem you can take a taxi on to the Herodion or Mar Saba. For longer trips, the Israeli bus company Egged serves all Dead Sea and Negev locations (see pp304–5). For those who only want to visit the Negev Desert, there are direct flights to Eilat with Arkia (see p303).

The volcano-like mound of the Herodion, a 1st-century-BC hilltop fortress

Key

═══ Motorway

──── Major road

····· Minor road

──── Scenic route

╍╍╍ Railway

▬▬▬ International border

■ ■ Disputed border/Ceasefire line

The waters of the Dead Sea, the most saline on earth and at their saltiest at the southern end, where crystalline pools are formed

❶ St George's Monastery

Road map C3. Route 1, 27 km (17 miles) E of Jerusalem. **Tel** (054) 730 6557. 🚌 from Jerusalem. **Open** 7am–4pm daily.

One of the finest hikes in the region is rewarded by the spectacle of St George's Monastery, an ancient retreat hollowed out of the sheer rock wall of a deep and narrow gorge. The monastery was founded in AD 480 around a cluster of caves where, according to tradition, St Joachim learned from an angel that Anne, his sterile wife and mother-to-be of the Virgin Mary, had conceived.

In AD 614 invading Persians massacred the monks and destroyed the monastery. It was partially reoccupied by the Crusaders in the Middle Ages, but only fully restored at the end of the 19th century. Some attractive 6th-century mosaics remain, and there is a Crusader-era church with a shrine containing the skulls of the martyred monks.

The monastery can be reached in 20 minutes on foot via a signposted track off the old Jerusalem–Jericho road. From a starting point on the modern road, hikers can take a more scenic path to the monastery, which follows along the full length of the Wadi Qelt gorge.

St George's Monastery, built into the cliff face of Wadi Qelt

Jericho, regarded as perhaps the world's oldest city

❷ Jericho

Road map C3. 🏠 17,000. 🚌 or taxi from Jerusalem. 🏨 daily. 🎪 Jericho Festival (Feb).

It is best to check with the authorities first before visiting the city to make sure it is safe for tourists as unrest has returned to the region.

Claimed to be the world's oldest city and with rich biblical associations, Jericho lies just a few kilometres north of the Dead Sea, 258 m (846 ft) below sea level, in the middle of the Judaean Desert. It owes its existence to the Ain es-Sultan Spring (the biblical Elisha's Spring), the same one that, 10,000 years ago in the late Mesolithic period, attracted a semi-nomadic population of hunter-gatherers to first settle here.

Islamic-era mosaic from Hisham's Palace

According to the Bible, Jericho was the first town captured by the Israelites under the leadership of Joshua. The Book of Joshua tells how, in order to possess the land promised to them by God, the Israelites brought down the city walls with a tremendous shout and a trumpet blast (Joshua 6). During Roman times, Mark Antony made a gift of the oasis town to Cleopatra of Egypt, who, in turn, leased the place to Herod the Great. Being at a lower altitude than Jerusalem, Jericho is notably warmer, and Herod wintered in a palace here, as had the Hasmonean rulers before him.

The Bible's New Testament mentions several visits to Jericho by Jesus, who healed two blind men and lodged at the home of the tax collector Zacchaeus (Luke 19: 1–10). Near the centre of town there is still the centuries-old sycamore tree up which Zacchaeus was said to have climbed in order to see Jesus.

Repeated Bedouin raids led to the decline of Jericho around the 12th century, and it wasn't until the 1920s that the town's former irrigation network was restored and the area was brought to bloom again. In 1948, the town took in more than 70,000 Palestinian refugees. The camps have since gone, and Jericho is now administered by the Palestinian National Authority.

Other attractions include **Tel Jericho** (also known as Tell es-Sultan), the sun-baked earthen mound that represents something like 10,000 years of continuous settlement. Most striking of all is a large stone tower with great thick walls that dates back as far as 7,000 BC.

A cable car service connects Tell es-Sultan with the Greek Orthodox **Monastery of the Temptation**, 2 km (1 mile) to the north. Like St George's in Wadi Qelt, this holy retreat has a spectacular location, perched high up on a cliff face. The views from its terraces are breathtaking. The monastery dates back to the 12th century and is supposedly built around the grotto where the Devil appeared to tempt Jesus away from his 40-day fast (Matthew 4: 1–11).

Hisham's Palace (Qasr Hisham) is an early Islamic hunting lodge built in AD 724 for the Omayyad caliph Hisham. It lies in ruins, destroyed centuries ago by an earthquake, but it is worth a visit if only to see a gorgeous floor mosaic depicting a lion hunting gazelles grazing under a broad leafy tree.

Environs

The baptismal site on the banks of the Jordan River, **Qasr el-Yehud** (see p32) is visited by fervent pilgrims keen to immerse themselves in the water and commemorate the event.

🏛 **Tel Jericho**
Open daily. 🅿 ▣

🏛 **Monastery of the Temptation**
Tel (02) 232 2827. **Open** 8am–4pm Mon–Sat. ♿

🏛 **Hisham's Palace**
Tel (02) 232 2522. **Open** 8am–5pm daily. 🅿

🏛 **Qasr el-Yehud**
10 km (6 miles) E of Jericho. **Tel** (02) 650 4844. ♿ ▣ 🌐 **parks.org.il**

❸ Nebi Musa

Road map C4. Route 1, 10 km (6 miles) S of Jericho. 🚌 to Jericho, then taxi. ♿

Although the claim is heavily disputed, Muslims revere the desert monastery of Nebi Musa as the burial place of Moses. There has been a mosque on the site since 1269, built under the patronage of the Mameluke

Nebi Musa, regarded by Muslims as the burial place of Moses

emir Baybars. In 1470–80 a two-storey hospice was added to accommodate visiting pilgrims. However, the attractive white-washed structures of the present day date from around 1820 and the days of Ottoman rule. The disputed cenotaph of Moses, covered with a traditional Islamic green drape, occupies the spartan, domed tomb chamber of the mosque.

Although the five-day festival of feasting and prayer that used to occur here each year now no longer happens, many Muslims still desire to be laid to rest in the large cemetery that covers the hills around the complex.

❹ Mar Saba Monastery

Road map C4. Off Route 398, 17 km (11 miles) E of Bethlehem. **Tel** (02) 276 2915. 🚌 Bethlehem, then taxi. **Open** 8am–5pm daily. Ring bell. No women allowed.

Located out in the wilds of the Judaean Desert, Mar Saba is one of the dozens of retreats built in this area from the 5th century on by hermits seeking an austere life of solitude and prayer. This particular monastery was founded in AD 482 by St Saba, a monk born in Cappadocia, Turkey, whose preachings were said to have impressed the Byzantine emperor Justinian. Despite a massacre of the monks by the Persians in the 7th century (the skulls are preserved in a chapel), the monastery survived to bloom in the 8th and 9th centuries, when its thick defensive walls housed up to 200 devotees.

Although only around 20 monks now live in Mar Saba, it remains a functioning desert monastery. As seen today, topped by bright blue domes, the complex largely dates to 1834, when it was rebuilt following a major earthquake.

An ornate canopy in the monastery's main church supposedly shelters the remains of St Saba, which were returned to the Holy Land only in 1965, having being carried off by the Crusaders and kept in Venice for seven centuries. The church walls are hung with icons and a lurid fresco depicting Judgment Day. Unfortunately, women are not allowed to enter the monastery, but the views of Mar Saba from a neighbouring tower (which women are permitted to climb) are alone worth the trouble of a visit.

The distinctive blue domes of the gorge-top monastery of Mar Saba

The hilltop Herodion, with sweeping views of the landscape

❺ Herodion

Road map B4. Route 356, 12 km (7 miles) SE of Bethlehem. **Tel** (057) 776 1143. ▣ Bethlehem, then taxi. **Open** 8am–5pm (winter: 4pm) daily. Closes 1 hour earlier Fri. ▨ ▧ on Sat, but call ahead. ♿

Dominating the desert landscape south of Bethlehem is the volcano-like mound of the Herodion, named for Herod the Great. He had this circular fortified palace built in 24–15 BC for entertaining, and to mark the defeat of his rival, Antigonus. It was long thought this might also have been his mausoleum and, after extensive excavations, a tomb believed to be Herod's was discovered in 2007, though this has been disputed.

During the Second Revolt in AD 132–5, the Herodion became the headquarters of the Jewish leader Bar-Kokhba. In expectation of a Roman attack, the rebels turned its cisterns into a network of escape tunnels.

Around the 5th century, the site became a monastery with cells and a chapel, where you can still see carved Christian symbols. Also identifiable are a massive round tower and three semicircular ones, ruins of the palace baths, the *triclinium* (dining room) and fragments of mosaics, all dating from Herod's time.

At the foot of the mound are the remains of the Lower Herodion, with the dry imprint of a large pool that, in Herod's day, served as a reservoir and centrepiece for ornamental gardens.

❻ Bethlehem

Perched on a hill at the edge of the Judaean Desert, Bethlehem is in biblical tradition the childhood home of David, who was named king here as he tended his father's sheep. It is also the birthplace of Jesus Christ and a major site of pilgrimage since the construction of the Church of the Nativity in the 4th century AD. The town flourished until Crusader times, but the following centuries witnessed a great reduction in population, reversed only after the 1948 War with the arrival of thousands of Palestinian refugees.

Getting to Bethlehem

The best way to reach Bethlehem is via Rachel's Crossing. To get to this checkpoint from Jerusalem, either catch bus No. 163 from Jaffa Road outside the Central Bus Station, or take a shared taxi *(see p309)* from Damascus Gate, or take a taxi. You will then have to walk through the checkpoint and take another taxi on the other side. Hire cars may be driven from Israel into Bethlehem, but check that your insurance policy includes the Palestinian Territories before setting out.

Exploring Bethlehem

Since 1995 Bethlehem has been under the control of the Palestinian National Authority, which has initiated a programme of economic recovery and tourism. Despite the huge number of pilgrims and chaotic urban growth, Bethlehem has retained a certain fascination, especially in the central area around Manger Square and in the souk just to the west. The souvenir shops are filled with kitsch religious objects, but also sell fine carved olive-wood crib scenes that local craftsmen have produced for centuries. No visitor should miss the **Church of the Nativity**

(see pp198–9) on Manger Square. Built in the 4th century over the supposed site where Jesus Christ was born, the church is one of the holiest Christian sites.

The prominent **Mosque of Omar** was built in 1860 and is the only Islamic place of worship in the town centre, despite the fact that Muslim residents now outnumber Christians in Bethlehem.

⛪ St Catherine's Church

Manger Square. **Tel** (02) 274 2425. **Open** summer: 6:30am–7:30pm daily; winter: 5am–5pm daily. **Closed** Sun am for services. ♿

Connected to the Church of the Nativity, St Catherine's faces a Crusader-period cloister *(see p198)*. The church was built by Franciscans in the 1880s on the site of a 12th-century Augustinian monastery, which had replaced a 5th-century monastery associated with St Jerome. On the right side of the nave, stairs descend to the grottoes of the Holy Innocents, St Joseph and St Jerome, which connect to the Grotto of the Nativity. These were used as burial places by Christians as early as the 1st century AD and contain the tombs of St Jerome and St Paula.

The church spires and towers of Bethlehem, birthplace of Jesus Christ

The Virgin Mary and Child, a relationship celebrated at The Milk Grotto

🔳 Rachel's Tomb
Hebron Rd. 🚌 163; there is also a special bus from Jerusalem (see website).
Closed 10:30pm–12:30am Sun–Thu, Shabbat & festivals. **W** keverrachel.com

On the road to Jerusalem is the tomb of Rachel, wife of Jacob and mother of two of his 12 sons. The tomb can be accessed only from the Israeli side. It is the third most holy site in Judaism and is also sacred to Muslims. The actual "tomb" consists of a rock covered by a velvet drape with 11 stones on it, one for each of Jacob's sons who were alive when Rachel died in childbirth. The structure around the tomb was built in the 1100s by the Crusaders and later altered many times, including in 1860 by Moses Montefiore (see p55). The site is visited by Jewish women who hope to conceive.

🏠 The Milk Grotto
Milk Grotto St. **Tel** (02) 274 3867.
Open 8am–noon & 2–5pm daily.
This grotto is considered sacred because tradition has it that the Holy Family took refuge here during the Massacre of the Innocents, before their eventual flight into Egypt. While Mary was suckling Jesus, so the story goes, a drop of milk fell to the ground, turning it white. Both Christians and Muslims believe that scrapings from the stones in the grotto help to boost the quantity of a mother's milk and also to enhance fertility.

The present building was put up by the Franciscans in 1872 on the site of a 4th-century church.

🏛 Baituna al-Talhami
Paul VI St. **Tel** (02) 274 2589.
Open 8am–1pm & 2–5pm daily. 📷
In an old Palestinian house on the town's main street, the Arab Women's Union has created this small but interesting craft museum. One room is given over to the embroidery typical of Palestinian women's dress, and to silver jewellery, which normally represented a family's fortune. The *diwan* (living room) is furnished with rugs, musical instruments and oil lamps. The kitchen contains old copper utensils and an oven. Examples of traditional hand-stitched embroidery are usually available to buy.

Bethlehem Town Map

① St Catherine's Church
② The Milk Grotto
③ Baituna al-Talhami
④ Rachel's Tomb
⑤ Church of the Nativity

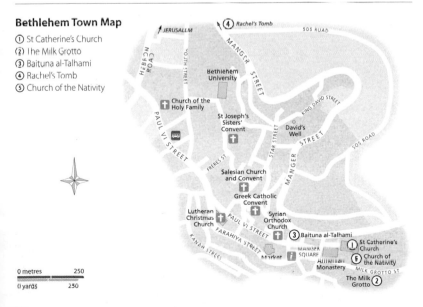

0 metres 250
0 yards 250

Church of the Nativity

The first evidence of a cave here being venerated as Christ's birthplace is in the writings of St Justin Martyr around AD 160. In 326, the Roman emperor Constantine ordered a church to be built, and in about 530 it was rebuilt by Justinian. The Crusaders later redecorated the interior, but much of the marble was looted in Ottoman times. In 1852, shared custody of the church was granted to the Roman Catholic, Armenian and Greek Orthodox churches, the Greeks caring for the Grotto of the Nativity.

Plaza in front of the Church of the Nativity, with the plain façade in the distance

★ Grotto of the Nativity
The grotto is the church's focal point. A silver star is set in the floor over the spot where Christ is said to have been born.

Nave
The wide nave survives intact from Justinian's time, although the roof is 15th-century, with 19th-century restorations. Fragments of high-quality mosaics decorate the walls.

Cloister of St Catherine's Church
Incorporating columns and capitals from the 12th-century Augustinian monastery that previously stood here, this attractive, peaceful cloister was rebuilt in Crusader style in 1948.

For hotels and restaurants in this region see p262 and p274

Painted Columns

Thirty of the nave's 44 columns carry Crusader paintings of saints and the Virgin and Child, although age and lighting conditions make them hard to see. The columns are of polished pink limestone, most of them reused from the original 4th-century basilica.

VISITORS' CHECKLIST

Practical Information
Manger Square. **Tel** (02) 274 2440. **Open** summer: 6:30am–7:30pm daily; winter: 5am–5pm daily. Grottoes closed Sun am.
  travelpalestine.ps

★ Mosaic Floor

Trap doors in the present floor, here and to the left of the altar, reveal sections of mosaic floor surviving from the 4th-century basilica.

★ Door of Humility

The Crusader doorway, marked by a pointed arch, was reduced to the present tiny size in the Ottoman period to prevent carts being driven in by looters. A massive lintel above the arch indicates the door's even larger original size.

KEY

① **Statue of St Jerome**

② **Other grottoes**, reached by these steps, contain the supposed tomb and study of St Jerome *(see p196)*.

③ **Altar of the Adoration of the Magi (Manger Altar)**

④ **St Catherine's Church** *(see p196)*

⑤ **Stairs to main church**

⑥ **Wall mosaics**, made in the 1160s, once decorated the entire church

⑦ **The narthex** was originally a single, long porch, with three large doors leading into the church and three onto the street.

St Jerome

St Jerome Writing (c.1604) by Caravaggio

Born at Stribo (not far from Venice), St Jerome (c.342–420) was one of the most learned scholars of the early Christian Church. He travelled widely and in 384 settled in Bethlehem, where he founded a monastery. Here, he completed a new version of the Bible *(see p28)*, inspired by the pope's suggestion that a single book should replace the many differing texts in circulation. His great work later became known as the Vulgate. Tradition places the saint's study and tomb next to the Grotto of the Nativity.

Caves at Qumran, where the hot, dry, desert climate helped to preserve the Dead Sea Scrolls

❼ Qumran

Road map C4. Route 90, 20 km (12 miles) S of Jericho. **Tel** (02) 994 2235. 🚌 from Jerusalem. **Open** 8am–5pm (winter: 4pm) Sat–Thu, 8am–4pm (winter: 3pm) Fri. 🅿️ ♿

Qumran is known chiefly as the place where the Dead Sea Scrolls were discovered. From 150 BC to AD 68, this remote site was the home of a radically ascetic and reclusive community, often identified with the Essenes. According to their school of thought, the arrival of the Jewish Messiah was imminent, and they prepared for this event with fasting and purification through ritual ablutions. These activities were rudely brought to a halt through conflict with the Romans.

The Essenes largely vanished from history until 1947, when a Bedouin shepherd boy looking for a lost goat happened upon a cave full of jars. These jars were found to contain a precious hoard of 190 linen-wrapped scrolls that had been preserved for 2,000 years. Following much study by academics, some of the scrolls are now on view in a purpose-built hall at the Israel Museum *(see pp140–41)*.

Visitors to Qumran watch a short film on the Essenes, with audio in eight languages, and view a small exhibition on the community before being directed to the archaeological site at the foot of the cliffs. Signs indicate the probable uses of different areas of the vaguely defined remains. The trail through the site is wheelchair accessible and has special signage for the visually impaired. From the site you can see the caves above where the scrolls were found.

❽ Ein Gedi

Road map C4. Route 90, 56 km (35 miles) S of Jericho. 🚌 from Jerusalem.

Ein Gedi is famous as a lush oasis in an otherwise barren landscape. Several springs provide plentiful water to support a luxuriant mix of tropical and desert vegetation. The site is mentioned in the Bible for its beauty (Song of Songs: 1–14) and as a refuge of David who was fleeing from King Saul (I Samuel: 24).

Protected as **Ein Gedi Nature Reserve**, the oasis is a haven for desert wildlife such as ibexes and rock hyraxes, which look like large rodents, while the more remote areas are the abode of the desert leopard. Two gorges, belonging to the Nakhal David and Nakhal Arugot rivers, are at the core of the reserve; these are crossed by a network of paths. The shortest walking tour takes about an hour and ends at the spectacular Shulamit Falls. A short way from the reserve's entrance are the ruins of a 5th-century-BC synagogue with mosaics and inscriptions in Hebrew and Aramaic.

Ein Gedi is also a popular spot with Dead Sea bathers. For a more luxurious experience, the **Ein Gedi Sea of Spa**, a further 3 km (2 miles) to the south, has hot sulphur baths and private access to the Dead Sea. The **Synergy Spa** at the Ein Gedi Hotel offers various treatments against a spectacular backdrop.

🏨 **Ein Gedi Nature Reserve**
Highway 90, Dead Sea. **Tel** (08) 658 4285 **Open** daily. 🅿️

🏨 **Ein Gedi Sea of Spa**
Highway 90, Dead Sea. **Tel** (08) 659 4813. **Open** daily. 🅿️ ♿ 🌐 eingediseaofspa.com

🏨 **Synergy Spa**
Kibbutz Ein Gedi. **Tel** (08) 659 4222. **Open** daily. 🅿️ ♿ 🌐 ein-gedi.co.il

Trail sign for one of the gorges in the Ein Gedi Nature Reserve

❾ The Dead Sea

The Dead Sea (which is actually a lake, not a sea) lies half in Israel, half in Jordan. It is 76 km (47 miles) from north to south and less than 16 km (10 miles) across. At 411 m (1,348 ft) below sea level, it is also the lowest point on earth. The water is so mineral-laden that it is around 26 per cent solid. The therapeutic qualities of the water and its mud have been touted since ancient times, and spas are dotted along its shores. However, the Dead Sea is endangered. Its water level has gone down 12 m (40 ft) since the beginning of the 20th century because its main source, the Jordan River, has been overexploited for irrigation purposes.

VISITORS' CHECKLIST

Practical Information
30 km (18 miles) E of Jerusalem.
Dead Sea Panorama Tel (05) 349
1133. Museum: **Open** 9am–5pm
daily. 🅿 **Wadi Mujib Nature
Reserve Tel** (06) 463 3589. 🅿
🎫 compulsory. 🌐 rscn.org.jo
**Bethany Beyond the Jordan
Tel** (05) 359 0360. 🅿 (includes
audio guide). ♿ 🎫 call ahead.
🌐 baptismsite.com

Transport
🚌 from Jerusalem for Qumran,
Ein Gedi, Masada and Neve
Zohar; from Amman for Amman
Beach, Dead Sea Panorama and
Wadi Mujib Nature Reserve.

Qumran is where the Dead Sea Scrolls were discovered.

To Amman

To Jericho and Jerusalem

Ein Gedi
A popular spot with sun-seekers, who flock to the beach, and nature-lovers alike, who trek through the lush vegetation of the nearby Nature Reserve (above).

Masada
Herod's mountaintop fortress, overlooking the Dead Sea (see pp204–5).

Israel

Jordan

Ein Bokek
A waterside spa resort with hotels, a beach and sanatoriums that make good use of the Dead Sea mud.

To Sodom and Eilat

Neve Zohar is a small hot-springs spa resort.

To Petra

Bethany Beyond the Jordan
Believed to be where Jesus was baptized by John (see p32), this site, with its various churches, is a popular stop for pilgrims. At the nearby Elijah's Hill, archaeological finds include the remains of a 5th-century monastery.

Amman beach
A public beach with showers. There are also several resort hotels a little to the north, where you pay for access to their private beaches.

Dead Sea Panorama
A lookout, restaurant and museum complex with breathtaking views.

| 0 kilometres | 20 |
| 0 miles | 10 |

Wadi Mujib Nature Reserve
A wildlife sanctuary that also has several guided trails, some of which involve wading through partially submerged canyons. Bookings for the trails must be made in advance through the Wild Jordan Centre in Amman (see p218).

Key
— Major road
— International border

The ancient city of Masada, the most visited archaeological site in Israel ▶

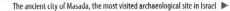

⑩ Masada

This isolated mountaintop fortress about 440 m (1,300 ft) above the banks of the Dead Sea was fortified as early as the 1st or 2nd century BC and then enlarged and reinforced by Herod the Great, who added two luxurious palace complexes. On Herod's death the fortress passed into Roman hands, but it was captured in AD 66 during the First Revolt by Jews of the Zealot sect. After the Romans had crushed the rebels in Jerusalem, Masada remained the last Jewish stronghold. Held by less than 1,000 defenders, it was under Roman siege for over two years before the walls were breached in AD 73.

Cable Car
The cable car operates daily between 8am and 4pm; otherwise it is a strenuous 45- to 60-minute climb up the twisting Snake Path.

★ Hanging Palace
Part of the large Northern Palace complex, the Hanging Palace was Herod's private residence. It was built on three levels; the middle terrace had a circular hall used for entertaining, the lower had a bathhouse.

KEY

① **Lower terrace**

② **Middle terrace**

③ **Upper terrace**

④ **Snake Path**

⑤ **Storerooms**

⑥ **The Water Gate** is at the head of a narrow, winding path to the reservoirs below.

⑦ **Southern Citadel**

⑧ **Western Wall**

⑨ **West Gate**

⑩ **The Roman ramp** is now the western entrance to the site.

Calidarium
Masada's hot baths are one of the best-preserved parts of the fortress. The columns, on which the original floor was raised to allow hot air to circulate underneath and heat the room, still remain.

Synagogue
Possibly built by Herod, this synagogue is thought to be the oldest in the world. The stone seats were added by the Zealots.

Cistern

At the foot of the mountain, Herod built dams and canals that collected the seasonal rainwater to fill cisterns on the northeast side of the fortress. This water was then carried by donkey to the cisterns on top of the rock, such as this one in the southern part of the plateau.

VISITORS' CHECKLIST

Practical Information
Road map C4. Off Route 90, 18 km (11 miles) S of Ein Gedi. **Tel** (08) 658 4207. **Open** 8am–5pm (winter: 4pm) Sat–Thu; sites close 1 hr earlier Fri & hols. 🅿️ 🚻 ♿ Sound-and-Light Show: Mar–Oct. **Tel** (08) 995 9333 for reservations.

Transport
🚌 from Jerusalem or Eilat.

Columbarium

This is a small building with niches for funerary urns; it is thought the urns held the ashes of non-Jewish members of Herod's court.

★ Western Palace

Used for receptions and the accommodation of Herod's guests, the Western Palace was richly decorated with mosaic floors and frescoes adorning the walls.

The Roman Siege of Masada (AD 72–73 or AD 73–74)

According to a 1st-century account by historian Flavius Josephus, the Roman legions laying siege to Masada numbered about 10,000 men. To prevent the Jewish rebels from escaping, the Romans surrounded the mountain with a ring of eight camps, linked by walls; an arrangement that can still be seen today. To make their attack, the Romans built a huge earthen ramp up the mountainside. Once this was finished, a tower was constructed against the walls. From the shelter of this tower the Romans set to work with a battering ram. The defenders hastily erected an inner defensive wall, but this proved little obstacle and Masada fell when it was breached. Rather than submit to the Romans, the Jews inside chose to commit mass suicide. Josephus relates how each man was responsible for killing his own family. "Masada shall not fall again" is a swearing-in oath of the modern Israeli army.

Roman catapult missiles

Remains of one of the Roman base camps viewed from the fortress top

⓫ Sodom

Road map C4. Route 90, 50 km
(31 miles) S of Ein Gedi.
🚌 from Jerusalem.

Biblical tradition holds that
the city of Sodom lay on the
southern shore of the Dead
Sea (Genesis 19). Its sinful
inhabitants, along with those
of neighbouring Gomorrah,
angered God, and he destroyed
the cities with "brimstone
and fire". Archaeologists now
favour Bab ed-Dhra in Jordan
as the likely site, but the name
Sodom remains attached to
a spot on the Israeli side of the
Dead Sea. There is nothing to
visit, but nearby are the two
spas of **Ein Bokek** and **Neve
Zohar**, famous for their
therapeutic centres, and a
public beach with freshwater
showers *(see p201)*.

Inland and 9 km (6 miles)
south of Neve Zohar is **Mount
Sodom**, a mountain composed
largely of rock salt. A well-
marked path goes up to
the top, from where you can
enjoy incomparable views of
the Dead Sea and the Moab
mountains in Jordan. You can
also go up by car: take the dirt
road that heads west off route
90 just north of the unattractive
Dead Sea Works plant. Another
signposted scenic hiking route
leads to what is known as the
Flour Cave. The cave gets its
name from the white crumbly
chalk coating that covers the
interior and the clothing of all
who visit.

A typically barren Dead Sea landscape
near Sodom

Spring-fed pool at Ein Ovdat in the shade
of canyon walls

⓬ Ein Ovdat

Road map B5. Route 40, 52 km
(32 miles) S of Beersheva.
Tel (08) 655 5684. 🚌 from Jerusalem.
Open daily. Summer: 8am–5pm
(to 4pm Fri & hols); winter: 8am–4pm
(to 3pm Fri & hols); last entry 1 hr
before closing. 🏞

At Ein Ovdat a white-walled
gorge gouged 200 m (656 ft)
deep into the desert floor
shades two icy-cold pools.
The larger of the pools is fed
by a waterfall with its source
in the rock face high above.
Archaeologists have found
traces of human presence
in this area that date back
perhaps 35,000 years,
suggesting that the springs
were known in antiquity.

A well-marked trail through
the gorge begins at a roadside
viewpoint 2 km (1 mile) south
of the turn-off for Kibbutz Sde
Boker. The trail ends with
a set of rough rock-cut steps
ascending the cliffs; the views
from these down the gorge are
spectacular. A path leads to a
roadside car park 7 km (4 miles)
south of the viewpoint.

⓭ Ovdat

Road map B5. Route 40, 60 km
(37 miles) S of Beersheva. **Tel** (08) 655
1511. 🚌 from Jerusalem. **Open** daily.
Summer: 8am–5pm (to 4pm Fri &
hols); winter: 8am–4pm (to 3pm Fri &
hols); last entry 1 hr before closing. 🏞

Located on a flat hilltop, the
ancient town of Ovdat was built
by the Nabataeans in the 2nd

century BC as a stopover on
the trade route between Egypt
and Asia Minor. It continued to
prosper under the Byzantines,
and most of what you see
today dates from the 4th or
5th century, including the
remains of houses, baths and
two churches. The smaller of
these has its original apse
and bishop's throne; a white
line divides the original and
reconstructed parts. The views
across the desert are excellent.
Below the hill you can make
out evidence of the network
of dams built by the Nabataeans
to channel rainwater towards
the dry land, enabling them
to plant vineyards and fruit
orchards. Ovdat was abandoned
after the Persian invasion of 620.
The Visitors' Centre has an
exhibition of archaeological
finds from the ancient site.

Partially reconstructed Byzantine-era ruins
at Ovdat

⓮ Hebron

Road map B4. 🗺 120,000. 🚌
🚢 daily.

Nestled among hills 40 km
(25 miles) south of Jerusalem,
Hebron is one of the most
densely populated towns
in the West Bank. Its fame
rests on its glassmaking, which
began in the Middle Ages and
has always been managed by
one single family.

This coloured glassware can
be found for sale in another of
Hebron's major attractions, its
medieval Arab souk, which has
some imposing Crusader-era
vaulted passageways.

The Tomb of the Patriarchs, mosque and burial site of Sarah, Isaac and Jacob

However, Hebron is a town undermined by troublesome political tensions. It is divided into two zones: the greater area is governed by the Palestinian Authority, but the town centre is occupied by Jewish settlers. Large numbers of Israeli soldiers maintain a constant peace-keeping presence. Friction between the two communities dates back to a 1929 pogrom in which the Arabs massacred Hebron's centuries-old Jewish community. After the Six Day War of 1967, the centre of town was resettled by militant Jewish colonists. Tension continues to erupt into occasional violence. For your personal safety, ask about the situation before making a trip to Hebron.

Hebron is regarded as a sacred place by the Jewish, Christian and Muslim religions alike; it was here they believe that Abraham buried his wife Sarah, in the Cave of Machpelah, purchased from the Hittite Ephron. The cave then became his own tomb and later that of his descendants Isaac and Jacob. Around 20 BC, Herod the Great sealed the cave and built a great hall over it. Under Byzantine rule the structure was turned into a church and then, after the Arab conquest of 638, a mosque. The invading

Crusaders attempted to reclaim the site for Christianity and built much of the present-day construction, but it was completed by Saladin as a mosque. In the 13th century the Mameluke ruler Baybars forbade non-Muslims from entering the building.

After the 1967 War the mosque remained Muslim, but access was granted to Jews as well. Today, the complex, known as the **Tomb of the Patriarchs** (Haram al-Khalil in Arabic), is divided into a Jewish synagogue and a Muslim mosque, each with its own entrance. It remains a bone of contention between the faiths; in 1994 Jewish colonist Baruch Goldstein entered the mosque and killed 29 Muslim worshippers.

⊙ ⊡ Tomb of the Patriarchs
Tel (02) 996 5333. **Open** 4am–10pm daily (except some religious holidays and during prayer times).

⑮ Beersheva

Road map B4. 🚹 200,000. 🚌
🚩 1 Hebron Rd, Beer Abraham, (08) 623 4613. 🛍 Bedouin market Thu.

The so-called capital of the Negev is a city that has grown rapidly and chaotically. In the Old Testament it is famous as the place where Abraham made a pact with Abimelech for the use of a well for his animals (Genesis 21: 25–33). Beersheva means "well of the covenant".

For centuries it remained little more than a Bedouin well until the Turks transformed the site into an administrative centre (which was the object of a valiant cavalry charge by the Australians in World War I).

Since the Israelis captured Beersheva in 1948, it has attracted many immigrants to become the country's fourth largest city.

There is an attractive grouping of an Ottoman-era mosque and Governor's House in the town centre, but the most interesting thing about Beersheva is the **Bedouin market**. This is held on the edge of town every Thursday from dawn and attracts hundreds of nomads. Besides the livestock and everyday objects bought by the locals, visitors can also buy traditional Bedouin handicrafts such as jewellery and copperwork.

Just outside town is **Tel Beersheva**, a city founded at the end of the 11th century BC and fortified around the time of Solomon. It was destroyed in the 9th century by the Egyptians but was rebuilt, remaining a bulwark of the southern frontier of Judaea until it was razed to the ground by the Assyrians. Remains include a 10th-century-BC city gate and a Roman fortress. There is also a museum of Bedouin life.

🏛 Tel Beersheva
6 km (4 miles) NE of Beersheva.
Tel (08) 646 7286. **Open** 8am–5pm (winter: 4pm) daily. Closes 1 hour earlier Fri. 🅿 ♿

Bedouin selling sheep at Beersheva's Thursday market

⑯ Makhtesh Ramon

Road map B5. Route 40, 80 km (50 miles) S of Beersheva. 🚌 from Beersheba. Visitors' Centre: **Tel** (08) 658 8691. **Open** 8am–5pm (winter: 4pm) Sun–Thu, 8am–4pm (winter: 3pm) Fri (last entry 1 hour before closing). 🚻 ♿

Makhtesh Ramon is Israel's most dramatic natural phenomenon: a crater some 40 km (25 miles) long, 9 km (5 miles) wide, with a depth of 300 m (1,300 ft). It is the largest of three craters in the Negev Desert, which scientists believe were formed more than half a million years ago by a combination of tectonic movement and erosion.

Traffic between Beersheva and Eilat has to cross Makhtesh Ramon, negotiating switchback roads that wind down to the crater floor and back up again. Nabataean caravans also travelled this way between Petra and Ovdat, and the ruins of an ancient caravanserai stand at the centre of the depression.

On the crater's rim is the town of Mitspe Ramon, the main base for exploring this part of the desert. The town's Visitors' Centre has exhibits on the geology of the great crater and its flora and fauna. It also has hiking maps – but make sure to take plenty of water if you go trekking here. In Mitspe Ramon you can also arrange to tour the crater by camel or jeep.

Spectacular geological scenery at Timna National Park

⑰ Khai Bar Yotvata Wildlife Reserve

Road map B6. Route 90, 35 km (22 miles) N of Eilat. **Tel** (08) 637 6018. 🚌 from Eilat. **Open** daily. Summer: 8am–5pm; winter: 8am–4pm. Closes 1 hour earlier Fri. 🎦 Obligatory, with departures every hour. 🚻 ♿

A caracal, one of the biblical species at Khai Bar

Khai Bar was founded with the aim of reintroducing some of the creatures named in the Bible, which have since vanished from the Negev. Most of the animals roam freely, safari-park style, in a 40-sq-km (15-sq-mile) territory in the Arava Valley. Visits can be made only by jeep in the company of a ranger guide. Native species in the reserve (not all of which receive biblical mention) include scimitar-horned oryxes, wild Somali donkeys, ostriches and the addax antelope with their curved horns. A Predator Centre houses wildcats, caracals (desert lynxes), foxes, leopards and hyenas in spacious enclosures.

⑱ Timna National Park

Road map B6. Route 90, 28 km (18 miles) N of Eilat. **Tel** (08) 631 6756. 🚌 from Eilat. **Open** 8am–4pm Sat–Thu, 8am–3pm Fri (to 1pm Jul & Aug). 🚻 🌐 parktimna.co.il

Ancient remains indicate working mines at Timna as far back as 3000 BC, and the Egyptians were mining copper here around 1500 BC. They left two temples dedicated to the goddess Hathor, protectress of mines. A hieroglyphic inscription in one of the temples mentions pharaoh Rameses III offering a sacrifice to Hathor. The mines continued to be worked under the Nabataeans and Romans before being abandoned. With the added attraction of some curious mushroom-shaped rock formations created by wind erosion, the area has been preserved as a national park. An underground passage gives access to the ancient mines, and you can see Egyptian graffiti representing ibexes and hunters armed with bows and arrows.

Visitors at Makhtesh Ramon, the largest crater of its kind in the world

For hotels and restaurants in this region see p262 and p274

⑲ Eilat

Road map B7. 🚗 50,000. ✈ 🚌
ℹ 8 Beit ha-Gesher St, (08) 630 9111.
Open 8:30am–5pm Sun–Thu,
8am–1pm Fri.

Lying at the end of the Gulf of
Aqaba, on a stretch of Israel's
12-km- (7-mile-) long southern
coast, Eilat is the only Israeli
town on the Red Sea. The town
is filled with hotels and tourist
villages, and is a centre for
diving and trips into the desert.
Eilat is similar in many ways to
Aqaba, which faces it from 6 km
(4 miles) away on the other
side of the Gulf. Along with an
equally stunning location, Eilat
also shares a similar history
to Aqaba. Now separated by
political boundaries, however,
it is Eilat that has prospered the
most. With the United Nations
partition of Palestine in 1947,
Israel was ceded this small
stretch of coastline, and Eilat
has since developed rapidly,
both as a port and as a popular
holiday resort with excellent
tourist facilities.

The bottom of the Red Sea is
the main attraction here. If you
don't want to dive to admire
this multicoloured ecosystem,

Coral Island, south of Eilat in the Gulf of Aqaba

there are glass-bottomed
boats as well as the "Yellow
Submarine". This large 23-m-
(75-ft-) long submersible leaves
from Coral World and cruises
out over the reef, descending to
a depth of around 60 m (200 ft).

The large **Coral World
Underwater Observatory** is an
oceanographic complex where
you can get a close-up view of
the marvellous marine life here.
It contains 25 tanks with more
than 500 species of fish, sponges,
corals and invertebrates. The
most interesting displays are
those with the larger creatures
such as sharks and sea turtles.
The main spectacle, though, is
at the underwater observatory

itself, which is 6 m (20 ft) under
water and gives a spectacular
live view of the local marine life
through its large glass windows.

Divers and expert swimmers
will be delighted at **Dolphin
Reef**, where small groups led by
an instructor can actually swim
with the dolphins and observe
their behaviour as they play,
swim and hunt.

The salt marshes just north
of Eilat are the feeding grounds
of many species of migratory
birds travelling between Africa
and Eurasia every spring and
autumn. The **International
Birdwatching Centre** has an
interpretation centre and
organizes guided birdwatching
tours. In season, the skies are
filled with thousands of storks,
flamingos and herons, as well
as eagles, hawks and buzzards.

By boat you can go to the
fabulous reefs off **Coral Island**
(or Pharaoh's Island), which lies
just across the Egyptian border.
Regular trips are run for divers,
but those wishing to land and
visit the 12th-century Crusader
fortress that dominates the
island will need to find a tour
that can arrange a group visa.

**🔲 Coral World Underwater
Observatory**
Coral Beach. **Tel** (08) 636 4200.
Open 8:30am–4pm daily. 🅿 ♿
ⓦ coralworld.co.il

🔲 Dolphin Reef
Southern Beach. **Tel** (08) 630 0100.
Open 9am–5pm daily. 🅿
ⓦ dolphinreef.co.il

**🔲 International Birdwatching
Centre**
Kibbutz Eilot, 2 km (1 mile) N of Eilat.
Tel (050) 767 1290. **Open** Oct–Jun:
Sun–Thu (am only). ♿ 📷

Swimming in the perfectly clear waters off the beach at Eilat

PETRA AND WESTERN JORDAN

While most visitors to Jordan come for the sole purpose of seeing the magnificent rock-cut city of Petra, many depart greatly impressed by the gracious and hospitable locals. Besides these attractions, Western Jordan has many fascinating archaeological sites from prehistoric, Roman, Byzantine and Crusader times.

Only partitioned off from Palestine in 1923 and made fully independent in 1946, the nation of Jordan has a maturity that belies its youth. That the kingdom is viewed as an anchor in the often turbulent sea of Middle Eastern politics is due, in large part, to the efforts of the late King Hussein (1953–99), who worked solidly to establish and maintain peace in the region. The extreme warmth and friendliness of the population is an expression of the stability Hussein secured for his country. Day-to-day patterns of life in Jordan are also shaped by a relaxed and tolerant interpretation of Islam. Tourists who have just visited neighbouring Israel may well appreciate the laissez-faire nature of the Jordanian people.

Although Jordan has an area of about 92,000 sq km (36,000 sq miles), around nine-tenths of this is made up of desert. Consequently, the population of approximately 5.5 million is concentrated in the northwest on a plateau above the Jordan Valley. Watered by the Jordan River and surrounded by mountains, this little pocket enjoys a lush greenhouse-like climate and is entirely devoted to agriculture. But south of Amman, the fertile plains abruptly end and give way to the vast stony desert that extends all the way down to the Red Sea. Largely shunned by the local populace, this is the region that visitors come to see. This is where you find the craggy sandstone landscapes out of which Petra was carved. Further south is Wadi Rum with its wide sandy oceans that provided a dramatic backdrop for the exploits of Lawrence of Arabia.

Ruins of the ancient Graeco-Roman city of Gadara at Umm Qais *(see p214)*

◄ The treasury at Petra, arguably the single most spectacular site in the whole Middle East

Exploring Petra and Western Jordan

Though possessing few sites itself, Jordan's modern capital, Amman, makes a very comfortable base from which to explore the northwest of the country. The Arab fortress at Ajlun, the Roman ruins at Jerash, the Byzantine mosaics of Madaba, and further mosaics along with splendid views at Mount Nebo are all within an hour's drive. If you can spare the time and secure the use of a car (self-drive or a taxi hired by the day), then Amman is certainly worth a couple of days. The Crusader castles of Kerak and Shobak are perhaps best visited while heading south, en route to the site that truly epitomizes the magic of the region, Petra. While it is possible to see the major attractions in just one day, Petra more than repays repeated visits: multiple-day passes are available. Accommodation is easy to find in the neighbouring town of Wadi Musa. Be sure also to leave enough time for the surreal rockscapes of Wadi Rum.

The impressive stone sweep of the colonnaded Oval Plaza at Jerash

Sights at a Glance

1. Umm Qais
2. Ajlun
3. Jerash
4. Amman
5. Mount Nebo
6. *Madaba pp220–21*
7. Kerak
8. Shobak
9. *Petra pp224–35*
10. *Wadi Rum pp236–8*
11. Aqaba

Getting Around

Most major tourist destinations can be reached by good, modern roads. There are two main routes south – take the King's Highway (Route 49) for Mount Nebo, Madaba, Kerak and Shobak, and the Desert Highway (Routes 15 and 53) to head directly to Petra and Wadi Rum. It is possible to fly between Amman and Aqaba and an inexpensive bus service connects all areas of the country. For many people, however, coach tours are the most comfortable way to get about.

Wadi Rum, where sandstone mountains rise sheer from the desert floor

For hotels and restaurants in this region see pp262–3 and pp274–5

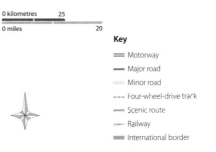

The Roman theatre in the shadow of modern central Amman

```
0 kilometres        25
0 miles             20
```

Key

- ▬▬ Motorway
- ▬▬ Major road
- ┈┈┈ Minor road
- --- Four-wheel-drive track
- ▬▬ Scenic route
- ▬▬ Railway
- ▬▬ International border

The Royal Tombs at Petra, a site that ranks with the Pyramids as a surviving wonder of the ancient world

For map symbols see back flap

❶ Umm Qais

Road map C2. 100 km (62 miles) NW of Amman. **Open** 7am–sunset daily.

Umm Qais is the site of the ancient Graeco-Roman city of Gadara. The ruins lie in lush hill country overlooking the Golan Heights and the Sea of Galilee. The city is well known from the Bible for Jesus's miracle of the Gadarene Swine, when he cast out demons into pigs (Matthew 8: 28–34). Since 1974, archaeologists have uncovered many impressive Roman remains, including a colonnaded street, a theatre and a mausoleum.

❷ Ajlun

Road map C3. 50 km (31 miles) W of Amman. 🛈 (02) 642 0115. Fortress: **Open** 8am–5pm daily (winter: 4pm).

The market town of Ajlun is dominated by the fortress of **Qalat ar-Rabad**, a superb example of Arab military engineering. Built in 1184–5, partly in response to Crusader incursions in the region, it was later used by the Ottomans up until the 18th century. At a height of more than 1,200 m (4,000 ft), it offers fantastic views over the Jordan Valley.

Environs
About 30 km (19 miles) northwest of Ajlun is **Pella**. Water, fertile land and, later, its location on two major trade routes were drawing settlers here well before 3000 BC. Its Roman-Byzantine ruins are today's attraction.

The Arab fortress at Ajlun, built to stem the Crusaders' advance

View of Jerash's Cardo, Agora (market place) and unusual Oval Plaza

❸ Jerash

Road map C3. 50 km (31 miles) N of Amman. 🚌 from Amman. **Tel** (02) 634 2471. **Open** Oct–Apr: 8am–4pm Mon–Thu, 9am–4pm Fri–Sun; May–Sep: 8am–7pm Mon–Thu, 9am–4pm Fri–Sun. 🎭 Jordan Festival (late Jul–early Aug). **Tel** (06) 566 0156.

Excavations of Jerash, known as Gerasa in classical times, began in the 1920s, bringing to light one of the best-preserved and most original Roman cities in the Middle East. It was during the Hellenistic period of the 3rd century BC that Jerash became an urban centre and a member of the loose federation of Greek cities known as the Decapolis (see p46). From the 1st century BC Jerash drew considerable prestige from the semi-independent status it was given within the Roman province of Syria. It prospered greatly from its position on the incense and spice trade route from the Arabian Peninsula to Syria and the Mediterranean. Jerash lost its autonomy under Trajan, but his annexation of the Nabataean capital Petra (see pp224–35) in AD 106 brought the city even more wealth. By AD 130 ancient

Detail of floor mosaic in St George's Church

Gerasa was at its zenith. Having become a favourite city of Hadrian (see p47), it flourished both economically and socially. After a period of decline in the 3rd century, it enjoyed a renaissance as a Christian city under the Byzantines, notably in the reign of Justinian (AD 527–65). The Muslims took over the city in 635, and it was badly damaged by a series of earthquakes in the 8th century. The final blow to the city was dealt by Baldwin II of Jerusalem in 1112 during the Crusades (see pp52–3). The city was reached through **Hadrian's Arch**, built in honour of the Roman emperor. Alongside is the **Hippodrome**, where Gerasa's chariot races and other sporting events were held. Today, re-enactment shows of these events take place every day (except Tue). A little way down the track is the **South Gate**, part of the 4th-century-AD city wall. To its left, and on a prominent rise, is first the **Temple of Zeus**, and then the **South Theatre**, which nowadays is used as a venue for the Jordan Festival (see p41). The most unusual feature of the Roman city is the **Oval Plaza** (1st century AD) which, with its asymmetrical shape, is a unique monument from the Roman world. The plaza, 80 m by 90 m (262 ft by 295 ft), is enclosed by 160 Ionic columns. Beneath its stone paving runs a complex drainage system. From here, going north, is the **Cardo**, a spectacular paved street about 600 m (2000 ft) long, which was lined with the city's major buildings, shops and residences.

Chariot tracks are visible in the stones. To the left lies the **Agora**, the city's main food market, which had a central fountain. At the Tetrapylon (crossroads) the Cardo meets a second major street, the **South Decumanus**, which runs east–west. Further along on the left side of the Cardo is the

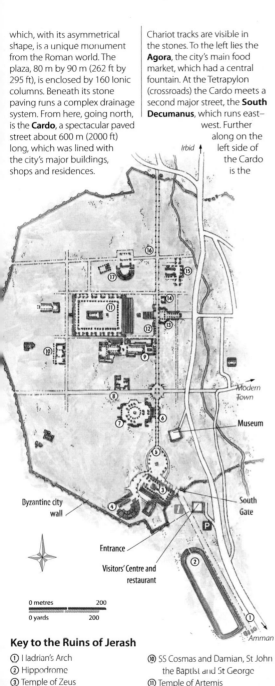

Temple of Zeus, which dates back to the 2nd century AD

2nd-century **Nymphaeum**, a lavish public fountain. One of its basins has a design of four fish kissing. Nearby is the impressive **Temple of Artemis**, the patron goddess of the city in Greek and Roman times.

Close to the Temple are the remains of several Byzantine churches. The largest is usually referred to as the **Cathedral**. There is also a complex of three churches, dedicated to **SS Cosmas and Damian, St John the Baptist** and **St George**, which dates back to AD 526–33 and has fine mosaic floors. Further along the Cardo, to the right, is the **Propylaeum Church** with the remains of an ornate plaza in front, while next to it are the ruins of an **Omayyad Mosque**. Beyond lie the unexcavated **West Baths**, which preserve a splendid domed ceiling. At the **North Tetrapylon**, once marked by a dome resting on four arches, the road to the left leads to the small **North Theatre**.

Allow at least half a day to see the ruins, and finish off with the **Museum**, displaying sarcophagi, statuary and coins.

Byzantine city wall

Modern Town

Museum

South Gate

Entrance

Visitors' Centre and restaurant

Irbid

Amman

0 metres 200
0 yards 200

Key to the Ruins of Jerash

① Hadrian's Arch
② Hippodrome
③ Temple of Zeus
④ South Theatre
⑤ Oval Plaza
⑥ Cardo
⑦ Agora
⑧ South Decumanus
⑨ Cathedral
⑩ SS Cosmas and Damian, St John the Baptist and St George
⑪ Temple of Artemis
⑫ Nymphaeum
⑬ Propylaeum Church
⑭ Omayyad Mosque
⑮ West Baths
⑯ North Tetrapylon
⑰ North Theatre

The reconstructed South Gate, the 4th-century AD entrance to Jerash

❹ Amman

Like Jordan itself, Amman is a modern creation, but one whose roots run deep into history. The hills of Downtown hosted the biblical capital of the Ammonites and the Roman city of Philadelphia, before the Omayyad Arabs built a palace on the same well-defended hilltop. In the modern age, Amman only began to prosper in the early 1920s when Emir Abdullah made it the capital of Trans-Jordan. Today, it is a bustling, modern and forward-looking Arab city of over two million people.

King Hussein Mosque, built on the site of a 7th-century mosque

Exploring Central Amman

Amman's most interesting district for the visitor is the Downtown area, with its bustling markets, interesting museums and fascinating Roman ruins. More than anything, Amman is a town of hills (jebels) and, of these, the most historically important is Jebel el-Qalaa, which rises north of Downtown. This is the site of the Citadel, a Roman temple and one of the city's main museums.

Downtown

The backstreet souks (markets) around Quraysh, El-Malek Faisal and El-Hashemi streets form the commercial hub of Amman. Shops here stock everything from marinated olives to gold jewellery, while pastry stalls, falafel stands and aromatic coffee and spice grinders also compete for the attention of passers-by. There are also several interesting souvenir stalls on El-Hashemi Street. The central **King Hussein Mosque**, built in 1924 on the site of a mosque erected in AD 640 by the caliph Omar, is the best attended in the city. Also nearby is the **Roman Nymphaeum**, built in AD 191 as a complex of pool and fountain, and

dedicated to the nymphs. Jordan's Department of Antiquities is excavating the Nymphaeum as part of an ongoing programme of restoration. There is no timescale for completion. In the Ras Al-Ayn area, the excellent Jordan Museum gives a detailed insight into Jordanian history and culture, going back several millennia. Among over 2,000 artifacts on display in this stylish building are the very modern-looking bug-eyed plaster statues from Ain Gazal, which are over 8,500 years old. The main attraction is a collection of copper-plated Dead Sea Scrolls (see p141). Check the website (www. jordanmuseum.jo) for opening times and other details.

🏛 Citadel

Jebel el-Qalaa. **Tel** (06) 463 8795. **Open** summer: 8am–6pm daily; winter: 8am–5pm Sat–Thu, 9am–4pm Fri. 🎫

For thousands of years Jebel el-Qalaa has served as the fortified heart of Amman. The Ammonite capital of Rabbath Ammon was situated here, but most of the remains visible today are part of what

was an Omayyad Palace, completed around AD 750 and destined to last for only 30 years. The large complex includes an impressive audience hall, a colonnaded street, a Byzantine basilica, a large cistern and the residence of Amman's local governor. The southern Roman Temple of Hercules, with its towering columns and ornately carved stonework, was built at the same time as the city's Roman Theatre and offers fine views over the city.

Ruins of the Temple of Hercules at the Citadel

For hotels and restaurants in this region see pp262–3 and pp274–5

Sights at a Glance

① Downtown
② Citadel
③ Archaeological Museum
④ Roman Theatre
⑤ Folklore Museum & Museum of Popular Traditions
⑥ Darat el-Funun
⑦ King Abdullah Mosque
⑧ Royal Automobile Museum
⑨ Wild Jordan Centre

```
0 metres        300
0 yards         300
```

Chequered *keffiyehs* – traditional Jordanian men's headwear

[Map of Amman with streets including JORDAN STREET, EL-HUSSEIN STREET, EL-HASHEMI STREET, showing Citadel, Temple of Hercules, Odeon, HASHMIYYEH SQUARE, Folklore Museum & Museum of Popular Traditions, Roman Theatre, Roman Nymphaeum, King Hussein Mosque, JEBEL EL-QALAA, JEBEL EL-JOFEH]

⑪ Archaeological Museum

Jebel el-Qalaa. **Tel** (06) 463 8795.
Open summer: 8am–7pm Sat–Thu, 9am–4pm Fri; winter: 9am–4pm daily.

This small museum at the Citadel records over 8,000 years of Middle Eastern history. Finds include Neolithic skulls and elephant bones from the Jordan Valley and several Nabataean artifacts from Petra *(see pp224–35)*. Look out also for the impressive doorway transported here from the Arab castle of Qasr el-Tuba in the Eastern Desert. Local finds include the graceful statue of Athena, from the nearby Roman Theatre, and the head of Tyche, the town god.

🎭 Roman Theatre

El-Hashemi St. **Open** summer: 8am–6pm Sat–Thu, 9am–6pm Fri; winter: 8am–4pm Sat–Thu, 9am–4pm Fri.

Amman's most obvious remnant from the past is its impressive Roman Theatre, dating from around AD 170 and with a seating capacity of about 6,000. It's a fine place to sit, meet the locals and take in the city. The back rows of the theatre were added later and carved out of an existing necropolis. At the foot of the theatre are a Corinthian colonnade and the old Odeon (a small theatre or meeting hall). The nearby Hashemite Square is a popular hang-out for local families.

⑪ Folklore Museum & Museum of Popular Traditions

El-Hashemi St. **Tel** (06) 465 1742.
Open summer: 8am–6pm Sat–Thu, 9am–6pm Fri; winter: 8am–4pm Sat–Thu, 9am–4pm Fri.

The vaults below the Roman Theatre house these two modest but interesting museums. The Folklore Museum has some traditional costumes, a Bedouin tent, fine examples of the *rababa* (a one-stringed musical instrument) and traditional coffee grinders. The second museum displays Circassian and Armenian silver jewellery, traditionally given to the bride on her wedding day, plus amulets made from Turkish coins and symbols representing the hands of Fatima. There are some fine mosaics from Jerash *(see p214–15)* and the baptism site of Wadi el-Kharrar.

VISITORS' CHECKLIST

Practical Information
Road map C3. 🚩 2,125,000.
🛈 Jordan Tourism Board, El-Mutanabbi St, Jebel Amman (Third Circle), (06) 567 8444.

Transport
✈

The Roman Theatre, built during the reign of emperor Marcus Aurelius

Exploring Amman

Although the majority of Amman's places of interest are concentrated in the neighbouring Downtown and Jebel el-Qalaa districts, it is well worth exploring further afield. Just west of the centre, Jebel Amman is the city's main hill, and is home to the Wild Jordan Centre and the landmark King Abdullah Mosque. West again, the upscale districts of Abdoun and, stretching to the north, Shmeisani boast the majority of Amman's shops and restaurants. The city is quite spread out, so taxi is the best way to get around.

The hilly landscape of the modern city of Amman

Darat el-Funun

Nimer bin Adwan St, Jebel el-Webdeh. **Tel** (06) 464 3251. **Open** 10am–7pm Sat–Thu. **W** daratalfunun.org

This art gallery, pleasant café and small garden dotted with archaeological remains offer a tranquil escape from the nearby Downtown bustle. The rotating exhibits of contemporary art, regular lectures and occasional music concerts make this the best place to tap into Amman's thriving arts scene. The main gallery is housed in a 1920s villa, next to the charming remains of a 6th-century Byzantine church, itself built on the site of a Roman temple. Above the church is the house in which TE Lawrence is said to have written sections of *The Seven Pillars of Wisdom*.

[C] King Abdullah Mosque

Suleyman el-Nabulsi St, Jebel el-Webdeh. **Open** 8am–11am & 12:30–2pm Sat–Thu, 9am–10am Fri. [image]

Amman's most impressive Islamic monument is the striking King (El-Malek) Abdullah Mosque,

completed in 1990 and dedicated by King Hussein to his grand-father. The soaring central blue dome covers the largest religious space in the city – the prayer hall can hold up to 7,000 worshippers. The cavernous, octagonal interior is decorated with fine Quranic calligraphy and several huge chandeliers. Remove your shoes when you enter the mosque. Women should wear a headscarf (provided). The attached small **Islamic museum** contains coins and examples of Islamic decorative arts.

[iii] Royal Automobile Museum

King Hussein Park. **Tel** (06) 541 1392. **Open** 10am–7pm Wed, Thu & Sat–Mon, 11am–7pm Fri. [image]
W royalautomuseum.jo

The former King Hussein was passionate about automobiles. This museum, 5 km (3 miles) northwest of the city centre, exhibits around 70 classic cars and

motorcycles from his own personal collection. These range from a 1916 Cadillac to an array of more modern Lotus, Ferrari and Porsche sporting models, all driven by the king. Also on display is the Mercedes-Benz jeep that carried the casket in his funeral procession in 1999.

[X] Wild Jordan Centre

Othman bin Affan St, Jebel Amman. **Tel** (06) 463 3589.
W rscn.org.jo

Jordan's innovative Royal Society for the Conservation of Nature (RSCN) runs this cutting-edge centre, which focuses on Jordan's natural heritage. The Wild Jordan Nature shop stocks products made by RSCN-operated development initiatives throughout Jordan, including natural handmade olive oil soaps from Ajlun, worked silver from Dana and Mujib, Bedouin-made candles from Feynan and hand-painted ostrich eggs from the Eastern Desert. The excellent café serves tasty and healthy lunches, and the terrace, in particular, affords fantastic views over Downtown.

This is also the place for information on ecotourism excursions to Jordan's many nature reserves; possibilities include hiking and canyoning in Wadi Mujib *(see p201)*, and the chance to see Arabian oryx in the wild at the Shaumari Wildlife Reserve.

The distinctive dome that caps the King Abdullah Mosque

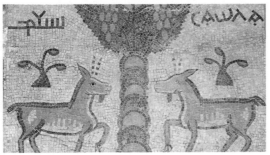

Detail of a mosaic from the Memorial Church of Moses on Mount Nebo

❺ Mount Nebo

Road map C3. 10 km (6 miles) NW of Madaba. 🚌 from Madaba, then a 4-km (2.5-mile) walk, or taxi. **Open** 7am–7pm daily (Oct–Apr: 5pm).

This mountain rises at the end of the long chain skirting the Dead Sea, and offers spectacular views of the Jordan River and Dead Sea 1,000 m (3,300 ft) below. It was from here that Moses saw the Promised Land just before he died (Deuteronomy 34: 1–5).

In the early 4th century a sanctuary, mentioned by the pilgrim nun Egeria (*see p36*), was built on Mount Nebo (Fasaliyyeh in Arabic) to honour Moses, probably over the remains of a more ancient construction. During the Byzantine period, the church was transformed into a fine basilica with a sacristy and new baptistry. Monastic buildings were added later.

Since 1933, reconstruction work has been carried out on the church, now known as the **Memorial Church of Moses**. Mosaics inside include a remarkable example in the Old Baptistry depicting farmers, hunters and an assortment of animals surrounded by geometric decoration. A Greek inscription dates it to AD 531. Next to the New Baptistry, a mosaic cross from the original church stands on a modern altar. Outside, the foundations of the monastery can be seen.

❻ Madaba

See pp220–21.

❼ Kerak

Road map C4. 🏔 19,000. 🚌 ℹ️ El-Mujamma St, (03) 235 4263.

The town of Kerak, on top of a hill with a sheer drop on three sides, is dominated by a magnificent Crusader citadel. Kerak was an important city (and for a time the capital) of the biblical kingdom of Moab. For this reason, the **castle** is also sometimes known as Krak des Moabites.

It was built in 1142 by the Frankish lord of Oultrejourdain, Payen le Bouteiller, to whom the territory had been ceded by King Baldwin II of Jerusalem in 1126. It was the pearl in the chain of fortifications that ran between Jerusalem and Aqaba, and replaced Shobak as the centre of Oultrejourdain. Under Reynald de Châtillon it resisted assaults by Saladin's troops in 1183 and 1184, but finally fell after a siege in 1188.

Arab repairs and additions in white limestone contrast with the Crusader parts built in dark, volcanic tufa. The upper courtyard, containing a much-damaged Crusader chapel, provides an exceptional viewpoint. Steps lead down to vast, dimly lit, vaulted rooms and corridors below ground. The lower courtyard gives access to a small **Archaeological Museum** displaying locally excavated artifacts.

🏰 **Castle**
El-Mujamma St. **Open** daily.

🏛 **Archaeological Museum**
Tel (03) 235 1862.
Open 9am–5pm daily. 📷

❽ Shobak

Road map C5. 60 km (37 miles) S of Tafila. **Tel** (03) 213 2138. 🚌 to Shobak village, then taxi. **Open** daily.

Shobak, isolated on a rocky, conical hill in rough, barren surroundings at 1,300 m (4,265 ft) above sea level, is perhaps the most impressively sited castle in Jordan. It was called Krak de Montréal, or Mons Regalis, and was the first outpost (1115) built beyond the Jordan River by King Baldwin I of Jerusalem to guard the road from Egypt to Damascus. It resisted many sieges until 1189, when it fell to Saladin's troops.

The towers and walls are well preserved and decorated with carved inscriptions dating from 14th-century Mameluke renovations, but the inside is ruinous. Near the gatehouse, a well with more than 350 dangerously slippery, spiral, rock-cut steps descends to a spring.

The impressive and well-preserved Crusader fortress at Kerak

❻ Madaba

Road map C4. 🏛 75,000. 🚌 from Amman. ℹ️ Hussein bin Ali St, (05) 325 3563.

According to the Old Testament, the Moabite city of Madaba was one of those conquered by the tribes of Israel. After changing hands several times, it flourished under Roman dominion and by the 4th century AD it had become an important centre of Christianity, with its own bishop. The town weathered invasions by the Persians and Muslims but declined under the Mamelukes, and was abandoned during the 16th century. It was not reoccupied until the late 19th century.

The main attraction is the fabulous mosaic map housed in **St George's Church** in the town centre. An icon of the Virgin Mary in the church is believed by Christians to incorporate a miraculous blue "helping hand". An **Archaeological Park** encompasses the remains of several more 6th-century churches, all with impressive mosaics, including one depicting scenes from the legend of Adonis and Aphrodite. The **Church of the Apostles** on the southern edge of town has a mosaic depicting the sea goddess Thetis surrounded by fish and sea monsters.

🏛 **St George's Church**
Open 8:30am–6pm daily (from 10:30am Fri & Sun). 📷

🏛 **Archaeological Park**
Open daily. 📷

St George's Church, also known as the Church of the Map

The Madaba Mosaic Map

In the late 19th century, clashes with the Muslim community led to a group of Christians from Kerak voluntarily moving to the long-uninhabited site of ancient Madaba. They were permitted to build new churches only on the sites of old ones. In 1884, while clearing such a site, the mosaic map was uncovered. It was incorporated into the new St George's Church but was badly damaged in the process. It wasn't until ten years later that scholars recognized the great historic value of the mosaic, which was probably made during the reign of the emperor Justinian (AD 527–65).

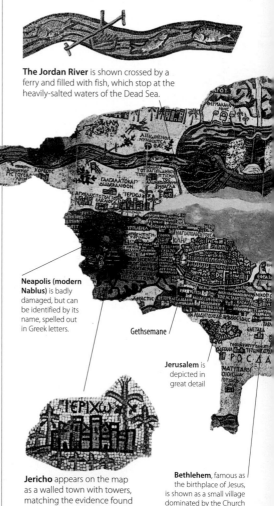

The Jordan River is shown crossed by a ferry and filled with fish, which stop at the heavily-salted waters of the Dead Sea.

Neapolis (modern Nablus) is badly damaged, but can be identified by its name, spelled out in Greek letters.

Gethsemane

Jerusalem is depicted in great detail

Jericho appears on the map as a walled town with towers, matching the evidence found at the site of Tel Jericho.

Bethlehem, famous as the birthplace of Jesus, is shown as a small village dominated by the Church of the Nativity.

For hotels and restaurants in this region see pp262–3 and pp274–5

The Madaba map, visited by up to a thousand visitors a day

Jerusalem as Depicted on the Map

In the 6th century, Jerusalem was still essentially the Roman city of Aelia Capitolina with its walls and gates, and the main streets of the Cardo Maximus and the Decumanus. Identifiable landmarks include Damascus Gate and the Church of the Holy Sepulchre, as well as the long-vanished Nea Basilica and Damascus Gate column.

Plaza in front of Damascus Gate with column

St Stephen's Gate

Golden Gate

Nea Basilica

Gate leading to Mount Zion

Damascus Gate

The Cardo Maximus was the colonnaded main street.

The Church of the Holy Sepulchre is shown topped by a golden rotunda, which was destroyed by the Fatimids in 1009.

Basilica on Mount Zion

Citadel (Tower of David)

Decumanus

Kerak sits on top of a high mountain.

Mamshit was a Nabataean city in the Negev Desert.

The Mountains of Sinai separate the desert to the north from the Nile Delta.

The Dead Sea is shown with two boats carrying salt and grain. The sailors have been hacked out, probably by Iconoclasts who objected to the representation of living beings in art.

Beersheva, although existing only in part, can be identified by the text – and by its accurate location in the western Negev Desert.

Pelusium was an important Byzantine-era city; it has long since disappeared.

Ashdod, an ancient port on the Mediterranean, remains an important deep-water harbour.

The Nile is depicted as flowing east–west rather than the reality, which is from south to north.

What the Map Shows

The map is oriented east–west rather than north–south, with Palestine on the left and Egypt's Nile Delta on the extreme right. The cities and villages are located remarkably accurately for the time, and they are represented in plan form, corresponding to a large degree with modern cartography.

Gaza was a major port in ancient times, with trade links to Egypt and Africa and, by its comparatively large size, the map accords it great importance.

Corinthian columns of the Temple of Artemis in Jerash, the Roman city of Gerasa ▶

⑨ Petra

Petra is one of the world's most impressive and atmospheric archaeological sites. Its marvellously preserved rock-hewn tombs and temples once encircled a thriving metropolis. There has been human settlement here since prehistoric times, but before the Nabataeans *(see p231)* came, Petra was just another desert watering hole. Between the 3rd century BC and the 1st century AD, they built a superb city and made it the centre of a vast trading empire. In AD 106 Petra was annexed by Rome. Christianity arrived in the 4th century, the Muslims in the 7th and the Crusaders briefly in the 12th. Thereafter Petra lay forgotten until 1812, when rediscovered by JL Burckhardt *(see p227)*.

The City of Petra
The city's main street leads to the Temenos Gate, entrance to the sacred precinct of Qasr el-Bint, Petra's most important temple *(see pp232–3)*.

★ The Monastery
The imposing façade of the Monastery, or El-Deir, is 47 m (154 ft) wide and 40 m (131 ft) high. This magnificent Nabataean temple may later have served as a church *(see p234)*.

Visiting Petra

- It is worth spending more than a day here. There are passes for one to three days.
- Cars allowed up to ticket gate but not beyond.
- Horses may be hired to take you the 900 m (half a mile) to the Siq entrance.
- Two-seater horse-drawn carts go from the ticket office to the Treasury. From there Petra can be covered on foot or camel.
- Basic food and drinking water available in Petra.
- Wear sunhat and high-factor sunscreen.
- Avoid wandering off main walk routes without guide and water supply.
- The visitors' centre near the Siq can arrange for guides.

Little P
(see p

Jebel
Umm Zaytuna

Jebel
El-Deir

Wadi El-Siyyagh

Jebel
El-Quray

Wadi ElThughra

Aaron's Tomb
(see p235)

Wadi Abu Ulloyqa

Wadi El Matah

Wadi Musa

Wadi El-Farasa

Wadi Ummrattam

Jebe
Attu

Key

-- Walk to Monastery *(see p234)*

-- Walk to High Place of Sacrifice *(see pp234–5)*

The Theatre
Carved into the mountainside by the Nabataeans, probably in the 1st century AD, this theatre follows the standard Roman design of the time. It was large enough to seat up to 7,000 people *(see pp228–9)*.

★ The Royal Tombs
These monumental façades sculpted into the mountain at the eastern end of the Petra basin create an awe-inspiring panorama when viewed from a distance *(see pp230–31).*

VISITORS' CHECKLIST

Practical Information
Road map C5. Wadi Musa, 260 km (160 miles) S of Amman. **Open** 6am–6pm (winter: 4pm) daily. 🎫 passes sold for 1, 2 or 3 days. 🚻 ask at the Visitors' Centre. Candle-lit tours: 8:30pm Mon, Wed & Thu. ℹ️ Petra Visitors' Centre, (03) 215 6044 or 215 6060 (6:30am–5pm daily). Do not photograph Bedouin without their permission. Museum: **Open** 9am–4:30pm (summer: 5:30pm) daily. 📷 💻

Transport
🚌 to Wadi Musa from Amman, Aqaba.

★ The Siq
Access to Petra is through this deep ravine, formed when a split in the mountain was swept clear by water from the Wadi Musa *(see pp226–7).*

Jebel El-Khubtha

P

← Wadi Musa Town

★ The Treasury
The best-known of all of Petra's magnificent temples, deliberately positioned at the end of the Siq for maximum impact, the 1st-century-BC Treasury takes its name from Bedouin folklore. They believed that the Khasneh el-Faroun (Treasury of the Pharaoh) was the magical creation of a great wizard who had deposited treasure in its urn *(see pp228–9).*

KEY

① High Place of Sacrifice *(see pp234–5)*

② Qasr el-Bint *(see p232)*

③ El-Habis Crusader fortress *(see p232)*

④ Old Museum *(see p232)*

⑤ Lion Triclinium *(see p234)*

⑥ Modern Museum *(see p232)*

⑦ Outer Siq

⑧ Mughar el-Nasara *(see p235)*

⑨ Tomb of Sextius Florentinus *(see p235)*

⑩ House of Dorotheos *(see p235)*

⑪ Petra Forum Hotel

⑫ Visitors' Centre

⑬ Ticket gate

⑭ Petra Forum Resthouse

⑮ Bab el-Siq

⑯ Siq entrance

0 metres 500
0 yards 500

The Siq: the Ancient Entrance to Petra

To reach the Siq, the narrow gorge that leads into Petra, you must first walk 900 m (half a mile) along the wide valley known as the Bab el-Siq. This prelude to Petra has many tantalizing examples of the Nabataeans' appetite for sculpting monuments out of mountainsides. The entrance to the Siq is marked by the remains of a monumental arch. It is the start of a gallery of intriguing insights into the Nabataeans' past. These include water channels cut into the rock, Nabataean graffiti, carved niches with worn outlines of ancient deities, Nabataean paving stones and eerie flights of steps leading nowhere. As the Siq descends, it closes in and at its deepest, darkest point unexpectedly opens out on Petra's most thrilling monument – the Treasury (see pp228–9).

Djinn Blocks
In Arab folklore these carved blocks, of which Petra has 26, house *djinn* (spirits). They may have been tower tombs.

Obelisk Tomb and Bab el-Siq Triclinium
Two rock-cut tombs on the way to the Siq stand one above the other. They seem to be one complex but are, in fact, separate. The upper, probably earlier, Obelisk Tomb shows Egyptian inspiration. The lower structure, known as the Bab el-Siq Triclinium (funerary dining chamber), is a superb illustration of the Nabataean Classical style (see p229).

A votive niche, to one side of the remains of the monumental arch supports, was reached by steps.

From the Ticket Gate, through the Siq, to the Treasury

It is about 1.5 km (nearly 1 mile) from the ticket gate to the end of the Siq. The route follows the course of a wadi which runs through the Siq and into the city. As the Siq descends, almost imperceptibly, it becomes deeper and narrower. At its narrowest point, the walls are only 1 m (3 ft) apart.

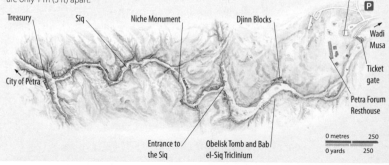

Treasury
Siq
Niche Monument
Djinn Blocks
Visitors' Centre
Wadi Musa
City of Petra
Ticket gate
Petra Forum Resthouse
Entrance to the Siq
Obelisk Tomb and Bab el-Siq Triclinium

| 0 metres | 250 |
| 0 yards | 250 |

Nabataean Pavements

The Siq was probably paved by the Nabataeans in the 1st century AD. Substantial stretches of this paving can still be seen. Next to the most extensive stretch is the Niche Monument *(see below)*.

Water Channels

The water channels were part of a sophisticated system of water conservation and flood prevention devised by the Nabataeans.

The Niche Monument

Carved into a free-standing rock, a quarter of the way along the Siq, is a small Classical shrine. Within the niche are two Djinn blocks, one of which has eyes and a nose.

The remains of the supports of the monumental arch consist of a carved niche flanked by pilasters.

Entrance to the Siq

In ancient times, the Siq was entered via a monumental arch. It fell in 1896, leaving only traces of its supporting structures.

View of the Treasury

The first breathtaking glimpse of the Treasury is when its pink-hued, finely chiselled façade suddenly appears through a chink in the dark, narrow walls of the Siq. It is a moment filled with powerful contrasts.

Johann Ludwig Burckhardt

In 1812, after lying hidden for more than 500 years to all except local Arabs, Petra was rediscovered by an explorer called Johann Ludwig Burckhardt. The son of a Swiss colonel in the French army, he was an outstanding student with a thirst for adventure. In 1809 he was contracted by a London-based association to explore the "interior parts of Africa". Three years later, after intense study of Islam and Arabic, he disguised himself as a Muslim scholar, took the name Ibrahim ibn Abdullah and set out for Egypt. On his way through Jordan, however, he was lured by tales of a lost city in the mountains. To get there, he had to persuade a guide to take him. Using the pretence that he wanted to offer a sacrifice to the Prophet Aaron, he became the first modern Westerner to enter Petra.

Burckhardt in the disguise he assumed to enter Petra

From the Treasury to the Theatre

Set deep in the rock and protected by the valley walls, the magnificent 1st-century-BC Treasury creates a formidable first impression of Petra. As its design had no precedent in the city, it is thought that architects from the Hellenistic Near East were brought in to create it. From the Treasury the path leads into the Outer Siq, lined on both sides with tombs of all sizes, some half buried by risen ground levels. At the end of the Outer Siq, in the midst of this great necropolis, is the Classical Theatre. Started by the Nabataeans and possibly added to by the Romans, it was a project requiring advanced engineering skills.

The Outer Siq
From the Treasury to the Theatre, tombs display a range of intermediate design styles. One, freestanding, uniquely combines Classical features with a crowstep used as a battlement.

Treasury Tholos
The central figure may be the Petran fertility goddess El-Uzza. Bullet marks in the tholos and urn have been made over the years by Bedouin attempting to release hidden treasure.

The Outer Siq
The artwork above shows some of the major constructions on the left-hand side of the Outer Siq as you walk from the Treasury to the Theatre. In reality, of course, the route bends and twists and on both the left and right sides are a great number of other tombs and features of architectural interest that could not be included.

Treasury Interior
A colossal doorway dominates the outer court *(left)* and leads to an inner chamber of 12 sq m (130 sq ft). At the back of the chamber is a sanctuary with an ablution basin, suggesting that the Treasury was in fact a temple.

The Architecture of Petra

The Nabataeans were adventurous architects, inspired by other cultures but always creating a distinctive look. The multiple crowstep can be seen as a design of the first settlers, whereas complex Nabataean Classical buildings reflect a later, cosmopolitan Petra. However, the dating of façades is very difficult, as many examples of the simple "early" style appear to have been built during the Classical period or even later.

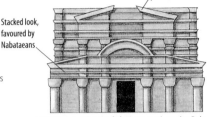

Multiple crowstep

This early design, seen in the Streets of Façades, was probably Assyrian-inspired. Fragments of the once brightly painted plaster pediments have been found.

Slot for primitive plaster pediment

Nabataean concave "horned" capitals, resting on "cushions"

Single-divide crowstep, lending height

This intermediate style, seen frequently in Petra, replaced multiple crowsteps with a huge single-divide crowstep, adding Classical cornices and pillars and Hellenistic doorways. This style continued well into the 1st century AD.

Stacked look, favoured by Nabataeans

Hellenistic broken pediment

Nabataean Classical designs, such as the Bab el-Siq Triclinium *(above)*, are complex, possibly experimental fusions of Classical and native styles.

Theatre Vaults
For access, there were tunnels either side of the stage. Inside *(right)* these were dressed with painted plaster or marble.

KEY

① **The vertical footholds** may have been to aid the sculptors.

② **Mounted figures** of Castor and Pollux, sons of Zeus, flank the portico.

③ **The eagle** was the symbol of the Nabataean male deity.

④ **"Attic" burial chambers** were a device to protect the dead from animals and tomb robbers.

⑤ **The single-divide crowstep** was a design devised by the Nabataeans to complement the Classical cornice.

⑥ **Stairway to High Place of Sacrifice** *(see pp234–5)*

⑦ **To the Streets of Façades**

⑧ **Tomb façades** were cut away when the rear wall of the Theatre was being made, leaving just the interiors.

⑨ **The stage wall** would have hidden the auditorium from the Outer Siq.

Streets of Façades
Carved on four levels, these tightly packed tombs may include some of Petra's oldest façades. Most are crowned with multiple crowsteps.

The Royal Tombs

Carved into the base of El-Khubtha mountain, a short detour to the right at the point where the Outer Siq opens out on to Petra's central plain, are the Urn, Corinthian and Palace Tombs. They are collectively known as the Royal Tombs, their monumental size suggesting they were built for wealthy or important people, possibly Petran kings or queens. These tombs and their neighbours are also remarkable for the vivid striations of colour rippling through their sandstone walls, an effect heightened in the warm glow of the late afternoon sun. Particularly striking are the Silk Tomb and the ceiling inside the Urn Tomb.

Panoramic view of the Royal Tombs from the direction of the ruined city

The Royal Tombs

First in the sequence of Royal Tombs is the towering Urn Tomb (far right), reached by a stairway. Its name refers to a relatively tiny urn on top. Further along is the badly eroded Corinthian Tomb, which seems to be modelled largely on the Treasury, and beyond that the Palace Tomb, thought to be based on Nero's Golden House in Rome.

Palace Tomb
The largest of all the Royal Tombs, the Palace Tomb had a grandiose façade on five levels, which was taller than the rock into which it was carved. The upper levels, since collapsed, had to be built up using large blocks of stone.

KEY

① **Of the four inner chambers**, only the middle two connect.

② **The Silk Tomb** gets its name from the beautiful streaks of yellow, grey, pink and brown, caused by wind and water erosion, which ripple across the walls and give them the appearance of shot silk.

③ **The central aperture** contains a badly worn statue of a man wearing a toga.

④ **Three burial chambers** are carved high in the façade.

Corinthian Tomb
There is no doubt that this was an important tomb in its day, but its design has baffled archaeologists because of its lack of symmetry. The doorways, each in a different style, are a clear illustration of this.

The Nabataeans

The Nabataeans were a people whose original homeland lay in northeastern Arabia and who migrated westward in the 6th century BC, settling eventually in Petra. As merchants and entrepreneurs, they grasped the lucrative potential of Petra's position on the spice and incense trade routes from East Asia and Arabia to the Mediterranean. By the 1st century BC they had made Petra the centre of a rich and powerful kingdom, extending from Damascus in the north to Leuke Kome in the south, and had built a city large enough to support 20–30,000 people. Key to their success was their ability to control and conserve water. Conduits and the remains of terracotta piping can be seen along the walls of the Outer Siq – part of an elaborate system for channelling water around the city. The Romans felt threatened by their achievements and took over the city in AD 106. Although the Nabataeans ceased to be an identifiable political group, Petra continued to thrive culturally for a time. In the end the transfer of trade from land to sea and two devastating earthquakes in the 4th and 8th centuries AD brought about the city's demise.

Sculpted head, possibly of a priest

Greek (left) and Nabataean pottery vessels found at Petra

Urn Tomb Interior
In AD 447 the Urn Tomb was turned into a church and two of the four recesses in the back wall were combined to make an apse. A Greek inscription records the consecration.

Urn Tomb Arches
Two levels of arches support the large terrace in front of the Urn Tomb. Their appearance earned them a place in Bedouin folklore as sinister dungeons underneath a law court.

The City of Petra

Just past the Theatre, the Outer Siq opens out into a wide plain. The ruins of the city of Petra are in the middle of this vast basin, and the path alongside the Wadi Musa leads down to the site. Today, fragmented remains of the main street and a few nearby buildings are almost all that is left of the great city that once filled the valley. The grand Roman-style Cardo would have been Petra's main artery, fringed with markets and leading to the city's most sacred temple, the Masr el-Bint. This building, like all the important buildings around the Cardo, would have been lavishly decorated. Traces of ornate plasterwork and marble veneer can still be seen on its walls and steps.

View of the ancient city of Petra from a point just past the Theatre

Modern Museum
Among the exhibits are a marble basin with lioness handles found in Petra Church and a small carved plaque of the Nabataean goddess al-Uzza *(left)* found in the Great Temple.

Qasr el-Bint el-Faroun
The name "Palace of the Pharaoh's Daughter" was a colourful invention of Bedouin mythology. The 1st-century-BC building was probably Petra's main temple, the huge slab of stone at the foot of the steps being an altar to the sun god Dushara, chief deity of the Nabataean pantheon.

KEY

① **The small El-Habis Crusader Fortress**, as its name suggests, was built by the Crusaders. While they were here, they also used the Qasr el-Bint as a stable.

② **The Old Museum** is in a rock-cut tomb built, unusually for Petra, with windows. It houses a collection of statuary.

③ Altar

④ Small temple

⑤ Lower market

⑥ Royal Palace

⑦ The Ridge Church

⑧ Northern city walls

⑨ Byzantine tower

⑩ **The Nymphaeum** was a grand public drinking fountain built where the Wadi Musa and the Wadi Mataha converge.

⑪ Shrine

⑫ Upper market

⑬ Roman house

⑭ Southern city walls

The Monastery (see p234)

Wadi Abu Ullayqa

Little Petra (see p...)

El-Habis Rise

Aaron's Tomb (see p235)

Temenos Gate
The imposing entrance to the sacred precinct of Qasr el-Bint had freestanding columns in front of its three massive, possibly metal-clad wooden doors. It probably dates from after the Roman annexation. The carvings of animal deities on its capitals are a Nabataean slant on an otherwise Classical design.

Temple of the Winged Lions
The name refers to the winged lions on the column capitals. It is also known as the Temple of al-Uzza as it may have been dedicated to this deity. The temple's monumental entrance was reached by a bridge across the Wadi Musa. Fragments of plaster painted with dolphins and floral garlands suggest rich interior decoration.

Petra Church
Superbly detailed 6th-century-AD mosaics adorn the aisles of this once large Byzantine basilica. A cache of 152 scrolls found here revealed details of daily life in Byzantine Petra.

Royal Tombs (see p230); Tomb of Sextius Florentinus (see p235)

Wadi El-Mataha

Wadi Musa

| 0 metres | 100 |
| 0 yards | 100 |

Theatre and Treasury (see pp228–9)

Great Temple
The grand entrance to this 1st-century-BC site led into a colonnaded lower precinct laid with hexagonal paving stones. Under the floor were extensive water ducts. Great stairways swept up to a 600-seat auditorium, of uncertain function. The decor was red-and-white stucco.

High Place of Sacrifice (see p234)

The Roman Cardo
The colonnades give the city's main street a Roman feel. They are thought to have been added after the Romans annexed Petra in AD 106. The street has been partly restored by Jordan's Department of Antiquities.

Other Sites Around Petra

Many of Petra's most famous sights can be visited in half a day. However, having come so far, it would be a pity not to explore more of this unique capital of a vanished civilization. A full day is enough to do the basic route from the ticket gate to the ancient city *(see pp232–3)*, taking in the Royal Tombs *(see pp230–31)*, and to include a walk to either the Monastery or the High Place of Sacrifice. Two days will enable you to do the basic route and both excursions and leave you with time to explore the area around the Tomb of Sextius Florentinus. Of the more distant sights, Little Petra can be visited in a day, while two days should be allowed for Aaron's Tomb.

High Place of Sacrifice: the round altar with the main altar behind

The Classical-style façade of the Lion Triclinium, located in a narrow side canyon

Walk to the Monastery

Just beyond the Qasr el-Bint *(see p232)* a path crosses the Wadi Musa. It leads past the Forum Restaurant to the start of an arduous but thoroughly worthwhile climb to one of Petra's most awe-inspiring and best-preserved monuments – the Monastery. The path, which cuts through the wadi, is paved in parts and features more than 800 rock-cut steps. The afternoon, when the sun is not directly in front, is the best time to do this walk.

A short detour off the main route, indicated by a Department of Antiquities signpost, leads to the **Lion Triclinium**. This monument, with the peculiar keyhole effect in the façade, caused by erosion, has blurred leonine representations of the goddess al-Uzza guarding its entrance. Its largely Classical façade has unusually ornate Nabataean features, such as "horned" capitals with floral scrollwork. After this, the path to the Monastery rises steeply. There

are occasional flights of steps through the winding and narrowing gorge, and several interesting carved monuments along the way. Finally, the path slips between two boulders and drops on to a wide, once-colonnaded, rock-cut terrace. Immediately to the right is the **Monastery**, Petra's most colossal temple, dedicated to the deified king, Obodas I, who died in 86 BC. Although it resembles the Treasury *(see pp228–9)*, it was never as ornate, even when statues adorned its niches. Its simple, powerful architecture, thought to date from the 1st century AD, is seen by many as the quintessential Nabataean Classical design *(see p229)*. The interior has one large chamber with an arch-topped niche where the altar stood. It came to be known as the Monastery because of the many Christian crosses carved on its walls.

The Monastery's massive tholos, crowned with an urn

Walk to the High Place of Sacrifice

Midway between the Treasury and the Theatre, a rock-cut stairway, marked at the start by several djinn blocks *(see p226)*, leads to the top of Jebel Attuf mountain. It is here, at 1,035 m (3,000 ft), that one of the best-preserved of Petra's many places of sacrifice is located. The ascent, while gradual, requires stamina and a good head for heights, and is best attempted in the early morning. The first part of the summit is a large terrace with two 6-m (20-ft) stone obelisks, possibly fertility symbols. The second, reached by a northwards scramble past the ruins of a small Nabataean building, is another plateau. Here, just beyond a rock-cut cistern, is the **High Place of Sacrifice**. In the centre of a large courtyard is a low offering table. Steps at the far end lead up to the main altar, which has a rectangular indentation in the top. The adjacent round altar has a basin with a carved channel, quite possibly for draining the blood of animal and human sacrifices. The nearby cisterns may have been used for ritual ablutions.

The path winding down the other side of Jebel Attuf into the Wadi Farasa valley is a spectacular stepped

Beautifully carved interior of the Triclinium, unusual for Petra

descent, sometimes with sheer drops. The first thing you see, carved into the rock face, is the **Lion Monument**, representing the goddess al-Uzza. It was originally a fountain, perhaps for pilgrims to the High Place, with water pouring from the lion's mouth. Water channels and the shape of the lion's head and legs can still be seen.

Thereafter, the path becomes a series of steps leading to the delightfully secluded **Garden Triclinium**. The tomb takes its name from the surrounding greenery. On top of the tomb is a large cistern. Further along, to the left, is the **Tomb of the Roman Soldier**, so called because of the remains in one of the façade niches of a figure wearing the uniform of a high-ranking Roman officer. Although Classical, the façade has Nabataean "horned" capitals on top of the pillars. Opposite is the façadeless **Triclinium**, thought to have been part of the Roman Soldier Tomb complex. It has the only carved interior in Petra and its niches, fluted half columns and cornice are superbly enhanced by the amazing bands of colour running through the walls and ceiling.

Further down the track is the relatively plain **Broken Pediment Tomb**, named after its most striking feature. Nearby is the elegant **Renaissance Tomb**, with the three urns above its arched entrance. Similar in style to the Tomb of Sextius Florentinus, it may date from the same period. Past this point the Wadi Farasa widens and the descent ends in the main valley, not far from the Qasr el-Bint (see p232).

Aaron's Tomb

This site is venerated by Muslims, Christians and Jews as the place where Moses's brother Aaron was buried. The white dome of the shrine can be seen from the High Place of Sacrifice, which may be a close enough viewing for most people. The journey there involves a three-hour ride on horseback and a hard three-hour climb to the top of Petra's highest peak – Jebel Haroun. For those determined to go, a guide and adequate supplies are essential.

Tomb of Sextius Florentinus

Beyond the Palace Tomb (see p230), along a track skirting the cliff, stands the **Tomb of Sextius Florentinus**. Despite its badly eroded north-facing façade, the beautiful and unusual details of its design are clearly visible. Above its entrance is a Latin inscription listing the positions held by Florentinus up to his last post as Governor of Arabia in AD 127. Further north is the **Carmine Façade** with its vivid striations of red, blue and grey. Continuing alongside the Wadi Mataha brings you to a rock-cut complex known as the **House of Dorotheus** because of two Greek inscriptions found here. On the other side of the wadi is a cluster of homes and tombs known as **Mughar el-Nasara**, including the fine

Tomb of Sextius Florentinus, Roman governor of the province of Arabia

The lonely mountaintop shrine of Aaron's Tomb, Petra's holiest place

Tomb with Armour. Local Christians were probably responsible for the many crosses etched into the walls.

Little Petra

This northern suburb of Petra, Siq el-Berid, has come to be known as Little Petra because it is like a miniature version of the main city. Situated 8 km (5 miles) north of Wadi Musa town, it is most easily reached by taxi. The journey on foot, north along the Wadi Abu Ullayqa, which starts just past the Qasr el-Bint, is hard, but rewarding. A guide is essential.

Little Petra seems to have been a largely residential settlement, as relatively few tombs have

Detail from ceiling of the Painted House

been discovered here. It may well have been where Petra's wealthy merchants had their homes. Just outside its Siq-like entrance, which was once controlled by a gate, are a large cistern and a Classical temple. The gorge, shorter than the one leading into Petra, contains a simple temple. As you emerge from the quiet of the gorge into the town, the incredible profusion of façades is overwhelming, with houses, temples and cisterns carved into every exposed rock face. Flights of steps shoot off in all directions, evoking images of a bustling urban centre. One of Little Petra's main attractions is the **Painted House**, with its plaster ceiling and walls delightfully decorated with flowers, vines, bunches of grapes, Eros with his bow and Pan playing his pipes.

❿ Wadi Rum

The desert landscape of Wadi Rum is one of the most awe-inspiring sights in the entire Middle East. Huge ochre-coloured rock pinnacles, weathered into bulbous, outlandish shapes, rise up 600 m (2,000 ft) from the flat valley floors, like islands in a sea of red sand. Hundreds of hiking and climbing routes wind their way up and around the many peaks. This area was once on a major trade route, and evidence of settlement here includes ruins of a temple built by the Nabataeans *(see p231)* and carvings and inscriptions left later by the Thamuds. Today the region, a UNESCO World Heritage Site, is still inhabited by semi-nomadic Bedouin tribes.

★ Lawrence's Spring
Not far from Rum village, this tranquil spring was described by TE Lawrence as "a paradise just 5 feet square". A Nabataean-built water channel can be seen nearby.

Rum Village
The main settlement is a rapidly growing Bedouin village. The Rest House on the outskirts offers spartan accommodation and simple meals.

Khazali Canyon
This steep defile is dotted with Thamudic inscriptions. It is possible to scramble 200 m (656 ft) into the canyon, starting on a ledge to the right.

KEY

① Nabataean Temple

② Abu Aina camp site

③ **Jebel Burdah rock bridge**
is spectacularly situated and can be reached via a moderately difficult climb.

Aqaba Petra

Jebel **Hubeira**

Jebel **Leyyah**

— Wadi Leyyah —

Wadi Rum

Jebel **Rum**

Wadi Rumman

Rum

Je **U** Ish

Jebe Umr Eji

Wadi

Jebel **Qattar**

Aqaba

0 kilometres — 4

0 miles — 2

Key
= Road

-- Walk

-- Hike/scramble

-- Four-wheel-drive/camel track

Rock Map at Jebel Amud
In a cave 20 km (12 miles) northeast of Rum is a rock marked with indentations and lines. It is thought by some to be a topographical map of the area, dating from around 3000 BC.

VISITORS' CHECKLIST

Practical Information
Road map C7. 30 km (19 miles) SE of the Desert Highway (Route 53). Turn off 45 km (28 miles) N of Aqaba. 🏍 🛆 advisable for visiting the desert. Jeeps, camels and guides available at the Rest House or in Rum village. Rest House: **Tel** (03) 201 8867. 💻

Diseh

Jebel Umm Anfus

Jebel Rashraasha

Seven Pillars of Wisdom
This spectacular peak, also known as Jebel Makhras, is named after TE Lawrence's famous book, not, as is often suggested, vice versa. Wadi Siq Makhras, just to the south, provides hiking access to Wadi Umm Ishrin and beyond.

Jebel Barrah

Barrah Canyon

Jebel Abu Judayda

bel iyyeh

Khor Al Ajram

Jebel Barrah
This large outcrop, seen here at its northern end, flanks beautiful Barrah Canyon, which is a stunning hike best negotiated from the south.

bel nm uth

③

Jebel Burdah

TE Lawrence (1888–1935)

Lawrence of Arabia, the most famous British hero of World War I, earned his nickname for his exploits fighting alongside the Arab tribes that revolted against Turkish rule in 1915. Sent to Mecca in 1916 to liaise with leaders of the revolt, he then led many Arab guerrilla operations in the desert, including attacks on the Hejaz Railway, some launched from Wadi Rum. He also took part in the capture of Aqaba and the advance on Damascus. *The Seven Pillars of Wisdom*, his account of the Arab Revolt, contains lyrical descriptions of the dramatic scenery around Wadi Rum.

★ Jebel Umm Fruth Rock Bridge
This dramatic natural phenomenon is one of several rock bridges in the area. It rises straight from the desert floor and can be climbed and crossed without difficulty.

Exploring Wadi Rum

There are essentially two main ways to explore the desert of Wadi Rum: through a combination of jeep and hiking, or by camel trekking. Jeeps allow you to travel further and faster, but the more traditional means of transport will bring you much closer to the stillness of the desert. Either way, make sure you carry lots of water and avoid travelling during the midday heat, especially in summer. For contact details of companies organizing Wadi Rum expeditions, see page 289.

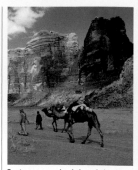

Tourists on a camel-trek through the canyons of the Wadi

Jeeps, the best way to cover large distances quickly in Wadi Rum

Jeep Tours

A wide range of jeep tour options is posted at the main reception gate, 7 km (4.5 miles) before Rum village. If you have not pre-arranged a trip, you will be allocated a driver here. It is possible to join up with other travellers to share the cost of a jeep. There are two main areas to explore: the main southern section of Wadi Rum and the less-visited northern scenery closer to the village of Diseh.

The most popular destinations include the striking red sand dunes of Jebel Umm Ulaydiyya,

the small oasis known as "Lawrence's Spring" and the narrow *siq* (gorge) of Khazali Canyon.

Other noteworthy attractions include the Nabataean inscriptions and petroglyphs of Anfaishiyya, the natural rock bridge of Jebel Umm Fruth and the various "sunset sites", which are all ideal places to witness the changing afternoon colours of the desert rocks.

Hiking

Many of the best trips offer a combination of jeep travel and hiking. The 5-km (3-mile) stroll through the towering walls of Barrah Canyon is a favourite option. Some hikes require a guide, such as the excellent hour-long scramble up to the Jebel Burdah rock bridge and the exciting half-day hike through labyrinthine Rakhabat Canyon.

Most trips require jeep transport to get you to the start of the hike. The only walk you can really do by yourself is from the visitor centre east to Makharas Canyon and back; take a guide if you are unsure of your route-finding skills.

Adventure Activities

An excellent alternative to making arrangements on the spot is to arrange a more active itinerary in advance with one of Wadi Rum's excellent Bedouin guides. Most can arrange jeep and overnight trips but you'll need a specialist for climbing or canyoning. Overnight trips that combine a jeep excursion, camel ride and some rock scrambling are very popular.

Camel trekking is fun but the pace is slow and can be highly uncomfortable after a couple of hours. Still, it is undeniably the best way to get a feel of the desert in classic "Lawrence" fashion. The three-day ride from Wadi Rum south to Aqaba is a challenging adventure.

Horse riding is possible on the periphery of the park, as is mountain biking over the desert flats.

It is well worth fitting in an overnight at a Bedouin camp during your visit. The larger fixed camps can be touristy but are fun nonetheless. The smaller ones shift location regularly and offer a more authentic, but also more basic, experience. The food is generally excellent; you may get to try *mensaf* (a Bedouin dish of lamb and rice) or, if you are lucky, a "Bedouin barbecue" – meat slow-cooked in a desert oven called a *zerb*. Reclining by an open fire, gazing at the stars and sipping a mint tea in the stillness of the desert is perhaps the quintessential Wadi Rum experience.

Hikers taking a break with their Bedouin guides

For hotels and restaurants in this region see pp262–3 and pp274–5

⓫ Aqaba

Road map B7. 🏚 62,000. ✈ 🚌
🛈 El-Koornish St (next to the Fort),
(03) 201 3363.

The only Jordanian outlet to the sea, Aqaba is a very important commercial port town. The relentless stream of heavy trucks going to and coming from Amman along the Desert Highway is clear evidence of this.

South of the town however, away from the busy port, the crystal clear waters are home to fabulous coral reefs. These are the main reason for Aqaba's popularity with visitors, as they offer some of the best scuba diving in the world. Closer to the shore, many other types of water sports also help to provide escape from the extreme summer heat. Large sandy beaches stretch out along the coast, bounded by modern hotels, and the steep mountains behind form a spectacular natural backdrop.

Aqaba's long and glorious past also provides it with some notable archaeological sites to visit. It is thought to be close to the site of biblical Ezion-Geber, the large port which is said to have been built by King Solomon. Its existence has, however, yet to be proved.

The town's deep fresh-water springs ensured that Aqaba became a popular caravan stop for merchants travelling between Egypt, the Mediterranean coast and Arabia. By the 2nd century BC, the now prosperous town had fallen under the control of the

Ruins of the old fortified Islamic town of Ayla, in modern Aqaba

Nabataeans *(see p231)*. Such prosperity saw it conquered by the Romans in AD 106, and later the Muslims in AD 630. Under Muslim control, Aqaba became an important stage on the pilgrimage to Mecca, and the Muslims built the fortified town of **Ayla** nearby to the north. After suffering a major earthquake in 748, the town was rebuilt, and thrived with an increasing sea trade. Following another earthquake in 1068 however, and then the Crusader conquests of the 12th century, the city was finally abandoned. You can visit the ruins at the Ayla digs, next to the coastal Corniche road. Much of the foundations of walls, towers and a series of buildings still remain. The **Archaeological Museum**, next to the tourist office,

Sign to Aqaba Aquarium

features material from the digs, as well as illustrating the history of Aqaba.

The other main archaeological site in Aqaba is the **Mameluke Fort**, set between the palm trees on La Côte Verte. Built in the 16th century, its portal now bears the coat-of-arms of the Hashemites, placed there after Lawrence of Arabia's troops conquered the port during World War I. The fort also served as a caravanserai for hundreds of years, and some restored rooms pay testament to this more peaceful role.

By going west past the industrial port and just beyond the ferry passenger terminal you will come to the small Aqaba Marine Science Station **Aquarium**. This contains a collection of the most important species of the varied flora and fauna in the Gulf of Aqaba, including moray eels and deadly stonefish. It also displays information on the campaign to protect the Red Sea.

🏛 **Archaeological Museum**
El-Koornish St (next to Fort). **Tel** (03) 201 9063 **Open** 8am–4pm daily. 🔲 🔲

🏯 **Mameluke Fort**
La Côte Verte. **Tel** (03) 201 9063.
Closed for renovation 🔲 🔲

🐟 **Aquarium**
South Coast (near ferry terminal).
Tel (03) 201 5145. **Open** 7:30am–3:30pm daily 🔲 🔲

Sailing boats anchored in the Gulf of Aqaba

THE RED SEA AND SINAI

Once coveted by Egypt's pharaohs for its reserves of turquoise, copper and gold, Sinai is now equally prized by tourists for its white, palm-fringed sands and the limpid waters of the Red Sea, rich with marine life. Its close association with key episodes from the Old Testament also makes the Sinai's mountainous interior an area of deep religious significance for Jews, Muslims and Christians alike.

The Sinai peninsula forms a triangle between the gulfs of Aqaba and Suez, two finger-like extremities of the Red Sea. Although the whole of Sinai is Egyptian territory, Israel and Jordan also have small stretches of Red Sea coast at Eilat and Aqaba respectively.

The word "Sinai" probably derives from "Sin", the moon god worshipped in Egypt under the pharaohs. But the region is better known through the Bible as the "great and terrible wilderness" negotiated by Moses and his people in their epic 40-year journey from Egypt to the Promised Land. It's here that God supposedly first spoke to Moses through the medium of a burning bush and here, on Mount Sinai, that Moses received the Ten Commandments. The peninsula has been crossed by countless armies, including that of the Israelis, who held the region from 1967 to 1982, when it was returned to Egypt under the terms of the Camp David peace treaty. In the years since then, tourism has boomed as southern Sinai and the peninsula's eastern coast have been developed with all-inclusive resorts, such as Sharm el-Sheikh. But the wilderness is far from tamed. Inland Sinai remains virtually uninhabited, with barren mountains sheltering hidden oases such as Feiran, with its thousands of date palms. More dramatic still are the underwater landscapes of the Red Sea, where vast coral reefs provide a home for more than 1,000 species of marine life, making for one of the world's richest dive sites.

Divers filming at Eilat's Dolphin Reef

◀ The incredible Coloured Canyon in Sinai

Exploring the Red Sea and Sinai

Most visitors head for where the mountains and desert meet the clear cool waters of the Red Sea; specifically, Eilat, Aqaba and, most picturesque of all, the Sinai peninsula's east coast. Its string of modern resorts, while uninteresting in themselves, are set against a backdrop of extraordinary natural beauty. Nuweiba, Dahab, Naama Bay and Sharm el-Sheikh are the largest and most well-developed tourism centres, but there are many smaller, more private beach retreats. St Catherine's Monastery can be visited as a day trip.

Aqaba, with a typical Red Sea scene of beach, palms and looming mountains

Sights at a Glance

① Taba
② Nuweiba
③ Dahab
④ Sharm el-Sheikh
⑤ Ras Muhammad National Park
⑥ *St Catherine's Monastery pp250–52*
⑦ Mount Sinai
⑧ Feiran Oasis

St Catherine's Monastery, an ancient walled retreat in the Sinai Desert

Getting Around

The coastal roads are good and the main resorts can be reached by car. Travelling in the Sinai interior is trickier, especially as foreigners are not permitted to stray off the main roads. Organized hikes or camel trips are perhaps the best options for those wanting to explore the desert. Buses serve coastal locations, as well as some places in the interior such as St Catherine's Monastery. Israeli and Jordanian visas and Sinai passes can be obtained at the borders *(see pp292–3).*

For hotels and restaurants in this region see p263 and p275

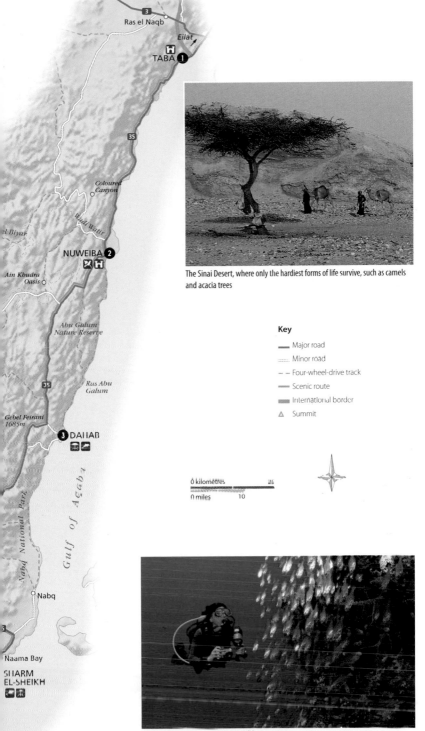

The Sinai Desert, where only the hardiest forms of life survive, such as camels and acacia trees

Key

—— Major road

═══ Minor road

– – Four-wheel-drive track

—— Scenic route

▬▬ International border

△ Summit

0 kilometres 20

0 miles 10

The underwater scenery and marine life of the Red Sea, which is every bit as stunning as the desert and mountain landscapes above

For map symbols *see back flap*

The Coral Reefs of the Red Sea

The Coral Reef is one of the richest ecosystems on earth. Visitors to the Red Sea cannot but marvel at the contrast between the barren, almost lifeless desert and the explosion of marine life on the coastal reefs. The waters are so clear that even from the surface you can appreciate the huge diversity of species inhabiting the reefs. Scuba divers can use the facilities of the many diving centres along the coast *(see pp286–9)*. Remember that a reef is an extremely fragile and threatened environment and divers should look but not touch.

View of lagoon and the shallow waters covering the reef-top

The edge of the reef is the best place for snorkellers to appreciate its wealth of marine life.

The lagoon teems with small colourful fish, including the fry of species found on the reef beyond.

Moray eel, emerging from its reef-wall lair

The clown fish protects itself from the sea anemone's stinging tentacles with a layer of mucus, using its host as a refuge from predators and for laying its eggs.

School of flag basslets, a very common species in the Red Sea

Manta rays are harmless plankton-eaters. Growing up to 6 m (20 ft) across, they are most common in open water or where there are strong currents.

Alcyonarians, brightly coloured soft corals

Corals, the Architects of the Reef

Corals are animals, colonies of polyps, which require very precise conditions of water temperature and sunlight to grow. They take many forms – from hard rock-like corals, such as *Acropora* species, to the horny gorgonians which project from the reef into the current to feed on microorganisms, to various soft corals. Most reefs are built over many thousands of years from the skeletons of hard corals.

Gorgonians filtering the water for plankton

An *Acropora* growing in still, shallow water

Feathery red plume of Klunzinger's soft coral

The sea fan is a horny coral, whose polyps emerge at nights to feed.

Jacks are usually seen in large schools in open water, but large solitary individuals will visit the reef.

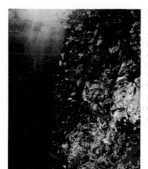

The reef wall, which plunges down to depths of 80 m (260 ft) or more, is home to an immense variety of corals, fish, crustaceans, sponges and many other forms of marine life.

Sea turtles are quite easy to spot in spring and autumn, especially between the Strait of Tiran and Ras Muhammad. They avoid the noisier, more developed stretches of the coast.

Shortnose blacktail shark

Coiled-wire coral

Despite their huge size, humphead wrasses (or Napoleon fish) feed on snails, crustaceans and small fish. Divers should resist the temptation to give them unsuitable food.

Black coral, so called for the colour of its skeleton

The jewel grouper, in common with the many other species of the family found in the Red Sea, prefers relatively shaded parts of the reef, where it preys on smaller fish.

Spotted sweetlips are usually found swimming in groups close to the reef wall. The name comes from their large blubbery lips. They make a noise that is clearly audible to divers, hence their other name – grunters.

An adult royal angel fish searches for sponges and other food on the reef. The young are more yellow with a large eyespot on the dorsal fin

Carvings on the Haggar Maktub, in the desert near Nuweiba

❶ Taba

Road map F5. 🚌

Since Israel returned ownership of the Sinai peninsula to Egypt in 1982, the small coastal town of Taba has served as a border post between the two countries. A pleasing stretch of beach is overlooked by a five-star hotel. Just under 20 km (12 miles) to the south is the resort of **Taba Heights**, which boasts some of the most luxurious hotels in Sinai, as well as an 18-hole golf course and a marina. There are views from the resort across the Red Sea to the Israeli, Jordanian and Saudi Arabian coastlines.

Between Taba and Taba Heights, just offshore is **Pharaoh's Island** (or Coral Island), which is dominated by an impressive Crusader fortress. Tickets for the boat across to the island are available from the Salah al-Din Hotel on the coastal road.

❷ Nuweiba

Road map F6. 🚌 🚢 from Aqaba (Jordan).

Nuweiba lies midway along the Gulf of Aqaba at the side of a promontory and consists of two distinct districts. To the south is the luxuriant Nuweiba Muzeina

oasis, which for centuries was a port for pilgrims going to Mecca. It now has many hotels and tourist villages. To the north is Nuweiba el-Tarabin, named after the Bedouin tribe that lives here. You can visit the ruins of the large **Tarabin fortress**, built in the 16th century by the Mameluke sultan Ashraf el-Ghouri.

The Nuweiba area is rich in beaches and diving and snorkelling sites.

Bedouin with his camel, outside Nuweiba

Environs

Nuweiba makes a convenient starting point for trips to the Sinai interior. One of the most fascinating is to the **Coloured Canyon**, a narrow sculpted gorge created by water erosion. Its sandstone walls have taken on many hues of yellow, red and ochre due to the slow process of oxidation of the ferrous minerals in the rocks. The canyon opening can be reached by car from the Ain Furtaga oasis, about 15 km (9 miles) from Nuweiba on the road west, and thence by following the Wadi Nekheil track.

Another fascinating trip uses a jeep track from Ain Furtaga through the immense Wadi Ghazala to **Wadi Khudra**. Midway along the track you will come to the Ain Khudra oasis, a lovely patch of palms and tamarisks seemingly wedged between the high, near vertical, red walls of the

canyon. If you continue a little further along the trail you will come to the solitary Haggar Maktub (Rock of Inscriptions). Since the Nabataean period, pilgrims going to Sinai have left graffiti carved on the rock.

Heading south from Nuweiba Muzeina along the coast leads you to the **Abu Galum Nature Reserve**. A maze of narrow wadis penetrates the interior, with an abundance of plants and wildlife, such as foxes, ibexes and hyraxes. The beach at Ras Abu Galum is usually deserted except for a few Bedouin fishermen.

❸ Dahab

Road map F6. 🚌

In Arabic the word *dahab* means "gold", and the name derives from the sand on the beautiful beaches. The crown of palm trees, the beaches and the light blue sea make this one of the most popular localities in Sinai. It has grown up around the old Bedouin village of Assalah, which still survives today. The many camping sites, simple hotels and beachside restaurants attract an array of mainly independent travellers who lend a raffish air to the town.

Many also visit for the world-class diving sites around Dahab. Among the most famous and dangerous are the "Canyon" and the "Blue Hole".

Raccoon butterfly fish with diver, off the coast of Dahab in the Gulf of Aqaba

Four Seasons Resort, one of numerous luxury hotels in Sharm el-Sheikh

Almost entirely surrounded by reef, the Blue Hole drops to a depth of 80 m (260 ft) only a few metres off the shore. Although many sites are for expert scuba divers only, there are still plenty of others suitable for beginners or snorkellers.

❹ Sharm el-Sheikh

Road map E7. ✈ 🚌 ℹ Tourist Office, Sharm el-Sheikh, (069) 366 4721.

Until the latter half of the 20th century, the most famous resort in Sinai was only a military airport. Situated on the western side of the Strait of Tiran, Sharm became famous when Egyptian president Nasser decided to block Israeli access to the Red Sea, thus provoking the 1967 War. Under Israeli occupation of Sinai, the first hotels were built and began to attract tourists, especially expert scuba divers. The Sharm el-Sheikh bay is still a military port, but the neighbouring Sharm el-Maiya bay has hotels, shops and small restaurants. Most of the tourist development, however, has focused on **Naama Bay**, a few kilometres to the north. This is the place that most people actually mean when they talk about Sharm el-Sheikh. It has a long beach with a host of luxury hotels and diving centres. Boats take snorkellers as well as scuba divers out to the open sea. Here, in the Strait of Tiran, you can

observe manta rays, sharks, dolphins and, occasionally, sea turtles. For those wanting to stay above water, tourists are taken in glass-bottomed boats to observe the coral reef from above. Other attractions include all manner of water sports, plus camel treks, quad biking and excursions inland.

Another spectacular sight is the long reef under the cliffs to the west of the **Ras Umm Sidd** lighthouse. Reachable from land, here you can admire a forest of gorgonians, huge Napoleon fish and, sometimes, barracuda.

Environs
A 29-km (18-mile) journey by jeep along the coast road north of Sharm el-Sheikh brings you to the 600-sq-km (232-sq-mile) **Nabq National Park**. This coastal park on the edge of

the desert boasts crystal-clear lagoons and the most northerly mangrove forest in the world, which extends for 4 km (2.5 miles) along the shoreline. The hardy mangroves are able to live in salt water, making this is an extremely important environment, linking land to sea. It is used as a feeding ground by migratory birds, including storks, herons and many species of birds of prey.

❺ Ras Muhammad National Park

Road map E7. 20 km (12.5 miles) S of Sharm el-Sheikh. ✈ 🚌 to Sharm el-Sheikh, then taxi. **Open** daily. 🛂 🔟

On the southern tip of the Sinai peninsula, where the waters of the Gulf of Suez and the Gulf of Aqaba converge, is a park instituted in 1983 to protect the incredibly varied coastal and marine environment. It includes extensive coral reefs, a lagoon, mangroves and a rugged desert coastline, and there is a series of well-marked trails leading to the most interesting spots. Among the most beautiful of these is the Ras Muhammad headland, the southernmost point in Sinai. Formed from fossilized corals, the headland is surrounded by beautiful reefs. The diving sites are very varied, with both reefs and wrecks to explore. There are also long, sandy beaches and a clifftop "Shark Observatory".

Gazelle at Ras Muhammad National Park

Entrance to Ras Muhammad National Park

School of anthias fish, likely to be seen during a dive at the isolated Brother Islands in the Red Sea ▶

❻ St Catherine's Monastery

A community of Greek Orthodox monks has lived here, in the shadow of Mount Sinai, almost uninterruptedly since the monastery was founded in AD 527 by Byzantine emperor Justinian. It replaced a chapel built in 337 by St Helena, mother of emperor Constantine, at the place where tradition says that Moses saw the Burning Bush. The monastery was named after St Catherine only in the 9th or 10th century, after monks claimed to have found her body on nearby Mount Catherine.

Library
The collection of priceless early Christian manuscripts is second only to that in the Vatican Library in Rome.

★ Icon Collection
Most of the monastery's 2,000 icons, such as this one of St Theodosia, are kept here. A selection is always on public view in the Basilica, while the most important icons are on display in the Treasury.

KEY

① **Round Tower**

② **The Walls of Justinian**, built in the first half of the 6th century, are part of the complex's original structure.

③ **The Chapel of the Burning Bush** stands where it is claimed the miraculous bush seen by Moses originally grew.

④ **St Stephen's Well**

⑤ **Dispensary**

⑥ **The Mosque** was created in 1106 by converting a chapel originally dedicated to St Basil.

⑦ **Monks' quarters**

⑧ **The underground cistern** was dug to store fresh water from the monastery's springs.

⑨ **The elevated entrance**, reached by a pulley system, used to be the only access.

⑩ **The Treasury** has on display important icons, manuscripts, vestments and works in silver.

The Burning Bush
This spiny evergreen is said to be from the same stock as the bush from which Moses heard God's voice, instructing him to lead his people out of Egypt to the Promised Land.

★ Basilica of the Transfiguration
This magnificently decorated church owes its name to the 6th-century Mosaic of the Transfiguration in the apse. It can be glimpsed behind the gilded iconostasis that dates from the early 17th century.

Bell Tower
This was built in 1871. The nine bells were donated by Tsar Alexander II of Russia and are nowadays rung only on major religious festivals.

VISITORS' CHECKLIST

Practical Information
Road map E6. Sinai, 90 km (56 miles) W of Dahab and Nuweiba. **Open** 9am–noon Mon–Thu & Sat. **Closed** Greek Orthodox hols. Offerings welcome. Guesthouse: Tel (069) 347 0353. Treasury: 🏛️ 🅦 **sinai monastery.com** 🅦 **saint catherinefoundation.org**

Transport
✈️ 10 km (6 miles) NE of monastery. 🚌 from Taba, Dahab or Nuweiba to St Catherine's Village (El-Milga), then taxi. Petrol available at monastery.

Monastery Gardens
In the orchard lies the cemetery, from which the monks' bones are periodically exhumed and transferred to the nearby Charnel House.

To Charnel House & Guesthouse

Visitors' entrance

Well of Moses
One of the monastery's main water sources, this is also known as the Well of Jethro, as Moses is said to have met his future wife, Jethro's daughter, here.

St Catherine of Alexandria

St Catherine is one of the most popular of early Christian female saints. Her legend, not recorded before the 10th century, recounts that she was a virgin of noble birth, martyred in Alexandria in the early 4th century. After being tortured on a spiked wheel (hence the Catherine wheel), she was beheaded. Her body was then transported by angels to Sinai, where it was found, uncorrupted, some six centuries later by the local monks.

A 14th-century painting of St Catherine holding a wheel

Exploring St Catherine's Monastery

Fortified by massive curtain walls, the monastery lies at the head of Wadi el-Deir (Valley of the Monastery), surrounded by high, red granite mountains. It is inhabited by about 20 Greek Orthodox monks, who follow the rule of St Basil, and the only buildings normally open to visitors are the Basilica and the Charnel House. Despite this and the constant crowds of pilgrims and tourists, the remote location in the heart of Sinai and spectacular, rugged scenery are awe-inspiring. For the reasonably fit, there are well-marked paths to the top of Mount Sinai and other nearby peaks.

Rock steps leading to the Gate of Confession on Mount Sinai

Inside the monastery

Entry to the monastery nowadays is through a small postern in the curtain wall, whose impressive thickness varies from 1.8–2.7 m (6–9 ft). Some sections of wall survive from the monastery's origins in the 6th century, but large-scale rebuilding took place in the 14th century, after an earthquake, and in 1800, on Napoleon's orders.

The monastery's Basilica was built in AD 527 with three aisles in typical Byzantine style. Eleventh-century, carved wooden doors open into the narthex (porch), where some of the monastery's splendid icons, all painted on wood, are displayed. The collection is exceptional for its size and quality, and because it contains the only examples of Byzantine

painting to have survived the Iconoclast era (726–843). Among them are a *St Peter* (5th–6th century), a *Christ in Majesty* (7th century), both in encaustic painting, and the *Ladder of Paradise* (7th century).

Carved cedar doors, made in the 6th century, lead into the central nave, which contains 12 columns topped by grey granite capitals and hung with icons showing the saints of the months of the year. The marble floor and coffered ceiling are 18th century. The iconostasis, dating from 1612, is by a Cretan monk, Jeremiah the Sinaite. The large figures represent Christ, the Virgin Mary and Saints Michael, Nicholas, Catherine and John the Baptist. Behind it can be glimpsed the exceptionally beautiful

6th-century Mosaic of the Transfiguration decorating the roof of the apse. It shows Christ surrounded by Elijah, Moses and the Disciples John, Peter and James. In the apse, (often closed), on the right, is a marble coffin containing the remains of St Catherine.

The Chapel of the Burning Bush, behind the apse and also usually closed to the public, is the holiest part of the monastery. It was built on the site where God is thought to have appeared to Moses for the first time (Exodus 3: 2–4). Tradition says that the bush itself (*see p250*) was moved outside when the chapel was built.

The library has over 3,000 manuscripts in Greek, Coptic, Syriac, Arabic, Georgian, Armenian and Old Slavonic. The oldest is the 5th-century *Codex Syriacus*, one of the earliest existing copies of the Gospels.

St Catherine's has, uniquely for a Christian monastery, a mosque within its walls. It was built for the Bedouin who worked in the monastery and also as a way of avoiding attacks by the Muslims.

Outside the walls

In the gardens (*see p251*) are the monks' cemetery and the Chapel of St Triphonius. The latter's crypt holds the Charnel House containing the bones of deceased monks. The robed skeleton is that of Stephanos, a 6th-century guardian of the path to Mount Sinai.

Moses receiving the tablets inscribed with the Ten Commandments, 6th-century wall painting

Chapel of the Holy Trinity on the summit of Mount Sinai

❼ Mount Sinai

Road map E6. Sinai, 90 km (56 miles) W of Dahab and Nuweiba.

According to tradition, Mount Sinai (Gebel Musa, the Mountain of Moses) is the biblical Mount Horeb, where Moses spent 40 days and received the Ten Commandments (Exodus 24). Two paths climb to the 2,286-m (7,500-ft) summit from behind the monastery, both requiring three hours' walking. The route said to have been taken by Moses is the most tiring as it consists of 3,700 rock steps called the Steps of Repentance. There are several votive sites along the way.

A cypress-shaded plain, 700 steps below the summit, is the so-called Amphitheatre of the Seventy Elders of Israel, where those who accompanied Moses stopped, leaving him to go to the top alone. It is also called Elijah's Hollow, as Elijah is said to have heard the voice of God here. It contains **St Stephen's Chapel** and is where people spending the night on the mountain are asked to sleep. This is also where the second, longer but easier, path joins the first. Camels can be hired to this point, but the final 700 steps have to be done on foot.

On the summit is the small **Chapel of the Holy Trinity** (often closed). It was built in 1934 on the ruins of a 4th- to 5th-century church and is said to be where God spoke to Moses from a fiery cloud. Nearby is a small, 12th-century mosque and the cave where

Moses spent the 40 days. The summit offers grandiose views, but is often crowded. If you join the many who go up to see the sunrise or sunset, take a flashlight and warm clothes.

The mountain lies at the heart of the St Catherine Protectorate, a conservation area recognized as a UNESCO World Heritage Site. The area is ideal for trekking. One of the longer hikes is to the top of Mount Catherine (Gebel Katarina), Egypt's highest peak. Angels supposedly transported St Catherine of Alexandria's body here, away from her torturers' wheel. Hikers can pick up informative booklets to trails in the area at the Protectorate Office in the nearby village of El-Milga, 3.5 km (2 miles) from St Catherine's Monastery. All treks must be done with a Bedouin guide, which is also arranged through the office.

❽ Feiran Oasis

Road map E6. Sinai, 60 km (37 miles) W of St Catherine's Monastery.

This is the largest and most fertile oasis in Sinai, verdant with date palms, tamarisks and cereal fields. Just south of the Bedouin village of adobe houses is a small, modern convent built with stone from the Byzantine bishop's palace which formerly stood here.

The oasis was the earliest Christian site in Sinai. Many chapels already existed here when, in 451, it became the seat of a bishopric. This governed St Catherine's Monastery until the 7th century, when Feiran's bishop was deposed for heresy and the city fell into ruin. Excavations have revealed its fortified walls, several churches and many other buildings. Feiran is said to be the place where Joshua defeated the Amalekites (Exodus 17).

Shaded gardens surrounding the convent in the Feiran Oasis

The Bedouin of the Sinai Peninsula

In Arabic the word *bedu* means "desert dwellers" and refers specifically to the nomadic tribes that live in Saudi Arabia, the Negev and Sinai. For centuries the Bedouin have lived in close contact with nature, depending for their livelihood on the breeding of sheep, goats and camels. Those in Sinai descend from the peoples who arrived from the Arabian Peninsula from the 14th to the 17th century. The last 20 years of the 20th century have seen a drastic change in their customs and traditions. Today, about 25,000 Bedouin live in Sinai. Many are still nomadic livestock breeders, while others live in permanent camps in wood and corrugated iron dwellings, making their living as guides or desert tour operators or by working in large hotels on the coast.

TRAVELLERS' NEEDS

WHERE TO STAY

Jerusalem offers an impressive range of accommodation: from the luxury of the King David and the American Colony hotels, to the plain but welcoming hospices of the various Christian communities, which cater to pilgrims and tourists alike. You will find even more varied options throughout the rest of the region. Across Israel, kibbutz hotels are moderately priced with good facilities and attractive country settings.

Those who want to cater for themselves will find many choices at a range of prices, from rented apartments to excellent youth hostels and camp sites. On both sides of the Dead Sea there are many hotels and health resorts, while along the Red Sea and Sinai coast, large tourist villages offer water sports at surprisingly reasonable rates. The listings on pages 260–63 give details on a selection of accommodation to suit every budget.

The grand exterior of the 19th-century Austrian Hospice *(see p260)*, Jerusalem

Grading and Facilities

There is no official hotel grading system in Israel, although hotels in Jordan do have their own rating system, with the best (four to five stars) being comparable to a standard international hotel. Most Israeli hotels lie within the medium to high price range, with excellent levels of service and amenities. Rooms are normally equipped with air conditioning, televisions and minibars, with other facilities often including fitness centres, pools and business suites. Most hotels also have bars and restaurants, and a large buffet-style breakfast is almost always included in the price of a room. Quite common, especially in Tel Aviv and more rural lodgings, are suites that include a kitchenette. For disabled travellers, most mid- and high-range hotels have wheelchair access and specially adapted facilities in at least

one room. In Jewish areas, many hotels are classed as kosher, and they observe the main Jewish religious laws. These have synagogues, kosher restaurants and automatic lifts which can be used during the Shabbat rest.

Larger hotels and tourist villages by the Red Sea offer private beaches, scuba diving and a range of water sports, while small beach camps in Sinai are basic but extremely cheap. Dead Sea hotels, often more akin to health resorts, are ideal for those in need of pampering, with their therapeutic hot spas.

Prices

Compared to Western standards, hotel prices in Israel are usually rather high, although the same level of accommodation and service will cost you significantly less in Jordan and, especially, in Sinai. Hotel rates fluctuate widely, depending on the season and the various Christian, Muslim and Jewish holidays, so make sure to verify the price before booking. The price of a room almost always includes breakfast, but not other extras. In Israel the room price also includes local taxes, although you can avoid the 17 per cent VAT by paying in foreign currency or by credit card. US dollars, especially, are taken almost everywhere, and all major credit cards are accepted.

In Jordan and Sinai the situation is slightly different. In the large hotels and tourist villages in Sinai, all costs over and above the basic room price are subject to double taxation if

paid together with the final bill, or on credit card. You can avoid this by paying in cash at the time. Also, listed room rates in Sinai and Jordan often exclude tax, which can be as much as 26 per cent, so make sure that you know the final cost. Credit cards are accepted in both Sinai and Jordan, but when using cash, note that while most major currency is taken in Sinai, you can only use dinars in Jordan.

Booking a Hotel

During certain periods of the year, such as Christmas and Easter, or during Jewish holidays – Passover, Rosh ha-Shanah, Yom Kippur, Sukkoth and Hannukah *(see pp40–43)* – finding accommodation can be a real problem, especially in Jerusalem. In Israel as a whole, you may also have difficulty finding a room during the hottest months of July and August, as this is the busiest time of year, with many Israelis also taking their own holidays.

It is, therefore, always wise to book well in advance, through centralized booking services or directly through hotel websites. The **Israel Hotel Association**, **Kibbutz Hotels Chain**, youth hostels and some local bed-and-breakfast associations have centralized booking services. The same also applies to many independent hotels and guest-houses. If you do need to make arrangements yourself over the phone, most hotel staff speak good English. **Airbnb** (www. airbnb.com) is also popular through the entire region, with locals offering rooms for rent.

◀ Diners at a restaurant overlooking the harbour at Old Jaffa

A reception room at the luxurious American Colony hotel *(see p260)*, Jerusalem

Kibbutz Hotels

These hotels were first established as a source of supplementary income for the largely agricultural kibbutzim, and are completely separate from the very basic type of accommodation offered to those on kibbutz working holidays *(see p288)*. Located mostly in the country, they are ideally placed for visitors wanting a relaxing rural break or a base near some of the region's archaeological attractions. Accommodation ranges from plain lodgings offering bed and breakfast, to very comfortable (albeit informal) hotel complexes with restaurants, swimming pools and other facilities. Most of the hotels are members of the **Kibbutz Hotel Chain** (KHC), which also offers some interesting package tours. Owing to their often remote locations, many kibbutz hotels are not served by public transport and are only convenient if travelling by car.

Kibbutz hotels are very popular among Israelis for their own vacations, especially during the Jewish holidays and in July and August. During these times, it is essential to book well in advance. Prices usually range between NIS 350–800 for a double room and breakfast, depending on the type of kibbutz and the season.

Zimmers

From the Yiddish meaning "room", zimmers are popular bed-and-breakfast guesthouses peculiar to Israel. Always located in rural areas, usually inside kibbutz or moshav communities, zimmers are found close to nature and often near historical attractions. Family-run and on a small scale, they come in many different forms, from simple guest rooms in somebody's garden to rustic romantic chalets. As they are hugely popular with Israelis for weekend breaks, they usually encompass a jacuzzi and satellite TV, and might have play areas and swimming pools. Kitchenettes come as standard, and breakfasts are optional but tend to be enormous and well worth the price. Rooms cost from around NIS 450 for a simple zimmer mid week, up to NIS 1500 for a luxurious chalet at weekends. The Galilee and the Golan have the highest density of zimmerim, but there is a growing number in the Negev as well. Several websites provide centralized booking for zimmer rooms.

Self-Catering

In Jerusalem and throughout the rest of Israel you can find a wide selection of properties to rent, from smart city apartments to luxury country villas. The cost can vary considerably, depending on the type of property you require, but if you are a large family or party, then it is usually much better value when compared to the same length of stay in a hotel. Two of the biggest agents dealing with rented holiday homes in Israel are **Isralet** and **Good Morning Jerusalem**.

Christian Hospices and Guesthouses

This type of accommodation, mainly in Jerusalem and near the holy sites, is a popular and less expensive alternative to hotels. Clean and simple, they are often centrally located and always include breakfast, with other meals optional. You don't have to be a practising Christian to lodge at the hospices, but at times the house rules can be quite strict (for example, the doors might be locked at 10 or 11pm). For unmarried couples it may also be difficult to find a double room. Many hospice guesthouses have over the years become bona fide hotels, with their own special charm and character. In these cases prices are slightly higher, although they are still good value when compared to the large hotels.

The terrace of the luxurious King David Hotel overlooking Jerusalem's Old City *(see p260)*

Holiday-makers relaxing on one of the beautiful beaches at Eilat, on the Red Sea coast

Youth Hostels

For those on a budget, youth hostels are ideal and often the cheapest places to stay in Israel. They are open to all over 18 years, so you will find a mixture of people staying at them, from young backpackers to older travellers. There are 19 **Israel Youth Hostel Association** (IYHA) hostels, affiliated to Hostelling International, to choose from. In addition, the independently run **ILH – Israel Hostels** group offers a high standard of accommodation in interesting villages, big cities and the main sites of tourist interest. ILH – Israel Hostels are often family-run, and members have been selected for their friendliness as well as their excellent facilities.

Hostels offer single, double and family rooms as well as the more usual dormitories, with prices starting between NIS 60 and NIS 250 per person. Israeli hostels are generally modern, with decent facilities and clean, simple accommodation. The price includes linen, and in the IYHA hostels it also includes breakfast and free Wi-Fi. In independent hostels you can pay for the room only and be entirely self-catering.

If you plan to stay at IYHA hostels for any length of time, you may want to pay for membership. While this is not compulsory, it does entitle you to preferential rates and gives discounts at some tourist sites. The IYHA can also provide full dinner at most of their hostels, and offers a good fly-drive package and an eight-day Taste of Israel tour.

Field Schools

There are ten Field Schools, run by the **Society for the Protection of Nature in Israel** (SPNI), that provide accommodation. These are located near some of Israel's major natural reserves and were established as a way of promoting a better understanding of the country's natural environment and history through organized educational holidays and summer schools. This is still their main focus, and so they usually host school groups during the week, which can make them noisy places to be, and some in fact only accept independent visitors at the weekend (eg Golan Field School). Even so, they can be a good option for families. The rooms are simple but clean, and all include a private bathroom and air conditioning. Most bedrooms sleep between four and six people, although some doubles and a few dorm rooms are also available. If you are paying on a room-only basis, the cost is generally less than NIS 190 per person. Booking in advance is obligatory.

Camping

There are camp sites across Israel for those wanting to spend time under canvas and visit more remote places. A few, run by the **Israel Nature and Parks Authority**, are located next to national parks and allow easy access to the sites. Many rural lodgings also provide tented accommodation, often huge structures that can sleep big groups. Prices start from NIS 40 per person, increasing at sites with better facilities. Some places will also hire out tents.

In Israel, camping rough is also quite common, particularly in the Galilee and the Golan. Choose a secluded area and leave the site tidy if you want to avoid problems. In the Negev Desert, south of Beersheva, there are designated night camping spots for trekkers. Patrols are made by park rangers to enforce this rule, in order to protect the local wildlife and environment. Places in the West Bank are no-go areas, as are all military and border zones. If in doubt, check first. Also be very aware of your possessions and personal safety, especially if in a remote area and alone. Make sure that you have protection against mosquitoes, and check thoroughly for other unwanted guests, such as scorpions.

Camp sites in Jordan and Sinai are much less common, with fewer facilities. They are found only in some of the more popular national parks and at some Red Sea beaches.

Jordan and Sinai

Parts of Sinai and Jordan offer the full spectrum of accommodation. Amman, in particular, has many international five-star chain hotels, including a Four Seasons, Grand Hyatt, Kempinski and Marriott, plus a healthy budget scene in the Downtown district. The choice is less wide at Wadi Musa (for Petra), and given the large number of visitors, it is wise to book in advance, especially in March/April and September/October (peak times). Elsewhere in Jordan the choice is greatly diminished, although the country is small enough that most sights can be visited from either Amman or Petra.

In Sinai, Sharm el-Sheikh and Taba offer top-class resort hotels,

many with prime beachfront locations, some boasting beautiful architecture, and all offering a full range of facilities, from multiple restaurants and bars to dive and watersports centres. Such is the abundance of accommodation, and with the decrease in tourism since the 2011 Egyptian Revolution, that a little Internet research can throw up some bargain room rates. Peak seasons are during the Muslim feasts of Eid el-Fitr and Eid el-Adha *(see p42)*, around Christmas and especially New Year, and during July and August; at such times you should book ahead.

There are hostels in Jordan and Sharm el-Sheikh affiliated to Hostelling International, as well as many cheap hotels that serve the same purpose. Dahab has a huge number of mid-range and budget options that all enjoy a seaside location. Nuweiba and other smaller Sinai

resorts often have simple bamboo-constructed huts for rent on the beach – these are popular with budget travellers.

Recommended Hotels

The hotels in this book have been carefully selected and are among the best in the region in their respective categories: luxury, boutique, family-friendly, pilgrim hospice and good-value lodgings. These categories highlight the available options that are unique to Israel, such as rural kibbutz hotels, and accommodation within historic buildings next to the holy sites. The choices reflect the wave of small boutique hotels opening up throughout the region, which provide an alternative to the established luxury of the large five-star chains. Given the generally high price of hotels in Israel, the list emphasizes places offering good value for money, including attractive hostels which provide comfortable private rooms, as well as dormitories. At the Dead Sea and along the Red Sea coast, the full spectrum of accommodation is presented, from self-contained all-inclusive resorts to small locally managed lodges and camps. The DK Choice category draws attention to establishments that are exceptional, perhaps for their outstanding private location, their emphasis on sustainability, or their community spirit

The rich interior of a room at the Auberge Shulamit *(see p261)*, Israel

DIRECTORY

Booking a Hotel

Israel Hotel Association
Tel (03) 517 0131.
w iha.org.il

Tourist Israel
w touristisrael.com

Travel In Israel
w israel-tours-hotel.com

Kibbutz Hotels

Kibbutz Hotels Chain (KHC)
Tel (03) 560 8118.
w kibbutz.co.il

Zimmers

w israel-tours-hotel.com
w zimmeril.com

Self-Catering

Good Morning Jerusalem
17 Ezrat Israel St, Jerusalem.
Tel (02) 623 3459.
w accommodation.co.il

Isralet
w isralet.com

Christian Hospices and Guesthouses

Christian Information Centre
Jaffa Gate, Old City, Jerusalem. Tel (02) 627 2692. **w** cicts.org

Youth Hostels

Israeli Youth Hostel Association (IYHA)
Jerusalem International Convention Centre Jerusalem.
Tel 1 599 510 511.
w iyha.org.il

ILH – Israel Hostels

w hostels-israel.com

Field Schools

Society for the Protection of Nature in Israel (SPNI)
Tel (03) 638 8688 or (057) 200 3030.
w teva.org.il

Camping

Israel Nature and Parks Authority
Tel *3639.
w parks.org.il

Where to Stay

Jerusalem

The Muslim Quarter

Austrian Hospice $$
Pilgrim hospice   **Map** 3 C2
37 Via Dolorosa, 97626
Tel (02) 626 5800
W austrianhospice.com
Spacious rooms in a beautiful
historic building. Garden café
and rooftop with Old City views.

Ecce Homo Convent $$
Pilgrim hospice   **Map** 4 D2
41 Via Dolorosa, 97626
Tel (02) 627 7292
W eccehomoconvent.org
Great-value modest rooms and
dormitory cubicles. Roman-era
ruins beneath and rooftop views.

The Christian and Armenian Quarters

Foyer Mar Maroun $
Pilgrim hospice   **Map** 3 B4
25 Maronite Convent St, 97111
Tel (02) 628 2158
W maronitejerusalem.org
Spotless rooms in an ancient
building. Welcoming staff and
dazzling rooftop views.

Christ Church Guesthouse $$
Pilgrim hospice   **Map** 3 B4
*Omar Ibn el-Khattab Sq, by Jaffa
Gate, 97604*
Tel (02) 627 7727
W cmj-israel.org
Constructed over Roman-era
foundations with a garden café
and church on site.

Knights Palace $$
Pilgrim hospice   **Map** 3 A3
Freres St, Nr New Gate, 14152
Tel (02) 628 2537
W knightspalace.com
Spacious, well-furnished rooms,
plus bar and courtyard on site.
Close to the Old City markets.

DK Choice

Lutheran Guesthouse $$
Pilgrim hospice   **Map** 3 C4
St Mark's Rd, 91140
Tel (02) 626 6888
W guesthouse-jerusalem.com
Nestled in an alleyway near
colourful markets, with all
the unique atmosphere of a
pilgrim hospice but without
the restrictions. There is a roof
terrace, garden patio and a bar.
Rooms have distinct stone walls
and simple furnishings.

The Mount of Olives and Mount Zion

Mount Zion $$$
Boutique   **Map** 1 B5
17 Hebron Rd, 93546
Tel (02) 568 9555
W mountzion.co.il
Characterful rooms with views of
Mount Zion. The building dates
from 1882.

Modern Jerusalem

Abraham Hostel $
Good value
67 HaNevi'im St, Davidka Sq, 94702
Tel (02) 650 2200
W abrahamhostels.com
Great amenities and excellent
tours at this modern hostel. Close
to Mahane Yehuda market.

Agron Guest House $$
Family-friendly   **Map** 1 A4
6 Agron St, 94265
Tel (02) 594 5522
W iyha.org.il
Large hostel with kosher facilities
and comfortable rooms in a
convenient location.

Jerusalem Hotel $$
Boutique   **Map** 1 C2
Nablus Rd, 97200
Tel (02) 628 3282
W jrshotel.com
Quaint rooms with Oriental decor
in a 19th-century Arab mansion.
Lively restaurant too.

**Notre Dame of Jerusalem
Centre** $$
Pilgrim hospice   **Map** 1 B3
3 HaTsankhanim St, 91204
Tel (02) 627 9111
W notredamecenter.org
Modern rooms in an imposing
historic building run by the
Vatican. Rooftop bar-restaurant.

Elegant, well-lit interiors at Austrian
Hospice, Jerusalem

Price Guide

Prices are based on one night's stay in
high season for a standard double room,
inclusive of breakfast, service charges
and taxes.

$	under $100
$$	$100 to $250
$$$	over $250

St George Landmark $$
Botique   **Map** 1 C2
6 Amr Ibn al-A'as St, 91692
Tel (02) 627 7232
W stgeorgehoteljerusalem.com
This hotel boasts east Jerusalem's
only rooftop pool, and is close to
Damascus Gate.

YMCA Three Arches $$
Family-friendly   **Map** 1 A4
26 King David St, 94101
Tel (02) 569 2692
W ymca3arches.com
Designed by the architect of the
Empire State Building; has good
sports facilities and restaurant.

American Colony $$$
Luxury   **Map** 1 C1
*1 Louis Vincent St, Sheikh Jarrah,
97200*
Tel (02) 627 9777
W americancolony.com
A 1902 hotel favoured by
diplomats. Indulgent rooms, lush
gardens and a Turkish courtyard.

David Citadel Hotel $$$
Luxury   **Map** 1 B4
7 King David St, 94101
Tel (02) 621 2121
W thedavidcitadel.com
Splendid modern hotel over-
looking the Old City, offering all
conveniences and fine dining.

King David Hotel $$$
Luxury   **Map** 1 B4
23 King David St, 94101
Tel (02) 620 8888
W danhotels.com
Historic hotel with classic rooms,
some with Old City views.

Mamilla Hotel $$$
Luxury   **Map** 1 B3
11 King Solomon St, 94182
Tel (02) 548 2200
W mamillahotel.com
High-tech facilities, top-class
dining, a fine pool and spa.

The Waldorf Astoria $$$
Luxury   **Map** 1 B4
26–28 Gershon Agron St, 9419008
Tel (02) 563 3333
W waldorfastoria3.hilton.com
Beautiful hotel with historical
origins, rebuilt to include luxurious
facilities. Overlooks the Old City.

Further Afield

Notre Dame de Sion Guest House $$
Pilgrim hospice
23 Haoren St, Ein Kerem, 95744
Tel (02) 641 5738
w notredamedesion.org
Beautiful gardens, valley views
and spacious, simple rooms.
Includes a health spa.

Ramat Rachel $$
Family-friendly
Kibbutz Ramat Rachel, 90900
Tel (02) 670 2555
w ramatrachel.co.il
Rooms are encircled by gardens.
Pool, tennis and spa facilities.

DK Choice

Hotel Alegra $$$
Boutique
13 Ha'achayot St, Ein Kerem, 95744
Tel (02) 650 0506
w hotelalegra.co.il
Stay in lavish designer suites
with arched windows and
Jerusalem-stone walls. There
is a splash pool, sauna and a
fine restaurant on site. The roof
terrace has loungers.

The Coast and Galilee

AKKO: Akkotel $$
Boutique **Map** B2
Salah al-Din St, Old City, 24112
Tel (04) 987 7100
w akkotel.com
Family-run hotel in a historic
building. Serves tasty food.

CARMEL FOREST: Carmel Forest Resort Spa $$$
Luxury **Map** B2
Near Kibbutz Beit Oren, 39100
Tel (04) 830 7888
w isrotelexclusivecollection.co.il
Peaceful escape south of Haifa.
Health treatments, tennis, yoga
and gourmet food. Full board.

HAIFA: Colony Hotel $$
Boutique **Map** B2
28 Ben Gurion Blvd, 35023
Tel (04) 851 3344
w colonyhaifa.com
Enviable location near Baha'i Gardens
and tastefully furnished rooms.

HAIFA: Dan Panorama $$$
Family-friendly **Map** B2
107 HaNassi Ave, 34632
Tel (04) 835 2222
w danhotels.com
High up on Mount Carmel with
stunning views. Great amenities.

Gracefully decorated rooms at Colony Hotel, Haifa

KFAR PEKI'IN: Peki'in Youth Hostel and Family Guesthouse $
Family-friendly **Map** C2
Kfar Peki'in, 24914
Tel (02) 594 5677
w iyha.org.il
Well appointed hostel in a Druze
village. Walking tours and inter-
action with locals.

DK Choice

NAZARETH: Fauzi Azar Inn $$
Good value **Map** C2
Old City, 16125
Tel (04) 602 0469
w fauziazarinn.com
This 200-year-old converted
mansion is at the heart of
Nazareth's ancient souk (market-
place). Some of the rooms have
hand-painted ceilings. Relax in
the vaulted stone courtyard or
on the sunny terrace.

ROSH PINA: Auberge Shulamit $$
Boutique **Map** C2
34 David Shuv St, 12000
Tel (04) 693 1485
w shulamit.co.il
Exquisite 1930s basalt stone
house with a highly recommended French restaurant.

SAFED: Artists' Colony Inn $$$
Boutique **Map** C2
9 Simtat Yud Zayin St, 13231
Tel (04) 604 1101
w artcol.co.il
Vaulted stone rooms in a pretty
house down a cobbled lane.
Jacuzzis and massages available.

SEA OF GALILEE: Pilgerhaus Tabgha $$
Pilgrim hospice **Map** C2
Migdal Tabgha
Tel (04) 670 0100
w heilig-land-verein.de
Historic building with well-
appointed rooms, bar and direct
access to the Sea of Galilee.

SEA OF GALILEE: Vered HaGalil Guest Farm $$
Family-friendly **Map** C2
Off Highway 90, 12385
Tel (04) 693 5785
w veredhagalil.co.il
Family-run ranch with wood-and-
stone cabins and cottages with
verandas. Restaurant plus spa.

SEA OF GALILEE: Scots Hotel $$$
Luxury **Map** C2
1 Gedud Barak St, Tiberias, 14100
Tel (04) 671 0711
w scotshotels.co.il
Historic hotel with five-star
facilities. Terraced gardens, spa
and seasonal pool.

TEL AVIV: Beit Immanuel Guest House and Youth Hostel $
Pilgrim hospice **Map** B3
8 Auerbach St, American-German Colony, 61027
Tel (03) 682 1459
w beitimmanuel.org
Austere rooms with high ceilings
and a pleasant garden café.

TEL AVIV: HaYarkon 48 Hostel $
Good value **Map** B3
48 HaYarkon St, 63305
Tel (03) 516 8989
w hayarkon48.com
Popular hostel two blocks from
the beach with great facilities.

TEL AVIV: Center Chic $$
Family-friendly **Map** B3
Kikar Dizengoff, 2 Zamenhoff St, 64373
Tel (03) 526 6100
w atlas.co.il
Hip, designer rooms in a Bauhaus
building. Roof garden with
loungers plus free bikes.

TEL AVIV: Port Hotel $$
Good value **Map** B3
4 Yirmeyahu St, 63507
Tel (03) 544 5544
w porthoteltelaviv.com
A mini-hotel with chic decor in
its rooms. Nightlife, cafés and
shopping are nearby.

For more information on types of hotels *see page 259*

TEL AVIV:
Alma Hotel & Lounge $$$
Boutique   **Map** B3
23 Yavne St, 6579201
Tel (03) 630 8777
w almahotel.co.il
Eclectic, vivid rooms in a 1920s
building. Top-class restaurant.

TEL AVIV: Dan Tel Aviv $$$
Luxury   **Map** B3
99 HaYarkon St, 63432
Tel (03) 520 2525
w danhotels.com
Smart, with beachside location,
attentive service and fine dining.

TEL AVIV: Diaghilev Live Art
Boutique Hotel $$$
Boutique   **Map** B3
56 Mazeh St, 65789
Tel (03) 545 3131
w diaghilev.co.il
Chic hotel with individually
furnished suites. Works of art
decorate the premises.

The Dead Sea and
the Negev Desert

EILAT: Eilat Youth Hostel
and Guest House $$
Good value   **Map** B7
7 Arava Rd, 88101
Tel (02) 594 5611
w iyha.org.il
Decent accommodation close to
the seafront and city centre.

EILAT: Herod's Palace $$$
Luxury   **Map** B7
North Beach, 18800
Tel (08) 638 0000
w herodshotels.com
High-class resort with attentive
service and superb dining.

EILAT: Orchid $$$
Luxury   **Map** B7
South Beach, 88000
Tel (08) 636 0360
w orchidhotel.co.il
Thai-inspired chalets and stun-
ning villas on a tropical hillside.
Free bikes and an on-site spa.

EIN GEDI: Ein Gedi Country
Guest House $$$
Family-friendly   **Map** C4
Kibbutz Ein Gedi, 86980
Tel (08) 659 4222
w ein-gedi.co.il
Rooms with creative furnishings.
Pool plus hiking nearby.

NEVE ZOHAR: Leonardo Club
Dead Sea All-Inclusive $$$
Luxury   **Map** C4
Neve Zohar, 86910
Tel (08) 668 9444
w fattal-hotels.com

Plush seating at Diaghilev Live Art Boutique Hotel, Tel Aviv

All-inclusive spa-hotel set among
palm trees. Private beach and
kids' activities.

JERICHO:
InterContinental Jericho $$
Good value   **Map** C3
Jericho-Jerusalem Rd
Tel (02) 231 1200
w ichotelsgroup.com
Modern hotel on the outskirts of
the city, with classic rooms, a
fitness centre, spa and pool.

KIBBUTZ LOTAN:
Kibbutz Lotan Guesthouse $$
Family-friendly   **Map** B6
Kibbutz Lotan, 88855
Tel (08) 635 6935
w kibbutzlotan.com
Set in idyllic surrounds, 20 minutes
from the Khai Bar Reserve, with a
seasonal pool and bird-watching.

MASADA:
Masada Youth Hostel $$
Good value   **Map** C4
Masada, 86935
Tel (08) 995 3222
w iyha.org.il
TVs and minibars in comfortable
modern rooms, plus a seasonal
pool, cafeteria and sun terrace.

DK Choice

MITSPE RAMON: ibike $$
Family-friendly   **Map** B5
4 Har Ardon, Spice Routes
Quarter, 80600
Tel (052) 436 7878
w ibike.co.il
This super-friendly guesthouse
has an inspiring approach to
healthy living. Rent bikes or take
guided tours into the Ramon
crater. The atmosphere draws
outdoor enthusiasts as well as
families. The rooms are cheerful
and there is a relaxing outdoor
area. Superb vegetarian fare
in the café.

MITSPE RAMON:
Beresheet Hotel $$$
Luxury   **Map** B5
1 Beresheet Rd, 80600
Tel (08) 659 8000
w isrotelexclusivecollection.co.il
Ultimate indulgence on the edge
of the crater with fine dining and
sublime pools.

Petra and
Western Jordan

AJLUN: Qalet Al Jabal Hotel $
Good value   **Map** C3
Al Qala' St, Halawa Crossing, Ad
Dayr, 26810
Tel (02) 642 0202
w jabal-hotel.com
Beautiful location on a hillside
with old-fashioned rooms and
delicious food.

AMMAN: The Boutique Hotel $
Good value   **Map** C3
32 Prince Mohammed St,
Downtown, 11101
Tel (07) 9797 0611
w the-boutique-hotel-amman.com
Freshly renovated rooms and
friendly service. Near historical
sites and lively markets.

AMMAN: Hisham $$
Good value   **Map** C3
Mithqal al-Fayez St, Jebel Amman,
11183
Tel (06) 464 4028
w hishamhotel.com.jo
Peaceful, family-run hotel with a
long history, plenty of character
and boutique touches.

AMMAN: Marriott $$
Luxury   **Map** C3
Isam el-Ajlouni St, Shmeisani, 11190
Tel (06) 560 7607
w marriott.com
First-class establishment in a
smart area, with elegant rooms
and personal service to match.

Key to Price Guide *see page 260*

AQABA: Kempinski Hotel   **$$**
Luxury   **Map** B7
King Hussein St, 77110
Tel (03) 209 0888
W kempinski.com
A stark exterior belies the sleek
luxury inside. Rooms with sea
views and a multi-layered pool.

DK Choice

DANA: Feynan Ecolodge **$$**
Boutique   **Map** C5
Wadi Feynan
Tel 079 748 7900
W feynan.com
Staffed by local Bedouin,
the Feynan holds true to its
environmental credentials.
The rooms feature candles and
calm desert tones, and there
is a charming library on site.
Hammocks on terraces offer
views of the Dana Biosphere
Reserve, the entry fee for which
is included in the room rates.

**DEAD SEA: Kempinski Hotel
Ishtar**   **$$$**
Luxury   **Map** C4
Dead Sea Rd, Sweimeh, 11194
Tel (05) 356 8888
W kempinski.com
Rooms, chalets and villas with
world-class facilities, including an
infinity pool and refined dining.

PETRA: Cleopatra   **$**
Good value   **Map** C5
Queen Rania St, Wadi Musa, 71810
Tel (03) 215 7090
W cleopatrahotel.com
Nice budget hotel with helpful
staff and an excellent buffet
dinner. Free shuttle bus to Petra.

**PETRA: Movenpick Resort
Petra**   **$$**
Luxury   **Map** C5
Tourism St, Wadi Musa, 71810
Tel (03) 215 7111
W moevenpick-hotels.com
Unbeatable location by Petra's
entrance. Arabesque designs in
the interior, and a soaring atrium.

PETRA: Petra Moon   **$$**
Good value   **Map** C5
Wadi Musa
Tel (03) 215 6220
W petramoonhotel.com
An excellent option with bright
rooms, good bar and rooftop
pool. Awesome buffet breakfast.

The Red Sea and Sinai

**DAHAB: Bishbishi Garden
Village**   **$**
Good value   **Map** F6
Mashraba St, Mashraba
Tel (069) 364 0727
W bishbishi.com
Rooms and chalets set in a garden
in a quiet part of Dahab. Bikes for
rent plus tours and diving.

DAHAB: Blue Beach Club **$**
Good value   **Map** F6
Lighthouse, Asilah, 46617
Tel (069) 364 0411
W bluebeachclub.com
Rooms with Arabesque touches
and sun terraces. Lively bar.

DAHAB: Nesima Resort   **$**
Family-friendly   **Map** F6
Mashraba
Tel (069) 364 0320
W nesima-resort.com
Well-presented rooms, many
with domed ceilings. Dive centre
and fantastic restaurant.

DK Choice

NUWEIBA: Basata   **$**
Good value   **Map** F5
*Sherif El Ghamrawy, Basata
village, 23 Nuweiba Rd*
Tel (069) 350 0480/1
W basata.com
Arabic for simplicity, Basata is a
rustic resort with stylish chalets
and huts, plus camping space.
Dinners are communal and
there is a kitchen for guests' use.
Snorkelling can be done nearby.

**NUWEIBA: Swisscare Nuweiba
Resort Hotel**   **$**
Family-friendly   **Map** F5
Corniche, Near Nuweiba City
Tel (069) 352 0640
W swisscare-hotels.com
A low-key resort with a peaceful
vibe. A huge pool and a private
beach, plus great diving nearby.

**SHARM EL-SHEIKH:
Oonas Dive Club Hotel** **$**
Good value   **Map** F7
Naama Bay
Tel (069) 360 0581
W oonasdiveclub.com
Friendly hotel with spotless,
simple rooms and a rooftop bar.
Snorkelling possibilities close by.

**SHARM EL-SHEIKH: Sharks Bay
Umbi Diving Village**   **$**
Good value   **Map** F7
Shark's Bay
Tel (069) 360 0942
W sharksbay.com
Chalets and budget huts, plus
diving and safari activities at this
resort with its own reef.

**SHARM EL-SHEIKH:
Four Seasons Hotel**   **$$$**
Luxury   **Map** F7
1 Four Seasons Blvd, 41632
Tel (069) 360 5555
W fourseasons.com
Oozing luxury, this cliff-side hotel
set in lush gardens has four
pools, diving facilities and
entertainment for kids.

**ST CATHERINE:
Bedouin Camp**   **$**
Good value   **Map** E6
El-Milga
Tel (069) 347 0457
W sheikhmousa.com
Well-maintained lodging and
excellent local food. Hiking trips
are their speciality. Breakfast
not included.

**ST CATHERINE: St Catherine's
Monastery Guesthouse** **$**
Pilgrim Hostel   **Map** E6
St Catherine
Tel (069) 347 0353
W sinaimonastery.com
Magical location adjacent to
the walled monastery and
orchards, with Mount Sinai
looming nearby. Simple rooms;
half-board.

TABA: Sofitel Taba Heights **$$$**
Luxury   **Map** F5
KM 42, Taba–Nuweiba Rd, 46621
Tel (069) 358 0800
W sofitel.com
All-inclusive resort occupying a
prime location in the Taba Heights
complex. It has a kids' club, private
beach, golf and spa.

One of the many beautiful pools at Kempinski Hotel Ishtar, Dead Sea

For more Information on types of hotels *see page 259*

WHERE TO EAT AND DRINK

Middle Eastern food is often overshadowed by more glamorous world cuisines, but its reputation and popularity is growing. Often simple and unpretentious, local food is tasty and always substantial. Israel, in particular Tel Aviv, is becoming known as a gastronomic destination. The constantly evolving restaurant culture reflects the huge interest in food, and many restaurants are of a very high standard, offering a wide range of innovative dishes sure to excite even the

most sceptical palate. Aside from the native cuisine, reflecting the broad ethnic mix of people, there are many restaurants offering international food. You can find Thai, South American, Japanese, Italian and French food, along with the ever popular American fast food. There are also many busy and informal cafés offering a cheaper, lighter menu. For a quick snack, street food revolves around the *shawarma*, houmous and falafel stalls, which can be found almost everywhere.

Arabesque, the restaurant in the American Colony Hotel *(see p270)*

Practicalities

In Israeli cities you will see people eating at all hours of the day, seated at restaurants and cafés or walking along with a falafel pitta. In the evening, people tend to eat late and spend a long time over their meals. Eating is a big social event, with children accepted in most restaurants. Dining, when possible, is alfresco, and restaurants often stay open until after midnight, especially during summer. However, most Jewish restaurants close for Shabbat (sundown on Friday until after sundown on Saturday), as well as for Yom Kippur, Shavuot, Holocaust Day, Remembrance Day and the first and last day of Sukkoth and Passover *(see p40)*.

The business lunch menu, offered in many restaurants from Sunday to Thursday (usually 12–4pm), is a great way of saving money and getting to enjoy top-notch dining in Tel Aviv and Jerusalem, with prices often half what they would be

on the à la carte menu. Service is not generally included in the bill; expect to tip around 10–15 per cent, depending on the type of establishment. Major credit cards are accepted in most restaurants throughout Israel.

Types of Restaurant

Food is a major part of Middle Eastern life, and there is a huge range of places to eat. Israeli food is a melting pot of flavours, reflecting the cultural mix of the nation and adopting influences from the Middle East, the Mediterranean and Eastern Europe. The main Israeli food is that of the Jews, largely the Oriental (Middle Eastern) and Ashkenazi (Eastern European) communities. Their food is as different as their origins. Oriental dishes revolve mainly around grilled meats and fish, stuffed vegetables and a range of *meze*. The Ashkenazi specialities are spicy stews, fish balls and stuffed pancakes, known as *blintzes*.

Other major ethnic groups have also brought their own unique dishes. Armenian favourites include spicy meat stews and sausages, while the Yemenites are famous for their *malawach* – large, flaky-pastry pancakes with various fillings. A more recent development is contemporary Israeli cuisine, which takes inspiration from the ethnic cuisines of the Diaspora and Arab regions and emphasizes locally grown ingredients, such as aubergine (eggplant), tomato, fish, dairy and *tahina*.

Aside from Israeli fare, you can also find restaurants serving international food and the usual fast-food chains. Café culture is huge, and if you are after something cheaper and less substantial, then cafés offer salads, pizzas, sandwiches and pasta dishes. They are also great places to sit and soak up the local atmosphere, and join in with Israeli life. The selection of restaurants is far more limited if travelling in Jordan or Sinai, however, where most are located in the hotels.

Dining outside in the spectacular setting of Petra *(see pp224–35)*

Bourj al-Haman Intercontinental restaurant, Jordan *(see p274)*

Kosher Restaurants

The Jewish dietary laws of *Kashrut* (literally, "fitness") determine many of the eating habits in Israel. To the outsider these can prove confusing, especially as you will find that not all Jewish restaurants adhere to these strict rules. What these laws mean in practice is that meat considered impure (for example, pork and rabbit), as well as certain types of seafood (anything without scales and fins), cannot be eaten. Animals that are permitted for consumption have to be slaughtered according to Jewish religious practice and cleansed of all traces of blood before cooking. Furthermore, during Passover, a kosher restaurant cannot serve any leavened food, such as bread or pastries.

The major complications of these laws revolve around the fact that meat and dairy produce can never be eaten together in the same meal. Dishes are consequently based on either one or the other, with many of the resulting problems deftly overcome through the use of dairy substitutes. Dairy-based restaurants are naturally a good option for non-meat eaters, as no meat is kept on the premises.

Vegetarian Food

As a vegetarian visiting the region, your dining options are wonderfully varied. Kosher restaurants serve all types of dairy-only food, such as creamy pasta and yogurt-based dishes, as well as many potato dishes and salads. Secular restaurants also have a large number of vegetarian options. Much of the cuisine is based around pulses, which are found in anything from houmous to hearty bean stews. Roasted and stuffed vegetables also feature, along with a variety of savoury pastries. For a quick vegetarian snack, the *falafel* is hard to beat.

Jordan and Sinai

Jordanian food is a mix of the Lebanese-Syrian-Egyptian fare common throughout the Middle East, mixed in with local Bedouin cuisine. Expect lots of good, fresh *meze*, salads and grilled meats, plus traditional specialities such as *mansaf*: lamb on a bed of rice sprinkled with pine nuts. You may also be offered *maqlubbeh*, which is steamed rice pressed into a small bowl then turned out and topped with slices of grilled aubergine (eggplant). Otherwise, places like Amman have plenty of international restaurants and cafés.

Food in the Sinai resorts tends to cater to the tastes of package holiday makers. Most restaurants are attached to hotels and favour Italian and other international dishes. Genuine Egyptian cuisine is rare, although the fish and seafood is excellent

Smoking

There has been a smoking ban in public places within Israel for many years. However, restaurants are allowed to have a completely separate smoking area, and smoking is allowed on terraces.

In Jordan and Egypt, tourists are allowed to smoke in restaurants, cafés and bars, except during Ramadan, when smoking is prohibited during daylight hours. Some restaurants do provide no-smoking areas.

Recommended Restaurants

The restaurants on the following pages have been carefully selected to give a cross-section of options from across the region: you'll find everything from international cuisine and home-cooking, to contemporary Israeli cuisine that offers a twist on traditional dishes, and street food staples. Also included are traditional Jewish and Middle Eastern eateries, with their strong emphasis on classic ingredients and timeless recipes, as well as many modern Mediterranean fusion restaurants, which might be influenced by North African, Levantine or other cuisines. Restaurants that have specialist meat, fish or vegetarian menus have been highlighted, as have those that carry a kosher certificate or do a business lunch deal. The contemporary Israeli cuisine options include some of the best restaurants in the region, and are mostly found in Tel Aviv and Jerusalem, with a few located in scenic countryside locations. The DK Choice category draws attention to the exceptional establishments, be it for their unique menu, long-standing reputation, or particularly stunning venues and views.

Fattoush *(see p272)*, popular for Middle Eastern cuisine in Haifa

The Flavours of Jerusalem and the Holy Land

The cuisines of the Holy Land are as varied as its people. Over the centuries, the region has embraced rich culinary traditions from around the Mediterranean, Central and Eastern Europe, the Middle East, North Africa and South Asia. Dishes brought by Jewish immigrants from Ethiopia have also appeared, and a growth in travel to East Asia has resulted in the food from this region becoming hugely popular. The local dining scene has come a long way since the spartan communal dining halls of the early kibbutzim, and an increasingly sophisticated gastronomic culture has transformed the restaurant scene.

Pomegranates

Fish seller's stall at Jerusalem's Mahane Yehuda market

Street Food

Stalls and storefront eateries offer a varied array of cheap, nutritious and relatively healthy "fast food". Falafel is an excellent option for vegetarians, as are houmous and *bourekas*, a filo pastry from the Balkans filled with salty *kashkaval* cheese, potatoes, spinach or mushrooms. Somewhat less well known is *sabih*, an Iraqi speciality that consists of potato chunks, fried aubergine (eggplant), a hard-boiled egg, salad, *tahina* (sesame paste), hot sauce and chopped parsley, served in a pitta. A carnivore favourite is *shawarma*, the local, often turkey-based, version of gyros or doner kebab. Griddled meats such as *me'urav yerushalmi* (a mixed grill of chicken livers, hearts and other offal) are served in, or with, a pitta.

Meze or Salatim

A meal typically begins with a large selection of starters (*meze* in Arabic, *salatim* in Hebrew). Middle Eastern restaurants serve *meze* either as a starter or as a full meal. Dishes you are likely to encounter include houmous (chickpea/garbanzo paste with olive oil, lemon and garlic), *tabouleh* (cracked wheat with masses of chopped mint and parsley, tomato,

Babaghanoush · Olives · Israeli salad · Kibbe · Pitta breads · Houmous · Pickled vegetables · Tabouleh

Some of the small dishes that make up a *meze* or *salatim*

Dishes and Specialities of the Holy Land

The traditional dishes you'll find served throughout the Holy Land range from stuffed grape leaves and *mansaf* (rice and lamb with a sour yogurt sauce), sometimes called the national dish of Jordan, to gefilte fish and chicken soup with matzo balls, favoured by Jews with roots in Eastern Europe. Popular Palestinian Arab specialities include *meze* salads and sumac-flavoured meat dishes such as *mussakhan*. About half of Israeli Jews have family roots in Asia and Africa, which is why the menus of ethnic restaurants often feature Moroccan couscous, fiery fish dishes from Libya, doughy *malawah* (pan-fried bread) and *jahnoun* (a heavy, slow-baked bread roll) from Yemen, and *kubbe* (or *kibbe*) from Iraq – also a Palestinian speciality.

Selection of sweets

Shashlik and kebab are, respectively, pieces of meat and spiced ground meat grilled on a skewer.

Outdoor markets offers superb fresh produce of the Holy Land

Local Produce

Israel has long been known for its excellent selection of cheeses, and a growing number of so-called "boutique" dairies has been setting ever-higher standards with their goats' and sheep's milk products. These go extremely well with classic Mediterranean specialities such as olives and extra virgin olive oil, produced with great pride by both Jews and Arabs. In both the Galilee and the Negev, travellers will often come across family-run roadside eateries where local farmers sell their own produce, such as delicious honey.

cucumber, oil and lemon), and *babaghanoush* (aubergine baked for a smoky flavour and then puréed), along with pickled vegetables and olives. *Kibbe* (cracked wheat and minced meat croquettes with onions and pine nuts) are among the few non-vegetarian dishes.

Fresh Fruit

The Bible is filled with references to the produce of the land, and today the Holy Land grows not only ancient favourites such as grapes, pomegranates, figs and dates, but also citrus fruits, which have been exported to Europe under the Jaffa labels since the 19th century. The largest type of citrus is the pomelo, a thick-skinned fruit that can grow to the size of a volleyball and is a speciality of the Jericho area. The fragrant Galia melon was developed in Israel. Watermelon is often eaten with chunks of salty Bulgarian cheese, similar to feta. Widely available exotic fruits include persimmon, kiwi and passion fruit.

Dried red peppers in the market at Shuk Levinsky, Tel Aviv

ON THE MENU

Baklava Honey-soaked chopped nut and filo pastries.

Cholent Sabbath lunch stew of beef, potatoes, carrots, barley, onions and beans.

Knafeh Palestinian pastry of cheese, crunchy wheat threads and very sweet syrup.

Kugel Egg noodle casserole, either sweet or savoury.

Labane Sharp, spreadable white "yogurt" cheese, often preserved in olive oil.

Za'atar Seasoning mix of hyssop, sesame seeds and salt.

Zchug Fiery red or green Yemenite condiment.

Falafel are deep-fried balls of mashed chickpeas (garbanzos) served stuffed into a pitta bread with salad.

Tilapia, or St Peter's Fish, is popular around the Sea of Galilee, simply grilled and served with lemon slices.

Jerusalem salad is a meal in itself, with olives, feta and sometimes pomegranate and za'atar sprinkled over.

What to Drink in Jerusalem and the Holy Land

Jews and Arabs alike adore coffee but have different ways of making it. It will be offered to you at any hour of the day or night. Teas of many kinds and herbal infusions are also popular. However, the hot, very dry climate makes water of the utmost importance. It is advisable to carry a bottle of it with you at all times and drink some before you feel thirsty to avoid dehydration. Israel now produces a lot of affordable medium- to high-quality wine. Beer is available in all the areas covered in this guide, but neither the Israelis nor the Arabs consume large quantities, preferring to go to cafés or coffee shops for socializing.

Enjoying outdoor café life on traffic-free Lunz Street in Jerusalem

Water and Soft Drinks

Bottled water

In the entire area described in this guide, bottled mineral water is readily available everywhere. Although tap water throughout Israel is safe to drink, it is more advisable to drink bottled water because it tastes better, especially in the Red Sea area, where tap water is so heavily chlorinated that it is unpalatable. Always make sure that the bottle is sealed when you buy water.

Bottled fruit juice is also popular, but remember that even juices that are sold as "natural" are really long-life juices produced on an industrial scale. Fruit juices freshly squeezed in front of you, especially citrus and pomegranate, are very good. All non-alcoholic beverages except for freshly squeezed juice are almost always served very cold and with a lot of ice (which may be made of heavily chlorinated water), so if you don't want your drinks this way, remember to say so when ordering.

Beers and Spirits

Many restaurants and cafés have draught beer, most of which is locally produced. The main Israeli beers are Maccabee, a slightly bitter, light lager, and Goldstar, which is reminiscent of British ale with a dash of malt. Taybeeh, similar to light, south German beer, is found in the Palestinian regions, East Jerusalem and some Israeli bars. Carlsberg is produced in Israel and Heineken in Jordan, both under licence, while most other major European brands are imported, especially into Israel.

Spirits are less widely available, but are always sold in hotel bars throughout the region. The commonest is arak, the typical Mediterranean distillate of anise.

Goldstar beer   Arak

Coffee and Tea

In Jewish areas, coffee and tea are drunk in European- or American-style cafés. The most widely available type of coffee is filter coffee, which is always served for breakfast in hotels. Many places also offer espresso coffee, but it is almost always rather weak. For a real espresso, you must ask for a *katzar* (strong coffee). What is called cappuccino sometimes has a huge amount of whipped cream added to it. Tea is almost invariably served in tea-bag form, and caffeine-free herbal tea (*zmachim*) is becoming increasingly popular.

Tea and coffee in Arab areas are drunk in coffee-houses (*qahwa*), which serve nothing else – except sometimes traditional water pipes (*nargileh*) to accompany the drink. Arabic coffee (also called *qahwa*) is strong

and aromatic because of the spices, in particular the cardamom, added to it. It is served in tiny cups holding only a few sips. If you do not specify little or no sugar, it always arrives heavily sweetened. To avoid a gritty texture, allow the sediment to settle in the cup first. Arabic tea (*shai*) is more aromatic and stronger than Western-style tea and is also drunk without milk and with a lot of sugar. In restaurants it is often served after a meal with fresh mint leaves (*naana*).

In Arab coffeehouses, if you want Western-style tea, ask for *shai-Libton*; in Arab or Jewish establishments, for Western-style coffee ask for *nes* (short for Nescafé).

Elaborate Arabic coffee set

Wine

Although the Middle East was the home of grape cultivation and wine-making, the first modern wineries in the Holy Land were founded in the mid-19th century. These included the Salesian estate (at Cremisan, near Bethlehem), which still operates today. For years it was the only producer of good, dry white wine, but its standards were later matched by the Latrun Trappist monks' winery, which uses French vines and wine-making techniques.

An Israeli Chardonnay

Today, there are over 300 wineries in Israel, providing a range of varieties and flavours, which reflect the range of climates across the country's small stretch of land. The number of vineyards then increased steadily and wine quality has improved dramatically since the early 1980s. The main wine areas are now: Golan and Upper Galilee at around 500 m (1,640 ft) above sea level, with ideal volcanic soil; Lower Galilee, the Jezreel Valley, the Mount Carmel region and Sharon, which are lower and more humid; Samson, the coastal plain south of Tel Aviv; and the hills of Judaea, which have poorer terrain and are very dry. A number of experimental vineyards in the Negev Desert are now in production.

The largest producers are the Carmel Winery, based in Zikhron Yaakov, whose Mizrachi "Private" series is especially good, and the Golan Heights Winery, based in Katsrin, whose main labels are Golan, Yarden, Gamla and Tishbi. Wines from small producers such as Kibbutz Tsora can be excellent.

Jordanian and Egyptian wines are very poor value for their price and, in both countries, imported wine is prohibitively expensive.

Israeli white wines, especially the Chardonnays and Sauvignon Blancs, are generally very enjoyable; often aromatic, sometimes fruity, smooth and full-bodied. Many of the reasonably priced whites are produced by the Golan Heights Winery.

Wine-Growing Regions of Israel

Key

- Golan, Galilee and the Jezreel Valley
- Mt Carmel and Sharon
- Samson
- Judaean Hills
- Negev Experimental Areas

Dalton
Meron • Katsrin
Haifa
Lavi • Sea Of Galilee
Zikhron Yaakov
• Tanakh
• Binyamina
Caesarea • Ayil
• Bakhan

Tel Aviv •
• Rishon le-Zion
Latrun
Gedera • • Jerusalem
Tsora • • Tkoa
• Hebron
Dead Sea

Arad •

Ramot Negev •

Sde Boker •

Negev Desert
Mitspe
Ramon •

0 kilometres 50
0 miles 30

Israeli red wines are also good, but, with some notable exceptions, tend either to lack body or to be slightly heavy. The grapes most commonly used are Carignan, Cabernet Sauvignon and Merlot, with many wines being a blend of the last two. Among the wines now produced by a growing number of small-scale, specialist wine makers are the fine Cabernets produced by Castel, and the Margalit reds.

Yarden white   Gamla Chardonnay   Tishbi Muscat

Carmel Mizrachi   Margalit red   Kibbutz Isora

Where to Eat and Drink

Jerusalem

The Muslim Quarter

Abu Shukri $
Houmous   **Map** 4 D2
63 El-Wad St, cnr Via Dolorosa, 97500
Tel (02) 627 1538
Simple sit-down restaurant on
the main alley between the
Western Wall and Damascus
Gate. Famous for the light and
sour houmous plates, but serves
other Arabic snacks as well.

Viennese Café $$
International   **Map** 3 C3
*Austrian Hospice, Via Dolorosa,
97626*
Tel (02) 626 5800
Delightful little oasis of calm
amid the bustle of the Muslim
Quarter; it has a pleasant indoor
area and a flowery garden where
guests can relax with a beer or
coffee and cake.

Modern Jerusalem

The Garden Restaurant $$
International   **Map** 1 C2
Jerusalem Hotel, Nablus Rd, 97200
Tel (02) 628 3282
Also known as Kan Zaman, this
covered terrace restaurant is a
great place to soak up some East
Jerusalem atmosphere. Oriental
decor, *narghila* pipes, alcohol
and a mix of Palestinian and
international dishes.

> **DK Choice**
>
> **Lavan** $$
> Mediterranean   **Map** 1 B5
> *Cinematheque, 11 Hebron Rd,
> 93546*
> **Tel** (02) 6673 7393
> Not only do the light meals
> served at Lavan appeal to all,
> but there are also fantastic
> views onto Mount Zion
> and the Old City walls to be
> enjoyed. A well-stocked bar
> accompanies pastas and pizzas,
> salads, fish and meat dishes,
> and fresh sandwiches. The
> Scandinavian-style interior
> perfectly fits the name of the
> place, which means white.

Link $$
Mediterranean
3 HaMa'alot St, 94263
Tel (02) 625 3446
Café-bistro in an old Jerusalem-
style building with a sun-dappled
courtyard. Known for its chicken
wings, juicy steaks and salads.

Little Jerusalem $$
Mediterranean   **Map** 1 A2
9 Ha-Rav Kook St, 94226
Tel (02) 624 4186   **Closed** *Shabbat*
A garden retreat, this restaurant-
cum-museum was artist Anna
Ticho's house. Expansive and
reliable menu, and regular
concerts to accompany dining.

Philadelphia $$
Middle Eastern   **Map** 2 D2
9 El-Zahra St, 97200
Tel (02) 532 2626
An East Jerusalem institution
famed for its Palestinian-style
stuffed vegetables, roasted meats
and fish, and a warm welcome.

Te'enim $$
Vegetarian   **Map** 1 B4
*Confederate House, 12 Emile Botta St,
Yemin Moshe, 94109*
Tel (02) 625 1967   **Closed** *Shabbat*
Charming old stone building
with arched windows that offer
great views of the Old City and
Mount Zion. Creative dishes
include Tom Yam soup.

Tmol Shilshom $$
Mediterranean   **Map** 1 A3
*3 Yoel Moshe Salomon St, Nakhalat
Shiva, 91316*
Tel (02) 623 2758   **Closed** *Shabbat*
Tucked away in a stone-built
1870s house, this mellow café-
restaurant-bookshop attracts book
lovers. Serves comforting mains
and mouthwatering desserts.

Village Green $$
Vegetarian   **Map** 1 A3
33 Jaffa Rd, 94221
Tel (02) 625 3065   **Closed** *Shabbat*
A canteen-style place with
everything from miso soup and
quiche to ratatouille and tofu
dishes. Mix-and-match salad
plates and pay by weight.

> **Price Guide**
> Prices are based on a three-course meal
> for one, including half a bottle of wine,
> tax and service.
>
> $ under $40
> $$ $40 to $80
> $$$ over $80

Adom $$$
Fusion   **Map** 1 A3
*The First Station, 4 David Remez St,
9354102*
Tel (02) 624 6242
Set in Jerusalem's renovated train
station, Adom stands out for its
stylish wine-bar feel. The French-
Israeli menu has something for
everyone. Business lunch deals.

Arabesque $$$
International   **Map** 1 C1
*American Colony Hotel, 23 Nablus
Rd, 97200*
Tel (02) 627 9777
This elegant restaurant at the
American Colony Hotel offers
great food. Try to get a table
in the Turkish-style courtyard.
The drinks list includes a number
regional wine varieties.

Cavelier $$$
Fusion   **Map** 1 A3
1 Ben Sira St, Nakhalat Shiva, 94181
Tel (02) 624 2945
Elegant, romantic bistro offering
meat and seafood classics from
France embellished with
Mediterranean touches.

Chakra $$$
Mediterranean
41 King George St, 94261
Tel (02) 625 2733
Fashionable choice with airy and
modern circular interiors. Meat
and fish dishes are Italian-based
with local flavours. Reserve
ahead. Or, try the café on the
upper level which offers a great

Table setting at Viennese Café, Jerusalem

breakfast and lunch menu. The drinks menu features boutique Israeli beers.

Darna — $$$
Moroccan   Map 1 A3
3 Horkanos St, 94235
Tel (02) 624 5406   **Closed** *Shabbat*
Moorish-inspired decor with Moroccan ceramics and cushions. Specialities include *mechoui* (roast lamb with almonds) and *harira marrakshia* (veal and lentil soup).

Dolphin Yam — $$$
Seafood   Map 1 A3
9 Shimon Ben Shatakh St, 94147
Tel (02) 623 2272
A Jerusalem favourite for fresh seafood, but serves meat and pasta too. Understated decor, seating on the sidewalk.

Mona — $$$
Mediterranean
12 Shmuel Ha-Nagid St, 94592
Tel (02) 622 2283
Housed in the historic Bezalel Art School, now a beautiful gallery. A fusion of Mediterranean flavours can be enjoyed indoors or alfresco.

Rooftop at Mamilla — $$$
Italian   Map 1 B3
Mamilla Hotel, 11 King Solomon St, 94182
Tel (02) 548 2230
Fresh pasta, grilled meat and fish, and delicious desserts to wrap up a great meal. Superb views over the Old City.

Sakura — $$$
Japanese   Map 1 A3
Feingold Courtyard, 31 Jaffa Rd, 94221
Tel (02) 623 5464
The city's best Japanese restaurant with authentic Asian furnishings. Japanese beers or saki to accompany little wooden platters of sushi and sashimi.

Further Afield

Abu Shukri — $
Houmous
4 Mahmoud Rashid St, Abu Ghosh, 90845
Tel (02) 534 2429
Popular spot renowned for its fabulous houmous. Offers sweeping views of the valley.

Azura — $
Traditional Jewish (Sephardi)
4 HaEshkol St, Mahane Yehuda, 94322
Tel (02) 623 5204   **Closed** *dinner daily; Shabbat*
Located in the Iraqi market, tiny Azura has been delighting

Outdoor seating at Rooftop at Mamilla, Jerusalem

customers since the 1950s. Kurdish and Turkish influences in dishes such as Sephardi chicken stew, *shakshuka* (eggs in a spiced tomato sauce), houmous or *kubbe* soup.

Burgers Bar — $
International
31 Emek Refaim St, German Colony, 93105
Tel (02) 561 2333   **Closed** *Shabbat*
Part of a burger chain, this branch is in the atmospheric German Colony and is widely acclaimed locally as serving the city's best burgers. Also offers other good-value meat dishes.

Rachmo — $
Traditional Jewish (Sephardi)
5 HaEshkol St, Mahane Yehuda, 94322
Tel (02) 623 4595   **Closed** *Shabbat*
A Jerusalem institution tucked away in one of Mahane Yehuda's colourful alleyways. Serves Jewish and Aleppo-style cuisine as well as houmous made with the owner's mother's secret recipe.

Karma — $$$
Italian
73 Ein Kerem St, Ein Kerem, 95744
Tel (02) 643 6643
Set in the pastoral village of Ein Kerem, this arched stone split-level restaurant has a lively yet relaxed vibe. Serves a number of meat and other dishes in very generous portions.

Machne Yuda — $$$
Contemporary Israeli
10 Beit Ya'akov St, Mahane Yehuda, 94322
Tel (02) 533 3442   **Closed** *Shabbat*
Hip spot with an open kitchen and country-style decor. Fresh ingredients sourced from the adjacent market are used in menus that change each week. Book ahead.

Majda — $$$
Fusion
The Blue House up the Hill, Ein Rafa, off Route 1, opp Abu Ghosh
Tel (02) 579 7108
This little restaurant in an Arab village is run by a Muslim-Jewish couple. The food is a fusion of Arab and Israeli traditions. Choose between shabby-chic interiors or tables in the herb garden.

The Coast and Galilee

DK Choice

AKKO: Humous Sa'eid — $
Houmous   Map B2
Benjamin of Tuleda St, Old City
Tel (04) 991 3945   **Closed** *Sat*
This no-frills Arab eatery, hidden in the heart of Akko's Old City, is reckoned as one of the best places for houmous. Bowls generously slicked with houmous are accompanied by piles of pickles, pitta and falafel. Note that queues can stretch down the street, and they often run out by 2pm.

Earthy, artistic decor at the Mona restaurant, Jerusalem

Colourfully decorated interiors at Fattoush, Haifa

AKKO: Uri Buri $$$
Seafood   Map B2
Lighthouse Square, HaHagana St, Old City, 24713
Tel (04) 955 2212
Located in an Ottoman mansion with shabby-chic decor and attentive service. Famous for their seafood dishes. Try the chef's tasting menu.

CAESAREA: Helena $$$
Mediterranean   Map B2
Old Harbour, Caesarea National Park, 30889
Tel (057) 944 3013
This romantic spot, overlooking Caesarea's ancient harbour, has charming interiors and a diverse menu. Groups of four or more can go for the good-value tasting menu.

GOLAN HEIGHTS:
Yaeli Café and Restaurant $$
Fusion   Map C1
Kfar Omanim, Aniam, off Rd 808, 12495
Tel (04) 682 1855
In the artists' village at Aniam, this typically Golani restaurant is welcoming and down-to-earth. Offers a range of European light meals with an Israeli twist. Great breakfasts.

HAIFA: Felafel HaZekenim $
Falafel   Map B2
18 HaWadi St, Wadi Nisnas, 33044
Tel (04) 851 4959
Enjoy legendary falafel in the lively lanes of the Arab area of Wadi Nisnas. Made with a secret recipe, the fried green chickpea balls are crispy and fresh.

HAIFA: Shawarma Hazan $$
Middle Eastern   Map B2
140 Jaffa Rd, 35252
Tel (04) 855 8075

A long-standing eatery hailed by many as the best *shawarma* place in Israel. Freshly made on the spot, lamb kebabs are stuffed into a pitta with parsley, onion, *tahina* and amba sauce.

HAIFA: Fattoush $$$
Middle Eastern   Map B3
38 Ben Gurion Ave, German Colony, 35023
Tel (04) 852 4930
The signature *fattoush* salad is a must. Sit under the trees on the terrace or lounge on silk couches in the Oriental-style chamber.

LOWER GALILEE: Dag Dagan $$
Seafood   Map C2
Kibbutz Hefzibah, near Beth Shean
Tel (04) 653 4359
Shaded picnic tables close to the Beit Alpha synagogue. Fish is the mainstay, but there are vegetarian and meat options too.

LOWER GALILEE:
The Herb Farm $$$
Fusion   Map C2
Road 667, Mt Gilboa, Lower Galilee, 19122
Tel (04) 653 1093   **Closed** Sun
Country-style restaurant on the Gilboa range with awesome views from the wooden terrace surrounded by herbs. The fresh, flavoursome dishes are mostly meat-based.

NAZARETH: Diana $$
Traditional Arabic   Map B2
51 Paul VI St, 16224; Grand New Hotel, 5050 St
Tel (04) 657 2919
With two branches, and over 30 years of expertise, Diana offers the best of Galilean cuisine. Delectable lamb dishes, an array of *meze*, Arab-style kebabs and *shishlik*, plus seafood.

NAZARETH: Tishreen $$$
Mediterranean   Map B2
56 El-Bishara St, 16000
Tel (04) 608 4666
An attractive, old mansion house with tiled floors, friendly staff and a warm atmosphere. Buzzing mix of locals and visitors. The unpretentious menu has plenty of choice for both carnivores and vegetarians.

ROSH PINA: Pina BaRosh $$$
Fusion   Map C2
8 HeChalutzim St, 12000
Tel (04) 693 6582
A short walk from Rosh Pina's galleries. Panoramic views of the Hula Valley and the Golan Heights from the terrace and the wine bar match the superb French-inspired food.

SEA OF GALILEE:
Ein Camonim $$
Vegetarian   Map C2
Hwy 85, 10 km W of Amiad Jct, 20109
Tel (04) 698 9680
Rustic eatery on a family-run dairy farm that uses fresh home-grown products, including the cheese. All-you-can-eat menu!

SEA OF GALILEE:
Israel's Kitchen $$$
Israeli   Map C2
Shavit Guesthouse, Moshav Arbel, off Rd 7717, Tiberias, 15282
Tel (04) 679 4919
The intimate home-cooked dinner and breakfast, handmade chocolates and excellent wines are worth the uphill drive from Tiberias. A hidden gem.

SEA OF GALILEE:
Marinado Banamal $$$
Kosher Meat   Map C2
Kibbutz Ein Gev, 14940
Tel (04) 665 8555
Premium-quality steaks, kebabs, salads and vegetarian options. Kids' menu, too. Seating on the boardwalk by the Sea of Galilee.

TEL AVIV: Abulafia Bakery $
Arab   Map B3
7 Yefet St, Jaffa, 68028
Tel (03) 682 8544
A classic Jaffa experience since 1878. Queue on the pavement for hot pitta topped with *zaatar* (mix of herbs) and olives, or a grilled *sambusac* stuffed with egg, potato and cheese. Open 24/7.

TEL AVIV: Ashkara $
Houmous   Map B3
45 Yermiyahu St, 62594
Tel (03) 546 4547
One of the best places in Tel Aviv for houmous. Indulge in a delicious lunch and then work it off by a walk in the riverside HaYarkon Park, one block away.

Al fresco breakfast at Pina BaRosh, Rosh Pina

TEL AVIV: Lehem Erez $
Sandwiches Map B3
52 Ibn Givrol St, 64361
Tel (03) 726 0077
The original branch of the chain offering gourmet sandwiches that fuse unexpected flavours and fresh salads. Perfect for breakfast or a casual snack.

TEL AVIV: Chadar Ochel (The Dining Hall) $$
Israeli Map B3
23 Shaul Ha-Melech Blvd
Tel (03) 696 6188
Bustling informal restaurant with muted decor in a courtyard by the Museum of Art. Serves traditional kibbutz-style food with a modern twist.

TEL AVIV: Elimelech $$
Jewish (Ashkenazi) Map B3
35 Wolfson St, Florentine, 66528
Tel (03) 681 4545
A quaint restaurant that has been serving Eastern-European Jewish food since 1936. Try chopped liver, chicken soup with matzo balls, schnitzel or the traditional Shabbat meal of *cholent* (a slow-cooked stew).

TEL AVIV: Il Pastaio $$
Italian Map B3
27 Ibn Givrol, 64078
Tel (03) 525 1166 **Closed** *Sat; Sun dinner*
Home-made pastas, lasagne and gnocchi, and a range of meaty mains. The risotto with porcini mushrooms and the tiramisu are delicious.

TEL AVIV: Moon $$
Japanese Map B3
50 Dizengoff St
Tel (05) 7942 6861
Sit at the black lacquer bar by the sushi conveyor belt, or at a table, for a selection of mini seafood and vegetarian delights.

TEL AVIV: Nanouchka $$
Eastern European Map B3
30 Lilienblum St, 65133
Tel (03) 516 2254
Fun, unconventional restaurant-bar with vibrant decor in its various rooms. Serves excellent Georgian cuisine which features lots of meat and pastry. Turns into a party place later on.

TEL AVIV: Orna & Ella $$
Mediterranean Map B3
33 Sheinkin St, 65232
Tel (03) 620 4753
Creative menu of light dishes with an Italian slant. Try the pumpkin *kubbe* and tamed sweet potato pancakes. Simple decor and a lovely terrace.

Tables awaiting diners at Mul Yam, Tel Aviv

TEL AVIV: Thai House $$
Thai Map B3
8 Rograshov St, 63808
Tel (03) 517 8568
Sample authentic spicy Thai dishes, many hailing from the Isan region, made with home-grown vegetables. Relaxed atmosphere and bamboo decor.

TEL AVIV: Brasserie $$$
French Map B3
70 Ibn Givrol, 64952
Tel (03) 696 7111
A 24-hour café-bistro with an Art Deco interior, serving unfussy French cuisine. The Friday brunch, served between 7am and 5pm, is hugely popular.

TEL AVIV: Herbert Samuel $$$
Contemporary Israeli Map B3
6 Kaufman St
Tel (03) 516 6516
Top-notch etablishment using the freshest ingredients. The seafood, salads and meat dishes can be ordered in half-sized portions. Stunning location on the promenade.

TEL AVIV: Margaret Tayar $$$
Fusion Map B3
HaAliya HaShniya Quay, Nr Jaffa, 68128
Tel (03) 682 4741 **Closed** *Sun*
Try authentic Tunisian, Libyan and Mediterranean food at this long-standing beachfront restaurant with a retro vibe. Expect slow service.

TEL AVIV: Mul Yam $$$
Seafood Map B3
Hangar 24, Tel Aviv Port, 63501
Tel (03) 546 9920
One of Israel's most exclusive restaurants, "Across the Sea" is located in the Port area, near many fashionable nightspots. Uses imported ingredients and has an incredible wine list. Business lunch available.

TEL AVIV: Raphael $$$
Contemporary Israeli Map B3
King David's Tower, 63143
87 HaYarkon St
Tel (03) 522 6464
Chef Rafi Cohen is renowned for his inventive flavoursome dishes, influenced by his Moroccan roots. Seaside views add to the experience.

DK Choice

TEL AVIV: Toto Restaurant $$$
Contemporary Israeli Map B3
4 Berkowitz St
Tel (03) 693 5151
This contemporary restaurant is known for its sharp flavours and unusual twist to Italian fare by chef Yaron Shalev. The chestnut gnocchi is delicious, but the fish and steaks are superb too. The restaurant boasts one of the best wine lists in the country. Reserve a much-coveted bar seat to best soak up the lively atmosphere.

UPPER GALILEE: HaTachana $$$
Steakhouse Map C1
1 HaRishonim St, Metula, 10292
Tel (02) 694 4810
Consistently cited as one of the best restaurants in the north, HaTachana specializes in succulent steaks. The cluttered cow-themed decor is strangely appealing. Great service.

UPPER GALILEE: Nechalim $$$
French & Italian Map C1
Gan HaTzafon shopping area, Road 99, near Kibbutz HaGoshrim
Tel (04) 690 4875
Romantic venue on the banks of a stream with a lush garden terrace. The speciality is fresh fish, but there are also seafood, meat and vegetarian dishes. Guaranteed to deliver a first-class dining experience.

Diners seated outside at Blue Fig, Amman

The Dead Sea and the Negev Desert

BETHLEHEM:
The Tent Restaurant $$
Middle Eastern **Map** B3
Shepherds' Field St, Beit Sahour
Tel (02) 277 3875
Inside a large Bedouin-style tent. Palestinian dishes are made with local ingredients. Try the *dajaj mahshi* (roast chicken stuffed with rice and pine nuts).

EILAT: Eddie's Hide-Away $$
International **Map** B7
68 Almogim St, off Eliot St, 88000
Tel (08) 637 1137
Old-style restaurant that has been an Eilat institution since 1979. Popular among locals. Steak, fish, shrimp, and pasta on the menu.

EILAT: Pastory $$
Italian **Map** B7
7 Tarshish St, 88000
Tel (08) 634 5111
Just north of the main beach with rustic Italian decor and an open kitchen. Home-made pasta, Tuscan-style sauces and desserts.

EILAT: The Last Refuge $$$
Seafood **Map** B7
Coral Beach, 88000
Tel (08) 637 2437
Gets the Israeli vote for the best seafood in town. Quaint nautical equipment reminiscent of New England embellishes the interior. Alfresco seating in summer.

EILAT: Marina Grill $$$
Mediterranean **Map** B7
Kings Wharf, North Beach, 88000
Tel (08) 636 3439 **Closed** *Shabbat*
Stylish place with a range of high-quality fish and meat dishes and excellent service. Try the *chraime*, a spicy fish dish traditional to Sephardi Jews.

MITSPE RAMON:
Chez Eugene $$$
Contemporary Israeli **Map** B5
8 Har Ardon, Spice Routes Quarter
Tel (08) 653 9595 **Closed** *lunch daily*
Mediterranean dishes, made with local Negev ingredients, served in a modern warehouse-style space with cool lighting. Be sure to leave room for the exquisite desserts.

Petra and Western Jordan

AMMAN: Hashem $
Houmous **Map** C3
Opposite Cliff Hotel, Downtown
Tel (06) 463 6440
Founded in the 1920s, this budget eatery is an Amman institution. Serves only two dishes: houmous and *fuul* (hot beans) with flatbread. Packed with locals 24 hours a day.

AMMAN: Blue Fig $$
International **Map** C3
Prince Hashem bin al-Hussein St, Abdoun, 11844
Tel (06) 592 8800
Hip, laid-back place to hang out on the city's fringes. Subtle lighting and modern design attracts chic Ammanis. Light bites, wraps and salads, and alcohol on the menu.

AMMAN: Fakhr el-Din $$
Middle Eastern **Map** C3
40 Taha Hussein St, between 1st and 2nd Circles, Jebel Amman
Tel (06) 465 2399
One of Jordan's best eateries, in a converted 1920s town house. Impeccable *meze* and grills. Reservations essential; book a terrace table in summer.

AMMAN: Reem al-Bawadi $$
Middle Eastern **Map** C3
Near Waha Circle, Tlaa al-Ali, West Amman
Tel (06) 551 5419
Excellent Arab cuisine in the informal setting favoured by Jordanian families. Seating inside or in a spacious Bedouin-style tent in the garden.

AMMAN: Romero $$
Italian **Map** C3
Near 3rd Circle, 11181, Jebel Amman, 11181
Tel (06) 464 4227
Tucked away down a leafy side street, with a warm atmosphere and authentic food made with fresh ingredients. The lounge-style Living Room is upstairs.

AMMAN: Tannoureen $$
Lebanese **Map** C3
Shatt al-Arab St, Umm Uthaina, West Amman
Tel (06) 551 5987
Among Jordan's best restaurants with elegant design and formal service. Exceptional *meze*, grills, fish and divine desserts. Alcohol and *narghila* (water pipe).

AMMAN: Wild Jordan $$
Organic **Map** C3
Othman bin Affan St, below 1st Circle, Jebel Amman, 11941
Tel (06) 463 3542
Café-restaurant perched on a hillside overlooking downtown Amman, with spectacular views from the terrace. Organic and locally sourced salads, wraps, soups and smoothies.

AQABA: Ali Baba $$
Lebanese **Map** B7
Princess Haya Circle
Tel (03) 201 3901
Located on a bustling corner, this long-established eatery is a favourite with locals and tourists. Fish and seafood, mixed grills and salads feature on the menu, along with beer.

AQABA: Bourj al-Hamam $$
Lebanese **Map** B7
Intercontinental Hotel, King Hussein St, North Beach
Tel (03) 209 2222
Exceptional Lebanese special-ities, particularly the fish dishes. A poolside terrace under palm trees looks out to the Red Sea.

AQABA: Romero, at the Royal Yacht Club $$
Mediterranean **Map** B7
Off the main corniche
Tel (03) 202 2464
A gated side road off Princess Haya Circle leads to the marina

and this lovely restaurant with waterfront views. The range of cuisines includes wood-fired pizza, pasta and Arabic meze.

DEAD SEA:
Kempinski Hotel Ishtar $$
International   Map C4
Dead Sea Rd, Sweimeh, 11194
Tel (05) 356 8888
At the Dead Sea, dining out is a case of picking a hotel. With beautiful natural surroundings and excellent Asian, Italian and Middle Eastern restaurants, the Kempinski is a top choice.

DK Choice

MADABA: Haret Jdoudna $$
Middle Eastern   Map C4
King Talal St, 11181
Tel (05) 324 8650
Serving top-quality authentic Jordanian cuisine, this is the place to indulge in grills and meze. Set in a historic building in Madaba's old quarter, with tables dotted around a foliage-filled courtyard. The decor is rustic and the ambience warm.

PETRA:
Movenpick Resort Petra $$$
International   Map C5
Movenpick Hotel, Wadi Musa
Tel (03) 215 7111
Top off the day at Movenpick, where Saraya offers extensive buffets and the formal Al Iwan has high-priced Mediterranean dishes. The roof garden is ideal for a sundowner.

UMM QAIS:
Umm Qais Resthouse $$
Middle Eastern & Italian Map C2
Umm Qais
Tel (02) 750 0555
In an Ottoman school within the ruins of the Roman city of Gadara, overlooking the Sea of Galilee and the Golan Heights. Salads, meze, grills and pasta

The Red Sea and Sinai

DAHAB: Blue House $
Thai   Map F6
Above Seven Heaven Hotel, Masbat
Tel (106) 717 7846
An unpretentious place with wooden tables and white-washed walls. Authentic dishes by the Thai chef. Vegetarians are also well catered for.

DAHAB: Nirvana $
Indian   Map F6
Near the Lighthouse, Asilah
Tel (06) 104 6061
Mouthwatering selection of fresh Indian food with beachside or patio seating. A popular spot for a drink.

DAHAB: Eel Garden Stars $$
International   Map F6
Asilah
Tel (102) 039 0412
In a quiet spot on the northern end of the beach with a wide-ranging menu of delectable local and Western dishes. The portions are very generous

DAHAB: Eldorado $$
Italian   Map F6
El Melel St, Asilah, 46611
Tel (069) 364 102
Home-made pasta and gnocchi with a host of delicious sauces, wood-oven pizza, breads and desserts. Good wine and stunning sea views

NUWEIBA: Blue Blue $$
International   Map F5
Hilton Coral Resort, 46625
Tel (069) 352 0320

International food with a distinctly Italian slant is served buffet-style at this eatery overlooking beachside gardens and pools.

DK Choice

NUWEIBA: Castle Zaman $$$
Slow-cooking   Map F5
2 km (1 mile) north of Basata
Tel (0128) 214 0591
Castle Zaman is not just about the amazing food. Relaxing by the turquoise pool and exploring the miniature castle hand-crafted by the owner is a one-of-a-kind experience. Raised on a cliffside, the castle affords extraordinary views of the Gulf of Aqaba. The slow-cooked meat and seafood spreads are fit for royalty.

SHARM EL-SHEIKH:
Abou El-Sid $$
Egyptian   Map F7
Naama Bay
Tel (069) 360 3910
This quirky, dimly lit restaurant serves up traditional Egyptian fare such as quail, stuffed pigeon and molukhiya (soup).

SHARM EL-SHEIKH: El-Fanar $$
Italian   Map F7
Ras Umm Sidd
Tel (069) 366 2218
Beautiful location right by the beach, next to a lighthouse. Serves some of the best pizzas in Egypt. Good wine list.

SHARM EL-SHEIKH: Sala Thai $$
Thai   Map F7
Hyatt Regency Hotel, Gardens Bay
Tel (069) 360 1234
Overlooking the Red Sea, this restaurant has terraces with hand-carved teak decor. Authentic and delicate dishes.

Warm interiors at Kempinski Hotel Ishtar, Dead Sea

For more information on types of restaurants *see pages 264–5*

SHOPS AND MARKETS

When it comes to shopping, the main attraction in Jerusalem is undoubtedly the souks, or bazaars, of the Old City. In comparison with the great bazaars of Istanbul or Cairo, Jerusalem's souks can seem small and overly touristy, but they still deserve exploration *(see pp152–3)*. The streets of the Old City away from the souks are also dotted with interesting small shops, handicraft centres, workshops and boutiques. Most other towns and cities throughout the Holy Land also have souks, with particularly good ones in Akko, Amman, Hebron and

Nazareth. Anybody intending shopping in the souks must become acquainted with the art of bargaining. In contrast to the traditional nature of the souk, bigger centres such as Jerusalem, Tel Aviv and Amman all possess modern shopping districts, as well as large American-style malls, filled with familiar brand names from the West.

In Jordan, the major tourist sites such as Petra and Jerash have small clusters of tourist-oriented shops where, sometimes, you can find local handicrafts and products of interest.

A typical fruit and vegetable stall

Opening Hours

Throughout the Holy Land there are often no strictly defined opening hours; it depends on the individual proprietor. In general, however, except for food shops, which open quite early, business activity begins at roughly 9am. Some shops close from 1 to 4pm, but most remain open all day until around 7pm. In Jerusalem's Old City and elsewhere, the souks don't really get going until perhaps 10am and they close around sunset. Many shops and stalls in the souks are closed all day Sunday, as many of the shop owners are Christian, although others are Muslim and they stay closed on Friday instead. During the holy month of Ramadan, Muslim-owned shops throughout the Holy Land close 30 minutes to one hour before sunset.

All Jewish-owned businesses in Jerusalem and throughout Israel close from Friday afternoon to sunset on Saturday for Shabbat (Sabbath). These shops are also closed during Jewish holidays *(see pp40–43)*.

How to Pay

Major credit cards, such as American Express, Visa and MasterCard, are accepted in almost all shops throughout Israel; travellers' cheques are not. In Jordan and Sinai, credit cards are less widely accepted. Only in top-end and mid-range hotels and international restaurants are cards usually accepted; in most places, you will have to pay in cash. It is usual to pay in the local currency (in Jordan and Sinai use of any other currency is illegal), but in Israel, if you are making a large purchase, it is

possible to get a discount by paying in US dollars. This is because transactions made in a foreign currency are not subject to Israeli VAT.

VAT Exemptions

A wide range of goods in Israel are subject to a Value Added Tax (*Ma'am* in Hebrew) of 18 per cent. Tourists are entitled to a refund on this for any purchases amounting to over 400 shekels (about US$100). Make sure the shop you buy from has a VAT (or tax) refund sign displayed. You need to ask the sales assistant for a special invoice showing the VAT paid in both dollars and shekels. This is then presented at the VAT counter at the airport at the time of your departure. You must have the purchases with you to cross-check against the invoice. Queues at this counter can be very long, so get there with time to spare.

Examining the wares at an Old City souvenir shop

Kenyon Malcha Mall in Malcha, Jerusalem

Department Stores and Shopping Malls

Israel has a rapidly growing number of large shopping centres and US-style out-of-town malls. Both are filled with standard mall-type outlets that sell everything from greetings cards to electronics items, most of which are imported from Europe and the United States. Jerusalem has several large malls, including one of the biggest in the country, the **Kenyon Malcha Mall**, out in the Malcha suburb of West Jerusalem. In the centre of the city, **Mamilla Alrov Quarter** is a high-end shopping strip with international and local stores as well as many attractive restaurants and cafés. Tel Aviv's biggest mall is the **Azrieli Centre**, in the base of three modern towers on the northeastern edge of town. More centrally located malls in Tel Aviv include the **Dizengoff Centre** on Dizengoff Street and the **Gan ha-Ir Shopping Centre** just north of Rabin Square.

As well as the shopping opportunities, Israel's malls are typically full of good, moderately priced restaurants, snack bars and cafés. Given that they are air-conditioned, they can be great places for pedestrians to escape from the often stifling heat outside.

Jordan's capital, Amman, has also succumbed to the mall craze. The city's biggest is **Mecca Mall**, out in the northwestern suburbs, which also contains a food court, cinema and bowling alley. There's also the smaller but more centrally located **Abdoun Mall**.

Markets

In addition to the souks of Jerusalem's Old City, there are lots of good buys at the **Mahane Yehuda** market in modern West Jerusalem *(see p135)*. Tel Aviv has **Carmel Market** *(see p176)*, which operates every day except Saturday, and, also in the same neighbourhood, the Nakhalat Binyamin **craft market** *(see p176)*, held every Tuesday and Friday. In Jordan, downtown Amman has several streets filled with colourful market shopping *(see p216)*.

Buying Antiques

In Jordan and Sinai it is forbidden to export any antique or archaeological find unless you have obtained special permission in advance. The border authorities are extremely thorough in their checks in this regard. On the other hand, in Jerusalem and Israel you may buy objects from excavations. For more details and for the addresses of some reputable dealers, see pages 152–3.

How to Bargain

Buying and selling in the Middle East is traditionally a highly ritualized affair, in which bargaining is far more than just haggling for a cheap price. The aim of the exercise is to establish a fair price that both vendor and buyer are happy with. As part of the process, a shop owner may well invite you to have a cup of tea or coffee and may literally turn the place upside down to show you something. You should not feel obliged to buy because of this. It is common sales practice and all part of the ritual.

Bargaining, by the way, is not socially acceptable in city centre shops, but it is unavoidable when in the souks if you don't wish to pay greatly over the odds.

The way to go about it is that once you identify an article that interests you, especially an expensive one, be brave enough to offer half the price quoted by the shop owner. Don't be put off by any feigned indignation on the part of the shopkeeper and only raise your next offer by a small amount. Through offer and counter-offer you should arrive at a mutually agreeable price.

Haggling over the price – time-consuming but essential to avoid paying over the odds

If you don't reach a price you think is fair then simply say thank you and leave. Making to walk away often has the effect of bringing the price plummeting down.

In theory, no one gets cheated because you, the buyer, have set the price yourself; it follows that you are happy with what you have agreed to pay, and the shopkeeper will certainly never sell at a loss.

Where to Shop in Jerusalem, Israel, Petra and Sinai

Jerusalem's souks are the first place to look for many of the items produced in this region (for shopping in Jerusalem, see pages 152–3), but there is also plenty of other good shopping in the Holy Land. Tel Aviv is probably Israel's finest shopping city, with several malls and markets, and lots of great boutique stores on and off Dizengoff Street. Amman, in Jordan, has a range of great arts and crafts items, many of which can also be found at stores in the more popular tourist destinations such as Madaba, Petra and Jerash.

Colourful Armenian ceramics for sale in Jerusalem

Religious Articles

For Christian religious items there are any number of shops in Jerusalem's Old City (see pp152–3). However, prices are generally lower in Bethlehem, which is where many of these items are made. One place worth visiting here is the **Holy Land Arts Museum** on Milk Grotto Street, which specializes in wooden objects with mother-of-pearl inlay and inlaid metalwork (damascene). For Judaica, visit the Jewish Quarter in Jerusalem's Old City and along central Ben Yehuda Street in Tel Aviv. Visit **Pninat-ha'kesef** in Tel Aviv for a wide selection of candlesticks and paintings.

Ceramics

Jerusalem is the place for beautifully coloured Armenian ceramics, but there are other styles produced elsewhere in the region. **Beit el-Badawi** in Amman sells the designs of local craftspeople who work in both traditional and modern styles. Pieces incorporate Arab calligraphy. Also in Amman, **Silsal Ceramics** is another good sales studio specializing in modern pottery.

For something really chic, visit **Blue Bandana** in northern Tel Aviv, which stocks a fine array of beautiful tableware, much of which is designed specially for the store.

Textiles and Rugs

The shops and market in the centre of Ramallah are a good place to look for densely embroidered Palestinian textiles. Cushions and bags made from Bedouin textiles are found in most souvenir shops in Israel. Prices vary little, but for Bedouin rugs you would do better to buy in Jordan. Madaba (see p220), in particular, is famous for its colourful rugs. These can be bought around town, but one recommended place is **Madaba Oriental Gifts**, which is opposite

St George's Church. **Shtihei Carmel** in Rehovot, near Tel Aviv, specializes in Carmel rugs.

Jewellery

Some of the region's most distinctive jewellery is made by the Bedouin. It is sold at the street markets of Nakhalat Binyamin (see p176) in Tel Aviv, in many of the boutiques in Jaffa and at the Thursday market in Beersheva.

For more contemporary pieces, **Agas and Tamar** is an upmarket boutique selling exquisite own-designed, one-off pieces. Even if your budget doesn't stretch this far, it's a beautiful shop in one of Tel Aviv's most interesting neighbourhoods.

Hebron Glassware

In Jerusalem, the first three shops on the left-hand side of David Street, going from Jaffa Gate, have the best selection of glassware. However, much lower prices are offered in the souk at Hebron. At Madaba in Jordan, **Madaba Oriental Gifts** has a good range of Hebron glassware, often at prices even lower than those in Hebron.

Cosmetics

The Arab town of Nablus is famed for its olive-oil soap, available at almost any East Jerusalem grocer's and in the Old City souks, especially on Khan el-Zeit Street. In Galilee the soap is sold in many souvenir shops, particularly in Nazareth, but at higher prices.

Craftsman hand-knotting the fringe of a rug

The reputed health-giving properties of the Dead Sea are exploited in the cosmetic products made by two companies, Ahava and Mineral. These are sold at all well-stocked pharmacies and at the Duty-Free Shop at Ben Gurion airport. When visiting the Dead Sea, you can buy directly from the **Ahava Factory**, north of Ein Gedi. It is open daily, but closes at 4pm on Fridays. There is also an **Ahava** at the Hilton Tel Aviv and a major outlet at the Ein Bokek spa resort on the Dead Sea shore.

A range of Dead Sea products is also sold at a shop called **Holy Treasures**, opposite St George Church in the town of Madaba, Jordan.

Souvenirs

Sandals, bags and belts are good articles to buy throughout the Holy Land. Copperware is also a good buy, notably coffeepots and trays, often etched with arabesque

patterns. A more exotic souvenir is a *nargileh*, or Arab water pipe. All of these can be found in Jerusalem and also in Amman, where a particularly good one-stop shopping opportunity is offered by the **El-Alaydi Jordan Craft Centre**, which has a vast selection of locally produced items, including Hebron glassware, Palestinian embroidery and Bedouin tent accessories.

In Madaba in Jordan, there is a complex of excellent **craft shops** just north of the Madaba Museum, offering everything from textiles to jewellery to mosaics. At Petra, look out for the **Made In Jordan** shop, which is near the entry gate to the site, and which has top-quality locally made items, including camel-hair shawls and olive oil. Decorative bottles filled with coloured sand are popular Jordanian souvenirs, especially at Wadi Rum and Petra.

Water pipes, or nargilehs

Making sand-filled bottles, Jordan's most prevalent souvenir

For a very different sort of souvenir, an extensive range of recordings of modern and traditional Jewish music can be found at **The Third Ear** in Tel Aviv. Alternatively, the **Bauhaus Centre** in Tel Aviv has a gift shop selling miniature models of some of the city's landmark 1930s architecture in the International Modern, or Bauhaus, style *(see p175)*, as well as books and prints.

DIRECTORY

Shopping Malls

Abdoun Mall
El Hashimi St, Abdoun, Amman, Jordan.
Tel (06) 592 0296.

Azrieli Center
132 Petach Tikva Hwy, Tel Aviv. **Tel** (03) 608 1199.

Dizengoff Centre
50 Dizengoff St, Tel Aviv.
Tel (03) 621 2416.

Gan ha-Ir Shopping Centre
71 Ibn Gabirol St, Tel Aviv.
Tel (03) 527 9111.

Kenyon Malcha Mall
Malcha, West Jerusalem.
Tel (02) 679 1333.

Mamilla Alrov Quarter
Tel (02) 636 0000.
w alrovmamilla.com

Mecca Mall
Mekka el-Mukkaramah Rd, Amman, Jordan.
Tel (06) 552 7943.

Religious Articles

Holy Land Arts Museum
Milk Grotto St, Bethlehem.
Tel (02) 274 2835.
w holylandarts museum.org

Pninat-ha'kesef
1/86 Ha'kishor St, Tel Aviv.
Tel (03) 518 1406.

Ceramics

Beit el-Bawadi
Fawzi el-Qawoaji St, Amman, Jordan.
Tel (06) 593 0070.

Blue Bandana
52 Hei Beyar, Kikar ha-Medina, Tel Aviv.
Tel (03) 602 1686.

Silsal Ceramics
Innabeh St, North Abdoun, Amman, Jordan.
Tel (06) 593 1128.
w silsal.com

Textiles and Rugs

Madaba Oriental Gifts
Madaba, Jordan.

Shtihei Carmel
Bilu Center, Rehovot.
Tel (08) 935 5557.

Jewellery

Agas and Tamar
43 Shabazi St, Neve Tzedek, Tel Aviv.
Tel (03) 516 8421.

Cosmetics

Ahava
Tel Aviv Hilton, Independence Park, Tel Aviv.
Tel (03) 522 0120.

Ahava Factory
Kibbutz Mitspe Shalem, Route 90, Dead Sea.
Tel (02) 994 5100.

Holy Treasures
Talal St, Madaba, Jordan.
Tel (05) 324 8481.

Souvenirs

Bauhaus Centre
99 Dizengoff St, Tel Aviv.
Tel (03) 522 0459.
w bauhaus-center.com

Craft shops
Haret Jdoudna Complex, Talal St, Madaba, Jordan.
Tel (05) 324 8650.

El-Alaydi Jordan Craft Centre
El-Kulliyah el-Islamiyah St, Jebel Amman, Amman, Jordan.
Tel (06) 464 4555.

Made In Jordan
Petra, Jordan.
Tel (03) 215 5900.

The Third Ear
48 King George St, Tel Aviv.
Tel (03) 621 5222.

What to Buy in Jerusalem, Israel, Petra and Sinai

Visitors on the lookout for unusual souvenirs, or the products of different cultures and ages, will certainly find something to their liking in Jerusalem, either in the souks and alleyways of the Old City, or in particular districts of the modern city. Some artifacts, such as pottery, brass and silver objects, Bedouin textiles and Arab jewellery, are sold throughout the Holy Land. However, in Jerusalem you will find an especially wide range of Jewish religious articles (while other places concentrate on Christian or Muslim items) and Armenian pottery.

Copper goblets

Firjan with spirit stove

Blue Hebron Glass

Most of this attractive glass, in shades of light blue and turquoise, is made to imitate Roman and Phoenician vessels. Some modern designs and full dinner services are also produced.

Copper- and Brassware

Copper plates, jugs, pots, trays and goblets, all usually engraved, are found everywhere. So, too, are traditional *firjan* (coffee pots) and large platters made of beaten brass.

Armenian Ceramics

The best-known decorative pottery is produced by the Armenian community, which has had a presence in Jerusalem since the 4th century *(see p111)*. It is characterized by the abundant use of blue and yellow, and of floral motifs. The designs are usually intricate and painted on a white background.

Silver and Pewter Jewellery

The Yemenite tradition of silver filigree work has been extensively adopted by religious and secular jewellers in the Holy Land. Look out also for attractive, modern pewter jewellery set with semi-precious stones, as well as traditional blue glass-eye and *khamsa* (hand-shaped) lucky charms, popular with Arabs and Jews alike.

Olive-wood Objects

Crucifixes, rosaries, Nativity scenes and figures of Christ, the Virgin Mary and the saints carved in hard, light-coloured and attractively grained olive wood make evocative souvenirs. The best come from the Bethlehem area.

Olive-wood sculpture

Blue glass-eye pendants

Modern brooch

Silver *khamsa*

Jewish Liturgical Articles

These often beautifully made objects include the *kippah* (male skullcap), *tallit* (pure wool prayer shawl), *kiddush* (blessing) cup, *besamim* (spice-holder), *mezuzah* (prayer container hung at front doors) and *shofar* (ram's horn blown for Yom Kippur).

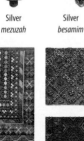

Kippah and tallit

Shofar

Silver *mezuzah*

Silver *besamim*

Rugs and Fabrics

Robust and vividly coloured Bedouin rugs, cushions and bags made from the cloth formerly used as Bedouin saddle covers, and traditional, finely embroidered Palestinian dresses are popular buys.

Bedouin cushion covers

Bedouin fabrics

Palestinian fabrics

Ancient Household Articles and Coins

Reputable dealers in finds from archaeological sites will often have attractive basalt, earthenware and stone kitchen vessels, small terracotta amphorae and Roman and Phoenician glassware. Coins from many historical periods are fairly plentiful, but beware of fakes.

Beauty Products from the Dead Sea and Nablus

A vast range of creams, soap, salts and Dead Sea mud, using the mineral properties of the unique Dead Sea salt, is sold to alleviate skin conditions. Nablus soap, which has olive oil and less than two per cent caustic soda as its only ingredients, is cheap, fragrant and long-lasting, and is good for use in dry climates.

Nablus soap

Dead Sea lotions

Local Delicacies

Specialist shops stocked with large sacks of nuts, dried fruits, pulses and dried vegetables are fascinating places to explore. They often sell spices, too. All these products make good buys as they are easy to carry and keep well at home.

Dried apricots

Chickpeas

Mulberries

Almonds

Pistachio nuts

Dried red peppers and aubergines

ENTERTAINMENT

If Jerusalem is, as Israelis often say, the city where they pray and Haifa is the city where they work, then Tel Aviv is definitely where they play. High culture is catered for by a fine modern opera house, several theatres and a busy dance and performing arts centre. Popular culture is supported by myriad bars, clubs and live music venues. While Jerusalem lacks the bustling nightlife of Tel Aviv, it has still established itself as a lively centre for a range of entertainment,

from music to dance to film and more. It boasts many bars, concert halls and cinematheques *(see pp154–5)*. Elsewhere, there is far less going on, although Jordan's capital Amman has several busy cultural centres and cinema complexes. Down on the Red Sea coast and in Sinai, entertainment is largely limited to bars and night-clubs. Local newspapers in Jerusalem, Tel Aviv, Jodan and Sinai are generally good sources of information for entertainment in these areas.

The Israel Philharmonic Orchestra

Information

The *Jerusalem Post* and the English-language edition of the newspaper *Ha-Aretz*, both of which are available throughout Israel, carry daily entertainment listings. Both also have extensive cultural supplements on Fridays with detailed listings of events for the week to come. There is also an English-language listings magazine *Time Out Tel Aviv*, published every two months and available free at certain bars and hotels. Tourist offices *(see p293)* also have abundant events magazines.

In Jordan, look out for the *Jordan Times* and the weekly *The Star*, or, when in Amman, visit **books@cafe**, an internet café-cum-bookshop whose notice boards provide the best way of finding out what's on in the capital.

In Sinai, look out for the monthly *Egypt Today*, which carries what's on information.

Classical Music

The Israel Philharmonic, one of the world's most prestigious orchestras, is based in Tel Aviv at the **Performing Arts Centre**. The neighbouring **Tel Aviv Museum of Art** also hosts regular chamber music concerts and other classical events in its Recanati Hall. Smaller venues include the **Felicia Blumenthal Centre** and **Einav Cultural Centre**, both of which host local and international classical musicans.

In the village of Ein Kerem *(see pp142–3)* near Jerusalem, young musicians give free recitals of chamber music every Friday at noon from October to May at the Fountain of the Virgin in the **Targ Centre**. In Amman, there's the large modern **Royal Cultural Centre**, which presents a varied performance

Classical street musician

programme of traditional Arabic music, theatre and dance.

Opera

Tel Aviv's Performing Arts Centre is home to the **New Israeli Opera**, a world-class company, which puts on four or five productions a year. The centre also frequently hosts visiting productions from Europe and America.

Rock, Jazz and Blues

Even in lively Tel Aviv, the live music scene is surprisingly disppointing. Local rock bands of variable quality perform most nights at **Zappa**, **Ozen Bar**, and also at **Mike's Place**, which is a foreigner-friendly bar down on the seafront. **The Container**, in a converted industrial warehouse in Jaffa Port, plays host to a wide range of live acts, from rock 'n' roll to techno. Its striking decor includes counters and tables made from old shipping containers and graffiti art on the walls. **Barbie** is host to a range of concerts, from Israeli rock to Russian hard rock. **Cafe Henrietta**, **Shablul Jazz Club** and **HaSimta**, all of which are in central Tel Aviv, feature jazz at least one night a week. Call or see the local press for details.

In Amman, weekly concerts of very varied music are put on by **books@cafe**.

Bars and Clubs

In Tel Aviv, the main cluster of bars is in the Nakhalat Binyamin district (see p176), particularly around the southern end of Rothschild Avenue and Lillenblum. The venue that has young hipsters queuing outside every night is **Nanuchka**, a rowdy but classy bar-restaurant with surreal decor and a permanent party vibe. Around the corner, the splendidly named **Rosa Parks** is a fashionable bar with a friendly vibe. There are also plenty of good late-night spots around the Cinematheque on Ha-Arbaa Street and up in the Old Port area (see p173).

Also up at the Old Port are a couple of super clubs, including the popular **ChinChin**, which has Israeli music on Tuesday nights. However, perhaps the most fascinating and singular club is **Ha-Hamman**, a strikingly beautiful, converted Turkish bathhouse in Jaffa.

For something more casual and laid-back, there's **Mike's Place**, down near the seafront in central Tel Aviv, or **HaMinzar**, a friendly, inexpensive bar that is popular with locals and tourists alike.

In Amman, there are plenty of bars and clubs in the uptown neighbourhoods such as Abdoun and Shmeisani. One

Tel Aviv's Suzanne Dellal Centre, renowned for excellence in modern dance

of the most popular places is the **Big Fellow Irish Pub**, which is run by the Sherton group. Drinks include, of course, Guinness, and there's Guinness pie to eat. **Champions** is an American-style sports bar at the Marriott, while the **Living Room** is an attractive lounge bar with a good, American-influenced food menu.

In Petra, do not miss the chance to have a drink at **Cave Bar**, which occupies a genuine 2,000-year-old Nabataean rock tomb. There's live Bedouin music most nights too.

In Sinai, bars and clubs are generally found in the many resort hotels.

Dance

The internationally known Bat Sheva company is the mainstay

Spontaneous outdoor dancing on the beach in Sinai

of modern Israeli dance. **The Israel Ballet**, based in Tel Aviv, is the only company in Israel that performs classical and neo-classical works. Contemporary dance, however, is very much alive here. The focal point of dance activity is the **Suzanne Dellal Centre**, a superb old Ottoman building at the heart of the historic southern Tel Aviv district of Neve Tzedek, which has benefited from extensive architectural renewal. In Jerusalem, dance can be seen at the Centre for Performing Arts in the Jerusalem Sherover Theatre complex, while Jewish and Arabic folk dancing performances take place on Monday, Thursday and Saturday evenings in the **YMCA** auditorium.

In Jordan, there are two well-established national folkloric groups. Both dance at the **Royal Cultural Centre** and, occasionally, at the Roman Theatre, both in Amman (see p217). Folkloric dance also features quite heavily at the Jordan Festival (see p41).

Dining, drinking and dancing al fresco in Atarim Square, Tel Aviv

Performers at a theatre festival

Theatre

Plays in Israel are normally performed in Hebrew (or, less commonly, Arabic). Some of the bigger theatres – such as Tel Aviv's **Ha-Bima Theatre** and **New Cameri Theatre** (and Jerusalem's Sherover Theatre, *see p155*) – have headphones providing English-language translation for some perform-ances, though there are a lot of performances in English as well. Productions, in all cases, range from revivals of the classics of world drama (both old and modern) to first-run stagings of new Israeli plays.

There are several theatre festivals throughout the year in Israel (*see pp40–43*), the most exciting of which is the **Akko Fringe Theatre Festival**, which stages some performances in the city's subterranean Crusader halls.

In Amman, theatre takes place at the **Royal Cultural Centre** and the **National Centre for Culture and Arts**. However, the premier theatrical event is the **Jordan Festival** (*see p41*), which brings together performers from all over the world to present their work amid the ancient ruins.

Cinema

Foreign films shown in Israel are not dubbed, but carry Hebrew subtitles. Cinemas are plentiful, especially in Tel Aviv, where complexes such as the **Rav-Chen 1–5** are modern, comfortable and air-conditioned. They tend to screen first-run Hollywood fare. The **Cinematheques**, of which there is one in Jerusalem (*see p154*) and one in Tel Aviv, specialize in art-house and independent films, as well as holding themed seasons

and retrospectives. Israel's biggest movie theatre complex is **Cinema City** in Tel Aviv, which has 21 auditoriums and three 3D screens.

There are several modern cinemaplexes in Amman offering recent releases, including the **Grand Zara** in the Zara Centre behind the Grand Hyatt and **Galleria**. Films are shown in their original language with Arabic subtitles.

Spectator Sports

Football is by far the most popular sport throughout the Holy Land. Two teams from Jerusalem play in Israel's premier league, Beitar and Ha-Poel. Matches take place in the **Teddy Stadium** at Malcha in West Jerusalem, which was opened in 1992.

Basketball is the next most popular sport. The Jerusalem team, Ha-Poel, plays in the Sports Arena near the Teddy Stadium, while the Maccabee Tel Aviv plays at the **Yad Eliahu Arena** just off the Ayalon highway.

Football is also followed religiously in Jordan. The two main teams in Amman are Wahadat and Faisaly. Games are mostly played at the **Jordan International Stadium**, in the Shmeisani district.

A basketball match at the Yad Eliahu Arena

Swimming

Almost all the large hotels have outdoor swimming pools; the YMCA in Jerusalem also has an indoor pool. You can also swim all year round at the **Jerusalem Swimming Pool** in the German Colony district, south of the centre.

The Red Sea is warm enough for year-round swimming; most resort hotels also have swimming pools. The Mediterranean is fine in summer but too cold from around October to April.

Children

For information on Jerusalem for children, see page 154. In northern Tel Aviv, the **Ramat Gan Safari Zoo** makes a good outing for children. You can drive through and observe the wildlife in its natural habitat. The **Children's Museum**, a short drive from Tel Aviv, has lots of fun, interactive exhibits. **Mini Israel**, which is just off the main highway that runs between Jerusalem and Tel Aviv, has over 350 miniature models of the Holy Land's important landmarks. South of Jerusalem, **Chava's Farm** offers a petting zoo with farm animals, donkey rides, goat-milking sessions, a play centre for babies and toddlers and a bouncy castle. It is open in August and September, but visits at other times of the year can be arranged by phone.

Tel Aviv's beach, starting to attract swimmers in spring

DIRECTORY

Information

books@cafe
Omar Ibn Al Khattab St
12, First Circle Jebel,
Amman.
Tel (06) 465 0457.
W **booksatcafe.com**

Classical Music

Einav Cultural Centre
71 Ibn Gvirol St, Tel Aviv.
Tel (03) 521 7763.

**Felicia Blumenthal
Centre**
26 Bialik St, Tel Aviv.
Tel (03) 620 1185.
W **fbmc.co.il**

**Performing Arts
Centre**
19 Ha-Melekh Shaul
Ave, Tel Aviv.
Tel (03) 692 7777.

Royal Cultural Centre
Al-Malekah Alia St,
Shmeisani, Amman.
Tel (06) 566 1026.

Targ Centre
Ein Kerem, near Jerusalem.
Tel (02) 641 4250.

**Tel Aviv Museum
of Art**
27 Ha-Melekh Shaul
Ave, Tel Aviv.
Tel (03) 607 7020.
W **tamuseum.com**

Opera

New Israeli Opera
Performing Arts Centre,
19 Ha-Melekh Shaul Ave,
Tel Aviv.
Tel (03) 692 7777.
W **israel-opera.co.il**

Rock, Jazz and Blues

Barbie
52 Kibbutz Gayulot St, Tel
Aviv. **Tel** (03) 518 8123.

books@cafe
See Information.

Cafe Henrietta
186 Arlozorov St, Tel Aviv.
Tel (03) 691 1715.

The Container
Warehouse 2, Jaffa
Port, Tel Aviv.
Tel (03) 683 6321.
W **container.org.il**

HaSimta
8 Mazal Dagim St,
Old Jaffa, Tel Aviv.
Tel (03) 681 2126.
W **hasimta.com**

Mike's Place
86 Herbert Samuel,
Tel Aviv.
Tel (03) 510 6392.

Ozen Bar
48 King George St, Tel
Aviv. **Tel** (03) 621 5210.
W **ozenbar.com**

Shablul Jazz Club
Hangar 13, Tel Aviv Port.
Tel (03) 546 1891.

Zappa
24 Raul Wallenberg St,
Ramat HaChayal, Tel Aviv.
Tel (03) 762 6666 or
*9080.
W **zappa-club.co.il**

Bars and Clubs

Big Fellow Irish Pub
Abdoun Circle, Amman.
Tel (06) 593 4766.

Cave Bar
Behind the Visitors'
Centre, Petra.
Tel (03) 215 6266.

Champions
Amman Marriott, Isam
el-Ajlouni St, Shmeisani,
Amman.
Tel (06) 560 7607.

ChinChin
3 Ha-Taaruha St, Tel Aviv
Port. **Tel** (054) 544 8444.

Ha-Hammam
10 Mifraz Shlomo St, Jaffa.
Tel (03) 681 3261.

HaMinzar
60 Allenby St, Tel Aviv.
Tel (03) 517 3015.

Living Room
Mohammed Hussein
Heikal St, Amman.
Tel (06) 465 5998.

Mike's Place
See Rock, Jazz and Blues.

Nanuchka
30 Lilenblum St, Tel Aviv.
Tel (03) 516 2254.

Rosa Parks
265 Dizengoff St, Tel Aviv.
Tel (03) 546 0091
or (054) 663 1006.

Dance

The Israel Ballet
4 Har Nevo St, Tel Aviv.
Tel (03) 604 6610.
W **iballet.co.il**

Jordan Festival
Jerash Festival Office,
Amman, Jordan.
Tel (06) 461 3300.

Royal Cultural Centre
See Classical Music.

**Suzanne Dellal
Centre**
5 Yehieli St, Neve
Izedek, Tel Aviv.
Tel (03) 510 5656.

YMCA
King David St, Jerusalem.
Tel (02) 569 2692.

Theatre

**Akko Fringe Theatre
Festival**
Tel (04) 955 2541.

Ha-Bima Theatre
Habima Square, Tel Aviv.
Tel (03) 629 5555.
W **habima.co.il**

Jordan Festival
See Dance.

**National Centre for
Culture and Arts**
Eden Al Haitham St,
Harjan, Amman. **Tel** (06)
569 0292 W **pacjo.org**

New Cameri Theatre
30 Leonardo Da Vinci St,
Tel Aviv. **Tel** (03) 606 0960.
W **cameri.co.il**

Royal Cultural Centre
See Classical Music.

Cinema

Cinema City
Gilot Junction, Tel Aviv.
Tel (1 700) 702 255.

Galleria
Abdoun Circle,
Amman, Jordan.
Tel (06) 593 4793.

Grand Zara
3rd Circle, Jebel Amman,
Amman, Jordan.
Tel (06) 461 3200.

Rav-Chen 1–5
Dizengoff Square, Tel Aviv.
Tel (03) 528 2288.

**Tel Aviv
Cinematheque**
2 Sprinzhak St, Tel Aviv.
Tel (03) 606 0800.

Spectator Sports

**Jordan International
Stadium**
Shmeisani, Amman.

Teddy Stadium
Agudat Sport Beitar,
Malkha, West Jerusalem.
Tel (02) 545 6279.

Yad Eliahu Arena
51 Yigal Allon St, Tel Aviv.
Tel (03) 537 6376.

Swimming

**Jerusalem Swimming
Pool**
43 Emek Refaim St,
Jerusalem.
Tel (02) 563 2092.

Children

Chava's Farm
Kibbutz Chafetz Chaim.
Tel (08) 859 3876.

Children's Museum
1 Mifratz Shlomo St,
Holon, Israel.
Tel (1 599) 585 858.

Mini Israel
Kibbutz Nacsho, Latrun.
Tel (1 700) 559 559.

Ramat Gan Safari Zoo
Ramat Gan, Tel Aviv.
Tel (03) 630 5328.

Sporting and Specialist Holidays

With terrain that runs from reefs rich in marine life to sometimes snow-capped peaks, and from coniferous forests to stony desert, the region offers a wide assortment of outdoor activities. Added to this, Israel is very much an "outdoors" society. As a consequence, the region is criss-crossed with hiking trails and treks, rivers are busy with rafts and canoes, parks offer opportunities for horse riding, and deserts for exploration by camel. All this is primarily for the locals, but visitors can enjoy these facilities too.

Windsurfing between Eilat and Taba in the Gulf of Aqaba

A clown fish swims by brightly coloured soft corals

Diving

Experienced divers claim that the Red Sea offers some of the world's best diving. The various scuba diving centres in Eilat, Aqaba and, especially, Sinai organize courses for beginners, as well as for more experienced divers who wish to qualify for the various international licences. Most centres hire out all the diving equipment you need (the daily rate is about $35–50), including, if desired, underwater photographic equipment.

Although the entire Red Sea teems with marine life, some of the richest dive sites are undoubtedly those within the Ras Muhammad National Park *(see p247)*, which is close to Sharm el-Sheikh at the tip of the Sinai peninsula. Dives in the park must be organized through a dive club.

While it is possible to sort out your own diving arrange-ments with a local company once you arrive, there are also many international agencies that specialize in Red Sea diving holidays.

In Eilat, reputable diving centres include **Aqua Sport**, which organizes daily boat excursions along the Sinai coast to less-dived locations, **Divers' Village** and **Marina Divers**.

In Sinai, some of the better outfits include **INMO** and the **Nesima Dive Centre** in Dahab, and the **Camel Dive Club**, **Emperor Divers**, **Oonas Dive Centre** and **Sinai Divers** in Sharm el-Sheikh. You can visit their websites *(see p289)* for more information.

For a different kind of diving experience, **Caesarea Diving** at the Caesarea National Park *(see p180)* on Israel's Mediterranean coast offers scuba trips that allow you to explore the submerged ruins of Herod's ancient harbour.

Snorkelling

Another way of viewing the rich marine life and beauty of the reefs is to snorkel. This has the advantage of being cheap and of not requiring any complicated equipment or specialized training. Dahab and Sharm el-Sheikh in Egypt *(see p247)* are the best locations, and each has plenty of snorkel-hire shops. It is also possible to snorkel in Israel at Eilat *(see p209)* and in Jordan at Aqaba *(see p239)*.

Water Sports

The windsurfing is good in the Gulf of Aqaba, particularly on the coast between Eilat and the border at Taba; there are plenty of places to rent boards, many of them near the small marina by the Club Med hotel. The region's centre for water sports is Eilat *(see p209)*, with everything from snorkels to jet skis for hire, plus a multitude of other activities, including paragliding and glass-bottomed boat trips. Israel's Mediterranean coast is more exposed, with dangerous currents, but there are water

A diver enters the Red Sea just off Aqaba in Jordan

sports activities at Tel Aviv and a few other coastal towns, such as Netanya.

In Egypt, all the larger Sinai resorts, including Taba Heights, Dahab and Sharm el-Sheikh offer extensive water sports facilities.

Rafting and Canoeing

Possibilities exist for rafting and canoeing on the Jordan River in the Golan Heights (see p185); these activities are supervised by **Abu Kayak** in the Jordan River Park, at Tel Bethsaida.

Desert Hiking

A large number of specialist organizations lead hikes throughout Israel. A good starting point for finding out about such trips is to visit the **Society for the Protection of Nature in Israel (SPNI)**. Its offices/ bookshops in Tel Aviv and Jerusalem carry a wide range of specialized maps and useful publications. The SPNI also runs plenty of hikes itself. Some of the best routes are around Maktesh Ramon (see p208) and Ein Gedi (see p200), and up in the Golan Heights (see p185).

The best hiking in Jordan is, without doubt, in and around Wadi Rum (see p236–8). Here you'll find trails that last anything from a couple of hours to several days, all of which are described in the essential *Treks and Climbs*

Trekking through the Negev Desert in Israel

in Wadi Rum, Jordan by Tony Howard and Di Taylor. There are numerous guide agencies based in the area; some of the better ones include **Bedouin Roads**, **Terhaal**, **Sunset Camp** and **Wadi Rum Adventures**. There is also some excellent hiking around Petra (see p224–35) and at Wadi Mujib (see p201). For more on treks and hikes visit the **Wild Jordan Centre** in Amman.

While not as magnificent as Wadi Rum or Petra, Egypt's Sinai peninsula has an interior that is starkly beautiful and well worth exploring; this can be arranged at most hotels in Nuweiba, Dahab or Sharm el-Sheikh. Some of the most rewarding trekking is around the St Catherine's Monastery region (see p250–52). All treks must be done with a Bedouin guide, and this can be arranged through the services of **Sheikh Musa**, a local Bedouin leader.

Camel Trekking

One of the best ways to explore the vast sandy expanses of Wadi Rum (see p236–8) is on the back of a camel. A wide variety of treks are available, ranging from half-hour explorations to overnight expeditions. It is also possible to arrange longer camel excursions from Wadi Rum – or Petra – down to Aqaba. These take from three to six nights, depending on the route. For more details contact an agency such as **Bait Ali**, **Bedouin Roads**, **Petra Moon Tourism**, **Sunset Camp** or **Wadi Rum Adventures**.

In Israel, the **Mamshit Camel Ranch**, near Dimona on Route 25 between Beersheva and Sodom, offers desert trips on camels. In Egypt's Sinai, camel trekking can also be arranged by most hotels in Nuweiba, Dahab and Sharm el-Sheikh.

Tourists enjoying a camel trek along the rugged shoreline of Egypt's southern Sinai

Visitors passing the Bab el-Siq Triclinium en route to Petra

Climbing

Wadi Rum (see p236–8) offers some of the Holy Land's best rock climbing, with the ascent of Jebel Rum high on most climbers' lists. For information on route options see the book *Treks and Climbs in Wadi Rum, Jordan* by Tony Howard and Di Taylor (easily available in Jordan) or try the website www.wadirum.net. Several guides offer instruction in basic climbing techniques, including **Wadi Rum Mountain Guides**, which is run by Attayak Aouda, one of Rum's best climbing guides. Experienced climbers should bring their own equipment.

Jebel Umm Adaami, near the border with Saudi Arabia, is Jordan's highest peak at 1,832 m (6,045 ft). It's a fairly easy hike to the summit, plus an hour-long jeep drive each way, and you can stop off at some interesting petroglyphs and lovely scenery en route.

Rope-assisted descents of spectacular gorges in Israel's Judaean Desert can be organized by the **Metzoke Dragot Centre**. The same company also offers climbing, hiking and jeep or truck excursions into the desert.

Horse Riding

Stables and riding schools are located throughout Israel, particularly in Upper Galilee, the Golan region and on the coast between Tel Aviv and Haifa.

Vered ha-Galil, just north of the Sea of Galilee, is the largest riding school in the country, while the **Haela Ranch** is conveniently close to Jerusalem, up in the hills east of the city.

In Jordan, it is possible to explore the desert landscapes of Wadi Rum on horseback. Among the agencies who can organize this are **Bait Ali** and **Jordan Tracks**. It is also possible to ride at Petra, although this is limited to a 1 km (half a mile) canter to the site entrance.

In Sinai, several resort hotels offer horse riding by the hour, while in Dahab, Bedouin rent horses on the beach.

Golf

Israel has precisely two golf courses and, of these, the **Caesarea Golf Club** is the only one that meets international 18-hole standards. The course, designed in 1961, passes through ancient Roman and Byzantine ruins. Egypt is marketing itself as a golfing destination and it has several courses. Two of these are in Sinai: the **Jolie Ville Golf Resort** at Sharm el-Sheikh, opened in 1998, and, further north, the **Taba Heights Golf Resort**, with its views across the Red Sea to Saudia Arabia and Jordan, which opened in 2006.

Birdwatching

Israel and Sinai lie on one of the principal bird migration routes between Europe and Africa and so are something of a birdwatcher's paradise. In Israel, interested parties should visit the **International Birdwatching Centre** (see p209), which is in Eilat, near the Arava border crossing with Jordan, a short distance northeast of the town centre.

In Jordan, the Royal Society for the Conservation of Nature organizes birding trips (visit them at the **Wild Jordan Centre** in Amman), typically out to the Azraq Wetland Reserve, which is about 80 km (50 miles) east of Amman. For information on birding in Sinai, and throughout Egypt, see www.birdinginegypt.com.

Working on a Kibbutz

Not as popular as it once was, Israel's pioneering, socialist-style kibbutz movement continues to employ young volunteers (traditionally between 18 and 32, although other ages are now accepted) from abroad to carry out manual work. Typical work involves picking fruit out in the fields, working on a factory production line or being attached to a dining room, kitchen or laundry. The kibbutz will normally expect a minimum commitment of two months, during which time volunteers work for their accommodation, meals and a small personal allowance, with one day a week holiday. The kibbutz facilities are

Volunteers working on a kibbutz in northern Israel

available to volunteers; these may include such things as a swimming pool or gym.

Volunteers usually apply through a special kibbutz office in their home country, although there is also a kibbutz office in Tel Aviv, through which online applications can be made (see the directory, below).

Hammams

Hammams are what are known elsewhere as Turkish baths. At one time, every Arab town would have had several such institutions. They were as much social centres as places to get clean. The advent of domestic plumbing has rendered them largely obsolete, but a handful remain. In Amman is the grand **Hammam el-Pasha**, which has separate areas for men and woman. In Aqaba (see p239), the **Aqaba Turkish Baths** are men-only – although women may visit by special appointment, in which instance they get the whole place to themselves.

DIRECTORY

Diving and Snorkelling

Aqua Sport
Coral Beach, Eilat, Israel.
Tel (08) 633 4404.
W aqua-sport.com

Caesarea Diving
Caesarea National Park, Israel. Tel (04) 626 5898.
W caesarea-diving.com

Camel Dive Club
Sharm el-Sheikh, Egypt.
Tel (069) 360 0700.
W cameldive.com

Divers' Village
Coral Beach, Eilat, Israel.
Tel (08) 637 2268.
W diversvillage.co.il

Emperor Divers
Dahab, Nuweiba and Sharm el-Sheikh, Egypt.
Tel (012) 350 2433.
W emperordivers.com

INMO
Dahab, Egypt.
Tel (069) 364 0370.
W inmodivers.de

Marina Divers
Coral Beach, Eilat, Israel.
Tel (08) 637 6787.
W marinadivers.co.il

Nesima Dive Centre
Dahab, Egypt.
Tel (069) 364 0320.
W nesima-resort.com

Oonas Dive Centre
Dahab and Sharm el-Sheikh, Egypt.
Tel UK (01323) 648 924.
W oonasdivers.com

Sinai Divers
Dahab, Sharm el-Sheikh and Taba, Egypt.
Tel (069) 360 0697.
W sinaidivers.com

Rafting and Canoeing

Abu Kayak
Jordan River Park, Beth Saida, Israel.
Tel (04) 692 1078.
W abukayak.co.il

Desert Hiking

Bedouin Roads
Wadi Rum, Jordan.
Tel (079) 589 9723.
W bedouinroads.com

Sheik Musa
St Catherine's, Egypt.
Tel (069) 347 0457.
W sheikmousa.com

Society for the Protection of Nature in Israel (SPNI)
13 Heleni ha-Malka St, West Jerusalem. Tel (02) 624 4605. 4 Ha-Shfela St, Tel Aviv. Tel (03) 638 8688.
W teva.org.il

Sunset Camp
Wadi Rum, Jordan.
Tel (077) 731 4688.
W wadirumsunset.com

Terhaal
48 Ali Nasuh Al Tahir St, Amman, Jordan.
Tel (06) 581 3061.
W terhaal.com

Wadi Rum Adventures
Wadi Rum, Jordan.
Tel (077) 747 2074.
W wadirumadventures.com

Wild Jordan Centre
Amman, Jordan. Tel (06) 533 7931. W rscn.org.jo

Camel Trekking

Bait Ali
Wadi Rum, Jordan.
Tel (079) 554 8133.
W baitalicamp.com

Bedouin Roads
See Desert Hiking.

Mamshit Camel Ranch
Mamshit, Western Negev, Israel. Tel (08) 943 6882.
W mamshit.co.il

Petra Moon Tourism
Petra, Jordan.
Tel (03) 215 6665.
W petramoon.com

Sunset Camp
See Desert Hiking.

Wadi Rum Adventures
See Desert Hiking.

Climbing

Metzoke Dragot Centre
Metzoke Dragot, Dead Sea, Israel.
Tel (08) 622 3014.
W metzoke.co.il

Wadi Rum Mountain Guides
Wadi Rum, Jordan.
Tel (079) 583 4736.
W rumguides.com

Horse Riding

Bait Ali
See Camel Trekking.

Haela Ranch
Nes Harim, Israel.
Tel (050) 444 3902 or (050) 444 3903.

Jordan Tracks
Aqaba, Jordan.
Tel (07) 9648 2801.
W jordantracks.com

Vered ha-Galil
Korazim, 20 km (12 miles) north of Tiberias, Galilee, Israel. Tel (04) 693 5785.
W veredhagalil.co.il

Golf

Caesarea Golf Club
Caesarea, Israel.
Tel (04) 610 9600.
W caesarea.com

Jolie Ville Golf Resort
Mövenpick Resort, Sharm el-Sheikh, Egypt.
Tel (069) 360 0635.
W jolieville-hotels.com

Taba Heights Golf Resort
Taba Heights, Egypt.
Tel (069) 358 0073.
W tabaheights.com

Birdwatching

International Birdwatching Centre
Near Arava Crossing, Eilat, Israel. Tel (050) 767 1290.
W eilat-birds.org

Wild Jordan Centre
See Desert Hiking.

Working on a Kibbutz

Kibbutz Programme Centre
6 Frishmann St, Tel Aviv, Israel.
Tel (03) 524 6154.
W kibbutz.org.il

Hammams

Aqaba Turkish Baths
King Hussein St, Aqaba, Jordan.
Tel (03) 203 1605.

Hammam el-Pasha
El-Mahmoud Taha St, Jebel Amman, Amman, Jordan.
Tel (06) 463 3002.
W pashaturkishbath.com

SURVIVAL GUIDE

PRACTICAL INFORMATION

The area covered by this guide is not very large, but because it includes the territory of three nations (Israel, Jordan and Egypt), as well as the Autonomous Palestinian Territories, getting about from one place to another may not always be straightforward. The political situation in this region is volatile, and you should make sure that there have been no significant changes to the international agreements between these countries before embarking on a trip that involves any crossing of borders. Israel, Jordan and Egypt all have their own tourist organizations, which have offices abroad (see p295 for the relevant contact details).

The King Hussein Bridge, one of the crossings between Israel and Jordan

When to Go

The region can be visited all year round, though July and August are unbearably hot. Egypt has virtually no rainfall at all, while Israel experiences some rain in winter, and the hilly regions of Jordan can see significant downpours (Dec–Mar). Winter nights can be cold throughout the region.

In Israel, religious holidays affect availability and prices. At Easter, accommodation in Jerusalem can be hard to find, so advance booking is essential.

Crossing Borders

There are three land border crossings between Jordan and Israel. The King Hussein Bridge crossing (also known as Allenby Bridge) is 16 km (10 miles) east of Jericho; the Wadi Arava, or Yitzhak Rabin Terminal, is 4 km (2 miles) from Eilat and 10 km (6 miles) from Aqaba; and the Sheikh Hussein Crossing, or Jordan River Border Terminal, is near Beth Shean in the north of Israel. Visit www.iaa.gov.il for opening times. Note that there

are hefty Israeli exit and Jordanian entry taxes to pay. Israeli fees can be paid online (www.clp.co.il).

To enter Sinai, you can take the ferry or catamaran departing every morning from Aqaba in Jordan to Nuweiba. You can also use the 24-hour border crossing overland from Israel at Taba.

Strict security measures are in place at all borders, so allow up to 2 hours for crossing. All borders are closed on Yom Kippur and the Muslim Feast of Sacrifice, except for Wadi Arava and Sheik Hussein, which are closed on the Muslim New Year. The King Hussein Bridge is also closed on Israeli holidays and some Islamic festivals.

Visas for Israel

Visitors must have a passport valid for at least six months. A visa is not required for citizens of Europe, North America, most South American countries, Australia and New Zealand. Visitors from most Arab, African and Asian countries do need visas and must obtain them from an Israeli consulate in their home country in advance. Visas are usually valid for three months.

Note that an Israeli stamp in your passport will bar you from entering some Arab countries, notably Syria and Lebanon. To avoid this, visitors are now given an entry card instead of an entry stamp on arrival at the airport and at land borders. However, it is important to confirm this with your consulate. A stamped passport facilitates the crossing of checkpoints when visiting the Palestinian Territories. At checkpoints between Israel and the Palestinian Territories, the police will examine your passport thoroughly and may carry out security checks.

Visas for Jordan

To enter Jordan you must have a passport valid for at least six months. You can obtain a single-entry tourist visa (US$30) upon arrival at Queen Alia airport; valid for one month. One-month visas are also issued at the Wadi Arava and Sheikh Hussein crossings. If entering Jordan at the King Hussein Bridge, you must obtain your visa in advance from the Jordanian consulate in your own country, Tel Aviv or Cairo. The fee to cross here is almost twice that at other crossings. Six-month multiple-entry visas must be arranged in advance.

Entry card for Israel, and visa required to enter Jordan

Visas for Egypt

A free 14-day Sinai Permit (for the Gulf of Aqaba coast and St Catherine's Monastery) is available at the Taba border for those travelling from Israel. If you plan to visit other parts of Egypt, you need a full visa, issued on the same day by the Egyptian consulate in Eilat. You can also get a Sinai permit on the boat from Aqaba or buy a full visa when you disembark at Nuweiba. Alternatively, you can arrange for a visa in advance from the Egyptian embassy in your home country, or in Amman, Aqaba, Tel Aviv or Eilat.

Travel Safety Advice

Visitors can get up-to-date travel safety information from the Foreign and Commonwealth Office in the UK, the State Department in the US and the Department of Foreign Affairs and Trade in Australia. Be sure to check the latest information and any warnings, particularly for the Sinai region.

Customs

The duty-free allowance in Israel is 250 cigarettes and 1 litre of spirits or 2 litres of wine. In Egypt and Jordan it is 200 cigarettes and 1 litre of alcohol (2 litres in Egypt). Valuable electrical items might be entered in your passport by customs officers to prevent them from being resold.

Tourist Information

Israeli tourist offices have brochures and maps, and can often help with finding accommodation. The sole information office covering the Palestinian Territories is in Bethlehem The only information offices in Jordan are in the main tourist destinations (Amman, Petra and Jerash); in Sinai there is one in Sharm el-Sheikh.

Admission Prices

Most archaeological sites in Jerusalem have an admission charge, while the majority of

Arab women in customary dress outside the Dome of the Rock, Jerusalem

religious sites ask for a small donation. In Israel, admission prices vary from NIS 10 to NIS 50. The 14-day Green Card (about NIS 150) allows for free entry to 65 different sites run by the **Israel Nature and Parks Authority**; a cheaper Green Card (NIS 105) allows access to any six of these sites.

Opening Hours

Because of the many religious holidays in the region (see pp40 43), opening hours for tourist sites vary greatly. As a rule, Jewish sites in Israel are open daily, except for Friday, when they keep restricted hours, and Saturday, when they are closed. Christian sites other than churches are closed on Sundays, while Muslim sites are closed on Fridays. Secular Israeli sites might be open on Saturdays but have a day's holiday during the week.

Petra, Jerash and other main sites in Jordan are open daily, but smaller sites and many museums close on Tuesdays. Some shops are closed on Fridays and Saturdays. Friday is the usual closing day in Egypt.

Language

In Israel all signs are bilingual (Hebrew/English), and most people speak some English.

In tourist areas in the Palestinian Territories, Sinai and Jordan, it is easy to find English speakers, though attempts to speak Arabic are appreciated. In more remote areas, it can be harder to get your message across without a basic grasp of the language. However, the

locals will try to communicate, even if it means resorting to sign language.

Etiquette

Israeli society is not that different from the West, except for ultra-Orthodox areas such as Jerusalem's Mea Shearim (see p129), where women should wear long skirts, long sleeves and high necklines, and men should wear long trousers and sleeves. Behaviour and dress should err on the side of conservatism in the Palestinian Territories and Jordan too. Muslim women usually cover their arms, legs and often their head in public, and men do not wear shorts. Visitors must be suitably attired in certain public places and at any holy site. In synagogues, mosques and churches, legs and shoulders must be fully covered. Cloaks may be provided for visitors who are deemed to be immodestly dressed. Remove your shoes before entering a mosque, and cover your head if you are a woman. At some Jewish holy sites, such as the Western Wall, men must cover their head. A paper kippah (skullcap) will be provided.

Smoking is banned in restaurants and bars in Israel, but in other areas of the region, cigarettes and nargilehs (water pipes) are ubiquitous. Intimate physical contact is taboo in Arab areas, with the exception of some Sinai beaches; Arabic couples are rarely seen even holding hands. In the region, photography at certain places, such as bridges and military installations, is prohibited.

Public Conveniences

Public toilets of the standard type found in the West are easily found throughout Israel. In Jordan they are much less common and a lot more rudimentary, but usually clean. In Sinai public toilets do not exist at all. It is wise to have a supply of tissue with you, since this is rarely supplied. Except in Israel, dispose of all paper using the bins provided, rather than by flushing it down the toilet, as the local plumbing cannot cope.

Taxes and Tipping

In Israel, it is standard to leave a 10–15 per cent tip in restaurants (depending on the level of service). VAT is added on to food bills, and some restaurants also add "security charges" that cover the cost of hiring armed guards. It is a nice gesture to leave a tip of around NIS 5 a day for cleaning staff in a hotel. Note that you are exempt from VAT on your hotel bill if you pay with a foreign currency – this can save nearly 20 per cent.

In Jordan, mid-range and expensive restaurants often add a 10 per cent service tax on top of the 16 per cent government tax. Cheaper places leave the tip up to you, 10 per cent being the norm. In Egypt, taxes adding up to 25 per cent are added to most restaurant bills, and it is customary to leave a further 10 per cent.

Travellers with Special Needs

In Israel many hotels, sites and museums are adapted for disabled use. The streets of Jerusalem's Old City are not easy to navigate, but there is a wheelchair route starting from Jaffa Gate. City buses have fold-out ramps, and the Light Rail is wheelchair-friendly too, with station platforms at the same height as the tram doors. Most stations on the Israeli train network have disabled

Caesarea National Park *(see p180)* has disabled access

access, and many national parks have wheelchair routes – even Masada is accessible. **Access Israel** is a website that lists suitable hotels, accessible sites and car-rental agencies, while **Yad Sarah** loans wheelchairs and other aids at no cost; it can also arrange airport pick-ups. **Mobility Rentals** delivers equipment to hotels and the airport.

Only luxury hotels in Jordan and Sinai are equipped for the disabled. Most sites are in rough terrain, so visits can be difficult, though parts of Petra are accessible by horse and carriage. In Sinai some dive centres, such as **Camel Dive**, make provisions for disabled divers. Locals are very willing to help out with any lifting.

Travelling with Children

Children are welcome at most hotels and restaurants. High chairs and baby-changing facilities are widely available, and it is easy to find familiar, unspiced food. In Israel, many museums provide useful educational materials for kids, and playgrounds proliferate in residential areas. It is best to get away from the cities and discover castles, tunnels and beaches that keep children enthralled.

The main downside is the extreme heat of summer; sunscreen and hats are necessary at all times.

Gay and Lesbian Travellers

Tel Aviv is a popular gay destination, with a Pride Parade each June and many gay-friendly events, clubs and restaurants. For local listings, consult **Gay TLVGuide** and **Gay Tel Aviv**. The scene in Jerusalem is much smaller, and conservative religious attitudes in the city mean same-sex couples can face discrimination in public. However, it still boasts a solid LGBT community and an annual gay pride parade. **Jerusalem Open House** works to promote pride within the gay and lesbian community.

In Palestinian areas, Jordan and Sinai, homosexuality is not tolerated. Appropriate behaviour is strongly advised.

Travelling on a Budget

Jerusalem and Tel Aviv are good for dormitory beds. Away from the major cities, lodgings in Israel can be expensive; however, **ILH – Israel Hostels** has more than 30 members providing shared rooms and kitchen facilities. Volunteering in a hostel is another option for cash-strapped travellers.

It is easier to travel on a budget in Jordan and, easiest of all, in Sinai, where beach huts can cost less than US$5.

In Israel, a recognized student card such as the **ISIC** (International Student Identity Card) allows discounts on most museum and sites, as well as 10 per cent off train fares. Egypt offers students 50 per cent off most site admissions, but student discounts do not exist in Jordan.

International Student Identity Card

Women Travellers

In Israel and the Palestinian Territories, lone females are sometimes subjected to verbal harassment from local males. This problem is most acute in

East Jerusalem and in the Old City and surrounding areas, such as the Mount of Olives. Incidences of rape have even been reported. Women should not walk alone in quiet or secluded areas after dark.

On Sinai's beaches and in tourist areas of Jordan, lone women may receive unwanted attention from men. Politely and firmly refuse any inappropriate suggestions; the tourist police are never far away should someone prove persistent.

Time

The time in Israel, Jordan and Egypt is 2 hours ahead of Greenwich Mean Time (GMT) and 7 hours ahead of Eastern Standard Time (EST). All three countries have daylight saving time (March–September).

A stall selling fruit and fruit juices on Shenkin Street, Tel Aviv

Electrical Adaptors

The electric current in Israel, Jordan and Sinai is 220V. Plugs in Israel are round-pronged and three-pinned, whereas in Jordan and Sinai they are round-pronged and two-pinned. It is a good idea to buy a good-quality adaptor prior to departure.

Responsible Travel

Awareness of green issues is growing in Israel, and plastic and paper recycling bins are common in residential areas. The weekly farmers' markets in East and West Jerusalem, Tel Aviv and other towns are good places to buy local products and support small-scale industries. There are also a number of eco-lodges and country cabins, and **Kibbutz Lotan** in the Negev offers a fully "green" experience.

"Wild Jordan", the tourism wing of the **Royal Society for the Conservation of Nature (RSCN)**, offers environmentally friendly tours and eco-quest houses. In Sinai, **Sheikh Sina Bedouin Treks** works with local Bedouin communities to run trekking excursions that respect the delicate mountain environment.

DIRECTORY

Embassies and Consulates

IN EGYPT

UK Embassy
7 Ahmed Ragheb St, Garden City, Cairo.
Tel (02) 2791 6000.
w gov.uk/government/world/egypt

US Embassy
5 Latin America (Tawfik Diah) St, Garden City, Cairo.
Tel (02) 2797 3300.
w egypt.usembassy.gov

IN ISRAEL

UK Consulate
19 Nashashibi St, Sheikh Jarah, East Jerusalem.
Tel (02) 541 4100.
w gov.uk/government/world/the-occupied-palestinian-territories

UK Embassy
1 Ben Yehuda St, Tel Aviv.
Tel (03) 725 1222.
w gov.uk/government/world/israel

US Consulate
18 Agron St, West Jerusalem. **Tel** (02) 622 7230. w jerusalem.usconsulate.gov

US Embassy
71 Ha-Yarkon St, Tel Aviv.
Tel (03) 519 7475/7551.
w israel.usembassy.gov

IN JORDAN

UK Embassy
Damascus St, Abdoun Amman.
Tel (06) 590 9200.
w gov.uk/government/world/jordan

US Embassy
Al-Umawayeen St, Abdoun, Amman.
Tel (06) 590 6950.
w jordan.usembassy.gov

Tourist Information

Egyptian Tourist Authority
UK: **Tel** (020) 7493 5283.
US: **Tel** (212) 332 2570.
w egypt.travel

Israel Ministry of Tourism
UK: **Tel** (020) 7299 1100.
US: **Tel** (212) 499 5650.
w goisrael.com

Jordan Tourist Board
UK: **Tel** (020) 7233 1878.

US: **Tel** (212) 949 0060.
w visitjordan.com

Palestinian Authority
Tel (02) 274 1581/2/3.
w travelpalestine.ps

Admission Prices

Israel Nature and Parks Authority
Tel *3639.
w parks.org.il

Travellers with Special Needs

Access Israel
Tel (09) 745 8080.
w aisrael.org

Camel Dive
Sharm el-Sheikh, Sinai.
Tel (069) 360 0700.
w cameldive.com

Mobility Rentals
Tel (03) 948 0401.
w mobilityrentalsisrael.com

Yad Sarah
124 Herzl Blvd, Jerusalem.
Tel (02) 644 4633.
w yadsarah.org

Gay and Lesbian Travellers

Gay Tel Aviv
w gay-tel-aviv.com

Gay TLVGuide
w gaytlvguide.com

Jerusalem Open House
w joh.org.il

Travelling on a Budget

ILH – Israel Hostels
w hostels-israel.com

ISIC
w isic.org

Responsible Travel

Kibbutz Lotan
Negev, Israel.
w kibbutzlotan.com

Royal Society for the Conservation of Nature (RSCN)
w rscn.org.jo

Sheikh Sina Bedouin Treks
St Catherine's, South Sinai.
w sheikhsina.com

Security and Health

Travel in Israel and the Middle East requires you to keep well informed about the current security situation. Political unrest in the region has at times resulted in acts of terrorism or rioting, and although this hardly ever affects tourists, it is wise to avoid any areas that are considered sensitive. Visitors rarely encounter crime, and there are next to no hazards in the form of dangerous animals or endemic diseases.

Israeli Defence Force soldiers at Damascus Gate

a year until the age of 40. Consequently, you will see armed soldiers around all the time, particularly at bus stations at weekends, when they are on the way to or from their bases.

Law and Order

Israel, Jordan and Sinai all have special tourist police, posted at major sites and resorts, to deal with any issues visitors may encounter. Most of these officers, who wear identifying armbands, speak English. The Jordanians also have a special form of tourist police, known as the Desert Patrol, in the Wadi Rum area. These officials are identified by their smart khaki uniforms, red-and-white checked headdress and by the fact that they often ride camels.

Regular Israeli police wear dark navy-blue uniforms and peaked caps. The border police, who wear a grey military-style uniform and a green beret, operate in the most sensitive areas of the country. The Palestinians have their own security forces, who come in many guises and maintain security within the Palestinian Territories.

Visitors will notice a large presence of military personnel on the streets in Israel. Every citizen (except Arabs and Orthodox Jews) must perform military service in the Israeli Defence Force (IDF) when they turn 18. The term of service is three years for men and two for women. Men serve for an additional 30 days (or less)

Personal Safety

As far as visitors are concerned, terrorism is not a major worry. Tourists have never been the target of terrorists, and most attacks have occurred well away from tourist sites. Naturally, you should be alert when in the streets, and also keep an eye on the local news. Among the most sensitive areas are the Haram esh-Sharif, West Bank towns such as Hebron, the Sinai coast and all border areas.

In Israel, you may have to undergo security checks on entering hotels, restaurants, bars, cinemas and malls. At the bus stations in Jerusalem and Tel Aviv, bags are searched or

A member of the Desert Patrol in Wadi Rum, Jordan

scanned. At many hotels in Sharm el-Sheikh, visitors are screened on entry. Always carry some identification with you, preferably your passport; indeed, it is essential to do so if you wish to enter the Palestinian Territories. Note that trouble often flares up on Friday after the noon prayers. Also be aware that you should not drive in ultra-Orthodox areas during Shabbat, when you risk stones being thrown at your vehicle. Should you be unlucky enough to come across a disturbance in the streets, move away from the scene quickly, and make it clear that you are a foreign tourist.

Security considerations mean that you should never leave your luggage unattended (especially in airports and bus stations), since it might cause alarm or trigger a reaction on the part of the security forces. Do not accept packages from anyone asking you to carry something for them.

Thefts, muggings and other similar opportunistic crimes are rare in the region. As a rule, all areas are considered safe for visitors, unless the visitor is an unaccompanied woman (see pp294–5).

Israeli policeman

In an Emergency

In an emergency in Israel, you can call 101 to request an ambulance or ask about the nearest casualty department. For the police, dial 100, and for the fire brigade, 102.

In Jordan, for ambulance and fire brigade services, call 199; for the police, 191. In Sinai, the number is 123 for an ambulance and 122 for the police. However, note that in both Jordan and Sinai the emergency services cannot be entirely relied upon, and you are probably better off taking a taxi to the hospital in a medical emergency.

Lost and Stolen Property

On the whole, Israelis and Arabs are very honest people. If you lose anything, it is always worth going back to the place the item was last seen or to the tourist police. Avoid leaving valuable objects in full view in your hotel room; put them in the hotel safe or leave them at the reception desk. Do not leave any items of value inside a car, particularly throughout the Negev, where break-ins are common. In the event of theft, contact the police and ask for a copy of the report. You will have to present this to your insurance company when you make your claim.

Hospitals and Pharmacies

The standard of care in Israeli hospitals is similar to that of other Western countries. In Sinai, Sharm el-Sheikh has a modern hospital, and in Jordan there are good private hospitals in Amman; Petra and Aqaba have government hospitals nearby, although you are advised not to use these. In Jordan, if you need a doctor, call into a pharmacy and ask for a recommendation, or call your embassy. Large hotels will also be able to direct you to a doctor. In Sinai, most large hotels have a resident doctor. For divers, the **Hyperbaric Medical Centre** in Sharm el-Sheikh is equipped with a recompression chamber.

Good pharmacies are easy to find in the region. If you need a specific medicine, it is wise to travel with your own supplies and keep a note of the product and its composition so that, if necessary, a pharmacist will be able to find a local equivalent. In Israel, the *Jerusalem Post* lists pharmacies that stay open late and during Shabbat and other holidays.

A small, well-stocked pharmacy in Jerusalem

Minor Hazards

No vaccinations are required before entering Israel, Jordan and Sinai, but doctors may advise inoculation against hepatitis A and B, tetanus and typhoid. There are no particular endemic diseases in the Middle East, but it is wise to take certain precautions, at least until you get used to the change in the diet. Drink mineral water (widely available), avoid food that has obviously been left standing for some time, and always peel fruit. In Jordan and Sinai, it is also sensible to avoid raw vegetables and not to use ice in your drinks. Always carry diarrhoea tablets, and consult a doctor or pharmacist if an upset stomach continues. Drinking large quantities of liquids is essential; the lack of humidity in the air causes rapid dehydration, even though you may not be aware of it.

Mosquitoes can sometimes be a nuisance, but there is no threat of malaria in the area. If you go diving in the Red Sea, be careful of sharp corals and be aware of which species of fish are poisonous and hence to be avoided.

Pharmacy sign in Israel

Israeli ambulance

Travel Insurance

When taking out travel insurance, consider the level of coverage provided for flight delays or cancellations, loss or theft of luggage, and dental expenses. Medical care in Israel is very costly, so do not travel without medical insurance. In Jordan and Sinai private medical treatment can be expensive. Your policy should cover at least the cost of repatriation. If travelling to remote or high-risk areas, consider a policy that covers emergency evacuation too.

Banking and Currency

Obtaining and exchanging money pose no problems in Israel, Jordan and Egypt. Credit cards are widely accepted in the main tourist destinations, and ATM machines are widespread and reliable. Cash and travellers' cheques can be exchanged at banks, exchange offices and in many hotels. The only issues to be aware of are the greatly varying levels of commission charged on transactions, and the limited opening hours of banks.

Official money exchange office in Jerusalem

Banks and Exchange Offices

Banks in Israel, Jordan and Sinai will exchange all major European currencies, but the most welcome is the US dollar. Be aware that banks tend to give the worst exchange rates for both cash and travellers' cheques while charging the highest commission. It is better to use one of the many exchange offices, such as **Change Point** and **Change Spot**, or a post office, as these do not charge commission at all.

Jerusalem's banking district is centred on Zion Square in the New City. There are several Arab exchange offices around Damascus Gate where it is

Automated teller machine (ATM) at an Israeli bank

possible to buy Jordanian dinars; however, Egyptian pounds are available only at the border. Western Union money-transfer facilities can be found in any post office.

In Israel, banks are generally open from 9am to 1pm, reopening for another hour from 4pm on Mondays and Thursdays. They are shut on Fridays and Saturdays, as are banks in Jordan. In Sinai, banking hours are similar to Israel, except that they are closed only on Fridays.

ATMs

Automated teller machines (ATMs), or cash dispensers, linked into international banking networks such as Cirrus, Maestro or PLUS can be found throughout Israel. Many ATMs will also dispense US dollars or euros, although exchange rates tend to be poor.

ATMs are less common in Jordan and Sinai, but all major tourist destinations have a reliable cash dispenser either within a high-end hotel or inside a shopping complex. English is always available as an on-screen language.

Credit and Debit Cards

Major credit cards, such as VISA, MasterCard, Diners Club and American Express, are widely accepted throughout Israel in shops, restaurants and hotels.

In Jordan and Sinai, most large hotels, expensive restaurants and some travel agents accept credit cards, but if you travel to smaller towns, be sure to have a decent supply of cash with you.

Debit cards are rarely used in the region at point of sale, although they can be used in ATMs in towns and cities.

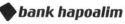

Logo of Bank Hapoalim

Currency

The national currency of Israel is the New Israeli shekel (NIS), referred to simply as the shekel. This is also the currency in the Autonomous Palestinian Territories, although a Palestinian national currency may be introduced in the future.

Jordan's currency is the dinar (JD), while in Sinai they use the Egyptian pound (LE). Note that these currencies are valid only in their home countries so, for example, it is not possible to spend excess Israeli shekels in Jordan. In addition, exchange rates between the three tend to be extremely bad. As a result, it is wise to use up all your shekels before leaving Israel and then to exchange dollars for dinars or pounds upon arriving in Jordan or Egypt.

Israeli Bank Notes

Israeli bank notes come in four different denominations: 20, 50, 100 and 200 NIS.

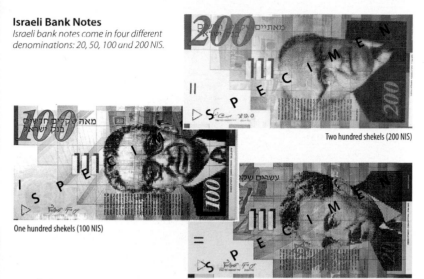

Two hundred shekels (200 NIS)

One hundred shekels (100 NIS)

Twenty shekels (20 NIS)

Israeli Coins

The shekel is divided into 100 agorot. There are coins to the value of 1, 2, 5 and 10 shekels, as well as 10 and 50 agorot.

Ten shekels

Five shekels

One shekel

Fifty agorot

Ten agorot

Jordanian Currency

The Jordanian dinar is divided into 1,000 fils and, confusingly, also 100 piastres (100 fils therefore equals 10 piastres). Notes come in denominations of 1, 5, 10, 20 and 50 dinars. Coins exist to the value of 5, 10, 25 and 50 piastres.

20 dinars

10 dinars

5 dinars

Egyptian Currency

The Egyptian pound is divided into 100 piastres. Notes come in denominations of LE 5, 10, 20, 50, 100 and 200. The 25- and 50-piastre notes have now been replaced by coins. Coins also exist to the value of 10, 20 and 50 piastres and one Egyptian pound (LE 1).

Ten Egyptian pounds (LE 10)

Five Egyptian pounds (LE 5)

Communication and Media

Visitors who plan to use their mobile phone while in Israel, Jordan and Egypt should check with their home service provider that it will work in the region. In all three countries, Wi-Fi connection is common in hotels and restaurants, which also makes it is easy to keep in touch with home via Skype. Israel's postal service is generally efficient, but letters to Europe and North America can still take a week or longer to arrive. The Jordanian and Egyptian postal systems are rather unpredictable.

A Jordanian man using a mobile phone in the desert

Telephoning in Israel and the Palestinian Territories

Visitors can rent mobile phones with local SIM cards from **IsraelPhones** at Ben Gurion Airport; the company also delivers rental phones to any location in the country. Rental rates start at US$1 per day, plus the cost of calls. If your phone is unlocked, you can buy a local SIM card and then pay as you go using top-up vouchers. Israeli networks, such as Orange and Cellcom, have coverage that extends to the Palestinian Territories. Likewise, Jawwal, the main Palestinian network provider, has coverage in Israel.

Israel's public telephones are operated by the national phone company, Bezek. They take prepaid phonecards, which are sold at post offices and shops. Palestinians in the West Bank have their own telephone network with their own phonecards; these do not work in Israel.

If you wish to dial abroad using Bezek (from a mobile, landline or public telephone), the international access code

is 014. Bezek competes with other telephone companies, including Golden Lines (012 to dial abroad) and Barak (013 to dial abroad). These rival services are often cheaper than Bezek, although charges also depend on the country you are calling.

Telephoning in Jordan and Sinai

As yet, it is not possible to rent a mobile phone during your stay in Jordan or Egypt. Pay-as-you-go SIM cards are a good and affordable alternative, though.

In Jordan, Umniah, Orange and Zain are the main network providers. International calls can also be made from one of the many unofficial telephone bureaux. Simply write down the number, and the desk clerk will make the call for you. These calls are charged by the minute and rates are reasonable. There are no public phones using phonecards in Jordan.

In Sinai, there are numerous shops and kiosks promoting local network providers Etisalat, Vodafone and Mobinil, and selling SIM cards. A SIM costs as little as US$1, and you can buy credit with vouchers (a small commission is often charged) or electronically. Public telephones that use phonecards are rare. Many hotels can provide an international line, but this is very expensive.

Internet

There are few Internet cafés in Israel. This is both because most Israeli families have Internet access at home, and because of the availability of free Wi-Fi hook-up in so many places, including Ben Gurion Airport *(see p302)*. Tel Aviv has entire streets where Wi-Fi is provided free of charge to residents and passers-by. Most hotels have either wireless access or computers available. Internet cafés are more prevalent, and significantly cheaper, in Palestinian areas.

books@cafe is an excellent Internet centre in the heart of Amman. There are also Internet cafés at Wadi Musa (Petra), Madaba and Aqaba. In Sinai, it is easy to find Internet cafés in Sharm el-Sheikh. Internet services are also available at many cafés in Dahab, Nuweiba and St Catherine's, and at many hotels. Online time is usually charged by the half-hour. Wi-Fi is also very common.

Logo of network provider Orange

Postal Services

Using the offices of **Israel Post** to send regular mail is straightforward. However, sending parcels or bulky items entails a series of security inspections. Depending on the branch, Israeli post offices have different opening hours, but all are closed during Shabbat. Postal rates vary according to the type of post and its weight, but a standard airmail letter to Europe or the

US costs the equivalent of US$1. For postal information in Israel, call 171. The Palestinian Authority has its own separate postal service for Gaza and the West Bank and issues its own stamps, but it is not as efficient as the Israeli service.

A letter posted in Jordan can take up to two weeks to reach Europe and a month for the US. Posting your letters at a five-star hotel or a main post office, rather than at a post box on the street, can help to speed things up. Jordanian post offices are closed on Fridays. Post from Sinai is also most easily sent from large hotels; stamps can be bought at shops and kiosks.

A typical post box

airport and in many hotels, has good insider information – particularly on Tel Aviv. The monthly *This Week in Palestine*, available in East Jerusalem and Arab parts of the Old City, lists events and activities taking place in the Palestinian areas. In Jordan, look out for the *Jordan Times*, published daily except for Fridays, and the weekly English-language *The Star*, published on Thursdays. Foreign newspapers and magazines are widely available, and they are usually just one or two days old. In Sinai, international newspapers are sold by shops and street vendors in Sharm el-Sheikh, and there are daily Egyptian English-language newspapers too.

Newspapers and Magazines

English-language readers are well catered for in Israel. The leading English-language publication is the daily *Jerusalem Post* (available online at www.jpost.com), which has no Saturday edition. *Haaretz* (www.haaretz.com) is the oldest national daily newspaper in Israel, with an English insert distributed inside the *International Herald Tribune*. Both *Haaretz* and the *Jerusalem Post* are worth picking up on Fridays for their extensive cultural supplements and entertainment listings. *Time Out Israel*, a free monthly magazine available at the

Television and Radio

Israeli TV has one state channel that shows a number of subtitled English-language programmes. Most hotels offer satellite channels showing movies and sports, as well as BBC, Sky News and CNN.

In Jordan, Channel 2 devotes plenty of screen time to US programmes, and it has English-language news nightly at 10pm. Most hotels have satellite TV, offering a wide choice of programmes.

Israel Radio is the national radio station. It broadcasts news in English each weekday at 6:30am and 8:30pm. In addition, there are various independent and army radio stations.

DIRECTORY

Telephone Prefixes

IN EGYPT
Country code: 20. Sharm el-Sheikh, Dahab, St Catherine's: 069.

IN ISRAEL
Country code: 972.
Jerusalem: 02. Tel Aviv: 03.
Haifa and the Northern Coast: 04.
Galilee and the Golan Heights: 04.
Negev and the Dead Sea: 08.
Coast south of Tel Aviv: 08.
Coast north of Tel Aviv: 09.

IN JORDAN
Country code: 962. Amman: 06.
Jerash: 02. Kerak, Petra, Aqaba: 03.

IN PALESTINIAN TERRITORIES
Country code: 972 (or 970 from some Arab countries). Bethlehem, Hebron, Jericho, Ramallah: 02.

Telephoning in Israel and the Palestinian Territories

IsraelPhones
w israelphones.com

Internet

IN ISRAEL

Change Internet
112 Dizengoff, Tel Aviv.
Tel (03) 529 1618.

Internet Café
31 Jaffa St, Jerusalem.
Tel (02) 622 3377.

IN JORDAN

books@cafe
Omar Ibn Al Khattab St 12,
First Circle Jebel, Amman.
Tel (06) 465 0457.

Friends Café
Off El-Yarmouk St, Madaba.

IN SINAI

Cyber Café
Hilton Sharm El Sheikh Fayrouz
Resort, Naama Day.
Tel (069) 360 0136.

Postal Services

Israel Post
w israelpost.co.il

A newsagent's shop in Tiberias, Israel

TRAVEL INFORMATION

The easiest way to reach the region is to fly direct. Jerusalem is served by Ben Gurion Airport, and there are also international airports at Eilat in Israel, Amman in Jordan, and Sharm el-Sheikh and Taba in Sinai. There are numerous daily flights to Ben Gurion and, with the area being a busy tourist destination,

it is possible to get cheap deals, especially if you are prepared to travel with a smaller, lesser-known airline, or take advantage of a charter package. There are currently no sailings to Israel from Europe, and travelling overland is an arduous business since all European trains terminate at Istanbul.

Arrival hall of Terminal 3 at Ben Gurion, Israel's main international airport

Flying to Israel

The Israeli national airline is **El Al**, which has direct flights to **Ben Gurion Airport** from most major European cities, as well as New York, Los Angeles and Toronto. Ben Gurion is also served by foreign airlines such as **Air France**, **Alitalia**, **British Airways**, **Lufthansa**, **Swissair**, **American Airlines**, **KLM** and **Delta**, and some low-cost airlines, notably **easyJet**. The high season is during the Jewish and Christian holiday periods, especially Rosh ha-Shanah, Passover and Easter *(see pp40–43)*. At such times fares are at a premium, and it can be hard to find seats.

It is always worth looking into flights to Eilat's **Ovda Airport**. This caters mostly to charter flights, which tend to have the cheapest fares. The drawbacks are that there are often restrictions on the dates you may travel and you have to make your own way up to Jerusalem and back, a bus journey of almost 5 hours each way.

Ben Gurion Airport

Ben Gurion Airport is located at Lod, about 22 km (14 miles) southeast of Tel Aviv and

45 km (28 miles) northwest of Jerusalem. Most international flights arrive at and depart from Terminal 3, where services include duty-free shops, cafés and restaurants, foreign currency exchange offices, phone-rental outlets, car-hire firms and tourist information and hotel reservation desks. The older Terminal 1 is used for domestic flights to Eilat, Haifa and Rosh Pina and for the check-in of a few low-cost international airlines.

Ben Gurion reputedly has the tightest security of any airport in the world. The time taken to thoroughly inspect every item of luggage means that passengers must check in at the airport at least 3 hours before departure.

Getting to and from Ben Gurion Airport

To travel from the airport to your destination, you can take a private taxi or a *sherut* (shared taxi, *see p309*), which is much cheaper. Private taxis take about 30 minutes to reach Tel Aviv. *Sheruts* leave from just outside the arrivals hall and set off once an hour or when full. They run through the night and during Shabbat, and will drop off passengers anywhere in the city. A *sherut* service also goes to Haifa, in the north.

A 24-hour train service links Ben Gurion to Tel Aviv, with connections to all four stations in the city. From the railway stations, taxis, *sheruts* or buses can take you on to a hotel.

To get to the airport from Jerusalem, book either a taxi or the **Nesher** *sherut* service the day before departure. Hotels can usually organize this; alternatively, call the number for licensed taxis at Ben Gurion Airport direct.

Flying to Jordan and Sinai

Jordan's main airport is **Queen Alia International Airport**. The national carrier,

El Al aeroplane taking off

Royal Jordanian Airlines, has direct services between Amman and most major European capitals, as well as New York, Chicago, Detroit and Montreal. Other major carriers flying into Amman include Air France, **BMI** and **Emirates**. Marka Airport, located about 5 km (3 miles) east of Amman, handles flights to Egypt, Aqaba and a few destinations in the Middle East. A third airport about 10 km (6 miles) north of Aqaba receives very few international flights. Flights to Amman are expensive; it is cheaper to fly into Ben Gurion or Eilat and take a bus across the border.

Sharm el-Sheikh Airport lies about 17 km (11 miles) north of town, connected by minibus and taxi. Several low-cost airlines fly from Europe to Sharm el-Sheikh. The international airport at Taba, 35 km (22 miles) from the

Outside the departure lounge of Sharm el-Sheikh Airport

border with Israel, is chiefly used by package tours and a few charter flights from Europe.

Getting to and from Queen Alia Airport

Queen Alia is 30 km (19 miles) south of Amman. Airport Express buses depart from outside the arrivals terminal hourly (7:15am–9:15pm) and go to Tarbarbour bus station;

from here, private taxis charge JD 2 for the journey to Downtown. Baggage is charged extra on buses.

Alternatively, you can catch a private taxi; these have fixed rates to destinations in the city. However, bear in mind that the official rate is some 15 times the bus fare.

Domestic Flights

Within Israel, domestic flights are operated by **Arkia**, El Al and **Israir**. With distances in Israel being so short, however, it only makes sense to fly internally to or from Eilat.

Royal Jordanian flies between Ben Gurion and Amman, while El Al and **Air Sinai** link Ben Gurion with Cairo, where you will have to change for Sharm el-Sheikh. Air Sinai does not have a website, so the easiest way to book a flight with them is via a travel agent.

DIRECTORY

Travelling Around Jerusalem, Israel, Petra and Sinai

By far the best way of getting around the region is by bus. Every town and city has a bus station, and inter-urban services are frequent and affordable. In comparison, rail networks are operational only within Israel, and sea transport is limited to just one route across the Red Sea.

Trains in Israel are modern and comfortable

Green Travel

For those concerned about their carbon footprint, Israel's size makes it easy to avoid internal flights. Even travelling to Sinai and Petra is most easily done (and cheapest) by land. Coach tours are affordable in Israel, taking visitors to several sites in one day in a way that is not feasible on public transport. The train is ideal for journeys along the coast north of Tel Aviv, but note that bicycles are not permitted on trains.

Travelling by Bus

Most long-distance bus routes in Israel are run by **Egged Tours**. Except for those to the Dead Sea region, services are frequent, with buses departing from Jerusalem to Tel Aviv every 15 minutes, to Haifa every 30 minutes and to Tiberias every hour. Simply turn up at the bus station and get a ticket for the next service, or buy one on board. The only route that can be booked in advance is the one to Eilat, and since there are only four buses a day, it is wise to do so.

Dan Buses operates mostly local buses in Tel Aviv and surrounding towns, but it also runs some short-distance inter-city routes in the Gush Dan and Shomron regions.

Given the small size of the country, journeys are feasible (the longest, Haifa–Eilat, is only 6 hours). Long-distance buses are comfortable and air-conditioned. There are no services on Shabbat (save for a limited service north of Haifa) nor on Jewish holidays *(see pp40–43)*. However, *sheruts (see p309)* still operate along major routes, such as between Tel Aviv and Jerusalem, during Shabbat.

Travelling by Train

Israel Railways' network comprises six lines, with Tel Aviv acting as a central hub. Most useful for tourists is the line from Tel Aviv to Nahariya, near the border with Lebanon. Running up the Mediterranean coast, this line serves important destinations

Cycling in Jaffa, a fun way to explore this area of Galilee

such as Haifa and Akko. The trains are swift, comfortable and inex-pensive, but services are very crowded on Sunday mornings and Thursday nights. Also, smaller stations tend to be some distance from the town centre, often requiring a taxi ride to reach them.

The Jerusalem–Tel Aviv train passes through some particularly lovely scenery but is slower than the bus. The journey takes one and a half hours, and there are 10–12 trains per day. The line for a fast train, taking under 30 minutes from inner Tel Aviv to Jerusalem, is due to be completed in 2018.

Red Sea Ferries

Aqaba in Jordan and Nuweiba in Sinai are linked by ferry and catamaran, both of which make one sailing each way, once a day. The ferry, which also carries cars, takes 3 hours, while the catamaran takes 1 hour. The catamaran is not significantly more expensive and is much more comfortable. Passengers can obtain a Sinai permit or a full Egyptian visa when travel-ling by either vessel *(see p293)*.

Cycling

The best regions for cycling are Galilee and the Golan Heights, where the scenery is at its most varied and the altitude helps to moderate the extreme heat of summer. Even so, from June to August it is best to plan to cycle only in the mornings, to avoid the high temperatures. The Negev is a popular destination too, with off-road biking through spectacular desert scenery.

In Tiberias, **Aviv Hotel** rents out bicycles to explore the shores of the Sea of Galilee *(see pp186–7)*; a full circuit can be made in just one day. Tel Aviv's seafront promenade is perfect for cycling. There are several hire companies, such as **O-Fun**, and some hotels offer free bikes to their guests. You can also pick up a bike at several stations around the city via the bike-sharing service, **Tel-O-Fun**. Registration to the scheme is necessary. In Jerusalem, **EcoBike** and **Bike Jerusalem** offer bikes to rent

Bright yellow taxis amid the busy traffic of central Amman

and bike tours. Note that the hills in and around the city can be quite a challenge.

Transport in the Palestinian Territories

There are two main public transport options in the Palestinian Territories: shared taxis and Arab buses. Buses and minibuses depart from two stations in East Jerusalem, one on Nablus Road (for services to Ramallah) and the other on Suleyman Street (for Bethlehem). Passengers have to change in Ramallah for services to Nablus and Jericho, and in or near Bethlehem for services to Hebron.

Arab shared taxis (known as service taxis; see p309) operate within the West Bank and are useful for getting between and around the towns.

In general, Arab buses do not go to Israeli towns, and vice versa. It is possible, however, to catch an Israeli Egged bus to the checkpoint outside Bethlehem or to the outskirts of Hebron.

Transport in Jordan

Jordan's main national bus company is **JETT**, which runs blue-and-white air-conditioned buses between the bus station on King Hussein Road in Amman and Aqaba, the Allenby Bridge and Petra. Booking your seat in advance is advisable.

Private buses for destinations in the north and west (including Ajlun, Jerash and the Allenby Bridge) depart from Tarbarbour bus station, located 7 km (4 miles) north of Downtown. All non-JETT minibuses heading south

(including services to Kerak, Petra and Aqaba) leave from Wahdat bus station, which is 5 km (3 miles) south of the city centre. A 10-minute walk downhill from the JETT bus station on King Hussein Road is Abdali bus station, from where you can catch a shared taxi to Syria. There are no scheduled bus services from Amman to the Dead Sea, so the only way to get there is by shared taxi or minibus. Buses from Aqaba to Petra leave between 8am and 2pm; after this time, you will have to hire a taxi. The trip takes about 2 hours.

While minibuses are becoming more widespread, shared taxis are still common in Jordan. A trip from Amman to Aqaba takes about 5 hours; from Amman to Petra about 3 hours.

To get about in Amman there are city buses, but the destination is indicated only in Arabic. Taxi drivers tend to be honest and use the meter. Only late in the evening or for longer journeys (such as to and from the airport) will you have to agree the price in advance.

Transport in Sinai

The resort towns of Sinai's east coast are served by Egypt's **East Delta Bus Company**. Services are very infrequent, however, with no more than four buses a day around the coast. Most of these buses are either coming from or heading to Cairo (which is 7 to 9 hours away). Only one early morning bus passes by St Catherine's Monastery, so check timetables carefully.

An informal shared-taxi service operates in Sinai, but it can take

see p309

DIRECTORY

Ministry of Transport

Tel *8787 (information for buses and trains throughout Israel).

Travelling by Bus

Dan Buses
Tel (03) 639 4444. [W] dan.co.il

Egged Tours
Tel (03) 920 3992.
[W] eggedtours.com

Eilat Bus Station
Ha-Temarim St.

Haifa Bus Station
Ha-Mifratz and Hof Ha-Karmel Stations.

Jerusalem Bus Station
224 Jaffa Rd.

Tel Aviv Bus Station
Levinsky St.

Travelling by Train

Israel Railways
Tel *5770. [W] rail.co.il

Cycling

Aviv Hotel
Tiberias. **Tel** (04) 672 3510.
[W] aviv-hotel.co.il

Bike Jerusalem
Jerusalem. **Tel** (02) 579 6353.
[W] bikejerusalem.com

EcoBike
Tel (077) 450 1650.
[W] ecobike.co.il

O-Fun
Tel Aviv. **Tel** (03) 544 2292.
[W] rentabikeisrael.com

Tel O-Fun
Tel Aviv. **Tel** *6070.
[W] tel-o-fun.co.il

Transport in Jordan

JETT
Tel (06) 566 4141 (Arabic only).
[W] jett.com.jo

Transport in Sinai

East Delta Bus Company
Cairo. **Tel** (02) 2405 3482.

time for the cars to fill up and the drivers can be reckless. Since taxis are quite cheap, it is best to negotiate a private vehicle for most trips around the peninsula. As an alternative, you can join an organized tour, which can be arranged in any resort town.

Travelling Around by Car

With well-maintained roads, light traffic (at least away from big cities and the coastal highway), short distances between towns and some enchanting scenery, Israel is a pleasure to drive around. In addition, car hire can work out to be incredibly cheap. The one black spot is other road users. Both Israelis and Arabs can be reckless behind the wheel, and road fatalities are high. While this should not put you off driving, you do need to be cautious. On the positive side again, Israel is full of small places of beauty and interest, often located well off any bus route, and having a car at your disposal can really open up the country.

Petrol station in Israel

What you Need

To rent a car, you must be over 21 years of age and in possession of a full, clean driving licence and an international credit card. An international driving licence is not necessary. Insurance is compulsory as part of any hire package. Be careful when booking online, since prices quoted often do not include insurance. All car-hire companies provide information on what to do and who to contact if you breakdown. Hire cars come equipped with a fluorescent vest and warning triangle; in the event of a breakdown, you should put on the vest before getting out of the car.

Driving in Israel

In Israel you should drive on the right-hand side of the road. At unmarked junctions, drivers give way to traffic on the right, and overtaking is done on the left (though be prepared for vehicles to undertake on highways). Only two roads operate a toll system: Road 6, which runs south to north (it will link Beersheva to Nahariya when completed); and a section of Road 1, which connects Ben Gurion Airport to Tel Aviv. Toll charges are automatically taken off the credit card you registered with the car-hire company, though some may ask you to sign a waiver whereby you agree not to drive on toll roads.

The speed limit in towns is 50 km/h (30 mph); on out-of-town roads, 90 km/h (55 mph). On some highways the speed limit is 100 km/h (60 mph), and on Road 6 it is 110 km/h (68 mph). Seat belts must be worn. Children under 15 must sit in the back, and children under four must be restrained in a suitable child's seat.

Traffic in and around Tel Aviv and Jerusalem is congested. Aim to avoid rush hour, which is roughly 7–9am and 4–6pm, though it is not unknown to encounter traffic jams in Tel Aviv even at 1am.

Road Signs in Israel

Although there is a lack of warning signs on Israel's roads, all places of interest are well indicated with brown signs. Road signs on highways are blue, and those within cities are green. Signs are in both Hebrew and English, and usually in Arabic too.

The lack of consistency in the transliteration of place names from Hebrew into English means that you could be following directions for Beersheva one minute and for Be'er Sheva the next. In this book we have tried to present place names as you will see them spelled on Israeli road signs, but local inconsistencies mean that this is not always the case.

Driving in the Palestinian Territories

Cars in Israel and the Autonomous Palestinian Territories have licence plates of different colours. Israeli cars have yellow plates, while Palestinian car plates are white with green numbers. Palestinian public transport vehicles have green licence plates with white numbers.

Cars with Palestinian number plates cannot easily cross checkpoints into Israel, but it is common for cars with Israeli plates to drive into Palestinian areas. However, it is inadvisable to drive to troublespots in the West Bank, such as Hebron. Cars rented in Israel are not insured for the Palestinian Territories. For this coverage, you will have to rent a vehicle from a company in East Jerusalem.

Two-way sign | Right-hand bend

Tourist site sign | Parking sign

Typically heavy traffic on the seafront promenade in Tel Aviv

Driving in Jordan

While driving is on the right, Jordanians seem to consider most other road rules open to interpretation. Overtaking takes place on both sides of the road, and right of way goes to those who hesitate the least. Main highways are well surfaced, with proper road markings, but minor roads are often in a poor state of repair. Speed limits are generally 100 km/h (60 mph) on open roads and 40 km/h (25 mph) in built-up areas. Take care on desert roads, where drifting sand can put the car into a spin if hit at speed. Direction signs are often positioned right at the junction, making it all too easy to drive past your turn-off.

Road sign at a busy city junction in Jerusalem

Driving in Sinai

There are few roads in Sinai, so driving routes are limited. Traffic is light, but it is mainly composed of buses and shared taxis; these tend to travel at high speed, paying little heed to other road users. Car drivers must be constantly on the lookout and ready to take evasive action.

Other than on recognized trails, off-road driving is not encouraged, since it can damage the fragile desert environment. Several such trails begin in the region of Nuweiba (see p246), where jeep tours with local Bedouin guides can be easily arranged.

Car Hire

Most international car-hire companies are represented in Israel, with offices (or counters) at Ben Gurion Airport and in Tel Aviv and Jerusalem. For the sake of convenience, it is better to use a firm that has a representative at the airport. Prices vary dramatically, so shop around before settling on a deal. Local companies, such as **Eldan**, frequently offer the best rates. Be aware that rental charges are usually quoted exclusive of insurance and collision waivers. Note that it is not allowed to take cars hired in Israel over into Jordan or Sinai.

Car hire is not very popular in Jordan and Sinai because there are so few roads. It also works out as very expensive when compared with getting around by other forms of transport, such as the bus or hiring a taxi for a day or two.

Petrol stations in Jordan, Sinai and even certain parts of Israel, particularly the Negev and Dead Sea areas, are few and far between. You are strongly advised to fill up your tank before setting off on any long journeys.

Hitch-Hiking

Known in Israel as *tremping*, hitch-hiking used to be a common way of getting about the country. It was particularly popular with soldiers heading home or returning from leave. However, a few incidents in the mid-2000s mean that hitch-hiking is unsafe, and soldiers are now banned from hitching. Visitors are advised against hitch-hiking while in Israel.

DIRECTORY

Car Hire in Israel

Avanti
Tel (077) 490 4800.
W avanti.co.il

Budget
Tel *2200.
W budget.co.il

Eldan
Tel (03) 557 9040 or *3524.
W eldan.co.il

Europcar
Tel (03) 622 2240.
W europcar.com

Good Luck
East Jerusalem.
Tel (02) 627 7033.
W goodluckcars.com

Hertz
Tel (1 700) 507 555.
W hertz.co.il

Sixt
W sixt.com/car-rental/israel

Car Hire in Jordan and Sinai

Europcar
W europcar.com

Hertz
Sharm el-Sheikh.
W hertzegypt.com
Amman. W hertz.jo

Oscar Car Rental
Amman. Tel (06) 553 5635.
W 1stjordan.net/oscar

Rent a Reliable Car
Amman. Tel (06) 592 9676.
W rentareliablecar.com

Getting Around Jerusalem

Most of Jerusalem's major historical and religious sites are concentrated in the Old City, which has to be explored on foot, since it is almost an entirely vehicle-free zone. Elsewhere, the Light Rail and bus networks will get visitors to more or less everywhere they want to go. This is just as well, as taxis tend to be too expensive for frequent use. The one time when visitors might have to use taxis is on Shabbat, when public transport stops running from mid-afternoon on Friday to sundown on Saturday.

Buses

Jerusalem's bus system is run by **Egged**. Buses are identified by a number displayed in the front window. To establish which route you need, visit the Egged website or ask at the tourist office by Jaffa Gate. Major bus routes include: No. 1 from the **Central Bus Station** to Damascus Gate, the Western Wall and Mount Zion; No. 9, linking the city centre to the Israel Museum; and No. 20, going from Jaffa Gate to Yad Vashem. Most buses run from about 5:30am until midnight. Night buses (Nos. 101–106) run from midnight to 3am on Thursdays and Saturdays (Sun–Thu in July and August).

East Jerusalem is served by Arab-run buses, which depart from two bus stations near Damascus Gate. Useful lines include No. 75 to the Mount of Olives, No. 21 to Bethlehem and No. 18 to Ramallah.

Line 99 Bus

A good, convenient way to discover the city is via a hop-on/hop-off ride on the Line 99 bus, also known as the Jerusalem City Tour. Run by Egged, the bus departs four times a day from the Central Bus Station on Jaffa Road. The circular route takes in most of the important sites outside the Old City in under 2 hours. There are no buses on Saturday.

Tickets can be bought on the bus or booked through your hotel reception. You can choose between one- and two-day tickets, and a guided tour is available on a multi-language personal listening device.

Mass Transit System

The Mass Transit System is the city's answer to heavy congestion. The system includes a Light Rail (tram) line and a Bus Rapid Transit (BRT) route.

The tram links Pisgat Ze'ev in the north (via Damascus Gate, Jaffa Road and the Central Bus Station) to Mount Herzl in the west. It is easy to use, fast, frequent and wheelchair-friendly. Buy a ticket from the dispenser at the stop and validate it in the machine on board.

An Egged bus, a popular way to travel around Jerusalem

Line 99 Bus Route

The clockwise circuit made by this bus passes many important Jerusalem landmarks. The bus makes numerous stops, but key points along the route include:

① Central Bus Station
② Mahane Yehuda Market
③ Mount Scopus
④ Jaffa Gate *(see p104)*
⑤ King David Hotel/YMCA *(see p126)*
⑥ Haas Promenade
⑦ Biblical Zoo *(see p142)*
⑧ Herzl Cemetery and Museum
    (see p142)

⑨ Yad Vashem *(see p142)*
⑩ Israel Museum *(see pp136–41)*
⑪ Knesset *(see p135)*

Key

— Old City walls

■ No. 99 bus route

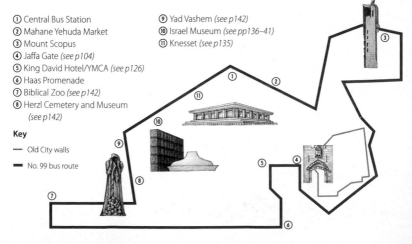

The BRT route runs along a dedicated bus lane from Talpiot in the south to Har Hozvim in the north, with stops near Jabotinsky, Agron and King George V streets.

The **CityPass** website has more details on both the Light Rail and BRT systems.

Tickets

Single one-way tickets can be purchased for use of the Light Rail and bus networks separately. Tickets, available from the machines at tram stops and in service centres, are valid for 90 minutes from the time of purchase and cost the equivalent of about US$2. Be aware that many journeys involve using both forms of transport in order to reach your destination. There are no return tickets. Visitors can also purchase the electronic top-up "smart card" (Rav-Kav), a multi-use card for travel on both the bus and Light Rail. A "personal" card is free and gives discounts on fares; otherwise the card costs 5 NIS if you do not provide ID proof. Insert your "smart card" into the machine when boarding a bus or tram. For those on a longer visit, monthly passes allow unlimited transport around the city for a set price.

Walking

The narrow streets and alleys of the Old City do not allow for vehicles, meaning this is pretty much a pedestrian zone.

Yellow Palestinian taxi

White Israeli taxi

Flat-soled footwear is essential, as many of the ancient streets are cobbled and slippery when wet. It is also easiest to get around the centre of the New City on foot, as Jaffa, Ben Yehuda and other streets are pedestrianized, and the lanes of Nakhlaot, Nakhalat Shiva and Yemin Moshe are largely impossible by car. Elsewhere, wide roads and aggressive traffic can make walking rather unpleasant.

Street signs are in at least two languages – Hebrew and English, or Arabic and English. In the Old City, they are in the scripts of all three.

Taxis

It is easy to find a taxi in Jerusalem. You can book one by phone, hail one on the street or find one at an official rank. Restaurant and hotel staff will always phone a cab for you. Taxis are white, with a yellow sign on top that is lit up if they are available. Occasionally, an

DIRECTORY

Buses

Central Bus Station
224 Jaffa Rd, Jerusalem.
Tel *2800.

Egged
Tel *2800 (information).
w egged.co.il

Mass Transit System

CityPass
w citypass.co.il

Taxis

Ambassador Taxis
East Jerusalem.
Tel (02) 582 6969.

Beit Hakerem Taxis
West Jerusalem.
Tel (02) 500 0101.

Rehavia Taxis
3 Agron St.
Tel (02) 625 4444.

Israeli driver may refuse to take you to an address in East Jerusalem, but Arab drivers are usually willing to venture into any part of West Jerusalem. All taxis have modern meters (which can print out a receipt on request), and you should insist that the meter be used. If it is not, you will pay a variable fare, which will be dependent on your haggling skills but will certainly be more than the meter would have indicated. Taxi fares are higher from 9pm to 5:30am, on Shabbat and holidays.

Shared Taxis

Known to Israelis as a *sherut* and to Arabs as a service (pronounced "servees") taxi, the shared taxi is a cross between a bus and a taxi. They operate fixed routes like a bus, but they run more frequently and, like a taxi, they can be hailed on the street. At the start of the route, drivers tend to wait until every seat is taken before setting off. There are no set stops; passengers indicate to the driver when they wish to be let off. Fares are similar to the equivalent bus ride and much cheaper than a taxi.

A taxi rank in Jerusalem

General Index

Acknowledgments

Dorling Kindersley would like to thank the following people whose invaluable contributions and assistance have made the preparation of this book possible.

Senior Managing Editor
Louise Bostock Lang.

Managing Art Editor
Jane Ewart.

Editorial Director
Vivian Crump.

Publishing Manager
Scarlett O'Hara.

Revisions Coordinator/Editor
Anna Freiberger, Rose Hudson.

Art Director
Gillian Allan.

Publisher
Douglas Amrine.

Main Consultants
Felicity Cobbing, Andrew Humphreys, Jonathan Tubb.

Translator
Richard Pierce.

Maps
Rob Clynes, James Macdonald (Colourmap Scanning Ltd).

Production
Imogen Boase, Marie Ingledew.

Additional Contributors and Consultants
Vanessa Betts, Jonathan Elphick, Professor Jonathan Magonet, Peter Parr, Amir Reuveni, Matthew Teller, Wolfgang Tins.

Visualizer
Joy FitzSimmons.

Additional Illustrations
Richard Bonson.

Additional Photography
Idris Ahmed, Vanessa Betts, Andy Crawford, Alistair Duncan, Mike Dunning, Steve Gorton, Noam Knoller, Ian O'Leary, Rough Guides/Eddie Gerald, Rough Guides/Paul Whitfield.

Revisions and Relaunch Team
Gillian Andrews, Sam Borland, Neha Chander, Samantha Cook, Emer FitzGerald, Camilla Gersh, Jasneet Kaur, Sumita Khatwani, Priya Kukadia, Priyanka Kumar, Esther Labi, Maite Lantaron, Carly Madden, Nicola Malone, Alison McGill, Loren Minsky, Sonal Modha, Helen Partington, Susie Peachey, Adrian Potts, Pollyanna Poulter, Lee Redmond, Alice Reese, Marisa Renzullo, Rockit Design, Ellen Root, Sands Publishing Solutions, Ankita Sharma, Azeem Siddiqui, Vinita Venugopal, Ya'arah Zikorel.

Editor
Jude Ledger.

Factcheckers
Tzipporah Johnston, Noam Knoller.

Proof Reader
Stewart J Wild.

Indexer
Hilary Bird.

Special Assistance
Sheila Brull, Egyptian Tourist Authority, Giovanni Francesio and Mattia Goffetti at Fabio Ratti Editoria, Efrat Goller at Keter Publishing, Tony Howard and Di Taylor at N.O.M.A.D.S. (New Opportunities for Mountaineering and Desert Sports), Israel Ministry of Tourism, Jordan Tourism Board, Amalyah Keshet and Tal Sher at the Israel Museum, Deborah Lipson at the Tower of David Museum of the History of Jerusalem, Hila Reuveni, Shelly Shemer at the Israel Wine and Gourmet Magazine. Special thanks to Massimo Acanfora Torrefranca.

Additional Picture Research
Julia Harris-Voss.

Photographic and Artwork Reference
Dale Harris, Ben Johnson, Albatros, Jerusalem.

Photography Permissions
The publisher would like to thank all the churches, museums, hotels, restaurants, shops, galleries and sights too numerous to thank individually, for their co-operation and contribution to this publication.

Picture Credits
a-above; b-below/bottom; c-centre; f-far; l-left; r-right; t-top.

Works of art have been reproduced with the permission of the following copyright holders: *Reclining Figure* (1969–70) Henry Moore, Gift of Maurice and Bella Wingrave, London. Through the British Friends of the Art Museums in Israel 174bc.

The publisher would like to thank the following individuals, companies and picture libraries for permission to reproduce their photographs:

Alamy images: Jon Arnold Images Ltd 10bc; The Art Archive 31cr; Art Directors & TRIP 58c; www.BibleLandPictures.c 13cr;

Tibor Bognar 218cla; Charles Bowman 208tr; Bruce Corbett 83cra; Luis Dafos 15br; Design Pics Inc 83crb; Paul Doyle 218br; Eddie Gerald 292cla; Nick Hanna 247tl; 287b; Hemis/Paule Seux 300cla; Israel images/Hanan Isachar 142tr; LOOK Die Bildagentur der Fotografen GmbH/Elan Fleisher 176tl; PhotoStock-Israel/Nir Ben-Yosef 302br; Shein Audio Visual 282cla; Jochen Tack 216bl; Steve Whyte 303tc; Danny Yanai 267c; **American Colony Hotel:** 264cla; **Ancient Art & Architecture Collection:** 32crb, 33cra, 34cra, 45br, 48cla, 51ca; R Sheridan 28tr, 45bl, 50bl, 54cb, 111cla, 111cl; **AKG, London:** 46crb, 50tl, 54tl, 58bl, 237br; Erich Lessing 24cl, 25cr, 33br, 34br, 49crb, 49br, 50cb, 96cla, 193c, 220ca, 220bc; Jean Louis Mou 63tl; **Fabrizio Ardito** 24bl, 30tr, 39cra, 107bl, 183tl, 221bc, 226tr, 228tr, 237tl, 237cb, 239tr, 239c, 310br, 311c, 318cl, 318cb, 319ca, 319tc; **ASAP, Jerusalem:** Eyal Bartov 38cl, 38cl; Bridgeman Art Library 31cr, 55bl, C.Z.A. 56ca; Hanan Isachar Itsik Marom 39cl, 39cb; Garo Nalbandian, Richard Nowitz Vivian Silver 57t; **Auberge Shulamit:** 259clb; **Austrian Hospice:** 256cla, 260bc, 270br.

Bank Hapoalim: 298cr; **Blue Fig:** 274tl; **Bridgeman Art Library:** *Christ Carrying the Cross* Eustache Le Sueur (1651) 35bl; 36bl; *Jerusalem from the Mount of the Olives* Edward Lear (1859) 37tl, *The Finding of the Saviour in the Temple* William Holman Hunt (1854–60) 37br; 44, 252br; Bibliothèque Municipale de Lyon 52clb; British Library 24cr, 25tc; Galleria Borghese *St Jerome Writing* Caravaggio (1604) 199b; Giraudon 30cl; Musée Condé, Chantilly 32bl; **British Library:** 26tr.

Colony Hotel, Haifa: 261tr, 264cla; **Corbis:** AFI IARFK II 41bl; Robert Bartow/Design Pics 144; Gianni Dagli Orti 28cl; Demotix/Alon Ershov 41cr; Design Pics/Peter Langer 250br; EPA/Jamal Nasrallah 284tl; EPA/POOL/AMMAR AWAD 43cr; Historical Picture Archive 55bc; Blaine Harrington III 132; Aaron Horowitz 266cla; Hulton-Deutsch Collection 56c, 57c, 58bc; Hanan Isachar 288br; Reuters/Ali Jarekji 217tc; Bruno Morandi 100-1; Richard T. Nowitz 55br; Science Faction/Eyal Bartov 39bl; George Steinmetz 202-3; Peter Turnley 59bc; Stuart Westmorland 248-9.

Diaghilev Live Art Boutique Hotel: 262tr; **Jo Doran:** 94cl; **Dreamstime.com:** Alexirina27000 75c; Antonella865 111cr; Aronbrand 124cl; Kushnirov Avraham 26-27c; Rafael Ben-ari 71tr, 141cra, 208bl; Vladimir Blinov 20, 112; Buurserstraat386 66cl; Kobby Dagan 27cr, 129br; Dunca Daniel 13tl; Danuer 23br; Davemontreuil 39clb; Designsstock 211b; Boris Diakovsky 38cb; Dnaveh 267tl; Dream69 243br; Joan Egert 39cl; Eldadcarin 190; Gkuna 39cb; Rostislav Glinsky 103tl; Gorshkov13 38clb, 125cra; Guter 185bl; Hugoht 80; Konstantin32 201cl; Kosmos111 240; , Iuliia Kryzhevska 181cl; Rafal Kubiak 142c; Liorpt 63cr; Lucidwaters 14tl; Markussevcik 11cr; Serge Novitsky 10cla; Sean Pavone 12bl; Zaid Saadallah 14hr, 38cr; Scaligor 28bl; Jozef Sedmak 28br; Slavapolo 35cb; Slidezero 168; Snake81 169b; Jacek Sopotnicki 62bl; Iryna Sosnytska 60-1, 164-5; Leonid Spektor 207tr; Alexey Stiop 128tc; Vitullia 22t; Vivoevale 15tl, Waj111 210, Daniel Weishut 281cr; Witr 223-4; Valeriya Zankovych 282bc.

Egged – Israel Transport Cooperative Society Ltd.: 308cr; **El Al Israel Airlines:** 312tc; **E.T.archive:** 52-3c, 53tr, 53br;

Mary Evans Picture Library: 36c, 37c, 52bl, 52br, 91tc. **ffotograff:** Patricia Aithie 54br, 119bc, 281cra, 282br; Charles Aithie 35clb, 63cra; **Gino Frongia** 28–29c, 38cla, 72c, 74tr, 107cla, 191b, 194bl, 258t, 296cla. **Cristina Gambaro:** 5ca, 66cla, 66clb, 69tc, 71c, 97bl, 103bl, 183c, 186br, 206tc, 296tr; **Eddie Gerald:** 34cla, 66bc, 82cla, 82cb, 115crb, 124crb, 128tr, 129bl, 178tr, 178bl, 187tl, 187crb, 199ca, 232bc, 242clb, 246c, 250cb, 251cra, 283tr, 283cr, 283bl, 284br, 297tc, 297c, 306cla, 306bc. **Getty Images:** AFP/Andre Brutmann 59crb; AFP/Jack Guez 297bc; **Gulbenkian Library:** 111bl.

Sonia Halliday: Laura Lushington 141bl; **Robert Harding Picture Library:** Adrian Neville 29cr; ASAP/Nalbandian 62tr; Gascoigne 32cl; **Hemispheres Images: Holmes Photography:** 253crb, Jean Holmes 53crb, Reed Holmes 236b, **Tony Howard:** 236cla.

Intercontinental Hotel, Aquaba: 265tl; **Hanan Isachar:** 4br, 5tr, 29tl, 29cra, 29crb, 35tr, 39crb, 40cra, 40bl, 41cra, 41br, 42cra, 42cb, 43cl, 43bl, 95tc, 96bl, 97tr, 97cra, 98cla, 104bc, 114br, 166cla, 170clb, 171br, 179tc, 179bc, 180tl, 180bl, 186cla, 193tr, 198cla, 198cb, 201clb, 204tr, 209bl, 220bl, 225crb, 230ca, 253tl, 276br, 278br, 304b; **www.israelimages.com:** 302cla; **Israel Ministry of Tourism:** 294tc; **Israel Museum, Jerusalem:** 48clb, *Destruction and Sack of the Temple of Jerusalem* Nicolas Poussin (1625–6) 49tr; 49cr, 53cra, 57b, *The Tzedek ve-Shalom Synagogue Paramaribo.* Suriname 1736, Elie Posner 136cla; *The Nuremberg Mahzor (Prayer book, according to Eastern Ashkenazi rite)* Southern Germany 1331. Scribes: Mattanyah; Jacob; Handwritten on parchment; brown and red ink, tempera, gold and silver leaf; square and semi-cursive Ashkenazic script. H: 50; W: 37cm, Ardon Bar-Hama 136clb; *Boy from South Tel Aviv* Ohad Meromi (2001) 136cra, *Gold-Glass base, Rome,* 4th century CE, Brown glass and gold leaf, Diam: 11.7; Th: 0.7cm. Acquired in 1966 through the generosity of Jakob Michael, New York, in memory of his wife, Erna Sondhelmer Michael; restituted in 2008 to the heirs to the Dzialynska Collection, Goluchow Castle, Poland, owners prior to World War II; acquired in 2008 by Dr. David and Jemima Jeselsohn, Zurich, and now on extended loan to the Israel Museum 137clc; *St. Peter in Prison (The Apostle Peter Kneeling)* 1631, Rembrandt van Rijn, Oil on panel, 59 x 47.8cm, Gift of Judy and Michael Steinhardt, New York, to American Friends of the Israel Museum, Avshalom Avital 137cra; *Mask from Horvat Duma, El Hadeb, southern Judean Hills,* Pre-Pottery, Neolithic B Period, 9,000 years ago, finely crystalline limestone, 22.3 x 15cm, Weight: 1.1kg, Gift of Laurence and Wilma Tisch, new York, purchasers of the Dayan Collection, Elie Posner 137crb; *The Cliff of Aval, Etretat,* Claude Monet, French, 1840-1926, 1885, Oil on canvas, 65.5 x 91.7cm. Bequest of Marie Dabek, Paris, to the State of Israel, in memory of Jack and Mimi Dabek On permanent loan to The Israel Museum, Jerusalem from the Administrator General of the State of Israel 137bl; *Jeanne Hebuterne seated* Modigliani (1918) 138tr, 138b, 139tr, 139c, 139br, 140cl, 141cl, 141c, 141cr, 205c; 140br; David Harris 138c, 141br; Ann Levin 140tr.

Paul Jackson: 178br, 179tc, 229cr, 231br; **www. Jerusalemshots.com:** 98crb; **Jordan Tourist Board:** 201crb, 238bl, 238cla, 238tr, 288tl.
King David Hotel: 126c, 257br; **Kempinski Hotel Ishtar:** 263bl, 275bc.
Magnum Photos: 58tl; **Mamilla Hotel, Jerusalem:** Rooftop at Mamilla 271tr; **Mona, Jerusalem:** 271br.
NHPA: Henry Ausloos 39br; **Richard Nowitz:** 5clb, 96br, 97c, 98bc, 99c, 166bl, 167tr, 167crb, 182cla, 182br, 192cla, 193b, 197tl, 204br, 205bl, 207br, 221tl, 227bl, 229bl, 234bc, 243tr, 246tl, 251tl, 251bl, 253bc, 279tr, 281ca, 293tr, 301bl.
Orange France Telecom: 300crb; **Cristine Osborne Pictures:** 167bl, 233cra, 252cla.
Pa Photos: Ariel Schalit 284c; **Pina BaRosh:** 272br; **Planet Popperfoto:** 56bl, 56br, 57c, 58br.
Zev Radovan: 4–5t, 24tr, 25clb, 26cl, 26bc, 27tl, 27tr, 32tr, 33clb, 46bl, 46br, 47cb, 47br, 55tl, 71bl, 75b, 107cra; **Fabio Ratti:** 76cl, 121br, 216tr, 217br; **Reuters:** Ronen Zvulun 59tl; **Rex Features:** 23cl; .Rex Shutterstock: Universal History Archive/UIG 57tr.
Peter Sanders Photography: 30bl, 30br, 31tl, 74cla; **Eitan Simanor:** 43cra, 48br, 186tr, 258b; **Jon Spaull:** 167cr, 212tr, 212bl, 213tr, 213br; **STA Travel Group:** 294br; **Superstock:** age fotostock 254-5; Fine Art Images 251br; Robert Harding Picture Library 290-1; Hanan Isachar 2-3.
Temple Institute Museum: 87tl; **Tower of David Museum of the History of Jerusalem:** Amit Geron 107tl.
Visions of the Land: American Colony Hotel 55crb; Tony Malmqvist 241b, 244tr, 244cl, 244cb, 244bl, 244bc, 244br, 245tl, 245tr, 245cra, 245cb, 245bl, 245br, 247c, 247br, 286tr; Beni Mor 33tl, 67tl, 68bc, 94tr, 95b, 118tr, 120tl, 120br, 181br, 184t, 184bc, 185tr, 188t, 188b, 194t, 195bl, 196t, 226cl, 237ca; Garo Nalbandian 30–31c, 39cla, 63br, 67cb,

72br, 73cr, 73b, 76bc, 77cr, 104tr, 104clb, 110tl, 110cra, 111cb, 111br, 116tl, 116tr, 117tr, 117bc, 128bl, 129tc, 189tl, 215br, 227tl, 227tr, 227c, 228cla, 228bc, 230tr, 230br, 231tr, 231tl, 232tr, 233cb, 234tr, 234cla, 235tr, 235tl, 235cr, 235bc, 239bl, 209tr, 250tr, 250cla, Basilio Rodella 47ca, 67cra, 68t, 68c, 70tr, 70c, 70b, 73t, 76tr, 77tr, 77b, 82bl, 83bl, 86t, 86c, 86bl, 88tr, 89t, 89c, 89b, 94ca, 96tr, 118tl, 121tl, 125cb, 126b, 127br, 130tr, 130bl, 130br, 131cl, 131br, 134tl, 134br, 135tr, 135br, 181c, 188cr, 189br, 194c, 196b, 200t, 204cl, 204cb, 205t, 205ca, 206bl, 207tl, 214tr, 214bl, 257tl, Studium Biblicum Franciscanum Archive 220–221c, 221cra; Ilan Sztulman 268cr, 268b, 269bl, 269clb, 269bc, 269cbc, 269brc, 269br, 277tl, all 280cla, 280crc, 280clb, 280cb, 280bcl, 280bc, 281tl, 281tc, 281tr, 281trr, 281cla, 281c, all 281crb; **www.VisitJordan.com:** 293clb.

Werner Forman Archive: British Museum 25br; **Peter Wilson:** 21b, 38tr, 38br, 171tr, 187br, 192bc, 215tr, 226–227, 231bl, 232c, 233tl, 236cb, 237bl, 242tr, 296bc, 307tl.

Front Endpaper - **Corbis:** Blaine Harrington III Rbl; **Dreamstime.com:** Vladimir Blinov Rbr; Eldadcarin Ltl; Hugoht Rbc; Kosmos111 Lbl; Slidezero Ltc; Waj111 Lbr

Pull Out Map: **Alamy Images:** imageBROKER

Jacket:
Front and spine – **Alamy Images:** imageBROKER

Special Editions of DK Travel Guides

DK Travel Guides can be purchased in bulk quantities at discounted prices for use in promotions or as premiums. We are also able to offer special editions and personalized jackets, corporate imprints, and excerpts from all of our books, tailored specifically to meet your own needs.

To find out more, please contact:
in the United States **specialsales@dk.com**
in the UK **travelspecialsales@uk.dk.com**
in Canada **specialmarkets@dk.com**
in Australia **penguincorporatesales@ penguinrandomhouse.com.au**

Hebrew Phrase Book

Hebrew has an alphabet of 22 letters. As in Arabic, the vowels do not appear in the written language and there are several systems of transliteration. In this phrasebook we have given a simple phonetic transcription only. Bold type indicates the syllable on which the stress falls. An apostrophe between two letters means that there is a break in the pronunciation. The letters "kh" represent the sound "ch" as in Scottish "loch", and "g" is hard as in "gate". Where necessary, the masculine form is given first, followed by the feminine.

In Emergency

Help!	Hatzilu!
Stop!	Atzor!
Call a doctor!	Azminu rofe!
Call an ambulance!	Azminu ambulans!
Call the police!	Tzaltzelu lamishtara!
Call the fire brigade!	Tzaltzelu lemekhabei esh!
Where is the nearest telephone?	Efo hatelefon hatziburi hakhi karov?
Where is the nearest hospital?	Efo bet hakholim hakhi karov?

Communication Essentials

Yes	Ken
No	Lo
Please	Bevakasha
Thank you	Toda
Many thanks	Toda raba
Excuse me	Slikha
Hello	Shalom
Good day	Boker tov
Good evening	Erev tov
Good night	Laila tov
Greetings (on the Sabbath)	Shabat Shalom
Have a good week (after the Sabbath)	Shavu'a tov
morning	boker
afternoon	akhar hatzohoryim
evening	erev
night	laila
today	hayom
tomorrow	makhar
here	po
there	sham
what?	ma?
which?	eizeh?
when?	matai?
who?	mi?
where?	efo?

Useful Phrases

How are you?	Ma shlomkha/shlomekh?
Very well, thank you	Beseder, toda
Pleased to meet you	Na'immeod
Goodbye	Lehitraot
(I'm) fine!	Beseder gamur
Where is/Where are…?	Efo…?
How many kilometres is it to…?	Kama kilometrim mipo le…?
What is the way to…?	Ekh megi'im le…?
Do you speak English?	Ata/at medaber/medaberet anglit?
I don't understand	Ani lo mevin/mevina
Could you speak more slowly, please?	Tukhal/tukhli ledaber yoter le'at, bevakasha?

Useful Words

large	gadol
small	katan
hot	kham
cold	kar
bad	lo tov
enough	maspik
well	beseder
open	patuakh
closed	sagur
left	smol
right	yamin
straight	yashar
near	karov
far	rakhok
up	lemala
down	lemata
soon	mukdam
late	meukhar
entrance	knisa
exit	yetzia
toilet	sherutim
free, unoccupied	panui
free, no charge	khinam

Making a Telephone Call

I'd like to make a long-distance call	Haiti rotze/rotza lehitkasher lekhutz lair/laaretz
I'd like to make a reversed-charge call	Haiti rotze/rotza lehitkasher govaina
I'll call back later	Etkasher meukhar yoter
Can I leave a message?	Efshar lehashir hoda'a?
Hold on	Hamtin/hamtini (Tamtin/tamtini)
Could you speak up a little, please?	Tukhal/tukhli ledaber bekol ram yoter?
local call	sikha ironit
international call	sikha benleumit

Shopping

How much does it cost?	Kama zeh oleh?
I would like…	Haiti rotzeh/rotza…
Do you have…?	Yesh lakhem…?
I'm just looking	Ani rak mistakel/mistakelet
Do you take credit cards?	Atem mekablim kartisei ashrai?
Do you take travellers' cheques?	Atem mekablim travellers' cheques?
What time do you open?	Matai potkhim?
What time do you close?	Matai sogrim?
this one	zeh
that one	hahu
expensive	yakar
inexpensive/cheap	lo yakar/zol
size	mida
shoe size	mida (midat na'alyim)
white	lavan
black	shakhor
red	adom
yellow	tzahov
green	yarok
blue	kakhol

Types of Shop

antiques shop	khanut atikot
bakery	ma'afia
bank	bank
barber's	maspera
bookshop/newsagent	khanut sfarim/ve'itonim
butcher's	itliz
cake shop	ma'adania
chemist's	bet merkakhat
clothes shop	khanut b'gadim
greengrocer's	yarkan
grocer's	makolet
hairdresser's	maspera
jeweller's	khanut takhshitim
market	shuk
post office	snif hadoar
shoe shop	khanut na'alyim
supermarket	supermarket
travel agency	sokhnut nesiyot

Sightseeing

bus station	takhana merkazit
bus stop	takhanat otobus
church	knesia
closed	sagur
library	sifria
mosque	misgad
park	park
synagogue	bet haknesset
taxi	monit
tourist information office	merkaz hameida letayar
town hall	bet ha'iria
train station	takhanat rakevet

Staying in a Hotel

I have a reservation	Yesh li hazma**na**
Do you have a free room?	Yesh la**khem khe**der pa**nui**?
double room	**khe**der zu**gi**
room with two beds	**khe**der im sh**tei** mi**tot**
room with a bath or a shower	**khe**der im she**rutim** ve amba**tia** o mi**kla**khat
single room	**khe**der ya**khid**
key	maf**te**akh
lift	ma'a**lit**
Can someone help me with my luggage?	**Mi**shehu ya**khol** la'a**zor** li im hamisva**dot**?

Eating Out

Have you got a table free?	Yesh la**khem** shul**khan** pa**nui**?
I would like to book a table	Hai**ti** rot**ze**/rot**za** lehaz**min** shul**khan**
The bill please	Kesh**bon**, bevaka**sha**
I am vegetarian	A**ni** tzimkho**ni**/ tzimkho**nit**
menu	ta**frit**
fixed-price menu	ta**frit** is**kit**
wine list	ta**frit** haye**inot**
glass	kos
bottle	bak**buk**
knife	sa**kin**
spoon	kaf
fork	maz**leg**
breakfast	aru**khat** bo**ker**
lunch	aru**khat** tzoho**ryim**
dinner	aru**khat** e**rev**
starter	ma**na** risho**na**
main course	ma**na** ika**rit**
portion	ma**na**
rare	mevu**shal** me'**at**
well done	mevu**shal** he**tev**

Food and Drink

almonds	shke**dim**
apples	tapua**khei** etz
apricot	mish mish
aubergine/eggplant	khatzi**lim**
beans	shu'**it**
beef	**ba**kar
beer	**bi**ra
bread	**le**khem
broad beans	ful
broccoli	**bro**koli
butter	khem'**a**
cabbage	kruv
cake	ug**ha**
carrot	**ge**zer
cauliflower	kru**vit**
cheese	gvi**na**
cherries	duvdva**nim**
chicken	off
chickpeas	**khu**mus
chips/fries	chips
chocolate	**sho**kolat
coffee	ka**fe**
cold cuts	pas**tra**ma
coriander	**kuz**bera
courgettes/zucchini	kishu**im**
crabs	sarta**nim**
cucumbers	melafefo**nim**
dessert	kinu**akh**
draught beer	**bi**ra mihakha**vit**
dry	ya**vesh**
eggs	bet**za**
figs	te'e**nim**
fish	dag
French beans	shu'**it** yero**kha**
fried	metu**gan**
fruit	pei**rot**
garlic	shum
grapes	ana**vim**
grey mullet	**bu**ri
grilled	al ha**esh**
grouper	**lo**kus
hard-boiled eggs	bet**za** ka**sha**
herbal tea	**tei** tzma**khim**
hot (spicy)	kha**rif**
ice	**ke**rakh
ice cream	**gli**da
kebab	shi**pud**
lamb, mutton	**ke**ves
lemon	li**mon**
liver	ka**ved**
meat	ba**sar**
milk	kha**lav**
mineral water	**my**im mine**ralim**
nuts	ego**zim**
olive oil	**she**men **zy**it

omelette	khavi**ta**
onion	bat**zal**
orange juice (freshly squeezed)	mitz tapu**zim** (tiv'**i** sa**khut**)
oranges	tapu**zim**
peaches	afarse**kim**
pepper (condiment)	**pil**pel
peppers (capsicums)	pilpe**lim**
pickles	khamutz**im**
plums	shezi**fim**
potatoes	tapu**khei** ada**ma**
prawns/shrimps	shrimps
red snapper	de**nis**
red wine	**yain** a**dom**
rice	o**rez**
roast	beta**nur**
salad	sa**lat** yera**kot**
salmon	sal**mon**
salt	me**lakh**
sandwich/filled roll	lakhma**nia**
sauce	ro**tev**
seafood	pei**rot** yam
smoked	me'u**shan**
soup	ma**rak**
spinach	te**red**
spinach beet (Swiss chard)	a**lei** se**lek**
squid	kala**mari**
steak	steik
strawberries	tut sa**de** (tu**tim**)
stuffed vegetables	memula**im**
sugar	su**kar**
tea	tei
tomatoes	agvani**ot**
trout	fo**rel**
turkey	**ho**du
vegetables	yera**kot**
vinegar	**kho**metz
water	**my**im
white wine	**yain** la**van**

Numbers

0	**e**fes
1	a**khad**
2	**shta**im
3	sha**losh**
4	**ar**ba
5	kha**mesh**
6	shesh
7	**she**va
8	shmo**ne**
9	**tei**sha
10	**e**ser
11	**a**ha**desreh**
12	**shte**mesreh
13	**shlo**shesreh
14	ar**ba**esre
15	kha**mesh**esreh
16	shesh**esreh**
17	shva**esreh**
18	shmo**na'esreh**
19	**tsha**esreh
20	es**rim**
21	es**rim** vea**khad**
30	shlo**shim**
40	arba'**im**
50	khami**shim**
60	shi**shim**
70	shiv'**im**
80	shmo**nim**
90	tish'**im**
100	me**a**
200	ma**tyim**
300	shlosh me**ot**
1,000	e**lef**
2,000	al**py**im
3,000	shlo**sha** e**lef**
4,000	**ar**ba e**lef**
10,000	asa**ra** e**lef**

Time

one minute	da**ka**
one hour	sha'**a**
half an hour	khet**zi** sha'**a**
Sunday	yom ri**shon**
Monday	yom she**ni**
Tuesday	yom shli**shi**
Wednesday	yom revi'**i**
Thursday	yom khami**shi**
Friday	yom shi**shi**
Saturday	sha**bat**
week	shavu'**a**
month	**kho**desh
year	sha**na**

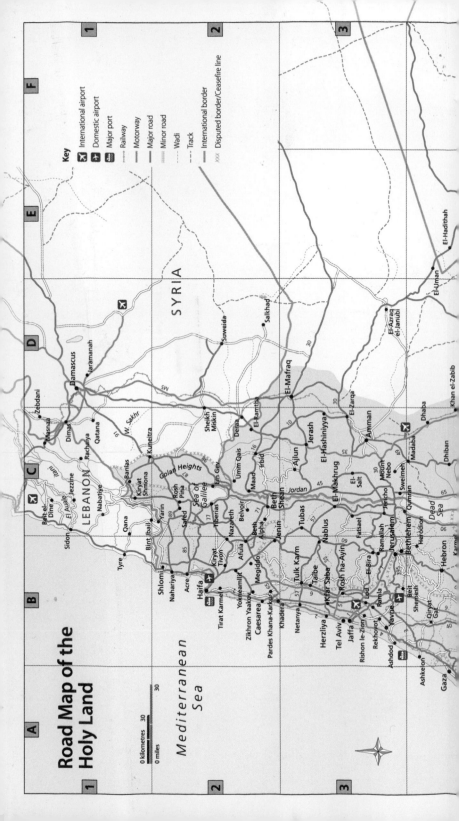

Road Map of the Holy Land

0 kilometres   30
0 miles   30

Key

✈	International airport
✈	Domestic airport
⚓	International port
	Major road
	Railway
	Motorway
	Major road
	Minor road
	Wadi
	Track
	International border
xxx	Disputed border/Ceasefire line

Mediterranean Sea

SYRIA

LEBANON

Golan Heights

Sea of Galilee

Jordan

Dead Sea

Damascus

Zebdani
Masnaa
Dima
Rachaya
Qatana
Beit el Dine
El Ayale
Jezzine
Nabatiye
Banias
Kiryat Shmona
Rosh Pina
Safed
Tiberias
Kuneitra
Sheikh Miskin
Deraa
El-Ramtha
Umm Qais
Maad
Irbid
Ajlun
Jerash
El-Hashiniyya
El-Mafraq
El-Zarqa
Amman
Sidon
Qana
Bint Jbail
Yarin
Nazareth
Beth Gev
Afula
Belvoir
Beth Alpha
Beth Shean
Tubas
Jenin
Nablus
Fatsael
El-Makhrug
El-Salt
Mount Nebo
Swiemeh
Madaba
Jericho
Qumran
Herodion
Bethlehem
Jerusalem
Ramallah
El-Bira
Beit Shemesh
Qiryat Gat
Hebron
Karmel
Dhiban
Khan el-Zabib
Dhaba
El-Uman
El-Azraq el-Janubi
El-Hadithah
Tyre
Acre
Nahariya
Shlomi
Haifa
Tirat Karmel
Zikhron Yaakov
Caesarea
Pardes Khana-Karkur
Yokneamlllt
Kiryat Tivon
Megiddo
Khadera
Netanya
Herzliya
Tel Aviv
Jaffa
Rishon le-Zion
Rekhovot
Ashdod
Ashkelon
Gaza
Yavne
Lod
Ramla
Rosh ha-Ayin
Tulk Karm
Kfar Saba
Talbe

W. Sakhr

A B C D E F
1 2 3

ON

• Damascus

SYRIA

JORDAN

DI
BIA

Modern Jerusalem
See pp122–131

The Muslim Quarter
See pp64–79

The Christian and
Armenian Quarters
See pp92–111

Jerusalem

MODERN
JERUSALEM

THE CHRISTIAN
AND ARMENIAN
QUARTERS

THE MUSLIM
QUARTER

THE JEWISH
QUARTER

THE MOUNT
OF OLIVES AND
MOUNT ZION

0 metres   800
0 yards   800

Further Afield
See pp132–143

The Jewish Quarter
See pp80–91

The Mount of Olives
and Mount Zion
See pp112–121